Revolutionising EU Innovation Policy

Klaus Gretschmann • Stefan Schepers
Editors

Revolutionising EU Innovation Policy

Pioneering the Future

Editors
Klaus Gretschmann
President of CATE
Stephanskirchen, Germany

Stefan Schepers
Henley Business School
Brussels, Belgium

T
26
.A1
R48
2016

ISBN 978-1-137-55553-3   ISBN 978-1-137-55554-0   (eBook)
DOI 10.1057/978-1-137-55554-0

Library of Congress Control Number: 2016941741

Printed on acid-free paper

This Palgrave Macmillan imprint is published by Springer Nature
The registered company is Macmillan Publishers Ltd. London

For Elke, coniugi carissimae,
without whose love, affection, and backing
I would not be who I am
Klaus

For my mother, Germaine Lijnen,
who taught me the values of Europe
Stefan

Preface

When in December 2011 the Polish government, while holding the rotating presidency of the Council of the EU, launched the initiative to set up a high-level expert group to look into EU innovation policy, its successes and failures and its needs for reform, then-Prime Minister Tusk and the Minister of Economy Pawlak had perhaps not imagined how important a contribution they were going to make to promoting more effective innovation and enhanced innovation policy in the European Union (EU). They had the good sense and courage to mandate us "to think outside the box," and we were fortunate that the equally visionary Irish and Italian Council presidencies asked us to continue the work.

The High Level Group on Innovation Policy Management (HLG on IPM) had three characteristics which were meant to substantially improve the creativity and serendipity of our discussions: (1) It had a tripartite composition, bringing together senior officials from the EU Commission and member states representing differing models of innovation, senior (innovation) managers from corporations of different sectors of the economy, and academic experts from different disciplinary backgrounds; (2) It was independent from the EU Commission and national governments and free from any instructions, and it operated under Chatham House rules to guarantee openness of discussions; (3) It was supposed to be rigorous in its analysis and bold in its conclusions and recommendations. This approach was in itself innovative in the EU context of advisory groups and think tanks. Its work was supported by a most dedicated research team, while the Polish presidency had entrusted EPPA, the management consultancy specialized in business-government interactions, with the overall organization. Former European Council President Herman Count Van Rompuy has lauded the independence and the quality of the work performed by this public–private arrangement.

The two reports of the HLG on IPM were submitted to the EU institutions in June 2013 and July 2014, in time for the then new 2014 Commission to be inspired when they envisaged necessary reforms. Although proud institutions hardly ever admit that they are being stimulated by outside advice and analysis, but rather claim to develop their own ideas and proposals, often they are silently grateful for being confronted with unorthodox, thought-provoking suggestions and recommendations.

In the course of our proceedings and discussions the idea was brought up that the HLG's reflections and ponderings, our arguments, background papers and proposals should not go unheard and gather dust on shelves or rest in peace in a bureaucrat's drawer but should rather be part of the public discourse on innovation and its role in business, politics and the European society at large. Against this backdrop, members of the HLG enthusiastically embarked when we were encouraged to publish a volume on *Revolutionizing EU Innovation Policy*. They were eager to thoroughly scrutinize our arguments and to draft many topics from scratch. The result is a selection of chapters by various contributors – interlinked like a monograph – containing many unorthodox and more or less radical ideas and suggestions on how to overhaul EU innovation policy, ideas which may be more profound and far-reaching than politically feasible in the near future.

Stephanskirchen, Germany   Klaus Gretschmann

Brussels, Belgium   Stefan Schepers

Acknowledgements

Chapter 7 – Stefan Schepers:
The author expresses his gratitude to Tristan du Puy and Léonard Tapié for their contributions.

Chapter 9 – Christoph Bausch:
The author would like to thank Eduardo Mulas for his research that contributed to this article.

Chapter 10 – Jean-Claude Thoenig:
Catherine Paradeise, Philippe Laredo and Ronan Stéphan have expressed comments and made suggestions that have been very stimulating. My special gratitude also goes to Stefan Schepers.

Contents

Contributors[1]

Christoph Bausch (R) served as a researcher and as the project manager of the High Level Group on Innovation Management. He currently works as a consultant at EPPA, a Brussels-based management consultancy specializing in business–government–society relations. He holds master's degrees in political science from the University of Vienna (A) and in international relations from King's College London (UK).

Maria Luisa Poncela Garcia (M) was appointed secretary general for science, technology and innovation of the Spanish government in 2013, and president of the board of directors of the Center for Industrial and Technological Development (CDTI) and of the executive council of the Barcelona Supercomputing Center (BSC). She developed her career both in the public and private sectors. In the public sector, she was previously director general for innovation and competitiveness, and she was nominated twice as head of the office of the secretary general of industry and the secretary general for innovation. In the private sector she climbed the career ladder as director of government affairs for Abbott Laboratories S.A. and as director general of Abbott Foundation, and she created her own company, Add Talentia SL. Additionally, she was a member of the executive council of the international technological organization Eureka for 8 years. She graduated in economics in 1982 from Zaragoza University (E), and obtained the competition exam of the National Corps of State Economists as well as of the chartered sales engineer's corps.

---

[1] (M) indicates a member of the High Level Group on Innovation Policy Management, (R) indicates a member of the research team which assisted the High Level Group on Innovation Policy Management

Klaus Gretschmann (M) is a former director-general of the EU Council of Ministers responsible for competitiveness, research, innovation, the Single Market, and industrial policy. Between 2012 and 2014 he served as chairman of the High Level Group on Innovation Policy Management. After an international career as a professor of public and international economics, he changed to politics as director-general for economics and finance in the German prime minister's office and as the prime minister's personal representative for G8 summits. He has authored numerous publications in seven languages, on integration, EU economic and monetary policy and competitiveness, etc. Today he is an independent advisor to EU governments and business leaders and has been awarded the Commander's Cross of the French Legion of Honor and the Federal Cross of Merit of Germany.

Andrew P. Kakabadse (M) is Professor of Governance and Leadership at Henley Business School, University of Reading (UK) and chairman of the directors' forum advisory board. He is vice chair of the supervisory board of the Academy of Business in Society. Before joining Henley Business School, Andrew was Professor of International Management Development, Cranfield University, School of Management from 1978 to 2012. He was awarded the title of professor emeritus in 2013. He was H. Smith Richardson Fellow at CCL, North Carolina, USA, 2005–2006. Andrew is a visiting professor at the University of Ulster, Ireland; Macquarie Graduate School of Management, Australia; Thunderbird School of Global Management, USA; Université Panthéon-Assas Paris II, France; Swinburne University of Technology, Australia; and an adjunct professor, Southern Cross Business School. His research covers boards, top teams and the governance of governments. He has published over 40 books, 88 book chapters, over 235 articles and 18 monographs. www.kakabadse.com.

Nada Korac-Kakabadse is Professor of Policy, Governance and Ethics at the Henley Business School, University of Reading. Nada is an elected member of European Academy of Science and Arts (EASA) and head of its EU Representation Office, Brussels. She has co-authored 19 books and has published over 190 scholarly articles. Her current areas of interest focus on leadership, boardroom effectiveness, governance, CSR and ethics, diversity, entrepreneurship, ICT impact on individuals and society, and the policy design of the state.

Egbert Lox (M) earned his master of science (1982) and PhD (1987) in chemical engineering at the University of Ghent (B) and started his career at the research laboratories of Degussa AG (D) and built up the R&D group for automotive emission control catalysts and assumed consecutive management functions. From 2006 to 2012 he was in charge of the corporate R&D team at Umicore (in B & D). Since 2013 he holds the position of senior vice president of government affairs, based in Umicore's headquarters in Brussels (Belgium). He is chairman of the board of directors of Innotek and represents Umicore in the board or executive committee of several industry associations. He lectures at the Department of Mechanical Engineering of the Karlsruhe Institute of Technology (D) and is a member of several university advisory councils and served as jury of PhD theses at European universities. He interacts with various RTOs by being member of the advisory board and/ or strategic evaluation and audit teams. He is author or co-author of about 130 technical papers; he is also co-inventor of more than 90 patents in the field of heterogeneous catalysis. He is the co-recipient of the 1998 A.T. Colwell Merit Award of the Society of Automotive Engineers (SAE) and a permanent member of the Royal Flemish Academy of Belgium for Sciences and Arts (KVAB).

Alberto di Minin (M) is Associate Professor of Management at the Scuola Superiore Sant'Anna in Pisa and a research fellow with the Berkeley Roundtable on the International Economy, University of California–Berkeley. He is social innovation fellow with the Meridian International Center of Washington, DC. Di Minin is currently the Italian representative on the SMEs and Access to Finance Programme committee for Horizon 2020 with the European Commission. At Sant'Anna, di Minin is teaching innovation management and innovation policy, he is the co-director of the Executive Doctorate in Business Administration Program, the director of the Confucius Institute of Pisa and of the Galilei Institute in Chongqing University. Di Minin's research deals with open innovation, appropriation of innovation and science and technology policy. Di Minin writes for Nòva, Il Sole24Ore. www.diminin.it.

Michel Praet (M), after graduating in economics, Université libre de Bruxelles, and completing the International Executive Programme (INSEAD), became adviser to Deputy Prime Minister De Clercq in 1982. After working as business development manager with Bull, he served as adviser to Deputy Prime Minister Verhofstadt and became head of the space, EC and Eurêka departments of the Belgian Science Policy Office, as well as chairman of the International Space Station Programme Board. In 1993, he became deputy director for marketing and sales at Alcatel Space in Europe. In 1999, he became head of the European Space Agency DG's Cabinet. He joined the private office of the president of the European Council, Herman Count van Rompuy, in February 2010, where he was, among other tasks, in charge of R&D, innovation, information society and culture. Since December 2014 he has been head of the EU relations for ESA. Praet is vice president of the Museum for Europe and vice president of the Palace of Fine Arts of Belgium.

Tristan du Puy (R) has a degree in political science from Sciences Politiques in Paris and is studying international economic policy at the same institution's school of international affairs. He studies law at Paris 1–Panthéon Sorbonne, and philosophy at Paris Ouest–Nanterre. He previously worked for the French Social Security EU representation office in Brussels and organized the 2015 edition of the Weimar Youth Forum on the topic of social Europe.

Morten Rasmussen (R) is currently an innovation consultant at CARSA responsible for designing and developing tenders for European organizations, in particular regarding digital and industrial innovation, entrepreneurship, and SME support at the EU level. He worked at the EU commission, DG Competition, on the preparation of reports on evaluation and strategy development and conducted research on market functioning in energy, telecommunications and transport sectors. Before that, he was at the permanent representation of Denmark to the EU. He holds a master's degree in European political economy from the London School of Economics (UK) and an degree in public policy from Roskilde University (DK).

Nicola Redi (M) is investment director in Vertis (I), with responsibilities on venture capital operations. He previously served as chief investment and technology officer of TT Venture, the first Italian technology transfer fund. Before working as a venture capitalist, Redi held European and global responsibilities in R&D management and operations within leading multinational companies such as Pirelli and Ideal Standard International. He was a member of the informal advisory board of the Italian Ministry for Education, University and Research. He teaches financing of innovation at the global MBA of the University of Bologna, new product development and business planning for new ventures at the international MBA of MIB School of Management and seed and venture capital at the international MBA of the University of Pisa. He holds an MS in aeronautical engineering from Politecnico di Milano, an MBA with honors from Bocconi School of Management, Milan (I) and a PhD from Aston Business School in Birmingham (UK). www.vertis.it.

Marco Rossi (R) holds degrees from King's College London and the London School of Economics and Political Science. He worked in the European External Action Service (EEAS) and as the directorate general for external policies of the European Parliament. He is currently a PhD researcher in the Department of European and International Studies, King's College London.

Stefan Schepers (M) served as secretary-general of the High Level Group on Innovation Policy Management. He is a visiting professor at Henley Business School, University of Reading (UK). Having been the first director general of the European Institute of Public Administration, in Maastricht (NL), he became a partner in EPPA, a management consultancy specializing in business–government–society interaction, advising business and government, based in Brussels (B). He has a master's degree in law, University of Leuven (B), and in advanced European studies, University of Strasbourg (F), and a PhD in political science, University of Edinburgh (UK). He is member of the senate of the European Academy of Sciences and Arts and a director of the Academy of Business in Society. He published on management and EU affairs and recently co-edited *Rethinking the Future of Europe* (2014). www.stefanschepers.eu.

Jean-Claude Thoenig (M) is a senior research fellow (em.) at the French Centre National de la Recherche Scientifique. He is affiliated with the Université Paris–Dauphine. A sociologist and political scientist by training, French and Swiss citizen, he was a professor at the Federal Institute of Technology (Lausanne), the associate dean and professor at INSEAD, a visiting scholar at Stanford, Harvard and the University of California–Berkeley. He co-founded various European professional associations and research institutions. He was a staff member of two French ministers. He was a consultant for top executives of multinational companies and for the European Commission. His contributions cover areas such as innovation management, public policy implementation and evaluation, intergovernmental relationships, and higher education and research institutions. His latest book co-authored with Catherine Paradeise is *In Search of Academic Quality* (Palgrave, 2015).

List of Figures

List of Tables

1

Revisiting Innovation: Revolutionising European Innovation Policy by Means of an Innovation Ecosystem

Klaus Gretschmann and Stefan Schepers

1 The EU in Need of a New Narrative

Both in economic and political terms, the EU is on life support. Its former attractiveness as an economic powerhouse, a political "soft power," and a much appreciated social model seems to be waning in the face of Eurozone troubles, the problems of migration and asylum seekers, or the political and military challenges at its borders. Far away from traditional integrationist thinking, which claims the EU has always been on an irreversible trend toward an ever closer union, today's analysts hold that the Union is losing its internal coherence, its historical significance, and economic usefulness.

K. Gretschmann (✉)
President, Competence and Advisory Team Europe (CATE), Germany
email: klaus.gretschmann@kgr-consilium.eu

S. Schepers
Director, European Public Policy Advisors (EPPA), Brussels
email: stefan.schepers@eppa.com

© The Editor(s) (if applicable) and The Author(s) 2016
K. Gretschmann, S. Schepers (eds.), *Revolutionising EU Innovation Policy*,
DOI 10.1057/978-1-137-55554-0_1

For many decades EU politicians have followed the guiding star of an ever closer union pursued by one method, supranationalism, without ever trying seriously other approaches, and ignoring the complex nationalities. However, recent crises have resulted in a sharp drop in the Union's attractiveness. For a variety of reasons, the EU has become most unpopular with her member states, peoples, and citizens. This is not merely due to the fallout from the financial and eurocrises, but rather the Union suffers from self-inflicted damage resulting from its contested, and sometimes self-serving, goals, governance methods, and culture of the past. Both have been made obsolete by new realities.

Political systems fray and decay Europe-wide. An increasing number of member states are afraid they may face "ungovernability," with dramatic consequences for the social and political glue holding the Union together (Gretschmann 2015).

Indeed, these appear to be the most testing and taxing times for the EU during its existence. Reasons for growing Euroscepticism abound. At its very heart seems to be the perception by the people in the streets that an elitist power cartel of pro-European agents, with disregard for the real problems citizens all over the Union are facing, has developed and has started a "power grab" from national governments beyond what is laid down in the treaties. They feel disempowered, alienated, and subject to forces they cannot control (Gretschmann 2014).

The EU in stormy seas is in urgent need of a new and attractive narrative, a positive, encompassing story to tell, and a fresh idea to follow. It requires a recipe for pioneering the future and bringing attractiveness and popularity back in. In order to be prepared for the challenges of the future, deep-running changes will have to be considered and paradigm shifts will be required: a move away from "bureaucratism" toward citizens' preferences, away from the "routinism" of the community method toward "innovationism," away from walking the beaten tracks toward new paths of revised principles and open and fluid structures of decision making. Talking about change while continuing in the old ways will not do!

The EU's internal cohesion will have to be restored, the European Common Good, which seems to be fading away, needs to be recalled and, last but not least, Europe as a whole, which is still lagging behind more active and agile emergent economies, needs overhaul and modernization.

All this implies revolutionizing the model of EU policy making, both in design and implementation, and to restart with new concepts and blueprints of reform.

What seems to the authors and contributors to this volume a most attractive narrative for Europe will be built on knowledge, education, research, technologies and, in short, INNOVATION.

In order to make use of such a narrative, we may need to revolutionize European innovation policies in order to move ahead toward a **European Age of Innovation** and a European innovation agenda.

2 Coming a Long Way from EU R&D to Innovation as a Promise

To be sure, Europe and, notably, the European Union has always been interested in research, science, and innovation as a means of modernizing European polities and economies.

Whereas the early years of the European communities did not see much in terms of research policy (Guzzetti 1995), except for some limited activities within the confines of the Euratom Treaty, a first push[1] occurred with the acknowledgment in the late 1960s that Europe suffered from a huge technology gap, vis-à-vis the USA and Japan. The seminal work of Jean-Jacques Servan-Schreiber (1968) about "Le défi americain" paved the way for thinking hard about what to do in order not to lose ground in international economic competitiveness. The result was a decision to pool resources and to synchronize national efforts in order to

* generate a genuine European value-added on top of national research benefits;
* provide cross-border, community-wide transparency and "usability" of research results;

---

[1] In 1965 already, the COM set up a working group called PREST (*Politique de la Recherche Scientifique et Technique*) and, in 1972, the internal work on a document pondering a European technology community had started.

- guarantee the critical mass necessary for large research projects, infrastructure, and funding;
- tie together transnational and interdisciplinary research;
- avoid duplication of the same research efforts in several member states;
- kick-start projects by providing funding from European sources;
- exploit EU-wide economies of scale; and
- activate, promote, and strengthen new research areas and activities of strategic importance for Europe's competitiveness, vis-à-vis the USA and Japan.

However, the approach was piecemeal at best. Innovations were connoted with universities or select enterprises or individual geniuses and inventors. Market forces alone were believed to steer and guide technology development and innovations either by demand pull or supply push. Market failures were the only legitimate reason for public policy to interfere. How far government involvement was to go was contested. Picking the winners by subsidization was no accepted strategy. And ever since, "innovations" have always been misunderstood in Brussels as just an extension of research and development (R&D) programs.

Along these lines, during the last 20 years the European Union has further developed an R&D policy, and it has tried to make it complementary to the research and innovation efforts of the member states. Some progress has been made, but it is still too slow and too limited to have a distinctive and lasting effect on Europe's growth and competitiveness. R&D[2] does not automatically lead to innovation in markets; intervening and flanking factors, such as legal provisions (EU and national ones), administrative support, entrepreneurial skills, risk propensity, and public opinion, etc., are not conducive to an innovation environment and need to be addressed and tackled simultaneously. Concomitantly, the removal of bottlenecks and obstacles to innovation has always been a tall order.

While innovation is widely considered as a key element to foster growth and prosperity, and would *excellently qualify for nurturing a new narrative of the EU*, the recent stalemate, if not outright decline, in

---

[2] The EU Treaty makes explicit reference only to R&D policy. Innovation policy is not mentioned but can be derived from a wider interpretation.

Europe's innovation record and in its investments in RDI (Innovation Scoreboard[3]) demonstrates that Europe is far from achieving its full potential and has to overcome many impediments and barriers, notably

* a disconnection between European governance and business interests and value chains;
* an exceedingly precautious approach to new ideas and inventions; and
* a neglect of public government innovation.

Commitments to politically stimulate and increase investment in research knowledge and innovation have been made ever since and, notably, over the past 10 years or so but have never been met in full. Evidently **creating** innovation, **commercializing** innovation, and **leveraging** innovation is easier said than done.

In parallel, theoretical and empirical research on innovation policy has gone from the recognition that innovation is decisive (exogenous growth models) and the study of innovation mechanisms (micro and sectoral) to the modeling of evolutionary and path-dependent processes and the interplay of technology and institutions. Policy makers have not taken into adequate account such research and its findings (Kok 2004; Aho 2006). A lot has been said and done about an encompassing approach involving, for example, ERC, EIT, JTI, Lead Markets, or CIP[4] about stakeholders, shareholders, producers, facilitators, knowledge workers, skills providers, and so on, but without much success and praise, not least due to lack of policy coherence.

Admittedly, we have come a long way. It has become general knowledge that (member) states should develop their innovation policies in the light of their specific characteristics and *inter alia* with the following objectives: establishing support mechanisms for innovative SMEs, including high-tech start-ups, promoting joint research between undertakings and universities, improving access to risk capital, refocusing public procure-

---

[3] The European Innovation Scoreboards provide a comparative assessment of research and innovation performance in Europe. The scoreboards help countries and regions identify the areas they need to address.

[4] All of these organizations are part and parcel of the recent EU research policy efforts: the European Research Council (ERC), the European Institute of Technology (EIT), Joint Technology Initiatives (JIT), and the Competitiveness and Innovation Programme (CIP).

ment on innovative products and services, and developing partnerships for innovation and innovation centers at the regional and local levels. And the icing on the cake would be a nice and attractive framework tying the national and local efforts together with the EU level.

3   Toward Revisiting Innovation in Europe

The European Union needs a *new grand vision* that can motivate people. Such a grand new vision could be founded on an *innovation paradigm*. Developing an *ecosystem of innovations* should be the overarching objective of the EU and of the member states for the next decades in order to *guarantee and promote the best possible living conditions for the largest number of citizens*. It appears clear that a narrative built upon an *innovation paradigm* can offer a nonconflictual, highly consensual, and attractive new compact, containing the glue for tying Europe together and integrating national and Union interests.

Innovation in all its guises is needed to manage the critical economic and societal issues of Europe of the first half of the twenty-first century, such as resource efficiency, climate change, healthy living and aging, food, energy, and resources security. To make it possible governance methodology and culture are necessary. Without it, the maintenance and furtherance of the European welfare model will be in jeopardy.[5] Innovation is an indispensable source of competitive strength and a precondition for Europe's model of "soft power" in world affairs (Tuomioja 2009).

However, in Europe, different cultural and sometimes ideological perceptions, and differing public governance or management fault lines, in particular between (and sometimes inside) the EU institutions and member states, hinder making efficient use of available intellectual capital and economic capabilities. Indeed, economic innovation requires much more than research that may lead, or not, to a new or improved product or use. It concerns also new methods of production or delivery of services, the development of a new market, or finding a new source of

---

[5] As recent calculations yield, the ratio of R&D needed per unit of GDP has gone up from 1:1 in the early 1990s to 3:1 twenty years later. Success rates of innovation still vary widely from 2.5 % at the lower end to 20 % at maximum.

supply of raw materials or manufactured inputs, or new design, or a new organization of industry, or management, or of public administration. Therefore, a traditional R&D approach to innovation is insufficient and ineffective and must be broadened to cover nontechnological innovations, including in the regulatory frameworks, procurement procedures, or intellectual property rights and standardization, to name but a few.

The emergence of novel concepts and products is often a result of improvisation, repeated trial and error, and the emergence of new tacit and explicit knowledge until some form of consolidation takes place. Innovation thus is a paradoxical process, combining, creativity and rigorous scientific method. It requires the opposite attitude from bureaucracy, which is about stable process and control in large entities; if it comes too early in innovation processes, it leads to inertia. But also beyond "managed innovation" independent thinkers, amateurs, and dreamers often provide the indispensable imaginative leaps, the fantasies and intuition that are often more useful than the much-praised "analytical rigor" when it comes to new ideas and innovations. Attempts to trigger nonconventional thinking and to open new ways both in universities, firms and politics, but also in civil society organizations, are still both a desideratum and a priority. A quadruple helix is far away still. Moreover, leadership and support in government systems is needed to create the optimal framework conditions to facilitate other actors, primarily but not exclusively companies and universities, to develop and manage the chain of actions that leads to innovation of products, services, and processes in the market.

Modern political leadership for innovation requires vision, strategy, consistency, and proper governance of cultural tools. It needs to pay attention to the whole chain of knowledge development in its broadest sense, to diffusion and absorption, and to its transformation in tangible applications, which bring economically and socially measurable benefits.

In the EU innovation requires a move beyond a culture of regulation and control toward a culture of mentoring and coaching of all actors and stakeholders. Stewardship tools are more suited to promote a culture of innovation and of change among various actors than traditional command and control approaches, which usually stifle diversity and creativity, two key ingredients for innovative thinking. This requires a real change of culture.

The analysis above pinpoints the crucial role of institutional arrangements as driving or at least supporting forces of innovation. The two forces of technology innovation and institutional innovation are deeply intertwined since new inventions, innovations, and technologies frequently are the source of disequilibria, which make it profitable or even indispensable to innovate institutional arrangements (North 1990). Institutions both constrain and structure human interactions, be they political, economic or social. Constraints, as North describes, are devised as formal rules (constitutions, laws, property rights) and informal restraints (sanctions, taboos, customs, traditions, code of conduct), which usually contribute to the perpetuation of order and safety within a market or society. Briefly stated, his works specify the process by which social, economic or political actors perceive that some new form of systemic organization (institutional arrangement) will yield a stream of benefits that makes it profitable to undergo the costs of innovating this new organizational form. These new arrangements are typically apt to realize potential economies of scale, reduce information costs, spread risk, and internalize externalities.

What may be drawn from the above is the necessary condition of alignment between inventions, innovations, technologies, and institutional settings—all of which involve governance regimes (private and public).

Today, governments' roles in innovation grow (Mazzucato 2013): Governments will increasingly become involved in technology, investing in a broad range of applications—from homegrown innovation incubators to local manufacturing sites that create jobs and manage geopolitical risk, not to mention potential ethical or civil rights issues about the use of new technologies. At the same time, governments should not forget their regulatory role but, rather, one adapted to the postindustrial economy and society. It also opens up new possibilities for institutional reform and governance innovation: As the innovation regime as well as governments' policies are becoming increasingly multilayer, multiactor, and hyper-complex, new modes of governance, citizens' participation, and transparency will be part of any innovation-promoting regime.

If the Douglas North proposition above can stand scrutiny, namely that every innovative technology/ process requires an adaptive and transformative government—that is, new institutional arrangements and new governance tools and regimes—then innovations in the public sectors, while also having regard for the political structures and processes, will be indispensable.

4   The Role of Business, the Stage-Gate-Model, and Beyond

That business is assigned a crucial role in the process of turning inventions and research results into innovations ready for the market is a truism. Equally well-known is the saying/ adage that research policy serves as a means to turn money into knowledge and innovation policy is a way to turn knowledge into money. And, last but not least, there is no doubt that institutional and policy adaptations need to take the processes of innovation carried out by business into account.

The classical innovation process inside enterprises consists of idea generation, idea selection and idea/ project management. The standard process for innovation management focuses on linear, nondisruptive, incremental innovation. The sequencing is described in the well-known Stage-Gate model (Cooper 2001, 2008). Stage-Gate is a value-creating business process and risk model designed to quickly and profitably transform an organization's best new ideas into winning new products. It enables firms to create a culture of innovation excellence—innovation leadership, top-notch teams, customer and market focus, robust solutions, alignment, discipline, speed, and quality.

The process helps prepare the right information, with the right level of detail, at the right gate to support the best decision possible, and allocate capital and operating resources (Fig. 1.1).

There is no question the Stage-Gate process has had a significant impact on the conception, development, and launch of innovative processes in firms. Yet, there have been consistent criticisms of it as the

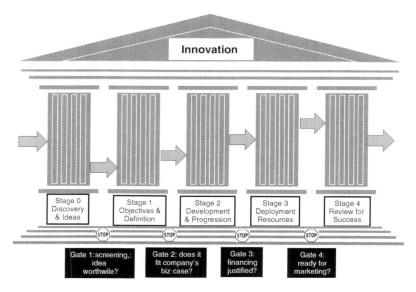

Fig. 1.1 Stage-Gate processes
Note: Author's interpretation and graphic account

world of innovation has moved on. Today it is faster-paced, less linear, far more competitive and global market and has become less predictable. The process of innovation is much more iterative than assumed in the SGP. Therefore, the model does not mirror innovation reality in the twenty-first-century firm.

In a very recent empirical study, Sarah Eckardt (2015) argued that the most crucial determining factor in firms' innovation processes is intrapreneurship.

Intrapreneurship (entrepreneurship within existing organizations) has been of interest to scholars and practitioners for the past two decades. Intrapreneurship is viewed as being beneficial for revitalization and performance of corporations, as well as for small- and medium-sized enterprises. The concept refers to pursuing and entering new businesses; the creation of new products, services, and technologies;

strategy reformulation, reorganization, and organizational change; and, finally, the proactiveness in pursuing innovations, competitiveness, initiative, risk taking, and competitive boldness.

In a similar vein, Ahuja and Lampert (2001) presented a model that explains how established firms create breakthrough inventions. They identify three organizational pathologies that inhibit breakthrough inventions: the familiarity trap, which favors the familiar; the maturity trap, which favors the mature; and the propinquity trap, which favors a search for solutions near to existing solutions. They argue that by experimenting with novel (the firm lacks prior experience), emerging (technologies are newly developed), and pioneering (technologies that do not build on any existing technologies) developments firms can overcome these traps and create breakthrough inventions. However, outside help through adequate innovation and technology policies may be supportive.

From very early on, Damanpour (1991) inquired into the factors determining innovation propensity and capacity in firms. A meta-analysis of the relationships between organizational innovation and thirteen of its potential determinants resulted in statistically significant associations for specialization, functional differentiation, professionalism, centralization, managerial attitude toward change, technical knowledge resources, administrative intensity, slack resources, and external and internal communication. Results suggest that the relations between the determinants and innovation are stable over time.

To focus on the innovation processes at the level of the firm involves no *mental gymnastics*; rather, it is absolutely necessary to be aware of how innovation works in business and thus in practice. Taking account of the basic intrafirm features is a prerequisite if innovation policy wants to make a difference and contribute to bringing about innovations. A skillful alignment between policy and business processes is imperative for any innovation policy to work. If the firm approach is complex and multidimensional, the (former) linear concept of EU innovation policy making and its implicit affinity to the SGP is no longer adequate. (See the contribution of Egbert Lox in this volume). Rather, a more complex and multilayered approach (Christensen 2011), such as an innovation ecosystem (Jackson 2011) approach is badly needed.

5   Shortcomings of Present EU Innovation Policy Approaches

* The success of the EU integration and cooperation process has led to such a high degree of complexity that the original methods of operation are no longer suited. There is an urgent need to rethink, within the confines of the treaties, how to bring about comprehensive stakeholder engagement and how to make this operationally possible through behavioral and procedural change and digitalization. In order to ensure policy coherence, not just within the Commission but also between the EU and member states, new approaches to impact assessment, to policy elaboration and to rule making and rule application in diverse contextual conditions must be found. In addition, the needs of the drivers of competitiveness and employment creation, industrial and service companies must become better aligned with the interests of national governments, visions, and welfare requirements.

* The gaps in competitiveness among member states are widening, with some advancing well in developing and implementing innovation in their economy and governance, others still at the stage of planning and piecemeal implementation, and still other countries just thinking about what to do, if anything. The European innovation ecosystem will become globally strong only if it is internally coherent and if all countries attain a minimum level of integration within it.

* It is clearly a collective European interest to ensure that all productive and innovative forces and opportunities are identified and used. This requires structural reforms in most if not all member states and in the EU itself, and a different use of EU instruments and funds to ensure that a level innovation playing field is rapidly created.

* The EU needs to organize technological and industrial cooperation in all sectors and across all regions. This requires a diversified yet strong approach for building new industries and European players of international standing as well as strengthening the ecosystem for innovation and investment. The pledge made in the Lisbon Strategy to provide the proper framework conditions for enterprise development and innovation are still not met in full.

* A key problem underlying the suboptimal design of EU innovation policy is the supranational governance model of the EU, once useful for creating a common market and a single currency but unfit for today's new challenges. It focuses far too much on regulating everything instead of operating with more sophisticated collaborative governance methods. Moreover, once it has opened a particular regulatory trajectory, it continues on it without regular and thorough evaluation of its effectiveness. No wonder European companies, and most of all small- and medium-sized ones and innovative start-ups, suffocate under complex, sometimes contradictory, shaky, and time-consuming regulations that benefit no one and neither stimulates research and innovation nor competitiveness or employment. Political debates tend to focus too much on "more or less Europe," but not on the cost-efficient functioning of its policy-making system, now designed half a century ago for a different political and economic context.

* What is badly needed is collaboration between research, business, governments, and the EU Commission, instead of silo thinking by each of them and mutual distrust. We must also dare to question regulatory capture in Brussels by a select number of nongovernmental organizations (NGOs) with their own agendas, whose impact on growth and employment is unclear, to say the least. Instead of fragmenting responsibilities for research, education, and enterprise policy, governments and the Commission should ensure convergence and cooperation, because they are the three pillars of global competitiveness on which the public income depends to finance Europe's cherished social model.

Europe does not lack the capacity to innovate; it has a broad fabric of innovation with certain elements already in place; but the framework conditions are lacking. It is confronted with problems of leadership and incoherence of vision and purpose. It struggles to create cumulative effects and critical mass. There is a rather inflexible culture of policy making and regulatory application. It suffers from organizational fragmentation, with multiple barriers to innovation in markets, and there is no encompassing of a systemic approach. Worse still, some innovation that is developed in the EU is appropriated elsewhere due to a lack of favorable framework conditions.

6 Innovation Ecosystems: Revolutionizing Innovation Policy

Innovation is the result of interaction among the "ecology" of actors. The "right" interaction between these actors is needed to turn an idea into a solution or a process, product, or service on the market. Therefore, the European Innovation Strategy model focuses on connectedness, the dynamics and the context in which a complex interaction of actors and agents, factors, sectors, and countries determining or hampering innovation is embedded.

We must acknowledge that innovation results from a complex process, combining curiosity, creativity, rigorous scientific method, and a suitable institutional framework of interaction. The emergence of novel concepts or processes, products or services, can only result from out-of-the-box thinking, improvisation, trial and error, and new tacit or explicit knowledge.

The traditional model of innovation uses scientific research as the basis of innovation and suggests that change is linear: from research via invention to innovation, to diffusion and marketing. However, this model has been acknowledged as incomplete and misleading. Rather, innovation is a result of the interaction among an "ecology" of actors. It is the "right" interaction between the actors that is needed in order to turn an idea into a solution or a process, product or service, on the market or in society.

The ecology model, first sketched out by Jackson (2011) provides a much richer picture of how innovation works, and how it can be stimulated and fostered. It focuses on connectedness, the dynamics and the context in which a complex interaction of actors and agents, factors, sectors, and countries determining or hampering innovation is embedded. Innovation and value creation require permanent strategic agility (Doz and Kosonen 2008), scanning the global context, scouting for opportunities, and attention to continuities or discontinuities in societies and economies.

We suggest in this volume the deployment of "innovation ecosystems": a set of ideas, institutions, instruments, policies, regulations, and factors that determine the level, direction, outcome, productivity, and degree of competitiveness from innovations. A realm characterized by clear, simple, efficient, smart, less complex, competition-based, and socially accepted features will be best suited and conducive to prompt promotion of innovation. Whereas the traditional linear model of innovation prioritizes scientific research as the basis of innovation, the model put forward in this book provides a much richer picture (Fig. 1.2).

The key objectives are to develop and promote an ecosystem of innovation that embeds innovation policies and activities into a flexible, dynamic, stimulating, and enabling environment. This ecosystem is intended to create value for society. It should enhance the quality of life for its citizens and the competitiveness of its enterprises. It should foster intelligent interaction between a variety of stakeholders (whether companies, local/ regional/ national authorities, or international systems like the EU and its institutions) and centers of knowledge creation such as universities and research organizations.

Reconstructing and unfolding the European innovation ecosystem will involve setting up

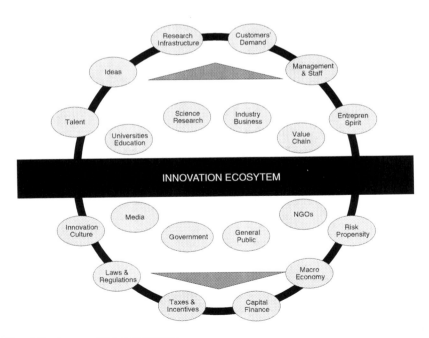

Fig. 1.2 Innovation ecosystem
Note: Author's compilation and garphic account

* a **network of formal and informal** public and private sector actors whose activities and interactions initiate, import, modify, and diffuse new technologies;
* the **communication flows and relationships** that determine the production, diffusion, and use of new basic or applied knowledge;
* a set of **individual actors**, whose incentive structures and competencies determine the rate and direction of technological learning and the volume and composition of change generating activities;
* **devices to create, store, and transfer knowledge**, skills, and artifacts that define new technological frontiers;
* **rules and political arrangements** for the framework guiding the innovation process, with particular attention to rules or practices that could hinder an innovation ecosystem;
* **a heterarchical**[6] **governance culture,** to develop stakeholder alignment and quadruple helix innovation;
* **a set of workable regulations** where nonfunctioning elements are repaired and adjusted to foster creative thinking and invention[7]; and
* **more space for regulatory interpretation** so rules are applied on the basis of reality evidence—less dogmatic and more flexible with regards to achieving desirable outcomes.

Once set up, this framework is supposed to ensure

* a cross-disciplinary and open-minded attitude;
* a reasonable but adequate propensity to risk; and
* strategic foresight, policy coherence, and flexible governance.

---

[6] A *heterarchy* is a system of organization where the elements of the organization are unranked (nonhierarchical) or where they possess the potential to be ranked a number of different ways. Definitions of the term vary among the disciplines: in social and information sciences, heterarchies are networks of elements in which each element shares the same "horizontal" position of power and authority, each playing a theoretically equal role.

[7] For example, consider antitrust laws, which were developed in the late nineteenth century in the context of the economic theories of the time. But today, many of those assumptions are irrelevant, thereby disregarding the value of ubiquity or non-convexities in new economic theories. Or take the idea of enacting short-term tax credits for research and development. R&D takes many years. If companies invest in a given year to take advantage of the R&D credit and, 2 years later, the tax code is changed, their investment may be lost. Therefore, tax credits do have some influence on business decisions.

In order to guarantee the functioning of the system, a complete revision and continuous monitoring of the methods, procedures, and output of governance within the various EU institutions and all member states, as well as of the interaction between themselves, and between them and the EU institutions, must also be achieved.

Building on those elements, the ecosystem will promote creative and bold thinking, free from useless bureaucratic constraints, and able to achieve innovative solutions that are eventually capable of addressing new challenges and specific problems.

The basis for innovation ecosystems requires

* openness and dialogue about the agendas of different stakeholders;
* overcoming short-termism through appropriate processes, and steering to build coherence and alignment within and between complex large public and private entities (corporations, governments, universities, etc.) about mission and objectives, and about interdependence of respective roles to achieve mega-societal objectives;
* understanding of how industrial dynamics and market functioning operate, how they can respond to economic and societal needs and demands, and which framework conditions are required to turn these into business opportunities;
* attention for the important role of creativity and for the innovation potential in so-called traditional industries and in agriculture;
* attention to the potential of young innovators and their needs and the removal of obstacles to start-up companies, including unintended side effects of certain forms of taxation;
* promoting entrepreneurship through lower entry costs and through fundamental changes in national bankruptcy laws;
* understanding the key role of public governance in putting the right framework conditions in place and hence the need for meaningful public administration innovation;
* understanding the (often global) research (radical or incremental) innovation chain, its funding costs before and at the point of market entry, and the time frame in different business sectors, and development of a comprehensive intellectual property protection;

* understanding the symbiotic relationships between large corporations and small- and medium-sized enterprises;
* result-oriented cooperation between public authorities, companies, and university research capabilities, with a preference for coaching over command and control functions, and ensuring engagement through a variety of incentives for all actors;
* interpretation of existing regulations in a way that stimulates innovation; and
* stable and coherent policy and regulatory frameworks, with minimum costs and fast procedures, which increase the probability of market success of innovation and hence facilitate its financing.

Because there is a certain probability that at least some enterprises launched in the ecosystem will fail, a healthy ecosystem should be structured to handle failures in a way that encourages cutting investment losses in the early stages of the enterprise. Ideally, the ecosystem is structured to recover and recycle resources (including human capital) that are released upon failure of an enterprise (Jackson 2011: 8). Therefore, besides assembling the actors who will contribute to the innovation ecosystem, a healthy ecosystem also provides a mechanism for building relationships and other intangibles between the actors, and entities within the ecosystem and those inside and outside the system.

To properly assess paradigm shifts and to align various agendas, it is essential to involve business leaders and other economic actors together and in close cooperation with the centers of knowledge creation, to contribute their understanding of markets and marketability. To make use of different perspectives and different modes of thinking and probing, we will need to establish a culture of deliberation and discourse. We will need tools that go beyond the technocratic and mechanistic stakeholder consultations that are the routine in Brussels. It is necessary in order to bring about a shared vision and mutual understanding and cooperation. If the EU wishes to promote and stimulate innovation, it needs to be innovation-bent itself—much more so than in the past.

We are in the midst of a major paradigm shift: the old approach to innovation policy no longer works and the new approaches are not matured enough yet. As a matter of fact, **innovation ecosystems** as social environments offering an all-encompassing and coherent policy strategy regarding innovation, permeate quite a lot of other areas, such as enterprise policy, smart regulation, affordable health, social reforms, and new ways of molding EU national policies.

The upshot of the line of argumentation outlined above is as follows: Both politics and business need to create and provide the right "innovation ecology," a laboratory of ideas, rules, procedures, etc., across disciplines, firms, and countries. This requires that stakeholders, shareholders, producers, facilitators, decision makers, knowledge workers, skills providers, etc., should all be involved and committed. **Then the innovation ecosystem approach may well be the best basis of a new narrative of a future Europe.**

7   A Plan of the Book and Its Rationale

As argued above, a whole set of largely unrelated individual initiatives does not make up an innovation system. Indeed, the EU and its member states have developed policies, programs, and projects to make innovation in Europe thrive. They have managed to develop an encompassing program such as Horizon 2020. However, so far the outcome is far from optimal. Stakeholders in science, business, and society alike remain skeptical and critical, to say the least.

Radical change in innovation policy seems indispensable, from fragmentation to coordination, from a narrow S+T orientation to an encompassing, holistic, and coherent strategy involving several policy areas, from a diffuse to a highly focused division of labor between all actors and stakeholders involved. This is what we mean by the Innovation Ecosystem Approach.

As outlined above many of the major issues deserve quite some more elaborate and in-depth analysis and reflection. In the following chapters the various authors and contributors will try to live up to this desideratum.

Benefits and rewards of innovation policies are the centerpiece of Morten Rasmussen's contribution: he explores the link between innovations and national macroeconomic parameters such as international competitiveness, growth and employment, and budgetary balance, etc.

The paper compares cross-country studies and rankings and deploys performance data and empirical analyses for determining a clear covariance between innovation-friendly policies, an ecosystem conducive to innovation and positive economic performance.

Whereas Rasmussen emphasizes the upside of comprehensive and stimulating innovation ecosystems, Klaus Gretschmann discloses the downsides and analyzes obstacles and opposition to innovation. He describes innovation as placed between "hype, rebuff, and new sobriety" and argues that albeit innovation has become the "magic formula" in today's intellectual debates, it is an error to assume that innovations are everywhere and always welcome. There is no such thing as a social consensus or a social compact about the unconditional promotion of innovation. Rather, the history of innovation is an unending story of resistance and opposition. A whole series of factors inhibiting innovation are discussed, such as personal attitudes to risk, intrafirm obstacles, institutional settings, the role of veto players, "groupthink" and "an intrinsic risk-adverse societal attitude" in European societies.

In their chapter entitled "Open Innovation and Clusters: Why Proximity Matters?" Alberto di Minin and Marco Rossi underline the significance of clusters for a stimulating innovation eco-system. They focus on three factors that make clusters particularly well fitted to develop effective and successful open innovation strategies: access to finance, cross-specialization, and local trust. The analysis focuses on how the peculiarly close-knit and cooperative environment that characterizes regional clusters can play a vital role in guaranteeing constant exchange and knowledge disclosure between different actors involved in a network, while at the same time significantly reducing costs. By encouraging this knowledge flow not only between local partners, but also between local competitors, clusters foster the constant exchange of data and solutions that underpin open innovation.

Innovations are produced everywhere, but there is wide disparity; while some countries or regions are in the top rank in terms of innovation, others are a lagging behind. The challenge to grow faster is to raise the "average" level of European innovation, to create a European ecosystem with the best performers, without leaving the rest behind. In this chapter Marisa Poncela analyzes the complexity of the governance system and the need to ensure coordination processes that facilitate long-term strategy planning (and implementation) and prevent short-term decisions that hinder innovation processes, aligning actors, priorities, and problems while preserving long-term policy coherence. Mechanisms to ensure horizontal interministerial policy coordination and mechanisms for top-down and bottom-up local-regional-national coordination will be highlighted. The importance of the impact assessments is underpinned and best practices and proposals to catalyze policy coherence are discussed.

Looking into a particularly important element of innovation, namely funding and financing, Nicolas Redi and Morten Rasmussen suggest that quite some fresh thinking is imperative in order to overcome financial barriers and frictions and provide the funds needed to kick-start innovations. Although steps have been taken to promote financing of innovation and R&D at the EU level, problems persist resulting from fragmented funding and financing, the lack of innovative financing strategies, reduced R&D budgets, and the way the funding is channeled into the market. Against this backdrop, Redi suggests innovative ways to make use of venture capital funding in cooperation with the setting up of a specific, earmarked European Investment Fund financing scheme and a new guarantee system to help absorb some financial risks innovations hold for investors.

In the chapter on collaborative governance, Stefan Schepers argues convincingly that a promising method for promoting innovation requires a fundamental change in the EU's governance approach. As he discusses the nature and past reform efforts of the European Union governance system from an historical perspective, he derives the urgent need for change in governance methods and culture in order to anchor innovation into the system. Economic paradigms calling for innovation will have to recognize that without equally significant governance innovation their case is lost. Both forms of innovation facilitate each other and contribute to the common good.

Andrew Kakabadse's contribution reasserts that a radical new vision to innovation policy is needed. This vision, based on an innovation ecosystem (ideas, institutions, policies, and regulation) can only be achieved through all-encompassing collaborative governance that is interactive and value generating. Kakabadse pinpoints the crucial role of institutional arrangements as well as a governance of alignment of all the driving forces and actors in favor of radical change and innovation, and this also requires innovation in corporate management.

Christoph Bausch questions the ability of the EU system of governance to help business and research unfold their innovative potential: the European Union is a complex system constituted by a myriad of different actors with often discordant political agendas and interests and a dominant, rigid, and regulatory approach. The central aim of EU governance when it comes to promoting innovation is to reconcile and align such divergence and translate it into solutions that serve the common European good. The author argues that notably the EU regulatory system is no longer able to successfully manage complex policies, as in the case of R&D or innovation, and is in strong need of overhaul.

Jean-Claude Thoenig emphasizes in his contribution that any competitive innovation ecosystem requires a stimulating higher education and research environment. Academic institutions are key contributors and stakeholders to fuel economic and societal dynamics. Building a stronger academic capacity inside the EU is an ambition. Yet, although the difference between the three basic models of higher education and research—the Anglo-Saxon, the German Humboldtian, and the French Napoleonic model—is slowly fading away, only a dozen or so of Europe's universities may compete with their U.S. counterparts. The EU has not yet reached a critical mass that will build up a competitive innovation ecosystem of its own. The author outlines the steps forward necessary to make European academia a player of the highest standards.

A most unorthodox yet equally interesting perspective on the European innovation ecosystem is opened up in Michel Praet's paper dealing with cultural diversity and political unity in Europe; two strongly intertwined forces which, on the one hand, determine innovation potentials and, on the other hand, are a result of innovative thinking. Culture and unity, both need creativity and innovation as fertile soil. Moreover, our "cultural industries" require cross-sectoral innovation and collaboration based on diversity and provide an important economic and cultural asset. Politics, Praet argues, need to foster cultural innovation and diversity lest it fall victim to the American style of culture industries (movies, music, etc.), which *per se* are much more homogeneous and streamlined, not least due to the large markets they serve.

Having considered innovation policy from various perspectives, the book ends with a chapter on foresight by Stefan Schepers, who summarizes principal challenges resulting from scientific, ethical, economic, ecological, and geopolitical developments. Foresight strengthens further the urgency of an innovative innovation ecosystem and governance and is a useful tool to explore the known interactions in complex systems, still leaving known unknowns that require special attention. Foresight studies can play a very useful role in developing alignment between stakeholders and in overcoming short-termism of electoral politics within innovated governance systems able to deal with the twenty-first century's problems. The EU could use foresight to position itself as a principal actor for solution development in its own and the global interest.

Eventually, in Chap. 14, we have assembled political recommendations to EU policy makers that are laid down in the two reports by the HLG on Innovation Policy Management, and a comment about the progress so far.

Our key conclusion is that Europe needs to work toward an innovation ecosystem that would unleash the dynamic interactions and feedbacks between the hitherto insufficiently coherent actions of the EU, national and local governments, large and small business, and universities and centers of learning across borders and economic sectors. Without a quantum leap in innovation and innovation policies, we will not be able to muster our economic problems and make our industries strong enough to compete on the global level. Addressing sector-specific innovation performance in areas such as advanced manufacturing, construction, energy, telecommunications, pharmacy, biotech, and transport, etc., will be indispensable for developing and strengthening a solid industrial base. And the most important and overarching task is to highlight the emergent narrative of a Europe unfolding its large innovation potential for pioneering and shaping our common future.

References

Aho Group Report. 2006. Creating an innovative Europe. http://ec.europa.eu/invest-in-research/pdf/download_en/aho_report.pdf.

Ahuja, G., and C.M. Lampert. 2001. Entrepreneurship in the large corporation: A longitudinal study of how established firms create breakthrough inventions. *Strategic Management Journal* Special issue: strategic entrepreneurship: entrepreneurial strategies for wealth creation. 22: 521–543.

Christensen, C.M. 2011. *The innovator's dilemma*. New York: Harper Collins.

Cooper, R.C. 2001. Stage gate international, innovation process. http://www.stage-gate.com/resources_stage-gate_full.php.

———. 2008. Perspective: The stage-gate idea-to-launch process—Update. http://www.stage-gate.net/downloads/wp/wp_30.pdf.

Damanpour, F. 1991. Organizational innovation: A meta-analysis of effects of determinants and moderators. *The Academy of Management Journal* 34: 555–590.

Doz, Y., and M. Kosonen. 2008. *Fast strategy: How strategic agility will help you stay ahead of the game*. Harlow: Pearson.

Eckardt, S. 2015. *Messung des Innovations- und Intrapreneurship- Klimas*. Wiesbaden: Springer.

European Commission—DG GROWTH. Innovation scoreboards (various issues). http://ec.europa.eu/growth/industry/innovation/facts-figures/scoreboards/index_en.htm.

Granieri, M., and A. Renda. 2012. *Innovation law and policy in the European Union: Towards horizon 2020*. Milan: Springer Italia.

Gretschmann, K. 2014. Forging the iron or chasing the wind? In *Rethinking the future of Europe*, eds. S. Schepers, and A. Kakabadse, 28–41. Basingstoke: Palgrave-Macmillan.

———. 2015. The EU in stormy seas: Beginning of the end or end of the beginning. In *A global perspective on the European economic crisis*, eds. B. Dallago et al. New York: Routledge.

Guzzetti, L. 1995. *A short history of European Union Research Policy*. Luxembourg: OPEC.

Jackson, D.B. 2011. What is an innovation ecosystem?. http://erc-assoc.org/sites/default/files/topics/policy_studies/DJackson_Innovation%20Ecosystem_03-15-11.pdf.

Mazzucato, M. 2013. *The entrepreneurial state*. London: Anthem Press.

North, D.C. 1990. *Institutions, institutional change and economic performance*. New York: Cambridge University Press.

Report from the High Level Group. 2004. Facing the challenge (chaired by Wim Kok). https://ec.europa.eu/research/evaluations/pdf/archive/fp6-evidence-base/evaluation_studies_and_reports/evaluation_studies_and_reports_2004/the_lisbon_strategy_for_growth_and_employment__report_from_the_high_level_group.pdf.

Servan-Schreiber, J.-J. 1968. *Le défi américain*. Paris: Denoel.

Tuomioja, E. 2009. The role of soft power in EU common foreign policy. *International symposium on cultural diplomacy*, Berlin, 30 July 2009, mimeographed. http://www.culturaldiplomacy.org/academy/content/articles/speakers/detailed/erkki-tuomioja/erkki-tumioja_-_the-role-of-soft-power-in-eu-common-foreign-policy.pdf.

2

The Benefits and Rewards of Innovation Policies

Morten Rasmussen

This chapter explores the link between innovation and national economic performance parameters such as international competitiveness, growth, and employment creation. It compares cross-country studies and rankings from major providers of comparative performance data and analyses the importance of innovation-friendly country systems for sound economic performance. Following a methodological reflection on the cross-study approach, it further discusses the effects of innovation on economic objectives, including performances in GDP, R&D, and employment. The assessment also integrates best practice examples and considers how innovation can be promoted from

The chapter is based on the paper titled, "The Micro and Macroeconomic Benefits of Innovation," from the publication *High Level Group on Innovation Policy Management* (2014): *Report & Recommendations*, June 2013. The chapter is updated on the basis of new empirical research and data from the most recent innovation and competitiveness rankings.

M. Rasmussen (✉)
Innovation consultant at CARSA, Former researcher at the
High Level Group on Innovation Policy Management, UK
e-mail: morten.ter@gmail.com or mrasmussen@carsa.es

an innovation policy management perspective: supportive of growth, jobs, and re-industrialization, as well as digitalization in markets and society. In this way, the chapter also links together the remaining chapters' recommendations on innovation policy to its economic impacts. In line with the remaining chapters of this book, it seeks to discuss how Europe can promote innovation capacity, capable of addressing the critical needs and societal challenges ahead, in a manner that is complementary to open innovation and innovation-ecosystem-building approaches, thus aspiring to collaboration models, co-creation, and user-driven innovation.

Overall, the chapter argues that despite some degree of variation, the cross-country studies comparison found that the top-performing countries in innovation were also those with the strongest performance in competitiveness and employment, pointing to a strong correlation between well-designed national innovation systems and good competitiveness conditions. Although there is no "one best way" to achieve top-notch innovation performance, as each country has its own specificities, including distinct industrial and business fabrics, certain similarities are found among the most innovative countries: efficient governance toolsets, consensus-building culture, integrative innovation strategies, targeted funding models, public–private partnerships, and successful commercialization of technological knowledge. Ample evidence shows that holistic and ecosystem-oriented approaches to innovation systems, with strengths in most dimensions, can significantly enhance innovation in markets, but also within organizations and public sectors, and thereby support competitiveness, employment, and value creation.

1   Cross-Study Comparison of National Innovation and Competitiveness Performance: Findings and Analysis

Academia, businesses, and policy makers alike acknowledge that research and innovation policy can be a very useful stimulant for economic development and social well-being (European

Commission 2010a; OECD 2007), but progress in Europe has been too slow to significantly catch up with the USA and Japan in innovation performance. Although the innovation gap is closing, Europe still finds itself struggling to keep up with the innovation leaders: the USA, South Korea, and Japan outperform the EU by, respectively, 22 %, 24 % and 14 %, according to the Innovation Union Scoreboard 2015 (European Commission 2015). Behind this picture, and among a number of causes, is a lack of capacity to compete on private R&D expenditures on innovation, patent applications, tertiary education, and public–private copublications, in comparison with the aforementioned countries (Eurostat 2014). At the same time, while China is still some distance away from aggregate EU innovation performance, it is catching up steadily, as exemplified through increased public R&D spending and the ability to attract highly skilled talents (OECD 2014).

In order to put the innovation gap in perspective, and with a view to address the linkages between the different components of national innovation ecosystems, we compare cross-study findings on innovation and competitiveness in this section. With this background, the insight gained from the cross-country studies will not only be used to assess the countries that make holistic and systemic endeavors to provide investments and guidance for innovation (both from policy and financial angles), but also to scrutinize the link between innovation-friendly country systems and economic performance (such as GDP growth and employment).

Starting with the rankings on innovation, we present comparative assessments of countries' innovation performance, based on Cornell University, The Institut Européen d'Administration des Affaires (INSEAD), the World Intellectual Property Organization's *Global Innovation Index World 2015*, the World Economic Forum's Global Competitiveness Report 2014–2015, and the European Commission's Innovation Union Scoreboard 2015, in Table 2.1 below.

Table 2.2 below compares competitiveness rankings on the basis of the World Economic Forum's *Global Competitiveness Report* 2014–2015 and IMD's *World Competitiveness Yearbook* 2015: both have undertaken

Table 2.1 Overview of innovation rankings

Rank	INSEAD's *Global Innovation Index* 2015	WEF's Global Competitiveness Report 2014–2015[a]	Innovation Union Scoreboard 2015
1	Switzerland (68.30)	Finland (5.8)	Sweden (0.7401)
2	UK (62.42)	Switzerland (5.7)	Denmark (0.7362)
3	Sweden (62.40)	Israel (5.6)	Finland (0.6764)
4	Netherlands (61.58)	Japan (5.5)	Germany (0.6763)
5	USA (60.10)	USA (5.5)	Netherlands (0.6473)
6	Finland (59.97)	Germany (5.5)	Luxembourg (0.6418)
7	Singapore (59.36)	Sweden (5.4)	UK (0.6365)
8	Ireland (59.13)	Netherlands (5.3)	Ireland (0.6282)
9	Luxembourg (59.02)	Singapore (5.2)	Belgium (0.6193)
10	Denmark (57.70)	Taiwan (5.1)	France (0.5906)
11	Hong Kong (57.73)	Denmark (5.1)	Austria (0.5851)
12	Germany (57.05)	UK (5.0)	Slovenia (0.5339)
13	Iceland (57.02)	Belgium (4.9)	Estonia (0.4890)
14	Korea. Rep. (56.26)	Qatar (4.9)	Czech Republic (0.4471)
15	New Zealand (55.92)	Norway (4.9)	Cyprus (0.4448)
16	Canada (55.73)	Luxembourg (4.8)	Italy (0.4389)
17	Australia (55.22)	Korea. Rep. (4.8)	Portugal (0.4032)
18	Austria (54.07)	Austria (4.8)	Malta (0.3966)
19	Japan (53.97)	France (4.7)	Spain (0.3854)
20	Norway (53.80)	Ireland (4.7)	Hungary (0.3692)

Drawing on: Cornell University, INSEAD, and the World Intellectual Property Organization (2015) the *Global Innovation Index World 2015—Effective Innovation Policies for Development*, Schwab, K. (ed.) (2015); *The Global Competitiveness Report 2014–2015*, Geneva, World Economic Forum; and European Commission (2015) *Innovation Union Scoreboard 2015*, Brussels, European Union

[a]The ranking from World Economic Forum's Global Competitiveness Report is based on the 12th pillar: Innovation, which is part of Subindex C: Innovation and sophistication factors

comprehensive studies of countries' performance along a wide range of competitiveness indicators and drivers.

Before analyzing the results, the methodological frameworks behind the different innovation assessment approaches requires some considerations. Differences in the criteria used, weights assigned, and methodology applied to capture innovation and competitiveness performance logically leads to variation in the innovation and competitiveness rankings by IMD,

Table 2.2 Overview of competitiveness rankings

Rank	WEF's Global Competitiveness Report 2014–2015	IMD's World Competitiveness Yearbook 2015
1	Switzerland (5.70)	USA (100.000)
2	Singapore (5.65)	Hong Kong (96.037)
3	USA (5.54)	Singapore (94.950)
4	Finland (5.50)	Switzerland (91.916)
5	Germany (5.49)	Canada (90.410)
6	Japan (5.547)	Luxembourg (89.411)
7	Hong Kong (5.46)	Norway (87.915)
8	Netherlands (5.45)	Denmark (87.077)
9	UK (5.41)	Sweden (85.921)
10	Sweden (5.41)	Germany (85.637)
11	Norway (5.35)	Taiwan (85.405)
12	United Arab Emirates (5.33)	United Arab Emirates (84.750)
13	Denmark (5.29)	Qatar (84.626)
14	Taiwan (5.25)	Malaysia (84.113)
15	Canada (5.24)	Netherlands (83.615)
16	Qatar (5.24)	Ireland (82.969)
17	New Zealand (5.20)	New Zealand (81.808)
18	Belgium (5.18)	Australia (80.452)
19	Luxembourg (5.17)	UK (79.932)
20	Malaysia (5.16)	Finland (78.447)

Drawing on: Schwab, K. (ed.) (2015) *the Global Competitiveness Report* 2014–2015, Geneva; and IMD (2015) *World Competitiveness Yearbook* 2015, Lausanne, Switzerland, IMD

INSEAD, IUS, and WEF. This is further explained in detail in Annex 1 and 2, which compares the overall methodology and data collection approaches used for scoping countries' innovative activities and competitiveness parameters.

Among the innovation rankings, the reports by INSEAD and WEF stand out for their broad scope concerning country selection and application of indicators. The WEF gives relatively high attention to soft data in the form of its Executive Opinion Survey, whereas INSEAD to a higher extent emphasizes hard data variables. Looking at competitiveness rankings, the IMD draws on 342 criteria, gives equal weight for all variables, and mainly relies on quantitative data. In comparison, the WEF study uses 114 criteria, attaches specific and unequal weights to each indicator, and emphasizes survey data with a weighting of 70 %. This suggests that the WEF assessment has strengths in its forward-looking indicators and up-to-date perceptions. In contrast, the report by IMD, in particular, but also INSEAD, values static and objective indicators higher, thus revealing more objectively past tendencies and performances. Yet, the common thread for all cross-study assessments is that they may not be able to grasp the impact of newly introduced innovation policies, as it will take some time before they influence performance.

Despite the differences in the exact ranking positions, the studies by the WEF, IMD, INSEAD, and IUS found many similarities in their findings on innovation and competitiveness. We can see that a number of EU member states, including Finland, Germany, the Netherlands, Sweden, Denmark, and Luxembourg, are consistently ranked among the most competitive countries. All the aforementioned countries make it into the top 20 ranking, according to both WEF and IMD's evaluation of competitiveness performance.

When we assess factors enabling a strong competitive performance, there is a corresponding significant tendency among the most competitive countries to perform either in the very top or well above average in innovation dimensions. The IMD, INSEAD, and IUS equally place countries such as Finland, Germany, the Netherlands, Sweden, Denmark, and Luxembourg among the most innovative countries. Overall, common for the countries with the finest innovation ranking achievements at the European or global level, they also tend to achieve a very high competitive position.

These findings are further supported by evidence on public and private R&D expenditures: the aforementioned EU countries with top competitiveness rankings all belong to the group of countries with the highest total expenditure on R&D as a percentage of GDP (European Commission 2015). The same observation holds if we consider the perceptions of company spending on R&D, according to the survey findings from WEF (Schwab 2015). Yet, and more important, although R&D funding has an enabling effect on innovation, it is only one part of many innovation dimension that must be addressed to support innovative activities.[1] R&D funding of innovation, whether public or private, requires

---

[1] See also Chap. 9 of this book, "Funding and Financing of Innovation—Fresh Thinking Required," for a discussion on the importance of R&D spending.

innovation-supportive policy framework settings and complementary efforts in order to ensure its transformation into markets.

Although, INSEAD's 2015 study shows differences between the input and output indices in terms of comparative country performance, the data and rankings still underline that the efforts countries undertake "to improve enabling environments are rewarded with increased innovation outputs" (Cornell University et al. 2015). This also accounts for faster employment growth creation, as the EU countries facing the largest economic impacts of innovation also had higher employment rates (European Commission 2013a). We can also observe a persistent—in some cases substantial—heterogeneity in innovation performance among the EU member states, following to some extent north versus south and east versus west dimensions (European Commission 2014). The member states, however, seem to converge on innovation performance as differences have become less significant since 2013 (European Commission 2015).

There is no single way to achieve top innovation performance, and each country has its own specificities, but the Innovation Union Scoreboard report found a wide range of commonalities among the most innovative countries. First, in order to achieve a high level of innovation performance, it requires the development of a balanced and holistic national innovation system, with high performance across many factors. As observed from the Innovation Union Scoreboard and the remaining cross-country studies, these include, but are not limited to, strengths in national research, public–private partnerships, collaboration among innovative small and medium-sized enterprises (SMEs), business R&D expenditures, PCT patent applications, and commercialization of technological knowledge facilitating knowledge transfer and rapid market use.

Another interesting perspective, if we also integrate dimensions of governance into this analysis on innovation performance, is that a correlation exists between, on the one hand, strong innovation and competitiveness performances and, on the other hand, the quality of governance. The World Bank's worldwide governance indicators measure governance performance according to: (1) voice and accountability; (2) political stability and absence of violence; (3) government effectiveness; (4) regulatory quality; (5) rule of law; and (6) control of corruption.

The six aggregate indicators are further based on 30 underlying data sources concerning perceptions of governance. If we consider the top 20 performances on governance (World Bank 2015), we can observe that the same countries (e.g., Sweden, Finland, the Netherlands, and Germany) also had top rankings on innovation and competitiveness, thus pointing to a strong correlation between the quality and efficiency of public services, rule of law, accountability, and countries benefiting from innovation and economic growth.

On the basis of the study rankings and criteria, and keeping the general conclusions of the linkages between innovation and competitiveness in mind, the following sections will offer further discussion on the link between innovation and a range of parameters, such as macroeconomic performance and GDP, R&D investments, and employment creation. References will also be made, where relevant, to the effects of innovation on private sector value creation and public sector services.

2   The Effects of Innovation on Macroeconomic Performance and GDP

Starting from a historical perspective, Europe has since the 1970s experienced a transformation from extensive growth (relying on capital formation and the existing stock of technological knowledge, and subject to diminishing returns) toward intensive growth relying much more heavily upon innovation (Eichengreen 2007). Since the mid-1990s, many nations have increased their efforts to integrate innovation-based economic growth by boosting jobs in key technological and manufacturing sectors. According to Atkinson & Ezell, it has led to a race for "global innovation advantage" whereby countries compete by "innovation chasing" in order to grow and attract high-value-added economic activities (Atkinson and Ezell 2012).

The OECD (2007) has further predicted that innovation will be "a crucial determinant of the global competitiveness of nations (p. 3)." Some countries have been able to take advantage of the opportunities offered by globalization and new technologies through efficient private sector and governance methods and are predicted to increase their competitiveness and growth rates. In general, the application of successful innovation policies and innovative activities, in markets as well as public sectors, enable countries to better utilize resources: by turning innovative ideas into new products, services, processes, and business models, better conditions are created for sustainable growth and competitiveness, quality jobs, and addressing European societal challenges (European Commission 2010a).

The benefits of innovation within one country are expected to lead to the diffusion of new technology, which contributes to increased knowledge and productivity and thereby also enables growth in GDP per capita growth.[2] According to Ahlstrom (2010), the importance of innovation for society concerns that even small upward shifts in the growth rate lead to important differences over time (Ahlstrom 2010). Yet, even very small reductions in growth diminish the potential benefits to the society (Barro and Sala-i-Martin 2004).

To develop strong, innovative capacity supportive of businesses and macroeconomic performance is a complex and challenging task that requires addressing many factors from a policy management perspective, while also taking into account the continuously evolving context of innovation and industrial and digital developments. In practical terms, innovation processes are widely recognized as characterized by multiple feedbacks and loops that influence and shape potential outcomes and their transformation into markets (Godin 2006). In addition to the role of research, development, and the application of scientific or technology advances, innovation processes are also shaped by such factors as market needs, marketing, networking, partnerships and, increasingly, users (Chesbrough 2003; European Commission 2015). Being competitive today, from a company point of view, therefore often requires simultaneous innovation along many dimensions, such as business models, partnerships, customer integration models, costumer experiences, and differentiated and personalized products and services.

---

[2] See, for example, W. J. Baumol and R. Strom, "Entrepreneurship and Economic Growth," in *Strategic Entrepreneurship Journal*, 1 (3–4), 2007, pp. 233–237; C. M. Christensen and M. Raynor, *The Innovator's Solution*, Boston: Harvard Business School Publishing, 2003.

Innovation can also be considered as an instrument of entrepreneurship that in turn facilitates competitiveness and growth. According to Romer, innovation is vital for the "entrepreneurial economy" since it leads to wealth creation (Romer 1986). Although entrepreneurs have a vital role in driving innovation, the constellation and coherence of European and national policies is imperative for supporting innovation performance. Given the complexity of factors and relationships necessary for a successful innovation strategy, the advancement of innovation requires efficient innovation strategies, framework conditions, modes of funding, reducing regulatory complexity and rigidity, facilitating industrial cooperation and public–private cooperation, and moving into next-generation industries. In order to meet global competition challenges and to achieve macroeconomic gains, countries must therefore excel in innovation and research by fostering the development of firms and institutions that are global leaders in their fields (Veugelers 2010). The central claim is that innovation has become one of the most important factors for countries' abilities to thrive in the global economy (Atkinson and Ezell 2012).

3   R&D Investments and Innovation Performance

Science and research are closely linked to innovation activities, not only by providing inspiration for business, but also by offering forecasts and guidance for policy making on the promotion of innovation and growth. Since the mid-1990s, investments in knowledge have increased more rapidly than investments in equipment and machinery across most OECD countries, and have exceeded the investments in equipment and machinery in such countries as Finland and the USA. As also outlined in the previous analysis, the best performing countries in R&D investments are also among the countries with the best competitiveness rankings.

From a business perspective, the advantages of investing in R&D is coupled to improvements in market shares and margins. Yet, the computation of the exact investment return of any particular company investment in innovation, whether through R&D or non-R&D

investments, is a hard task, even within a single company. This further complicates the process of allocating resources for innovation activities. However, if we turn the question around, the alternative is to consider the potential opportunity costs of not investing in innovation and thereby the ability to launch innovation in markets. Put differently, the cost of not supporting or developing innovation (in its different forms) is linked to the market opportunities that the company fails to address. The avoidance of innovation therefore hinders a company's ability to enter into new markets, attract new customers, and benefit from new revenue streams and market shares.

The economic crisis has however led to a decline in R&D expenditures in many EU countries, although with significant variation between countries, sectors, and actors (European Commission 2013a). There is also a significant gap between the EU and innovation leaders such as the USA on private R&D investments. The gap can, to some extent, be explained by the focus on medium-tech sectors in Europe, in contrast to new high-tech and high-growth sectors, which are more dominant in the USA. The EU has recognized that the low R&D spending, from public as well as private sources, may restrict Europe's innovation performance and endanger future competitiveness, and that R&D investments are an important element in enabling growth in Europe (European Commission 2013a).

As previously alluded to, R&D expenditure is however only one of many interlinked sources that pushes forward innovation. R&D investments also require conversion into market value and wide-ranging complimentary reforms of the settings relevant to a country's innovation model.

3.1   Country Examples on R&D Practices

Focusing specifically on the relation between R&D and economic performance, our cross-study findings revealed that Finland, as an example, has consistently ranked at the forefront of innovation investment and innovative performance. Finland had the highest R&D intensity among EU countries (3.32 % of GDP) in 2013 (Eurostat 2013). Central to its innovation system is a collection of business accelerators funded by the government and private enterprises and strong public–private partnerships facilitating knowledge transfer and rapid market use.

Tekes, the innovation agency in Finland, and the venture capital fund Finnvera, aim to find and support early stage companies. They have funded over 60 % of well-known Finnish innovations between 1985 and 2007. In 80 % of cases, the funding was found to have a significant impact on companies' performances (Hyytinen et al. 2012). Of the 49 million Euros they contributed in 2011 to innovative companies seeking rapid growth, one-third was directed to firms in the Vigo acceleration program, from which around 130 companies are currently receiving funding. The cumulative turnover of these companies increased from 10 to 250 million Euros in 4 years. In terms of the growth company ecosystem in Finland, several attributes define these firms such as being younger (less than 10 years), smaller (less than 20 employees), ICT and knowledge intensive, and being targeted by venture capitalists. When assessing the efforts to improve innovation policies on research and technological performance, we can observe that Finland is among the top performers in producing scientific articles and triadic patents per capita. The entrepreneur-friendly Finnish environment has supported a significant number of start-ups and new clusters. This is also reflected in companies' performances in new-to-market product innovations. In addition, since the 1990s, Finland has systemically outperformed the OECD and EU15 average performance in labor productivity growth (Tekes 2012).

Germany's experience echoes that of Finland. Fornahl, Broekel and Boschma's study found evidence that German biotech firms' performances, including their patent activity, were enhanced through public modes of funding such as R&D subsidies to joint R&D projects with two or more partners, network partners, and close cognitive distance of collaborative partners within a cluster (Broekel et al. 2011). Although a country's specific policy and framework conditions make it difficult to transfer experiences that worked under certain conditions, these lessons can be applied in other contexts.

The Small Business Innovation Research (SBIR) program in the USA,[3] often used as a reference model, and equally an inspiration source for the new EU SME Instrument, seeks to help develop the capacity of domestic small businesses to conduct research and development. In particular,

---

[3] For more details, see https://www.sbir.gov/.

it addresses the shortage of high-risk, early stage research funding, while also integrating commercial potential criteria. Funding is provided in the form of grants or contracts; 11 federal agencies in the US participate, and they are tasked to allocate 2.8 % of their R&D budgets to the program. Funding is provided in three phases: exploration of feasibility and technical merit (phase 1); R&D efforts to support development and expansion of phase 1 results (phase 2); and commercialization of R&D efforts (phase 3). According to an evaluation by Wessner, the SBIR program plays a catalytic role during the early stage of a technology development cycle (Wessner 2008). With a shortage of private sector sources available, it helps young firms determine the potential market of a given product or service and potentially enable them to grow rapidly through venture capital financing. Some lessons learned from the SBIR program include that just 2–3 % of funded SMEs become a big hit (Wessner 2015). This further calls for a broad and holistic innovation framework, but also long-term policy action and clear objectives, to help bring R&D results into markets.

4 Innovation, Entrepreneurship, and the Employment Effects

As innovation and entrepreneurship in advanced economies through decades and centuries has been followed by employment growth, it points to a positive long-run economic impact of innovation on employment. In this context, several studies, including Audretsch et al. (2001); Baumol (2004); Carree and Thurik (2003); and Schumpeter (1912), have outlined the spillover benefits of entrepreneurial activities. This provides a strong case for reorienting public policies and funding toward supporting these activities in the economy. After all, it is not just the entrepreneur but the entire society that possibly may gain from these activities.

In this context, a study by the European Commission (2012a) found that 85 % of the net new jobs in Europe between 2002 and 2010 were created by SMEs. In another study, the European Commission (2013b) has also underlined that employment growth heavily depends on high-growth innovative firms, as the quantity of jobs they create, directly or indirectly, is disproportionately large.

Framework conditions, the level of regulatory complexity and rigidity, and the access to public and private modes of finance are all important factors for businesses creating new jobs. They allow businesses to set up targets for innovation, to scale up and to reduce time and resources spent on dealing with the anticompetitive side effects of regulations or policies and chasing after scarce sources of finance; instead, it enables businesses to focus on research, development, production, delivery, and marketing, among others, of goods and services.

The long-term view is also critical for realizing the benefits of innovation. Many studies fail to find a significantly positive relationship between entrepreneurship and growth—but the studies that covered 10 and more years provide clear evidence on the relationship, while also highlighting the long-term perspective of the economic effects of innovation (Nystrom 2008).

However, an important perspective needs to be put forward in this context. In order to secure a positive spillover effect on European employment levels, it requires that the innovative entrepreneurial-driven businesses are able to fill new job openings with workers from European countries. A profit-seeking company is incentivized to search for the best possible employees, according to the required skill-sets, even if this implies an offshoring of its production facilities. As a consequence, there are high demands for upgrading skills—for example, according to the new needs and opportunities in digital and advanced manufacturing sectors. Put differently, the EU member states need to enhance the demanded set of skills and also popularize technological topics. Yet, it also requires finding a balance, since talent flows and brain gains lead to accumulation of human capital, equally supportive of growth and innovation in the European business landscape.

The automation in industry and digitalization in markets and society, which are enabled through the availability of big data, mass customization and the Internet of Things, are highly beneficial in terms of productivity and new business opportunities. Yet, their effects on the European labor markets do require targeted policy responses, in order to mitigate circumstances where capital replaces labor. According to Frey and Osborne, 47 % of the occupational categories are at risk of being automated, including technical writing, legal work, accountancy, and a range of white collar occupations (Frey and Osborne 2013). The share of employment is also increasingly moving away from manufacturing and toward services in the advanced economies. Also digital literacy, which is becoming more of an essential life skill, is becoming a key challenge, with many disadvantaged groups partly disconnected from digital trends, including in particular those persons over the age of 55. Therefore, strategies and efforts are needed to develop advanced skills in manufacturing and IT-related fields through educational attainment and by removing obstacles to the demand of advanced manufacturing technologies, while also making the service sector more competitive and capable of absorbing dislocated workers. In many "modern services," ICT, for example, creates new growth and high-productivity sectors (Dadush 2015), including in finance, telecommunications, business process outsourcing, and software, and is thus an important future source of new jobs. Ghani et al. (2011) noted that the range of modem services capable of being digitized and traded at the global level is continuously expanding.

4.1   Country Examples on the Employment Effects of Innovation Investment

In the following section, some country examples on the employment effects stemming from innovation investments will be addressed. Although the role of large firms and corporate "locomotives" in job creation is essential, jobs are increasingly generated by new, surviving growth firms. According to Nordic Innovation (2012), gazelles (young firms with a minimum of 20 % annual growth) have had a considerable impact on job creation relative to their absolute numbers.

Between 2006 and 2009, 214 Norwegian and 92 Finnish gazelle firms increased employment by 10,594 and 8,447, respectively (without considering the indirect employment effects). Between 2006 and 2009, 691 growth companies were found in Finland. On average they grew by 74 people during the period, and in total generated more than 51,000 new jobs, accounting for almost half of the new jobs created in Finland during this period. Here it should be kept in mind that the innovation programs also take time to realize.

German industry has a strong international competitive position concerning high-quality, high-performance, innovative products. The backbone of German manufacturing is small to mid-sized firms. These companies are in many cases committed to keeping factories at home: though they aim for the highest profit possible, they are not under the same pressure from shareholders to show consistently growing profits each quarter (Schuman 2011). This allows them to take a long-term view and find ways of staying profitable while still manufacturing in Germany.

Many of those countries (Germany, Finland, and Sweden) who strengthened their innovation strategies and R&D investments prior to the economic crisis also experienced subsequent recovery and employment growth (European Commission 2013a; OECD 2007). The countries with relatively high economic prosperity, but lagging behind in building a knowledge-based productive economy, are those that have suffered the most in terms of employment. In other words, prosperity in Europe seems unlikely to be sustained over time without high levels of innovation (World Economic Forum 2012).

A number of barriers exist for innovative approaches to job creations: lacking framework conditions, regulatory complexity and rigidity, funding possibilities, and the skill quality of workers (World Bank 2012). Also, employment is likely to increase in more productive firms, whereas employment in less productive firms tends to decrease. It therefore seems that innovation and employment creation are strongly coupled in the long run, although innovation may imply shifts in employment across sectors. This in turn requires a well-designed labor market and policies aimed at helping displacing movers find new jobs.

5   Overall Findings

Through interlinked steps, this chapter has identified country systems performing well in innovation—with wide-ranging and holistic policy management frameworks to support it—and proves the importance of innovation for competitiveness. The chapter further discussed the link between innovation and a range or parameters, such as macroeconomic performance and GDP, and R&D performance and employment creation.

The main finding of this chapter is that a more encompassing approach to innovation policy management is required, which should be rooted in a holistic and ecosystem-oriented approach, to achieve growth and employment in Europe. The cross-study comparison found a strong correlation between innovation and competitiveness; the most innovative countries were also among the most competitive. Evidence also suggests that efforts that countries undertake (input) are rewarded in terms of improved innovation outputs and market activities that create value.

There is no single way to achieve top innovation performance, but commonalities were found among the most innovative countries: efficient governance toolsets, well-designed framework conditions, innovation strategies, and funding modes, as well as strengths in national research, public–private partnerships, and commercialization of technological knowledge. Evidence from the best innovation systems indicates that R&D expenditure and well-targeted business accelerators had a significant impact on research output and quality as well as on companies' growth, job hiring, and new-to-market product innovations. While the top-performing countries in innovation and competitiveness had some of the highest R&D expenditures, a simple increase in R&D spending may not necessarily lead to growth and quality job creation. There is a strong need to supplement R&D spending with an encompassing innovation policy and financing toolbox, including efforts to transform public and private R&D expenditures into a market context. Put differently, countries should constantly innovate along several dimensions to differentiate in a crowded, highly competitive field. An ineffective innovation model proves to be due to lack of priorities, criteria, and benchmarks for selecting projects, as well as low excitement around newness and change and unintended side-effects resulting from policies and regulatory complexity.

Innovation enables companies to transform themselves into a completely different type of business, and by bringing innovation to the market, firms facilitate economic growth. The spillover effects—direct and indirect employment—of this process extend throughout the entire economy. The economic impacts provide a strong rationale for a system redesign that reorients policies, funding modes, and regulations and their application toward fostering the growth of innovative firms and giving European innovation a new momentum.

6   Annex 1: Overview of Key Innovation Criteria

	INSEAD's Global Innovation Index World 2015	WEF's Global Competitiveness Report 2014–2015	Innovation Union Scoreboard 2015
Scope	The Global Innovation index 2015 (GII) analyses innovation performance among 141 economies.	The WEF's Global Competitiveness Index (GCI) focuses on 144 countries' competitiveness performance, but is in this section only related to its innovation assessment.	The Innovation Union Scoreboard (IUS) provides a comparative assessment of the relative strengths of the EU Member States' national innovation systems.
Criteria	The GII is structured around two sub-indices. The *Innovation Input Sub Index* draws on the following pillars: (1) institutions; (2) human capital and research; (3) infrastructure; (4) market sophistication; and (5) business sophistication. The *Innovation Output Sub-Index* consists of: (6) knowledge and technology outputs; and (7) creative outputs.	The innovation pillar, which belongs to the *Innovation and sophistication index*, captures: (1) capacity for innovation; (2) quality of scientific research institutions; (3) company spending on R (4) university-industry collaboration in R (5) government procurement; (6) availability of scientist and engineers; (7) PCT patent applications; and (8) intellectual property protection.	The IUS assessment distinguishes between three main types of indicators: (1) *Enablers* focusing on human resources, research systems, and finance and support; (2) *Firm Activities* capturing firm investments, linkages and entrepreneurship, and intellectual assets; and (3) *Outputs* drawing on respectively innovators and economic effects.

(*continued*)

	INSEAD's Global Innovation Index World 2015	WEF's Global Competitiveness Report 2014–2015	Innovation Union Scoreboard 2015
Weight	The overall GII score is the average of the Input and Output Sub-Indices, which both has the same weight in the calculation of the overall GII scores (although the Output Sub-Index only consist of two pillars).	The computation of the score is based on aggregations of scores from the indicator level, mainly qualitative data. The survey asked for responses on a scale from 1 and up to 7 which is the best possible outcome.	The performance is measured using an indicator obtained by an aggregation of the 25 IUS indicators ranking from lowest possible performance of 0 toward the maximum of 1.
Data Collection	A total of 79 indicators are used: 59 hard data variables, 5 survey questions and 16 composite indicators from international sources. Data stems mainly from 2012 to 2014.	The calculation of the innovation performance draws almost entirely on soft data from the WEF's annual Executive Opinion Survey (2014 data).	The IUS uses statistics from Eurostat and international sources. Indicators rely mainly on data from 2013 and 2012, while limited indicators are based on 2010 and 2009 data.

7 Annex 2: Overview of Key Competitiveness Criteria

	WEF's *Global Competitiveness Report* 2014–2015	IMD's *World Competitiveness Yearbook* 2015
Scope	The WEF applies the Global Competitiveness Index (GCI) measuring the microeconomic and macroeconomic foundations of national competitiveness in 144 countries.	The *WCY* assesses and ranks 61 countries' ability to create and maintain an environment which stimulates firms' competitiveness.
Criteria	The GCI assesses 12 pillars grouped into 3 sub-indexes: (1) the Basic requirements sub-index covering institutions, infrastructure, macroeconomic environment, and health and primary education; (2) the Efficiency enhancers sub-index focusing on higher education and training, goods market efficiency, labor market efficiency, financial market development, technological readiness and market size; and (3) Innovation and sophistication factors sub-index addressing business sophistication and innovation.	The *WCY* analyses 342 ranked criteria linked to 4 factors: (1) an macroeconomic evaluation of the domestic economy; (2) the extent to which government policies are conducive to competitiveness; (3) the extent to which enterprises are encouraged by the national environment to act in an innovative, profitable and responsible manner; and (4) the extent to which firms' need of technological, scientific and human resources are meet.
Weight	The GCI score presents a weighted average of the various factors and the computation is based on aggregations of scores from the most disaggregated level to the overall GCI score. The GCI takes stages of development into account, by giving a higher weight to the sub-indicies deemed more relevant for a given economy based on which stage it is located in.	Each of the four competitiveness factors are further divided into five sub-factors which, independently on the number of criteria they contain, are given the same weight in the overall consolidation of results. The overall ranking of the *WCY* thus stems from aggregating the results of the 20 sub-factors.

	WEF's *Global Competitiveness Report* 2014–2015	IMD's *World Competitiveness Yearbook* 2015
Data collection	The WEF cooperates with over 160 partner institutes worldwide and relies on quantitative data from internationally recognized agencies and national authorities (mainly data from 2013 to 2014). When a more qualitative assessment is required or quantitative indicators are deemed insufficient, it draws upon data from the WEF's annual Executive Opinion Survey (EOS): the 2014 version of the EOS consists of more than 14,000 surveys with executives, which represents an average of 100 respondents per country.	IMD cooperates with 55 partner institutes and draws on hard data from international organizations when measuring competitiveness (e.g., GDP). Soft data from IMD's Executive Opinion Survey of 6234 respondents in 2015 integrates business executives' perceptions of competitiveness. Hard data represents a weight of approx. 2/3 in the overall ranking; the survey data is given a weight of 1/3.

8 Annex 3: Measurement of Innovation

Innovation surveys	Several methods and approaches have been developed to measure innovative activities. It can be measured through innovation surveys whereby innovating firms are asked about their activities. However, this kind of qualitative measurement finds it hard to distinguish between genuine innovative activity and the introduction of best practice, which already is in place in other firms (i.e., is it new to the world or new to the firm or market).
Input indicators	Another way of determining innovation is through input indicators such as the recorded level of R&D expenditures. Yet, although this indicator indicates broad differences among market actors in terms of the rate of innovation, it is less capable of assessing the exact timing or level of innovation.

(*continued*)

(continued)

Output indicators	Output indicators such as IPRS, including trademarks, designs and, in particular, patents, have also been analyzed to measure innovative activities. The advantage of using patents as an indicator is firstly that they in many cases can be a forerunner to innovative activity and secondly that much data are available on patents. Patents might however only indicate inventions, which not turn into innovation or become commercialized in markets.
Innovation indexes	Lastly, innovation indexes, such as the European Innovation Scoreboard addressing the country level, have been applied to take into account the different measures of innovation. It can be based on a weighted sum drawing on the specific value which each input, output or survey measure has been given.

References

Ahlstrom, D. 2010. Innovation and growth: How business contributes to society. *Academy of Management Perspectives* 24(2): 11–24.

Atkinson, R., and S. Ezell. 2012. *Innovation economics: The race for global advantage*. New Haven: Yale University Press.

Audretsch, D.B., T. Aldridge, and A. Oettl. 2006. *The knowledge filter and economic growth: The role of scientist entrepreneurship* Discussion Paper on Entrepreneurship, Growth and Public Policy, 0611. Jena: Max Planck Institute of Economics.

Barro, R.J., and X. Sala-i-Martin. 2004. *Economic growth*. Cambridge, MA: The MIT Press.

Baumol, W.J. 2004. *The free-market innovation machine: Analyzing the growth miracle of capitalism*. Princeton, NJ: Princeton University Press.

Baumol, W.J., and R. Strom. 2007. Entrepreneurship and economic growth. *Strategic Entrepreneurship Journal* 1(3–4): 233–237.

Broekel, T., D. Fornhal, and R. Boschma. 2011. What drives patent performances of German biotech firms? The impact on R&D subsidies, knowledge networks and their locations. *Papers in Regional Science* 90(2): 395–418.

Carree, M.A., and A.R. Thurik. 2003. The impact of entrepreneurship on economic growth. In *Handbook of entrepreneurship research*, eds. D.B. Audretsch, and Z.J. Acs, 437–471. Boston/Dordrecht: Kluwer Academic Publishers.

Chesbrough, H. 2003. The era of open innovation. *MIT Sloan Management Review* 44: 35–42.

Christensen, C.M., and M. Raynor. 2003. *The innovator's solution*. Boston: Harvard Business School Publishing.

Cornell University—INSEAD and the World Intellectual Property Organization. 2015. The Global Innovation Index World 2015—Effective Innovation Policies for Development.

Dadush, U. 2015. Deindustrialization and development. http://www.voxeu.org/article/deindustrialisation-and-development.

Eichengreen, B. 2007. *The European Economy since 1945: Coordinated capitalism and beyond*. Princeton: Princeton University Press.

Eurostat. 2014. *Europe 2020 indicators—Research and development*. Luxembourg: Eurostat.

———. 2013. Seventh Community Innovation Survey—Highest proportions of innovative enterprises in Germany, Luxembourg and Belgium. Eurostat News release 5/2013, 11 January 2013.

European Commission. 2015. *Innovation Union Scoreboard 2015*. Brussels: European Union.

European Commission. 2015. *Open Innovation 2.0—Yearbook 2015*. Directorate-General for Communications Networks, Content and Technology. Brussels: European Union.

———. 2014. Europe more innovative but regional differences persist. Press release, IP/14/198, 4 March 2014. http://europa.eu/rapid/press-release_IP-14-198_en.htm. Accessed 20 Sep 2015.

———. 2013a. *Innovation union scoreboard 2013*. Brussels: European Union.

———. 2013b. State of the innovation union 2012—Accelerating change.

———. 2012a. Do SMEs create more and better jobs? Press release, IP-12-11, 16 January 2012. http://europa.eu/rapid/press-release_MEMO-12-11_en.htm?locale=en. Accessed 20 Sep 2015.

———. 2010a. Europe 2020: A strategy for smart, sustainable and inclusive growth.

Frey, C. B. and M.A. Osborne 2013. The future of employment: How susceptible are jobs to computerisation. OMS Working Papers.

Ghani, E., A.G. Goswami and H. Kharas 2011. Can services be the next escalator? http://www.voxeu.org/article/can-services-be-next-growth-escalator. Accessed 30 Sep 2015.

Godin, B. 2006. The linear model of innovation: The historical construction of an analytical framework. *Science Technology & Human Values* 31(6): 639–667.

High Level Group on Innovation Policy Management. 2014. *Report & recommendations.* June 2013.

Hyytinen, K. et al. 2012. Funder, activator, networker, investor: Exploring roles of Tekes in fuelling finnish innovation. Tekes Review 289/2012.

IMD. 2015. *World Competitiveness Yearbook 2015.* Lausanne, Switzerland: IMD.

Nordic Innovation. 2012. The Nordic growth entrepreneurship review 2012— Final report. Nordic Innovation Publication, 25.

Nystrom, K. 2008. Is entrepreneurship the salvation for enhanced economic growth? A review of the empirical evidence of the effect of entrepreneurship on employment, productivity and economic growth. *CESIS Paper* 143: 163–178.

OECD (2007). Innovation and growth—Rationale for an innovation strategy. http://www.oecd.org/science/inno/39374789.pdf. Accessed 8 Sep 2015.

OECD. 2014. *Science, technology and industry outlook 2014.* Paris: OECD Publishing.

———. 2007. Innovation and growth—Rationale for an innovation strategy. http://www.oecd.org/science/inno/39374789.pdf. Accessed 8 Sep 2015.

Romer, P. 1986. Increasing returns and long-run growth. *Journal of Political Economy* 94(5): 1002–1037.

Schuman, M. 2011. Does Germany know the secret to creating jobs? Time magazine. 25.02.2011. Available at http://business.time.com/2011/02/25/does-germany-know-the-secret-to-creating-jobs/. Retrieved on 17.03.2016.

Schumpeter, J.A. 1912. *The theory of economic development.* Cambridge, MA: Harvard University Press.

Schwab, K., ed. 2015. *The global competitiveness report 2014–2015.* Geneva: World Economic Forum.

Tekes. 2012. The impact of Tekes and innovation activities 2012.

Veugelers, R. 2010. Young leading innovators and the EU's R&D intensity gap. Bruegel Policy Contribution.

Wessner, C. 2015. Charles Wessner at EASME presenting U.S. SBIR programme. Presentation at EASME, Brussels, June 13.

Wessner, C.W. 2008. *An assessment of the SBIR program* National Research Council (US) Committee for Capitalizing on Science, Technology, and Innovation. Washington, DC: National Academies Press.

World Bank. 2015. Worldwide governance indicators. http://databank.world-bank.org/data/reports.aspx?source=Worldwide-Governance-Indicators. Accessed 28 Sep 2015.

———. 2012. Innovation for job creation—Background note for the world development report 2013.

World Economic Forum. 2012. Global competitiveness report 2012–2013.

3

Icarus or Sisyphus: Innovation Between Hype, Rebuff and New Sobriety

Klaus Gretschmann

1 Introduction

For the past 50 years or so, innovation (technical progress and the modernization of economies and societies) has been a ground-laying principle in the Western world, not least in Europe. More recently though, and with the arrival of the computer, the internet, smartphones, Silicon Valley entrepreneurs, and the digitalization of the world, a real hype about innovation has emerged.

With the rise of new technologies and new avenues toward the future, a new world of possibilities and a radical shift of our knowledge frontiers have become a reality. Politics and institutions are making every effort to stimulate and condition innovation everywhere in our societies, economies, and polities. Therefore, not surprisingly, the innovation imperative (Marklund et al. 2009) has risen to overarching prominence.

K. Gretschmann (✉)
President, Competence and Advisory Team Europe (CATE), Germany
e-mail: klaus.gretschmann@kgr-consilium.eu

© The Editor(s) (if applicable) and The Author(s) 2016
K. Gretschmann, S. Schepers (eds.), *Revolutionising EU Innovation Policy*,
DOI 10.1057/978-1-137-55554-0_3

Innovation has become the "magic formula" in today's intellectual debates about global competition, job creation, and growth, meant to help solve fundamental problems such as the financial crises, demographic developments, deadly diseases, catastrophes, or air pollution, just to name a few.

In its broadest sense innovation is more than just research or generating new ideas that may or may not lead to a new or improved product or technology. It also covers new modes of production, delivery of services, the development of new markets, finding new sources of supply, new materials or new design, or new business models and modes of organization in industry and in public administration.

However, it is an error to assume that innovations are everywhere and always welcome. There is NO such thing as a social consensus or a social compact about the unconditional promotion of innovation. Rather, the history of innovation is an unending story of resistance and opposition (Hauschildt and Salomo 2007, p. 178). The problem of barriers to innovation is not a new one, even though its forms, forces, and elements have varied over time. Already in 1912, Schumpeter referred to "a steady antagonism vis-à-vis change" in the process of creative destruction (Schumpeter 1912, p. 108).

This is because innovations are often accompanied and characterized by high levels of risk, uncertainty, complexity, opaqueness, and fundamental change. Innovation is neither a good nor a bad thing *per se*; rather, its assessment depends on its effects and impacts on the social and economic welfare of a society—the ways in which we work, live, and exist.

Therefore, innovations oftentimes find both consent and support with some but may trigger massive reticence, resistance, and opposition with others. Nonetheless, lip service in favor of abstract "innovation" and the call for unfolding innovation potential is *en vogue* today. Everybody who is in the public limelight, be it politicians, entrepreneurs, business leaders, scholars, or association officials, is enthusiastic to demonstrate that they are on the bright side of modernizing our economies and societies.

As there will be winners and losers from any process of innovation, and since turbulences and adaptive requirements accompany every innovation, this "love of innovation" is lukewarm at best. As a matter of fact, what we can observe today are "go-getters" and "procrastinators," drivers and constraints in the "war theater" of innovation (Govindarajan and Trimble 2010).

Innovation policies today are either of an *Icarus* type[1] (too high-flying, falling down hard), or of the *Sisyphus* kind[2] (rolling something uphill again and again but unable to hold it). The former mirrors the aggrandizement of and the hype about innovation as well as a lack of scrutiny, whilst the latter reflects a new sobriety—the continuous hard work involved and required from us all if we wish to prompt, develop, and make best use of innovations.

2   Trailblazing the Future: The Long and Stony Road to Innovation

In the Europe of 2015 the received view maintains that the prospects for prosperity—economic, social, and environmental—over the next 25 years will strongly depend upon actively encouraging deep changes and tectonic shifts far greater than those experienced in the twentieth century. Realizing the full potential of tomorrow's innovations and their contribution to human well-being is considered a function of the capacity to embrace dynamic change and the stimulation of innovations across all aspects of human life.

If we wish to build our future on *innovation as a principle*, we will have to pave the way. At times it may be a high road, sometimes a thorny trail. Everything depends on the right, stimulating environment—an inspiring innovation ecosystem[3] will have to be created and unveiled.

---

[1] According to Greek mythology, Icarus dared to fly too close to the sun on wings of feathers and wax. In spite of warnings that the Sun would cause the wax to melt, he became ecstatic with the ability to fly and ignored the warning. The feathers came loose and Icarus plunged to his death in the sea.

[2] For various crimes against the gods, Sisyphus, the king of Corinth, was condemned to an eternity of hard labor. His assignment was to roll a great boulder to the top of a hill. Every time Sisyphus, by the greatest of exertion and toil, attained the summit, the boulder rolled back down and the labor and troubles started all over again.

[3] In this volume see the chapter entitled "Rethinking and Revolutionizing European Innovation by Means of Innovation Ecosystems."

The standard innovation policy model based on the assumption that research institutes, entrepreneurial activities, and high-tech firms should be stimulated and encouraged in linear manner from invention to innovation, and diffusion is overly simplistic. Any negative impacts should be solved through ex-post-regulation and other compensatory measures. We have argued above (see chapter on innovation ecosystems) that this model is counterproductive and that a new approach is the tall order of the day.

The concept of an innovation ecosystem lays emphasis on the interaction and information flowing among a multitude of people, enterprises, and institutions. Innovation is the result of the interaction among an ecology of actors, rules, and institutions. It is the "right" interaction that is needed in order to turn an idea into a solution or a process, product, or service on the market.

So, what is badly needed is collaboration between research, business, governments, and also EU institutions, instead of silo thinking by each of them and mutual distrust. We must also dare to question regulatory capture by a select number of players. Instead of fragmenting responsibilities, governments should ensure convergence and cooperation.

The digital revolution has laid the groundwork for today's Great Transformation[4]: It has changed the way we work and live almost beyond recognition. As Carly Fiorina (2007, p. 177) has stated so aptly:

> The future is digital, virtual, mobile and personal—a future in which everything physical and analog can be represented in digital form; where anything can move anywhere because it exists in cyberspace and can be networked; where virtual reality can be someday as compelling as physical reality; and where individuals can control myriad actions, events and information and knowledge on their own behalf.

Digital technology offers new access to production, logistics, consumption, health care, and education, etc., while blurring boundaries between industries. The power of the individual will grow, new political

---

[4] The original "Great Transformation" is the seminal work of Karl Polanyi, which was first published in 1944. It deals with the social and political upheavals that took place in England during the rise of the market economy.

decision modes will emerge (*internet democracy*), and new competitors will show up, disrupting industries and creating new business models. Twenty years from now we may look back on the present as a time when rapid and continuous innovation changed almost everything about the way we live and how we produce, consume, communicate, interact, and participate in our polities.

No doubt it will be indispensable to develop a vision of technological possibilities, involving computing, genetics, brain technology, new materials, renewable energy, transportation, environmental tools, and others.

Ralph-Christian Ohr contrasts continuous and incremental innovations as evolution, with radical and discontinuous leaps to completely novel offerings, opening up new business and growth trajectories which can be described as revolution.[5]

Evolution accounts for the majority of innovation activities in most firms and organizations. However, it *only* optimizes and improves existing trends and products along their trajectories. Revolutionary innovation, in turn, explores new-to-the-world opportunities and creates new business potential. Revolutionary innovators ask questions based on the limitations of existing solutions and offer new solutions to existing problems of which no one else has thought.[6]

In order to remain competitive or win a new competitive edge, we do need both revolutions and evolutions. This in turn will help to operate sustainable, efficient, and socially beneficial innovations. Some innovations are at risk of failing because they might be driven in the wrong direction, not aligned with the properties of the innovation ecosystem in which they operate. Consequently, the existing businesses may die, the novel idea dies, or both die.

Beyond dispute, there are a myriad of risks associated with advances in new technologies and innovative avenues toward the future. If trailblazing and pioneering for our future is the tall order of the day, we do need to tackle and control the following:

---

[5] See http://timkastelle.org/blog/2012/08/evolutionary-and-revolutionary-innovation/.

[6] Former senator and attorney general of the USA, Robert F. Kennedy so nicely paraphrased George Bernard Shaw's quote: "Some people see things as they are and say why? I dream things that never were and say why not?"

- Tomorrow's technologies may contain destructive potential that will be both powerful and difficult to control. They could pose threats to the natural and human environment.
- Through new breakthrough innovations the world becomes more diversified, complex, and technology-dependent, and a diminishing control over our physical or social systems may result.
- Problems related to ethics, values, and mindsets loom. Innovative technologies such as human cloning or artificial intelligence will pose major challenges to ethical and cultural standards, and will strain people's tolerance of the novel and unknown.
- Closely related is the risk of over- or under-regulation of new developments. Either can thwart the desirable or fail to constrain the un-desirable.
- The enthusiast who is so optimistic about an innovation that he neglects the social, economic, and political constraints and overlooks the secondary side effects of innovations may jeopardize innovations.
- In a similar vein, a very recent study by VCI (2015) concludes that business and politics are equally required to improve the framework conditions for making "innovation tick."
- This involves primarily the fostering of a "culture of innovation" and of society's open-mindedness, vis-à-vis innovation and change.
- However, the biggest risk that we face is the failure to embrace the huge potential that new technologies and innovations hold for improving the condition of humankind and the state of nations (Coates 1998).

However, we cannot neglect that there could be an important clash between the radical possibilities opened up by innovations and technological change and vested traditions, habits, and relationships. Adopting new attitudes, accepting alternative approaches to risk management, and equipping people for new decision-making structures is of paramount importance for meeting the challenge of nurturing an innovation-driven economy and society and preparing them for the future.

In short, it is imperative to strengthen a culture of innovation in enterprises, universities, and the society at large. Moreover, we need to raise curiosity and risk propensity. Disruptive and incremental innovation need to be equally promoted. We need to unhinge ideologies for the sake of reality, and confidence and trust in science need reinforcement. Benefits and risks must be communicated freely and honestly. This all makes up the essence of trailblazing the future through innovations in the face of major obstacles and sometimes fierce opposition.

3 Skepticism, Opposition, and Barriers to Innovation

3.1 Factors Inhibiting Innovation

In spite of lip service to the contrary, skepticism, vis-à-vis technological modernization, and often outright refusal to accept new knowledge and complex innovations prevail. At all levels of innovation policy and management opposition can be found. There is no generic "welcome culture" for innovation in Europe.

In order to promote our ability to innovate we need to identify, analyze, and anticipate barriers and opposition to innovation. The following key factors for either stimulating or inhibiting innovation have been identified in the literature (see list below). These factors have a cumulative influence on any innovation.

Barriers and obstacles to innovation include

* Personal attitudes toward change
* Organizational openness and innovation culture
* Regulations and bureaucracy (licensing, approving authorities)
* Asset availability (skills, knowledge, manpower, finance)
* Risk propensity or aversion
* Lack of social acceptance (for health, environment, social, etc., impact)
* The number and strength of veto players
* Sound and fully fledged innovation ecosystem.

As depicted in Fig. 3.1, which is derived from a broad body of diverse literature, factors have been merged and weights have been attached in terms of percentage values of their "barrier significance": Intrafirm

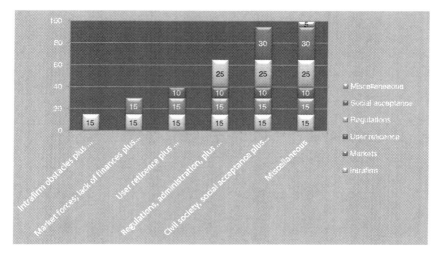

Fig. 3.1 Capability to innovate as a function of opposing forces (100 % opposition standing for complete paralysis; 0 % opposition indicating full mobilization)

obstacles account for 15 %, market forces 15 %, user reticence 10 %, regulations 25 %, social acceptability 30 %, and miscellaneous 5 % (author's own estimates, KG).

Personal obstacles such as career outlooks, job security, promotion, rise or fall in the firm's hierarchy, etc., go hand in hand with organizational impediments, such as coordination among departments, the NIH syndrome,[7] loss of departmental power and influence, etc., with technical

---

[7] The not-invented-here (NIH) syndrome refers to internal resistance in a company against externally developed knowledge. Although previous research has shown that firms can benefit significantly from external knowledge inflows in terms of firm performance and innovativeness, such positive effects from external knowledge sourcing cannot be taken for granted. The adaption of external knowledge requires flexible processes facilitating changes in the company's vision, strategy, and culture and a welcoming attitude of employees toward externally generated knowledge. If such an attitude of the employees is missing, they can show resistance toward external knowledge and fail to realize the expected benefits for the company. This is the essence of the NIH syndrome. Hussinger and Wastyn (2011), ZEW STUDY, http://ftp.zew.de/pub/zew-docs/dp/dp11048.pdf.

frictions—how a new product, business model, etc., affects organizational processes and stability and, last but not least, vested powers and interests. Additionally, project management and funding requirements (at whose cost?) may cause trouble—also under the heading "intrafirm barriers."

Moreover, as emphasized in the theory of veto players (Tsibelis 2002) it is particularly important to identify those parties and agents that are powerful enough to block the development and implementation of path-breaking decisions and ideas: a veto player is a person, group or institution whose agreement or consent is indispensable for any decision or measure necessary for change. In other words, veto players can block innovations. If veto players are in the game, three parameters measure their power: (1) their number, (2) their internal cohesion and political/economic or social weight, and (3) the policy congruence among them and with society at large.[8]

But these are not the only barriers and obstacles to innovation.

As a recent study by German VCI (2015)[9] has shown convincingly that internal opposition in enterprises, research institutions, or administrations is only one side of the coin. Even more important seem to be external obstacles such as regulations and bureaucracy, licensing and clearance, the social acceptance or the general cooperation, and political support (VCI 2015, p. 52). Some obstacles work cumulatively against innovations: approving authorities are reticent and stall for time whenever interest groups or the civic society spell out resistance, when doubts are expressed about externalities and impacts, or when competitors ponder complaints in terms of competition law and other issues. A long process of risk assessment is then to be expected. Examples abound: crops and genetic engineering, pharma and drugs, clinical studies, genomics, nanotech, and the use of big data, etc.

Better communication, information, cooperation, and dialogue between science, industry, politics, and civil society, combined with rigorous innovation impact assessment, may be a means to attenuate such opposition and forces of inertia. An honest and pristine balance between

---

[8] In the case of Germany, R.G. Heinze, 1998 has convincingly analyzed such mechanisms leading to a "blocked society" not able to react flexibly to change pressure and new opportunities.

[9] Innovationen den Weg ebnen (VCI, Sept. 14, 2015).

risks and benefits (a risk-reward ratio or RRR) of innovations may help to put social concerns at ease and make scientific analysis more credible and authentic.

Misconceived and rigid regulation is a major impediment to innovation. As a general rule, regulation results from a long thought and consensus building process among political decision makers, with more or less successful involvement of a variety of skeptical stakeholders. It is based on the calculation of so-called external costs[10] and their effect on a social welfare function.[11]

Some spectacular accidents such as Bophal, Seveso, river pollution, and diseases, etc., brought issues that had been previously the exclusive domain of scientists and experts into the public limelight and thus to political attention.

(Un)fortunately, nothing lasts forever and the rapid evolvement of scientific discovery and innovation can make existing regulation obsolete. Institutional and legal inertia often prevents timely regulatory innovation and change. Just continuing a particular regulatory trajectory without regular checks of its impact and costs, and without re-examination of the goals and objectives themselves, is fundamental to hindering innovation and a main barrier to modernization.

3.2   Resistance to Change

One of the best approaches to explain resistance to or acceptance of innovations can be found in Gatignon and Robertson (1991). The authors consider multiple areas where resistance to innovations occurs before and throughout the innovation process, and they understand resistance to innovation as a special case of general resistance to change.

---

[10] An external cost occurs when producing or consuming a good or service implies imposing a cost upon a third party.

[11] A social welfare function describes the state of well-being of a society and ranks social states as more or less desirable for every effect from political measures or decisions. Inputs of the function include any variables considered to affect the economic welfare of the society as a whole.

For many of those involved, innovation means change, notably a kind of change to which they will be subject and the implications of which they can neither understand nor control. Thereby, reticence and resistance arises.

No matter whether triggered externally or internally, every initial response by individuals or organizations is either resistance or openness depending on personal or institutional preconditions. On the individual level, the reaction of those involved and affected by an innovation often prompts an emotional and spontaneous response of rejection, protest, or even active boycotting. Although active resistance can also occur rationally—that is, after careful deliberation—more often than not it is determined by norms, standards, values, and seasoned patterns of institutional response. For example, commitment to religious principles may prompt some to resist certain medical practices, irrespective of their technical merit, or membership of a labor union demands resistance to innovations that might jeopardize jobs and employment. In such cases, group norms and institutional identification can predetermine resistance to or acceptance of innovations (Turner 1991). Today "Groupthink" (Janis 1982, p. 244), is a major threat to any innovation, often disguised in rational arguments and criticism of scientific research methods.

This phenomenon can be observed within groups of people, in social networks or in organizations of the civic society, in which the desire for intragroup harmony and conformity results in an irrational or dysfunctional outcome. Group members try to minimize conflict and reach a consensus without critical evaluation of alternative viewpoints by actively suppressing dissenting opinions and isolating themselves from outside influences.

Whereas the media coverage often focuses primarily on the negative reactions to innovations, recent surveys show that the basic attitudes of the citizens in Europe, vis-à-vis science and technology (S&T), are primarily positive. As depicted in Fig. 3.2, there is both a strong interest in S&T and an overwhelmingly positive feeling about the impact of S&T in the European Union.

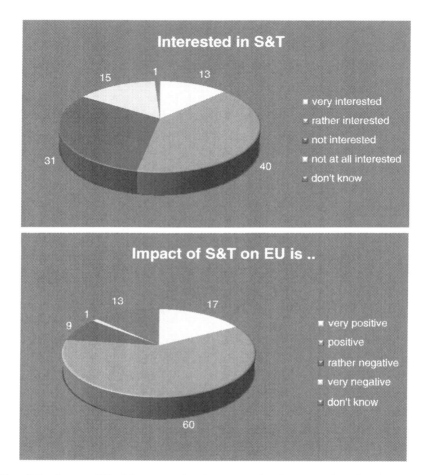

Fig. 3.2 Survey EU citizens' attitudes toward science and technology (28 member states; 27,563 respondents; year: Nov. 2013)
Source: http://europa.eu/rapid/press-release_IP-13-1075_en.htm

To be sure, attitudes and reactions with respect to innovations are often based on incomplete and biased information, distorted communication, and a lack of knowledge on the part of the respondents. Therefore, attention must be paid to both preconditioned attitudes of resistance or acceptance and the ways benefits and risks are communicated. As it happens, innovations include continuous or discontinuous change, and resistance to change is inevitably higher against the latter: discontinuities and break-ups are more difficult to swallow than smooth, nondisruptive transformation.

3.3   Risk and Attitudes toward Innovation

As Guenther Dueck (2013) has argued convincingly, four types of players can be identified by their attitudes, vis-à-vis novel ideas and innovations:

(a) *Frontrunners and aficionados* who are eager to see new things and ideas developed, accomplished, and tested. This is a very small group.
(b) *Open Minds*, or people who are receptive to new ideas but who do not wish to be protagonists and pioneers but rather followers. This is a pretty large group.
(c) *Close Minds* are those who are rather skeptical and distrusting of novel ideas and technological progress, and who will follow suit only when a large number of proponents is already leading the way.
(d) *Antagonists* are principally hostile and negative toward anything new and remain strictly opposed to novelties.

Factors that determine a positive attitude vis-à-vis an innovation or at least help create a constructive attitude have been identified by Rogers (2003, S. 222 f.):

* personal advantages from innovations
* a high degree of compatibility with personal, environmental, and organizational and ideological predispositions
* a good understanding and low complexity of an innovation
* testability, observability, and affinity.

On top I regard the following factors as decisive:

* positive reference groups and social networks
* charismatic leaders and convincing promoters
* a general pro-innovative societal spirit.

If these factors exist, we may assume a high probability for acceptance and a positive attitude in favor of innovations and change (Siegrist 2008).

Opposition to change is never solely built on emotional and psychological dispositions. Rather cognitive and rational arguments play a major role, and notably the perception and management of risks. An honest and unobstructed discussion about the risk from novel ideas, products technologies, or business processes is indispensable. And we may need a critical mass of rational arguments put forward by proponents and promoters to make an innovation work, and enforceable (Currall 2006).

Siegrist et al. (2010) have pointed out that "laymen's" risk perceptions often differ starkly from experts' assessments of risks. Yet, the vision of both groups needs to be taken into account in order to deal successfully with risk-driven opposition. As beliefs can be corrected only by personal experience, and most people have no experience with innovations and their consequences, trust plays a major role. Those concerned or affected by innovations must rely on reassurances made by expert scientists whose "language" they hardly understand. Only trust in experts can help moderate the process of social amplification as described in the seminal work of Slovic and others (Pidgeon et al. 2003).

Slovic (2000) pointed out that high public concern about a risk issue—be it nuclear energy, fracking, biotech, etc.—is associated with distrust of the "industry managers" responsible for the issue while low public concern (e.g., medical use of radiation) is associated with trust in risk managers (doctors). So, trust in risk management is negatively correlated to risk perception. In the same vein, any success or failure of risk communication largely depends on whether or not there are trusted communicators.

Against this backdrop, we see innovation and risk management being viewed as partners, not adversaries. When properly fused, the two areas can help organizations and polities pursue opportunities that risk-averse attitudes might leave in the drawing room.

Help to overcome risk problems associated with innovation may also come from the State: As innovations and the development of new technologies do require a vision, a mission and lots of money spent from upstream research to downstream commercialization, all accompanied by serious risks, the State can act as risk absorber, agenda setter, stimulator, and enforcer against opposition.

Since, as a rule, the private sector or the venture capital industry is often much more risk-averse than government agencies, it is easier for the latter to fund capital-intensive and high-risk projects through public money, thereby socializing some of the financial risks through taxation. This active—and often catalytic—role governments assume to cover risky investments in future technologies is excellently described and analyzed in Mazzucato's work (2013) about the entrepreneurial state.

One way to attenuate the role of risk as an impediment to innovation might be the use of qualitative "Risk/ Reward Ratios" to deal with related promises and perils: borrowed from financial investment theory, a risk-reward ratio is used by many investors to compare the expected returns of an investment to the amount of risk undertaken to capture these returns. What we need in order to cope with innovation resistance is a kind of social and qualitative RRR.

Such an RRR would take into account, on the one hand, the social (perceived) risks from innovations and, on the other hand, the (expected) social rate of return—that is, the collective reward from an innovation. As shown in Fig. 3.3 below, in a four-quadrant matrix, several possibilities exist:

When both risk and reward are low, as in Q1, no incentive and no opposition will exist, and innovations are unlikely. When reward is low and risk is high, as in Q2, innovations will not materialize. Q3 depicts a constellation in which risk is low and the social rate of return is high; here innovations are unhindered and will be promoted without doubt. The most difficult problems arise in Q4 where both the rewards and the risks are high. Here we are faced with a clear trade-off, which is hard to balance.

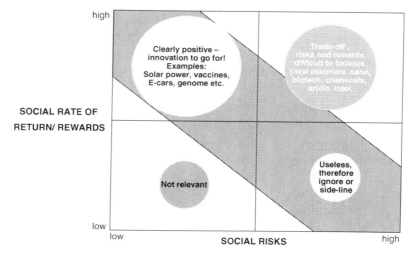

Fig. 3.3 Qualitative risk-reward relationship

4   Europe: Prototype of the Risk-Averse Society?

4.1   The Changing Concept and Context of Risk

Today, Europe seems to be moving toward a *risk avoidance culture* rather than *a risk management culture*. Instead of understanding risks as potential sources of human progress and technological development, today risk connotes dread, uncertainty, instability, dangers, and threats. In such context it is often conceived as a prime obstacle to innovation.

It has not always been like this! From Gutenberg's printing press to CERN's accelerating protons, from Pythagoras' theorems to Marconi's radio, Europe can look back on a proud tradition of entrepreneurship and discovery. Throughout the centuries, the relentless pursuit of new knowledge and innovative ways of doing things has made our societies strong, prosperous, and safe.

However, when investors buy stock, surgeons perform operations, engineers design machines, entrepreneurs launch new businesses, astronauts explore space, or politicians run for office, risk is an inescapable companion. Whereas in the past centuries risk was perceived as a force of fate in the face of which we seemed helplessly in the hands of the gods' mercy, modern times are characterized by a change in the perception of risk as calculable and controllable, weighing and measuring its consequences, unleashing an approach that considers risks as opposed to opportunities. As Peter Bernstein (1996, p. 1) in his seminal book *Against the Gods: The Remarkable Story of Risk,* has put it succinctly: "The revolutionary idea that defines the boundary between modern times and the past is the mastery of risk."

Indeed, the concept of risk has undergone a radical transformation. Today's concept of risk is a product of modern times and did not exist in this form before the industrial revolution in the nineteenth century. Until then, people knew dangers as natural phenomena, such as hunger, illness, or natural catastrophes, and attributed these dangers to external powers lying outside of human decision or influence.

Industrialization challenged the idea of risk and danger as purely natural phenomena and subsequently replaced it with the notion of risk being created by humans themselves. This occurred with the rise of science, technology, and new mathematical techniques, especially in the field of contingency analysis, which created a new approach to risk and its assessment.

Industrialization shifted the responsibility from gods to humans and their decisions and actions. As Frank Furedi pointed out (2005), natural disasters are no longer seen as "natural" events, but people automatically suspect human responsibility behind a catastrophe, so that they get redefined as preventable.

Graubard (1990, p. v) explains, "It is perfectly obvious that the concept of 'risk' has taken on wholly new dimensions in recent decades and is today being reflected on in ways that would have been almost inconceivable even a few years ago. The older idea, that risk is essentially a wager, which individuals take in the hope of gaining something significant, substantial, has almost disappeared from common parlance."

In a most brilliant paper, Stefan Schepers (2016) analyzed the problems of risk-averse western societies. He identified the increasing difficulties between industry and EU institutions and governments about risk assessment and management, the introduction of precautionary principles in the EU treaties and the move toward a hazard-based approach, based on deep-rooted cultural changes in Western society. We can observe widespread doubt about the advances of science and technology that are seen to produce new risks manufactured by various industries, which may potentially affect everyone and are creating a high degree of social uncertainty. Schepers concludes that scientific argumentation alone does not suffice to provide an impartial and sober reflection of reality **as risk perception is itself a social construct.**

4.2   The Precautionary Principle

Over the last two to three decades, the European risk regime has changed significantly. Regulatory politics and policies have not only become more visible and contentious, but they have also become more stringent and risk-averse, particularly compared to other parts of the world like the USA and Asia.

Regulations reflect this trend toward ever stricter interpretations of risk, increasing the time and impediments to access the market for needed medicines, alimentation, and new technologies. Thereby, the EU itself is often seen as contributing to a climate of increased risk aversion and playing a major role in changing the quality and dynamics of European regulatory policies. The most notorious result thereof is probably the unconditional use of the precautionary principle[12] enshrined in the EU treaties in 1999, by which the EU laid the groundwork for its general approach to risk. According to the Commission the precautionary principle[13] may be invoked when a phenomenon, product, or process may have a dangerous effect, identified by a scientific and objective evaluation, if this evaluation does not allow the risk to be determined with sufficient certainty.

---

[12] See http://eur-lex.europa.eu/legal-content/EN/TXT/?uri=URISERV:l32042.

[13] The precautionary principle is detailed in Article 191 of the Treaty on the Functioning of the European Union (EU). It aims at ensuring a higher level of environmental protection through preventative decision taking in the case of risk. However, in practice, the scope of this principle is far wider and also covers consumer policy and European legislation concerning food and human, animal, and plant health.

Although the Commission emphasizes the importance of "finding the correct balance so that proportionate, nondiscriminatory, transparent, and coherent decisions can be arrived at" to provide the required protection and allow for innovative development, the reality is unfortunately somewhat different. The potentially negative effects on innovation result from the fact that by focusing primarily if not exclusively on possible risks and dangers, the precautionary principle disregards those dangers that might occur, or could be exacerbated, if new technological development is hindered and prevented.

The precautionary principle is Europe's risk policy framework and guideline for policy makers on how to assess and manage risk and uncertainty. Initially developed in the context of environmental protection, the principle has gradually found application in other fields of policy such as human health, food, genetically modified organisms (GMOs), and chemicals, etc. According to the Commission, the principle has the following objective:

> Finding the correct balance so that proportionate, nondiscriminatory, transparent and coherent decisions can be arrived at, which at the same time provide the chosen level of protection, requires a structured decision making process with detailed scientific and other objective information. This structure is provided by the three elements of risk analysis: the assessment of risk, the choice of risk management strategy and the communication of the risk.

The emphasis on the precautionary principle must be seen as related to the rise of the civil society and NGO movements in the Western world. Essentially, a specific development took place in the last couple of decades and produced a new set of societal norms, values, and expectations. These led to a redistribution of power between citizens and governments accompanied by an increasing lack of trust in public authorities and public bodies.

The most prominent criticism of the precautionary principle concerns its most essential notion, namely that it reverses the burden of proof, so that those proposing a new technology, for instance, have to assure that it will not cause any damage. It provides governments with the possibility to impose regulatory measures based upon the barest potential of harm, be it to humans or the environment. These measures can be taken even if there is no strictly scientific proof and detrimental effects from political intervention cannot be excluded.[14]

In its most radical form the precautionary principle compels the innovator to prove that his innovation will (by 100 % surety) never cause any harm whatsoever to public health or the environment before it can be allowed to enter society.

The precautionary principle thus risks missing its actual purpose—the protection of humans and the environment—and creating even more risks, or more dangerous ones.

As Peter J. May (2003: 397) pointed out, "any regulatory regime entails finding a balance between how tight controls should be in promoting consistency and accountability versus how much discretion should be granted in promoting flexibility and innovation. The prescriptive approach emphasizes control and accountability (whereas) the performance-based approach desires to promote flexibility with accountability for results." Unlike in many other parts of the world which move toward, or have already implemented, a performance-based and differentiated sectorial-based approach, the prescriptive approach is predominant in Europe.

Against this backdrop, in 2013, 12 of the largest corporations in Europe submitted a letter to the European Commission (EC), urging them to adopt an "Innovation Principle"[15] as a counterweight to the precautionary principle to be taken into full consideration during policy and legislative processes.

The principle is meant to ensure that whenever policy or regulatory decisions are under consideration *their impact on innovation* should be assessed and addressed. It sets out to provide a new and positive way of ensuring that policy makers fully recognize social and economic needs

---

[14] The USA, for example, has not adopted the precautionary principle but relies on several court decisions and scientific guidelines for risk regulation (e.g., the 1980 Benzine decision). Generally speaking, before risk regulation gets enacted in the USA, "significant risk" must be (scientifically) demonstrated. Hence, unlike the EU's proactive approach, US regulation authorities wait for evidence of harm before regulating.

[15] http://www.riskforum.eu/uploads/2/5/7/1/25710097/innovation_principle_one_pager_5_march_2015.pdf.

for both precaution and innovation. It is therefore intended to be used to improve the quality and application of EU legislation and, as a result, to stimulate confidence, investment, and innovation by balancing risk of innovation and of hindering innovation.

5 How to Communicate Innovation: Respect Opponents, Mobilize Proponents, and Rely on Honest Brokers

Although often recommended as a remedy, information and communication will not suffice to overcome prejudice and preconceptions. More importantly, communicated trust and beliefs are indispensable means to help reach a more balanced verdict on any innovation.

What is required for a fair assessment of both the potential and the perils is an early dialogue between civil society, politics, economics, and business. Politicians will have to alter their widespread role as doubters and objection raisers into the roles of mediators and honest brokers who should equally emphasize the gains and virtues of innovations and new technologies and their possible risks and perils, where they exist.

Public suspicion of governments' abilities to deal with danger and risk is reinforced by deficient communication. Governments still tend to rely on outdated models of risk communication, and view the public as an essentially naïve audience. In this vein a one-way process is usually applied: a huge amount of technical and scientific data is just thrown at and disseminated to the public in a desperate effort to raise "understanding," to counteract "irrational" opinions and to build support. (Botterill and Mazur 2004).

This approach does not mesh well with academia and civil society as it runs the danger of making assessment subject to government or industry interests. More successful communication strategies call for a more democratic and differentiated approach and focus mainly on three dimensions (Slovic 1999):

* the complexity of the risk concept and the inadequacies of viewing risk analysis as an exclusively scientific enterprise;
* the recognition that risk and risk assessment are socially constructed; hence, science and technical judgments are blended with important political, social, and cultural factors; and
* the appreciation that the way in which risk is defined and by whom is central to how assessment, management, and communication materialize.

Moreover, scientific research alone will never suffice to convincingly communicate either the benefits or the risks of an innovation. Scientists and engineers should work to establish the objective facts and figures, and it is essential that social scientists and communication experts work on how the public perceives and appraises new ideas, technologies, or innovations.

That an inconspicuous attitude, the non-meddling and the non-communication by scientists, may be crucial for the general public to refuse an innovation has been emphasized by H Jon Entine (2011: 79):

> Scientists have largely remained silent when the public discussion turns to the tradeoff of benefits and risks .... They are often unwilling to engage in controversial issues that could endanger their funding and research.... The public interprets the unwillingness of scientists to engage those who campaign against chemicals as an implicit validation of their dangers. Those who do speak out are often…branded as industry apologists. Maybe the best we can hope for is that brave scientists, scientifically literate journalists, and government officials, who are responsible for translating science into regulatory policy, will take the public's best interest into account… [and] resist the irrational and often regressive impulse stirred by the scare tactics that are so common today.

In order to turn destructive into constructive opposition, promoters need be found—expert and knowledge promoters, power promoters, and process or relation promoters (Hauschildt 1999)—who are able to reduce the "distance" between proponents and opponents and promote mutual understanding. According to Hauschildt and Chakrabarti (1988), power promoters are able to pull the strings in an organization due to their hierarchical position and thereby can enforce innovation processes upon "refuseniks" and "Luddites." Knowledge promoters track down and fix weaknesses and constructive glitches. In doing so they can communicate the usefulness or significance of an innovation and convince procrastinators. Process promoters are integral mediators between power and knowledge promoters; they also act as a link between intraorganizational and outside administrative forces and help with a smooth change of innovation processes and attitudes of those involved. Such a promoter model is required on all levels, be it in firms, research institutions, or politics, etc. (Hauschildt and Salomo 2007, p. 207).

Efforts have to be made to involve well-reputed academic bodies, such as the Royal Society in the UK, the National Science Foundation in the USA, the ERC, the DFG, Frauenhofer, or the European Academy of the Sciences and the Arts, for using the current state of knowledge for innovation assessment. Interagency "impact subgroups" could be formed to coordinate communication and information and to organize public outreach and media work. It is indispensable to redouble efforts to be thorough, transparent, timely, and honest in disseminating and communicating results.

We seem to be living in a world out of balance—a surplus of politics and ideology and a deficit of ideas and scientific rigor. Such a world where ideologies prevail and rationality is bounded needs radical overhaul in order to succeed in creating a successful and sustainable innovation society in Europe.

References

Bernstein, P.L. 1996. *Against the gods. The remarkable story of risk.* New York: Wiley.

Botterill, L., and N. Mazur 2004. *Risk & risk perception: A literature review.* A report for the rural industries research and development corporation. Australian Government.

Coates, J. 1998. The next 25 years of technology: Opportunities and risks. In *OECD, 21st century technologies*, 33–46. Paris.

Currall, S. C. 2006. What drives public acceptance of nanotechnology. www.nature.com/nature.nantechnology.

Dueck, G. 2013. *Das Neue und seine Feinde*. Frankfurt a. M: Campus.

Entine, J. 2011. *Scared to death. How chemophobia threatens public health*. New York: American Council for Society and Health.

Fiorina, C. 2007. *Tough choices*. London: Penguin.

Furedi, F.. 2005. *Politics of fear: Beyond left and right*. London: Continuum Press.

Gatignon, H., and T.S. Robertson. 1991. *A propositional inventory for new diffusion research*. Englewood Cliffs, NJ: Prentice-Hall.

Govindarajan, V., and C. Trimble. 2010. Stop the innovation wars. *Harvard Business Review*. https://hbr.org/2010/07/stop-the-innovation-wars.

Graubard, S.R. 1990. Preface to the issue "risk". *Daedalus* 119(4): v–vi.

Hauschildt, J., and S. Salomo. 2007. *Innovations management*. München: Vahlen.

Hauschildt, J. 1999. Widerstand gegen Innovationen—destruktiv oder konstruktiv. *ZfB* 2(99): 1–20.

Hauschildt, J., and A. Chakrabarti. 1988. Arbeitsteilung im Innovationsmanagement. *ZfO* 57: 378–388.

Heinze, R.G. 1998. *Die blockierte Gesellschaft*. Opladen: Westdeutscher Verlag.

Hussinger, K., and A. Wastyn. 2011. In search for the not-invented-here syndrome: The role of knowledge sources and firm success. ZEW Discussion Paper No. 11-048.

Janis, I. 1982. *Groupthink*. Houghton Yale.

Marklund, G., N. Vonortas, and Ch.W. Wessner, eds. 2009. *The innovation imperative: National innovation strategies in the global economy*. Cheltenham: EE Publishers.

May, P. J. 2003. Performance-based regulation and regulatory regimes. Law and Policy 25: 381–401.

Mazzucato, M. 2013. The entrepreneurial state: Debunking public versus private myths. N.Y. Anthem.

Pidgeon, N., R.E. Kasperson, and P. Slovic. 2003. *The social amplification of risk*. Cambridge: Cambridge University Press.

Polanyi, K. 1944. The great transformation. 11th edn. 1971. Boston: Beacon Press.

Rogers, E.M. 2003. *Diffusion of innovation*. New York: Free Press.

Schepers, S. 2016. The risk averse society: a risk for innovation? In *Sustainability in a digital world*, ed. C.H. Lohmann and T.H. Ossurg. Berlin: Springer.

Schumpeter, J. 1912 (reprint 1983). Theory of economic development. Brunswick: Transaction Publishers

Siegrist, M., T.C. Earle, and H. Gutscher. 2010. *Trust in risk management: Uncertainty and skepticism in the public mind*. London: Earthscan.

Siegrist, M. 2008. Factors influencing public acceptance of innovative food technology and products. *Trends in Food Science and Technology* 19: 603–608.

Slovic, P. 1999. Trust, emotion, sex, politics, and science: Surveying the risk-assessment battlefield. *Risk Analysis* 19(4): 689–701.

———. 2000. *The perception of risk*. New York: Taylor and Francis.

Tsibelis, G. 2002. *Veto players*. Princeton: Princeton University Press.

Turner, J.C. 1991. *Social influence*. Baltimore: Brooks.

VCI 2015. Innovationen den Weg ebnen. https://www.vci.de/vci/downloads-vci/publikation/vci-innovationsstudie-langfassung.pdf.

4

Open Innovation and Clusters: Why Geographical Proximity Matters

Alberto Di Minin and Marco Rossi

1 Introduction

The 2008 crisis is still casting a long shadow upon the European Union's growth, and its magnitude has been felt well beyond the purely financial sphere, impacting Europe's social fabric and mentality like few other events in the recent past (European Commission 2014). Above all, the last few years have shown the vulnerability of the international and European financial system and the perils large and small companies are unavoidably exposed to within an intensely interconnected, interdependent macroeconomic system. Like in previous periods of global financial downturn, market failures have led to a widespread loss of trust in the

A. Di Minin (✉)
Associate Professor, Istituto di Management, Scuola Superiore Sant'Anna, Pisa, Italy
e-mail: a.diminin@sssup.it

M. Rossi
PhD Candidate, Department of European and International Studies, King's College London, London, UK
e-mail: marco.rossi@kcl.ac.uk

overall financial system on the part of small and large investors alike, as well as to a sensible increase in risk perception (Baumol et al. 2007). It is therefore hardly surprising to find out that the crisis has exacted a heavy toll on a significant number of innovative activities, being risky and bold investment one of the foundations upon which revolutionary and forward-thinking research has always evolved.

Against a background of uncertainty, a significant number of firms and entrepreneurs are now looking at new and old ways to improve their resilience and, in some cases, to stimulate once more the flow of investments and resources by exploiting the tools offered by open innovation (Chesbrough 2003). Indeed, business scholars have identified open innovation as a powerful strategy to cope with the downturn (Chesbrough and Garman 2009; Di Minin et al. 2010). Predictably, many actors have turned toward forms of collaborative networking to reinforce their innovative capacity and make use of each other's strengths to leverage capital and knowledge and exit the impasse. By focusing their activity at the local and regional level, several European firms, particularly medium-sized companies and start-ups, have sought to compensate for the loss of risk propensity on the international stage by improving cooperation within a narrower geographical scope, bounding to local research centers, universities, and even former competitors. Those agglomerations, known as *clusters*, have been subject of copious studies since the work of Alfred Marshall (1920). Local specialization of assets was a pivotal idea for economist and Nobel Prize winner, Paul Krugman (1991), the concept of clusters gained centrality in industrial dynamics literature as Michael Porter created a link between local agglomerations and competitive advantage (Porter 1998), and sociologists such as Annalee Saxenian (1994) and Manuel Castells (1994) explicitly applied this concept to high-tech industries.

As a result of decades of work by scholars and policy makers, clusters are today a central concept within innovation ecosystems. This chapter will look not only at the definition of such agglomerations, but also at the features that have made them such a valuable model for a variety of entrepreneurs and a recurrent staple of institutional discussions on growth and innovation (NESTA 2012; European Commission 2014). Perhaps more importantly, the chapter will highlight those factors that make clusters particularly suitable as vehicles and vectors of open innovation. Therefore, after having offered a brief overview of the concept of cluster itself, the analysis will focus on three such distinctive attributes: **access to finance**, which allows a number of actors, such as small and medium-sized enterprises (SMEs), but also larger companies that do not benefit from R&D capabilities, to gain access to a broad range of financial resources and funds, otherwise precluded to small stakeholders; **cross-specialization of assets** as internal learning and specialization produced within firms can contribute to more innovative solutions; and **local trust**, key in guaranteeing continuous exchanges and knowledge disclosure.

2   The Parallel Path of Clusters and Open Innovation

From a theoretical point of view, the idea that a certain number of firms and industries within a defined geographical space can join forces and improve their productivity by gathering together or, in other words, by "clustering," is hardly new or peculiar to contemporary literature. The concept can be traced back s to the period between the late nineteenth and the early twentieth century, during the decades that witnessed the zenith of Western technological development and, at the same time, its descent into a period of long-lasting conflict. By that period, Marshall had observed how, even in the already, vastly interconnected business environment of the time, "industrial districts" and agglomerations could thrive on tight historical linkages and innovative exchanges between local actors (Marshall 1920). In more recent periods, clusters resurfaced in the innovation literature with the work of Michael Porter. Porter saw those agglomerations of geographically related and highly specialized companies, research centers, and institutions as a fundamental part of what the Harvard scholar himself defined as the "diamond model," as well as key drivers of microeconomic competitiveness (Porter 1990; Porter 2007). According to Porter, proximity might create a stimulating business environment where companies can thrive, while at the same time drawing from each other's pool of skilled labor and expertise to source inputs, acquire knowledge and information and, therefore, generate complementarities (1998).[1]

---

[1] Porter defines clusters as "geographical concentrations of interconnected companies and institutions in a particular field" (Porter 1998, p. 197).

More recently, other authors have reinstated the importance of location and the pivotal role of proximity in spearheading innovative research. Those authors did so by analyzing the great high-tech clusters in the USA, such as the ones devoted to create revolutionary IT tools in the Silicon Valley, California (Saxennian 1994), or cutting-edge defense solutions designed jointly by governmental institutions—such as the Defense Advanced Research Projects Agency and other private actors (Kenney and Florida 2004, and more recently Mazzucato 2013). Notwithstanding differences in approaching the issues of financing, externalities, and learning, as well as in establishing the exact degree to which the state and the private sector interact in the process, all the analyses agree upon the fact that persistent communication, knowledge sharing and transparency at the heart of successful clustering. Unsurprisingly, this aspect might well turn clusters into enablers of dynamics that Henry Chesbrough defined as "open innovation" (2003; 2006).

Open innovation draws upon the increasingly substantial volume of knowledge modern companies are now surrounded by, produced by agents like universities, research centers and, more importantly, other companies that would normally be counted among the competitors. According to Chesbrough, such bountifulness of external resources should stimulate companies to adopt an outward-looking policy in their quest for new sources of innovation, instead of treating information, know-how, and even a highly qualified workforce as jealously guarded assets, and the production of innovation as a purely "internal" pursuit conducted within insulated R&D unit (Chesbrough 2003). With the aim of defying a certain corporate parochialism, companies should try to engage multiple parties, suppliers, and competitors in common endeavors, in a process of assets exchange and externalization (inside-out) or of absorption of external ideas (outside-in). Indeed, it is hard not to notice how a number of elements that are an integral part of the open innovation paradigm can fit well within the cluster model. In fact, a number of distinctive features of cluster systems seem designed to benefit from and, at the same time, to productively channel the advantages offered by open innovation. For example, local companies can exploit geographical proximity to maximize the advantages offered by promoting greater openness and a culture of exchange. Much in the same way, the accurate knowledge of the local context and the presence "on the ground" of many firms involved in a cluster can allow them to quickly scout for new innovative initiatives and immediately capitalize on them, as well as to exploit each other's pool of qualified and professional expertise. In addition, it should not be forgotten that, since open innovation is largely reliant on mutual exchanges of sensitive information—turning trust into a key factor—local connections promoted by clusters can significantly encourage firms to exchange knowledge without excessive reserves and therefore favor circulation of innovative solutions and best practices alike. To limit the scope of the analysis, this chapter will focus on three particular elements that link geographical agglomerations of entrepreneurial activities—clusters at the head—to open innovation: access to funds, cross-assets specialization, and local trust.

3   Access to Funds: The Advantages of Visibility

Whatever the model adopted by companies, start-ups, or any other industrial actor, securing available capital remains an inescapable condition in guaranteeing the success of an enterprise (Mazzucato 2013). This is particularly true of the high-tech and scientific sectors, where investment in R&D and the constant quest for innovative solutions requires a continuous flowing of capital and a solid financial basis. Most of the time, such financial commitment relies heavily on the action of venture capital funds, angel investors and, depending on the country, a relevant support from the state and national agencies. However, since the very beginning of the financial crisis, access to funding on the part of smaller enterprises, especially SMEs, has been made increasingly difficult due the worsening economic context and a number of related factors (OECD 2009). Recurring issues include lack of liquidity, strict credit and bank lending conditions, scarce inclination toward risk, but also fragmentation and a poor or scarcely promoted presence on financial markets are just the most prominent among the trends that have impinged upon the activity and, at times, even the survival of SMEs. To add to those dynamics, state aid to SMEs has also witnessed a sharp decline in recent years, a trend which has particularly noticeable in some of the EU's member states most affected by the crisis. Even though recent statistics seem to indicate a relative upturn, with some commentators going as far as to suggest that with the exception of the years immediately following the crisis, small businesses have benefited from a constant (or at least undiminished) credit flow (Freeman 2013), the situation for most SMEs remains one of recurrent uncertainty. In the brief analysis that follows, this chapter will look at how clusters can acquire a central place in revitalizing access to funding thanks to their collaborative nature and diversification.

As already mentioned above, while responses to this contingency have varied widely from state to state, both national entities and organizations have emphasized more and more the need to make use of the rich toolkit of instruments offered by open innovation in order to reverse the trend (European Commission 2014). One of the main novelties introduced by the open innovation paradigm lays in its emphasis on collaborative endeavors and its distinctive knowledge-sharing culture (Chesbrough 2003; Baldwin and von Hippel 2011). In this specific case collaboration and knowledge, as well as information exchange, should not be seen as something circumscribed to the mere production process. Conversely, the competitive advantage offered by clusters can extend well into the network of institutional and financial interactions necessary to obtain funds and credit. This fact is particularly relevant in contexts where access to funding is more "institutionalized" and where access to relevant political and governmental actors involved in R&D is no less important than private credit and lending, a frequent occurrence in some EU countries. Considering those premises, it is clear that clusters present an ideal set of features that can come into play when attempting to attract capital and channel indispensable funds.

In a number of cases, for example, the sectorial nature of clusters, which frequently focus on a specific sector and draw upon a pool of local, specialized knowledge, represents a key advantage in the search for capital and investments. This is mostly due to the fact that in many cases, and even more frequently when looking at early stage investment and "seed" capital, venture funds and angel investors tend to require an extremely precise overview of the business in question before committing to a risky financial operation. While this factor might benefit above all technological enterprises with higher a prospective of high returns, such as those dealing with nanotechnologies, aerospace, and high-end IT, it is nevertheless true that the other sectors might also attract funds thanks to the cohesion of a particular cluster and the quality of the research underpinning its production. This is evident, for example, in the case of a number of enterprises dealing with niche sectors, whether in technology or consumption goods. When we take into account the US-based venture capital industry, this has always been identified as extremely regionally concentrated and highly co-specialized (Smith and Florida 2000; Kenney and Florida 2004; Mazzucato 2013). It is also important to notice how the close interaction between public and private, significantly fostered by the clusters' structures, can result into a model that mitigates the shortcomings of the both sectors while increasing their strengths through complementarity. This model, which combines the strategic capacities and research power of universities and local epistemic communities to the business experience and proactivity of single enterprises, whatever their field, can prove more appealing and reliable to investors looking for a safe destination to their long-term investments. Another element worth pointing out is also the (all too frequently) overlooked role universities and research centers can play in attracting state funding and in providing useful institutional contacts to clusters they are part of. This contribution turns out to be particularly important in EU countries such as France, Italy, or Spain, where large structural funds for innovative projects are more frequently provided by the state rather than by private actors—as it occurs in the Anglo-Saxon context—and public universities tend to have strong bounds with ministries and governmental agencies. Eventually, it is also important to notice how, when developing within or around capitals and important cities in general, clusters can acquire high visibility by exploiting the urban milieu they are grounded in, therefore creating potential for investments and giving the cluster itself additional leverage. In conclusion, while certain contingent factors—cumbersome bureaucratic processes being just one of them—can prevent clusters from obtaining adequate funding, it can be said that clusters constitute an effective vehicle to leverage funds by exploiting the interactivity and network-based mentality promoted by the open innovation model.

4   Cross-Assets Specialization: Sharing Is Better

As already highlighted in the previous paragraph, the capacity to attract a substantial and, above all, constant flow of investment constitutes a pivotal and unavoidable issue in the survival of clusters. However, while funds do indeed matter, due attention should be given to what might be considered as the core strength that makes clusters such effective structures in promoting innovative projects and to leverage the capital necessary to bring them forward. This specific element, which can be defined as "cross-assets specialization," represents a unique feature of the cluster model and, in a way, the most evident bridge between the geographically tight entrepreneurial agglomerations and the open innovation paradigm (Cooke 2005). While laying the basis for the concept of openness in innovation, different authors, including Chesbrough himself (2003) have repeatedly drawn attention to the capacity of firms to go beyond their original inwardness in R&D and sourcing for solutions among the ranks of potential partners and, when the opportunity arises, even of potential competitors. The following analysis will look at how clusters, due to their geographical distinctiveness, can exploit openness and knowledge produced by their components to produce innovative solutions and avoid stagnation.

When looking at the particular case of assets sharing, it is especially important to focus on the role knowledge plays in clusters. In certain cases clusters can present themselves as agglomerations of already powerful companies, research centers, or universities, most of which could easily produce their own share of groundbreaking innovation through their internal R&D capabilities. Some of the great California or East Coast high-tech clusters are a prominent example. However, particularly at the European level, it might be said that actors aggregate into clusters to obtain a bigger outcome out of a small pool of individual resources. Cooke and Morgan's (1998) analysis on what they call "associational economy" presents evidence of regional co-specialization in various powerhouses of European competitive advantage. In such contexts, the advantage of close proximity translates into the opportunity to capture knowledge produced by actors that are external to the firm or the research center in question. It would be logical to assume that such "knowledge externalities" would only be willingly shared by an actor only with close partners. Nevertheless, it can be noticed how the local dimension of clusters favors a looser approach, given that human and commercial interaction between actors coexisting within close proximity lead to an unavoidable exchange of ideas. This intentional and unintentional flow of knowledge, sometimes defined as *knowledge spillover*, can be seen as a central element allowing actors within clusters to enter a virtuous cycle of innovative production (Breschi et al. 2005; Huang and Rice 2013).

As such, the knowledge produced and circulated within a cluster, be it regional or smaller in scale, can assume different forms and can be transferred in different ways, but it is more frequently exchanged in the form of the abovementioned assets. In line with the variety of actors composing a cluster, those assets can vary in nature. In the case of firms, particularly if specialized in a highly technical sector like manufacturing, assets can be human, taking the form of skilled labor. When the expertise of this labor capital is shared between companies, employees do not only contribute to a common depository of knowledge, but they also convey a considerable amount of learning acquired within their own firms, thus magnifying their influence. Assets sharing can also involve the common use of a specific market information, allowing the actors to access a wider array of consumers and, in the future, create a new pool of potential clients. When research-intensive communities—universities in particular—are also brought into the equation, assets tend to become more "intangible," but not for this reason are they less important. The relevance of universities and public research centers is experienced in various industries: for example, Kenney and Mowery (2014) provide evidence of the role the various campuses of the University of California had in fostering local collaboration and the development of cluster dynamics. Particularly for a small firm, partnering with universities and dynamic start-ups can provide unique intellectual assets that include, among the others, the possibility to access state-of-the-art R&D solutions and to scout for fresh talent. At the same time, companies would benefit from a range of important institutional connections, which in the long term might result in obtaining state funding and favorable policy linkages

(Röttmer 2011). Eventually, it is possible to observe that local knowledge and reputation itself constitutes a fundamental asset and an extremely important tool to attract investments and resources from much bigger firms that do not necessarily lie within the geographical limits of the cluster, but can become precious partners on the long run.

Those factors do not always concur to determine the success of a cluster; nevertheless, they contribute to make its survival and productivity more likely even in front of systemic adversity, strengthening its resilience and capacity to generate new solutions. Overall, firms located within geographical proximity tend to outperform their competitors when it comes to patenting, creating, and marketing innovative products (Jaffe, Trajtenberg and Henderson 1993; Howells 2002; Distefano et al. forthcoming). However, an important body of literature has been warned about considering assets sharing within clusters as the only path to success. While the ability of clusters to make the best of externalities remains important, strong in-house R&D and the capacity to protect innovative discoveries is still essential to the rise and fall of numerous companies (Chesbrough and Crowther 2006). In a way, even firms successfully embedded in a cluster system cannot avoid finding a "golden middle" between internal and external learning, if they do not want to lose their competitive advantage and, due to the interconnectedness they share, compromising the major tools that open innovation offers.

5   Trust: The Intangible Strength of Local Networks

Of all the factors facilitating the growth of open innovation within and through clusters, trust is perhaps the most interesting and, at the same time, the most easily overlooked. This can be attributed to the fact that the concept of *trust* itself is as intangible and ambiguous a concept as it is inescapable, particularly when looking at relations between strongly interconnected actors. On the one hand, trust figures prominently in literature pertaining to regional and local innovation systems and networks (Möllering 2006; Murphy 2008). Quite predictably, clusters are no exception to this trend. In fact, the subject has been debated, if not always in considerable depth, in several recent works. On the other hand, some authors see trust as too much of an intangible (if precious) asset, no more than a marginal and undefined influence in economic transactions. To some extent, both positions hold a certain amount of truth. It can be pointed out that trust remains, as this paragraph will argue, an element in the creation of clusters, but also the result of successful clustering (Paniccia 1998; Ring and Van de Ven 1994). Through an overview of the existing literature, the following analysis will look at clarifying the role of trust within clusters and why clusters represent an ideal milieu for trust to take root. Above all, this passage will highlight the role of trust in reinforcing clusters' inner cohesion and in contributing to both greater efficiency and the exchange of specialized knowledge, which remains the lymph of open innovation.

While it is important to remember that a precise definition of trust might be the cause of endless etymological debate, a functional description of what trust implies and its contextualization within the framework of innovation networks—clusters in the first place—constitutes a helpful starting point for this analysis. Trust has been seen by some authors as the factor guaranteeing a degree of mutual honesty and transparency (Fukuyama 1995, p. 26) between two or more actors who identify with a certain community, thus posing significant limits to the rise of "opportunistic behavior" (Williamson 1993). When considered in such terms, trust can also be seen as an element mitigating the feeling of risk and uncertainty for the partners involved in a particular collaborative endeavor. In addition to the alleviation of risk, trust is also an easily recognizable element in situations of strong mutual dependence (Granovetter 1985). No less important, trust implies that the actors involved in an exchange, being it at an interpersonal, informational, or economic level, share a certain sets of norms and aim toward achieving a common objective. From a broad point of view, trust can therefore be understood as the combination of transparency, lack of opportunism, and an understanding of shared norms that exist between people or other entities involved in a particular dealing or a set of relationships. In light of those considerations, trust can be recognized as a key underlying element of a myriad of successful interactions, among them financial, scientific, or industrial, which can shape an innovation system.

However, among the many networks and interactions through which innovation can be generated, clusters present a number of distinctive features that allow trust not simply to develop but also to become a significant instrument in generating innovative solutions. Not surprisingly, trust is more easily achievable among actors who share a common background, both cultural and geographical, a factor that is greatly facilitated by the geographical proximity bounding together different clusters' actors (Boschma, Balland, and de Vaan 2014, pp. 246–248; Schilling and Phelps 2007; Wong 2010). In fact, not only does such proximity guarantee the belonging of the clusters' actors to a common normative background but it does also allow the actors themselves to assess their reciprocal accountability without necessarily exercising a continuous, stiffening, and formal mutual scrutiny (Lazerson and Lorenzoni 2007). Indeed, even though quality assessment and control remain important, increasing emphasis is placed on reputation and reliability, which are naturally consolidated in time through collaboration (Uzzi 1997). An important consequence of this trend is the stronger proclivity of clusters' firms and enterprises to take risk and pour both investments and knowledge into a common objective, for uncertainty can be swiftly mitigated through growing accountability. Additionally, it is possible to observe how this informal atmosphere of trust and accountability developing within the cluster can frequently result in a greater efficiency of the firms' activities and in a significant reduction in transaction costs, the latter being tamed by the lack of opportunism (Orstavik 2004, p. 211). However, from the viewpoint of open innovation, the key contribution of trust within clusters is certainly the intensification of information and knowledge exchange, which allow the different agents/partners to fully benefit from a continuous flow of externalities. For instance, on the development of Silicon Valley, Saxenian (2006) clearly points the fact that people in such agglomerations tend to be more loyal to the cluster and their project, rather than the company they are employed with. In this regard, trust is a fundamental factor, and local industrial dynamics lead partners to rely the more and more on each other's research and learning capabilities, on the development of projects that necessarily cut across an individual institution's boundaries. In turn this dynamic leads to a self-enforcing mechanism based on the accumulation of both "codified" and "tacit" knowledge (Huang and Rice 2013, p. 107).

Whether trust can be considered an exclusively "virtuous" element in the development and durable success of clusters remains an object of debate. If there is little doubt that greater freedom to share specialized knowledge in a close-knit network of partners can significantly strenghten a firm's creativity and resilience, excessive trust might have a negative effect on some of the firms involved. For example, an uneven reliance on externalities and partners' resources might lead a firm to become too dependent, if not subjugated to other agents. At the same time, a long-standing collaboration might lose steam or the adequate "level of tension" (Bidault and Castello 2010) necessary for fruitful debate to take place. It might nevertheless be said that the advantages of a trustful environment can compensate for such shortcomings, since a cluster might easily recover its competitiveness by flexibly adjusting to new conditions and needs. Eventually, trust remains a pivotal instrument and a key factor in making clusters efficient vehicles of open innovation.

6   Conclusion: Stepping into the Future and Connecting Clusters Within Ecosystems

On June 22, Commissioner Moedas[2] pointed to the fact that a new beginning for the European Research Area needs to be grounded on the ideas and principles of open innovation strategy: "We need open innovation to capitalise on the results of European research and innovation. This means creating the right ecosystems, increasing investment, and bringing more companies and regions into the knowledge economy." Consistent with such view, this chapter has argued that the concept of open innovation, as it was originally coined, and as it has been applied by companies and institutions worldwide, has a fundamental regional dimension, as some of its fundamental drivers such as access to finance, co-specialization of assets, and trust are rooted in the idea of industrial clusters. Geographical proximity, far from representing an element of parochialism within a fully globalized financial and market system, can represent a key competitive advantage.

---

[2] Speech delivered by Commissioner Carlos Moedas in Brussels on June 22, 2015 "Open Innovation, Open Science, Open to the World".

Clusters can achieve such advantages by becoming vehicles of open innovation, a paradigm that works particularly well thanks to the structure of clusters themselves. On the one hand, SMEs but also larger companies that try to connect to a local context, can benefit immensely from the networking opportunities created by the cluster structure. Firms can leverage on the strong position, greater visibility, vast connections, and even reputation offered by the cluster in order to leverage funds in periods of financial strain, thus avoiding a likely failure. On the other hand, the availability of both tangible and intangible assets within a cluster, like specific technical know-how, institutional connections provided by research institutions, or a pool of skilled personnel, allows businesses to remain up to date with the latest discoveries and innovations. Even universities and public research infrastructures can gain from such a virtuous cycle, which allows the best talent to experience firsthand the reality of the entrepreneurial world and, in certain cases, to go on working within that very environment. Eventually, geographical proximity also favors the development of trust, an intangible element that stimulates the generation of best practices and, even more important, encourages firms to diffuse their internal learning and research. However, even the most effective model can quickly lose its advantage in the fast, ever-changing global environment, where innovative ideas can become outdated as quickly as they are produced. Indeed, clusters do manage to frequently manage to bring the local and regional realities of innovation to national, even international prominence, acting as small-scale innovation ecosystems. Yet, clusters can themselves become isolated and inward-looking, soon exhausting their innovative propulsion. The end of the clusters' life cycle can be caused by the very same reasons that contributed to its success: excessive trust in local expertise can cost competitive advantage; strong relations can, in the long term, turn into inactivity; and ideas can come to stagnate even within the supposedly thriving borders of a cluster. While pursuing local open innovation dynamics, clusters can close off the world and become inward-looking places. As several reports have stressed (NESTA 2008; European Commission 2014; HLG 2014), it is exactly by avoiding becoming prisoners of the same boundaries that guarantee their prosperity that clusters can further prosper within the globalized world. This goal can only be achieved through further integration of the clusters within broader innovation ecosystems, which in turn can connect them to other clusters, thus favoring crossfertilization and the development of open innovation dynamics, not only within clusters but also between international centers of excellence.

References

Baldwin, C., and E. von Hippel. 2011. Modeling a paradigm shift: From producer innovation to user and open collaborative innovation. *Organization Science* 22(6): 1399–1417.

Baumol, W.J., R.E. Litan, and C.J. Schramm. 2007. *Good capitalism bad capitalism and the economics of growth and prosperity.* New Haven: Yale University Press.

Bidault, F. and A. Castello. (2010). Why too much trust is death to innovation, MIT Sloane Management Review, 51 (4). http://sloanreview.mit.edu/article/why-too-much-trust-is-death-to-innovation/.

Boschma, R., P.A. Balland, and M. de Vaan. 2014. The formation of economic networks: A proximity approach. In *Regional development and proximity relations*, eds. A. Torre, and F. Wallet. Cheltenham: Edward Elgar.

Breschi, S., F. Lissoni, and F. Montobbio. 2005. The geography of knowledge spillovers: *Conceptual issues and measurement problems.* In *Clusters, networks, and innovation*, eds. S. Breschi and F. Malerba. Oxford: Oxford University Press.

Castells, M., and P. Hall. 1994. *Technopoles of the world. The making of 21st century industrial complexes.* London: Routledge.

Chesbrough, H. 2003. *Open innovation: The new imperative for creating and profiting from technology.* Boston: Harvard Business School Press.

Chesbrough, H., and A.K. Crowther. 2006. Beyond high tech: Early adopters of open innovation in other industries. *R&D Management* 36: 229–236.

Chesbrough, H., and A. R. Garman. 2009. How open innovation can help you cope in lean times. *Harvard Business Review.*

Chesbrough, H., J. West, and W. Vanhaverbeke. 2006. *Open innovation: Researching a new paradigm.* Oxford: Oxford University Press.

Cooke, P. 2005. Regional knowledge capabilities and open innovation: Regional innovation systems and cluster in the asymmetric knowledge economy. In *Clusters, networks, and innovation*, eds. S. Breschi, and F. Malerba. Oxford: Oxford University Press.

Cooke, P., and K. Morgan. 1998. *The associational economy. Firms, regions, and innovation.* London: Oxford University Press.

Cowan, R. 2005. Network models of innovation and knowledge diffusion. In *Clusters, networks, and innovation*, eds. S. Breschi, and F. Malerba. Oxford: Oxford University Press.

Di Minin, A., F. Frattini, and A. Piccaluga. 2010. Fiat: Open innovation in a downturn (1993–2003). *California Management Review* 52(3): 132–159.

Distefano, Fabio, Giacomo Gambillara, and Alberto Di Minin. 2016. Extending the innovation paradigm: A double 'I' environment and some evidence from BRIC countries. *Journal of the Knowledge Economy* 7(1): 126–154.

European Commission. 2014. *Open innovation 2.0 yearbook*. Luxembourg: Publication Office of the European Union.

———. 2015. *Open innovation 2.0 yearbook*. Luxembourg: Publication Office of the European Union.

Freeman, A. 2013. Challenging myths about the funding of small businesses.... Demos Finance Report. http://www.demos.co.uk/files/DF_Finance_for_Growth_web.pdf?1378216438.

Fukuyama, F. (1995). *Trust: The social virtues and the creation of prosperity*. New York: Free Press.

Granovetter, M. 1985. Economic action and social structure: The problem of embeddedness. *American Journal of Sociology* 91(3): 481–510.

High Level Group (HLG) on Innovation Policy Management. 2014. Blueprint: The way forward to improve people's lives. Inspiring and Completing European Innovation Ecosystem. HLG Secretariat: Brussels.

High Level Group. 2015. *Blueprint: The way forward to improve people's lives*. Brussels: Inspiring and Completing European Innovation Ecosystem. HLG Secretariat.

Howells, J. 2002. Tacit knowledge, innovation and economic geography. *Urban Studies* 39(5–6): 871–884.

Huang, F., and J. Rice. 2013. Does open innovation work better in regional clusters? *Australian Journal of Regional Studies* 19(1): 85–120.

Ja/e, Adam B., M. Trajtenberg, and R. Henderson. 1993. Geographic Location of knowledge spillovers as evidenced by patent citations. *Quarterly Journal of Economics* 108(3): 577–598.

Kenney, M., and R. Florida, eds. 2004. *Locating global advantage*. Stanford, CA: Stanford University Press.

Kenney, M., and D. Mowery. 2014. *Public universities and regional growth*. Palo Alto: Stanford University Press.

Krugman, P. 1991. *Geography and trade*. Cambridge, MA: MIT Press.

Lazerson, M.H., and G. Lorenzoni. 2007. The firms that feed industrial districts: A return to the Italian source. In *Clusters, networks, and innovation*, eds. S. Breschi, and F. Malerba. Oxford: Oxford University Press.

Marshall, A. 1920. *Principles of economics*. London: Macmillan.

Mazzucato, M. 2013. *The entrepreneurial state: Debunking public vs. private sector myths*. London: Anthem.

Möllering, G. 2006. *Trust: Reason, routine, reflexivity*. Oxford: Elsevier.

NESTA 2008. Towards an innovation nation. *NESTA Policy Briefing* (March). http://www.nesta.org.uk/sites/default/files/towards-an-innovation-nation.pdf.

OECD. 2009. *Measuring entrepreneurship a collection of indicators*, 2009 edn. Paris: OECD.

Orstavik, F. 2004. Knowledge spillovers, innovation and cluster formation: The case of Norwegian aquaculture. In *Knowledge spillovers and knowledge management*, eds. C. Karlsson, P. Flensburg, and S. Hrte. Cheltenham: Edward Elgar.

Paniccia, I. 1998. One, a hundred, a thousand of industrial districts: Organizational variety in local networks of small and medium-sized enterprises. *Organization Studies* 19(4): 667–700.

Porter, M. 1990. The competitive advantage of nations. *Harvard Business Review* 68(2): 73–91.

Porter, M. 1998. Clusters and the new economics of competition. *Harvard Business Review* November–December.

———. 2007. *The competitive advantage of nations: With a new introduction*, (10 pr. ed.) edn. Basingstoke: Palgrave Macmillan.

Ring, Peter, and Andrew Van de Ven. 1994. Developmental processes of cooperative interorganizational relationships. *Academy of Management Review* 19(1): 90–119.

Röttmer, N. 2011. *Innovation performance and clusters: A dynamic capability perspective on regional technology clusters*. Dresden: Gabler.

Saxenian, A. 1994. *Regional advantage*. Cambridge, MA: Harvard University Press.

———. 2006. *The new argonauts: Regional advantage in a global economy*. Cambridge, MA: Harvard University Press.

Schilling, M.A., and C. Phelps. 2007. Interfirm collaboration networks: The impact of network structure on rates of innovation. In *Entrepreneurship, innovation, and the growth mechanism of the free-enterprise economies*, eds. E. Sheshinski, R.J. Strom, and W.J. Baumol. Princeton, NJ: Princeton University Press.

Smith, D.F., and R. Florida. 2000. Venture capital's role in regional innovation systems: Historical perspective and recent evidence. In *Regional innovation, knowledge and global change*, ed. Z.J. Acs. London: Pinter.

Uzzi, B. 1997. Social structure and competition in interfirm networks: The paradox of embeddedness. *Administrative Science Quarterly* 42(1): 35–67.

Williamson, O. 1993. Calculativeness, trust, and economic organization. *Journal of Law and Economics* 36(2): 453–486.

Wong, A. 2010. Angel finance: The other venture capital. In *Venture capital: Investment strategies, structures and policies*, ed. D. Cumming. Hoboken, NJ: Wiley.

5

Policy Coherence for Developing and Steering Innovation Ecosystems

Marisa Poncela-Garcia

1   Introduction

Innovation is a very popular term, widely used by many policy makers convinced about its role in promoting economic growth and creating new (often high-skilled) jobs. An increasing amount of evidence (OECD 2014) has identified a robust relationship among them. Moreover, innovative and knowledge-based economies and businesses have proven to be more resilient to the economic crisis than traditional ones (OECD 2015).

Innovation is essentially the result of a complex and usually lengthy process that may start with basic research and ends up with the introduction of new technologies, processes, products, or services into the market. Many actors are involved in this procedure: researchers, technologists, and businesspeople, as well as a wide range of entities such as public, private, or mixed R&D centers; innovative companies; and public and private funding agencies. The technological developments behind an innovation

M. Poncela-Garcia (✉)
Secretary-General for Science, Technology and Innovation,
Government of Spain, Madrid, Spain
e-mail: marisa.poncela@mineco.es

© The Editor(s) (if applicable) and The Author(s) 2016

97

K. Gretschmann, S. Schepers (eds.), *Revolutionising EU Innovation Policy*,
DOI 10.1057/978-1-137-55554-0_5

may be protected through intellectual property rights and are a relevant source of income for innovative companies. Similarly, those companies that acquire intellectual property may obtain a competitive advantage by reducing their production costs and/or increasing their sales. As a result, the economies where innovations are produced or acquired gain direct and indirect benefits from the innovative processes.

As awareness across the world has increased about the benefits of innovation, the demands for ways to enhance it have similarly increased. This has led to a focus on the nature and efficiency of the processes related to innovation. Traditionally, it was thought that the translation of research into innovation followed a linear model. However, present conceptualizations focus on the systemic nature of the process, highlighting the interactions between all the factors and actors participating in it for value creation. Thus the term "innovation ecosystem" is now broadly used, which can be defined as "the set of ideas, institutions, policies, and regulations that will determine the direction, outcome, productivity, and degree of competitiveness from innovation" (HLG-IPM 2013). Strong and efficient innovation ecosystems have some similarities such as strengths in research areas (regarding both talent and excellent research facilities), cooperation between business and research centers, public and private partnerships, substantial private investment in R&D activities, commercialization of technological knowledge facilitating transfer, rapid market use, and patent revenues from abroad.

Public administrations have a crucial role in these successful systems as they are a source of funds for the initial processes behind research and innovation, and also create the right environment to increase their outputs and efficiency.

2   A European Perspective on Innovation Performance

Europe is a key producer of scientific knowledge and technological breakthroughs but often these are commercialized outside Europe, due to global competition for R&D talent and the increasingly global nature of innovative enterprises. Therefore, R&D policies need to focus on constructing a favorable environment for innovation and commercialization, which are most relevant for our economies.

To address this challenge, the European Union launched in 2010 "Innovation Union" (EC 2011), one of the seven flagships announced in the Europe 2020 strategy (EC 2010). It included 34 commitments related to the reinforcement of European knowledge base and the reduction of its fragmentation, the enhancement of the transfer of good ideas into market, the improvement of social and territorial cohesion, the development of European innovation partnerships, and the coordination of member states (MS), R&D international cooperation programs and activities. It also identified the responsibilities of each actor in the European Union for reforming research and innovation systems, and measuring the progress made.

A recent report from the European Commission (EC 2014a) states that "excellent progress has been made in delivering on each of the Innovation Union blocks." Indeed, many instruments have been launched to address the different blocks identified in the "Innovation Union," such as the following, which will be addressed later in this chapter:

* **Horizon 2020**, the new research and innovation framework program, which encompasses all phases of the innovation cycle and has secured greater private investment in key technological sectors.
* **Instruments devoted to ease access to finance**, such as the Risk-Sharing Finance Facility (jointly set up by the European Commission with the European Investment Bank Group) or the increase of instruments such as precommercial public procurement.
* The setup of **innovation-friendly regulations**, such as the revision of the state aid framework for R&D&I.
* **Instruments devoted to improve social and territorial cohesion**, such as Smart Specialization Strategies as an ex ante conditionality for investment priorities on R&D and innovation activities.
* **Development of European innovation partnerships.**

The recent creation of a **European Fund for Strategic Investments** (EFSI), linked to the launch of an investment plan for Europe (EC 2014b), is also relevant.

It will take some time for the impact of these initiatives on the European innovation ecosystem to be known and evaluated. Their impact is likely to have been reduced, as a result of the global financial and economic crisis. For instance, the quantitative target of the European Union established in its strategy, "Europe 2020," "to invest 3 % of its GDP in R&D&I activities" (EC 2010) has not been reached and, according to Eurostat (2013 data),[1] only 14 % of EU-28 member states were devoting resources equal or above this value. The present postcrisis budgetary situation in most member states does not allow for increases in expenditures. Many countries were forced to reduce their investments in this sector during the last financial crisis, which has been particularly apparent since 2012.

The High Level Group on Innovation Policy Management (HLG-IPM), established under the Polish Presidency of the Council of the European Union has recently undertaken a thorough review of the challenges the European Union faces on innovation. It identified the need in promoting a radical change in European innovation policies "from a narrow science and technology orientation to an all-encompassing holistic and coherent strategy involving several policy areas, from a diffuse to a highly focussed division of labor between all the players and stakeholders involved" (HLG-IPM 2013). As mentioned in the introductory chapter of this volume, the HLG-IPM identified seven policy priorities for the improvement of the European innovation ecosystem. According to the members of this group, the most urgent priority is the improvement of policy coherence across the European Union. This issue is also a major driver for other priorities set up by this group, such as reducing regulatory complexity and rigidity, eliminating obstacles to the provision of new funding for innovation, reinterpreting competition law, or developing an inclusive view of intellectual property. This chapter focuses on this particular topic of policy coherence.

---

[1] See http://ec.europa.eu/eurostat/statistics-explained/index.php/Europe_2020_indicators_research_and_development.

3   Addressing Policy Coherence Across Europe

The HLG-IPM identified the existing fragmentation in innovation policy through EU institutions and among member states, and between them and EU authorities. Coherent public governmental policies create a clear framework that will support the innovation process. Those policies should be framed around providing the right business environment, including reducing regulatory complexity and rigidity, facilitating industrial and public–private cooperation, and moving into next generation technologies and businesses.

As member states have developed their overall R&D&I strategies in recent years, alignment with the Innovation Union and Horizon 2020 objectives has increased. This is particularly the case of the Spanish strategy 2013–2020, which shares three of its four pillars with Horizon 2020. This alignment reduces the fragmentation and incoherence among MS policies, with clear benefits for improving their innovation subsystems, whether through industrial leadership and scientific excellence, and the promotion of public–private partnerships to address key societal challenges.

However, achieving overall policy coherence across Europe is not an easy task. To begin with, there is not a uniform European innovation ecosystem as revealed the Innovation Union Scoreboard (IUS) (Fig. 5.1). This aggregated indicator reflects the large differences in the performance of the innovation subsystems of the 28 member states of the European Union. The last available report (EC 2015) shows a small number of "innovative leaders" (four member states), with some "innovative followers" (seven member states), a vast middle class of "moderate innovators" (13 member states), and a few "modest innovators" (three member states).

These dissimilarities are even more open to public inspection when regional innovation ecosystems (EC 2014d) are assessed (Fig. 5.2a). These geographical divergences have historical and economic grounds: regional innovation performance is very much related to the ratio of their GDP in regards to the average European Union GDP (Fig. 5.2b). This suggests that innovation policies of member states and regions are designed to address the particular challenges their systems face within competitive global environment. It is not surprising that the innovative leaders would

Fig. 5.1 Classification of European Union Member States according to the Innovation Union Scoreboard 2015 (EC 2015)

promote policies to attract talent and investments from across the world, including from other European member states, while the modest innovators would promote policies to maintain or improve the talent and investments they badly need for the improvement of their system.

Cultural or historical differences are also a barrier to aligning innovation policies across Europe. Less innovative European areas may have limited expertise in defining proper strategies, policies, instruments, and actions for the improvement of their innovation subsystems. Some key

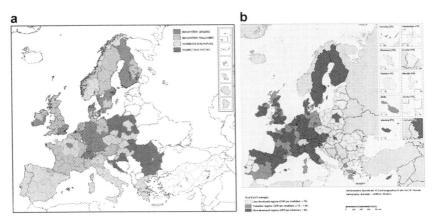

Fig. 5.2 (a) Classification of European Union Regions according to the Regional Innovation Scoreboard 2014 (EC 2014d); (b) Regional Gross Domestic Product (GDP) per inhabitant in NUTS2 regions over the 2007–2009 period as percentage of EU-27 average
Note: NUTS stands for Nomenclature of Units for Territorial Statistics. NUTS2 regions have a population ranging between 0.8 and 3 million inhabitants. The information provided in Fig. 5.2b was the basis to establish regional eligibility for structural funds (2014–2020). (Eurostat 2014)

actors of their subsystems may not accept they have a role to play in supporting policy makers designing innovation ecosystems. Those regions will probably face more difficulties than other regions as their stakeholders and citizens may not be completely aware of the need to change the current drivers of their economy. These challenges have been already experienced when developing Smart Specialization Strategies (RIS3), which would allow them to spend European Structural and Investment Funds (ESIF) for R&D&I activities.

Funding also remains a challenge for many less innovative areas, as shown in the ratio between public and private share of their GDP in R&D&I activities (Fig. 5.3). While the overall EU-28 share of the private sector is 64.2 % of the total, large differences are experienced across member states, ranging from 22.6 % (Latvia) to 77.3 % (Slovenia).

These differences affect the capability of the system of absorbing the talent and the scientific and technological developments promoted by member state public investments in R&D&I. Moreover, it will also limit the capacity

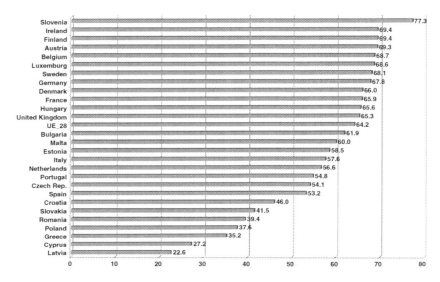

Fig. 5.3 Percentage of private investment over total country investment in R&D&I activities. EU-28 Member States
Note: 2012 data; FECYT 2014

of their systems to absorb innovations performed elsewhere. Therefore, R&D&I member state public policies aimed to improve their innovation systems must be tailored to their own characteristics (EC 2014c).

However, coordination and synergies among the approaches developed by the different member states to improve their systems will support the expansion of the quality and the efficiency of the EU innovative system. Collaboration between countries on their national R&D&I agendas can help, but this needs to be managed in a way that prevents an explosion in the number of initiatives, which become impossible for customers to navigate or governments to properly manage them.

A completely coherent innovation policy across Europe is neither feasible nor desirable. However, greater alignment between European, national, or regional institutions is badly needed and should be achievable. Many examples can be provided on the lack of internal incoherence of policies and actions in this regard.

At the EU level, the revision of the state aid guidelines at the European level has reduced some of the burdens to R&D&I investments (through reducing thresholds for notification, broadening the categories of aid, and allowing greater flexibility to finance innovative businesses). However, they still represent barriers for innovation improvement. Furthermore, they do not work well with those rules for the European Regional Development Fund (ERDF).

Similarly, government departments at the member state or regional level have developed sectoral policies and regulations to protect or enhance particular sectors or areas, resulting in incoherent frameworks negatively affecting not only the overall innovation performance of the administered territory but also their agricultural, industrial, environmental, and social progress.

This incoherent approach in public policies related to innovation is very unfortunate as public governance is crucial for creating the favorable environment that is needed to improve the European innovation ecosystem. In fact, some of the weaknesses the HLG-IPM highlights, such as problems of leadership and incoherence of vision and purpose, reduced cumulative effects and critical mass, inflexible culture of policy making and regulatory application, organizational fragmentation, multiple barriers to innovation markets, and the absence of an encompassing systemic approach, are behind this.

One of the recommendations the HLG-IPM proposed to solve this problem is to have an overarching authority with full responsibility for innovation and competitiveness within the EU institutions and in each member state.

In Spain the Council on R&D&I policies was established in 2012 to ensure the coordination of the national and regional policies. The relevant sectorial national ministers plus regional R&D&I responsible and the ones that participate. This council has recently approved the new road map of Spanish research infrastructures. The coordination at a more technical level is performed through the Network on Public R&D&I Policies (REDIDI), which ensures the coordination of regional and national programs. This network has proved to be very useful for exchanging knowledge, expertise, and good practices related to the definition and follow-up of regional RIS3.

The HLG-IPM also identified as a challenge the lack of policy coherence when sectors and clusters are involved. Some efforts are underway to solve or ease it at the European Union level. Joint technology initiatives have been developed, which aim to coordinate and design the actions needed to enhance European competitiveness in crucial economic sectors. However, their implementation would be improved by allowing a more open competition between the industrial stakeholders directly leading the initiative and other agents. The development of sector and crosssector perspectives to determine where the competitive advantages of Europe may lay dormant, as the HLG-IMP proposed, would probably provide a better framework in this regard.

These sectoral visions, which affect different national and regional departments and many R&D&I actors, including business, are under development in some countries. In the case of Spain, sectoral views are under development for Transport, Bioeconomy, BioHealth, and Energy. These visions will be complemented with overviews considering horizontal issues such as Key Enabling Technologies, ICT, advanced manufacturing, materials, or territorial development. Once national and regional sectoral priorities are set, after a thorough revision of strengths and weaknesses, it will be much easier to achieve the coordination of particular programs at the European level.

An appropriate environment has to be created first in order to construct such visions. National policies can support technological platforms led by business associations where the different actors in a given sector could work together to define specific programs or actions to achieve those sectoral visions. When these platforms are federated at the supranational level, they provide an opportunity to support collaboration and coherence within the EU.

The HLG-IPM identified the implementation of peer review processes as another mechanism by which policy coherence could be improved. This would enable modification or removal of underperforming policies and programs. Although some institutions, such as the European Commission, are already applying this principle, it is not widely spread across R&D&I public national and regional administrations.

4   National Perspectives: Efforts Made to Improve Internal Innovation Policy Coherence

Since the structure, size, and effectiveness of member states innovation systems greatly varies across the European Union, the policies developed to improve them should be tailored to their specific needs. Therefore, each member state must identify those necessities and design the strategies, programs, and instruments that are required to address them. The internal coherence of those components of public innovation policies is highly needed to increase the efficiency of the system and thus the overall economic growth and employment of a particular country.

In this section we focus on a successful initiative carried out by one European Union member state, Spain, to improve the internal coherence of their innovation policies.

4.1   The Need for Internal and External Policy Coherence in the Spanish Innovation System

Spain clearly needs to improve the number and size of innovative enterprises to have a sustainable innovation system able to absorb the knowledge generated in the country. It accounts for an 11.3 %[2] of the citable European scientific production, and has a great potential to be transferred to business. The Spanish Research Council (CSIC) is the eighth and thirteenth best world institution in the number of citable publications and number of citations of its publications in the dossiers of international patents,[3] respectively. However, CSIC revenues from patent licenses just represent 0.13 % of its budget.

The integration of more and greater innovative companies that could take benefit of the R&D results of Spanish researchers is thus a highly desirable objective. When analyzing the world's top 2,500 companies investing in R&D&I, only three Spanish companies are among the top

---

[2] See http://www.scimagojr.com.
[3] See http://scimagoir.com.

100 European investors (EC 2014e) compared to the 16 UK enterprises included in that particular shortlist. The increase in the number of strong innovative companies would probably be the only means to sustainably increase the size of the system as the current private share of the total investment performed in Spain in the sector is close to 50 %, away from the 65–70 % range recorded in countries leading the European innovation, such as Germany and the UK.

The Spanish economy would largely benefit from the increase in the knowledge absorption capacity that would be associated with the intensification of private investment in innovation as the Spanish patents and associated revenues would also augment, thus providing further fuel to the system. It should be noticed that Spain just produced 3.04 triadic patents per million inhabitants in 2011, nine times less than UK records (OECD 2014).

New public national policies have been recently introduced to further strengthen the Spanish national system, under the overall framework set out in the Spanish Strategy on Science, Technology, and Innovation[4] (2013–2020). This seeks to accelerate the internal transformation of knowledge into innovation by supporting scientific excellence, attracting talent, and promoting academia and industry cooperation, while orienting a significant amount of research to address relevant social challenges. Specific funding instruments have been implemented to support this, complemented with other financial instruments designed to leverage higher investment from the private sector into R&D&I activities.

However R&D&I policies and instruments provided by the Spanish central administration are just part of the picture. The European context provides an excellent opportunity to increase the size and quality of the Spanish system through cooperation and competition with other European agents. To best benefit from this framework, the national policies and instruments are aligned with Europe 2020 strategy and Horizon 2020, and the most competitive Spanish agents are encouraged to participate in its different subprograms.

Equally, the regional context is also very important as large differences in the innovation systems and the economic structure of the 17 Spanish

---

[4] See http://www.idi.mineco.gob.es/stfls/MICINN/Investigacion/FICHEROS/Spanish_Strategy_Science_Technology.pdf.

Autonomous Communities are quite evident (see Fig. 5.2). The regional authorities are also developing policies and instruments to improve their innovation subsystems; some of them are heavily dependent on the use of structural funds that the European Union provides. (Spain is the third EU-28 member state in receiving such funds, with an 8.1 % share of the total cohesion funds envisaged for the 2014–2020 period.) In fact, the European Union has required that these funds be used to support existing regional smart specialization strategies.

This overall framework provides an excellent opportunity for improving the coherence of the Spanish innovation system at the regional, national, and European level in order to increase the efficiency of the midterm investments that are to be performed. Figure 5.4 illustrates the complexity of the process.

However, ensuring internal and external coordination and coherence of public policies and instruments is not just a Spanish matter, and it even exceeds the European context (OECD 2011). To address it, the Spanish authorities have established the Network on R&D&I Public Policies (REDIDI).

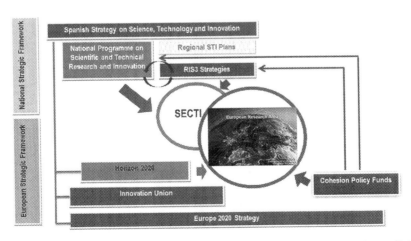

Fig. 5.4 Coordination of European, National and Regional public policies and instruments to improve the Spanish innovation system
Note: author's compilation and graphic account

4.2   The Spanish Network on R&D&I Public Policies (REDIDI) to Reinforce Internal and External Coherence Public Policies

The Network on R&D&I Public Policies has been established to:

* promote the design, implementation and further development of the adequate frameworks for public support to innovation;
* increase the efficiency of the funding mechanisms provided at the regional, national, and European levels for implementing the existing R&D&I public policies, avoid potential overlaps in the definition of programs, and usage of resources;
* increase the cooperation among the different administrative levels, generate synergies;
* improve the information systems and channels;
* propose ways of improving the usage of the different funding schemes (especially ERDF funds), and prioritize knowledge or sectoral areas.

It was launched back in 2011 and is presently chaired by the Spanish Ministries of "Economy and Competitiveness" (MINECO, responsible of the R&D&I policy at the national level) and "Finance and Public Administrations" (MINHAP, responsible of the management of the ERDF funds at the national level). The Network encompasses the Territorial Agents of Innovation (TAIs) designed by each autonomous community, with each regional administration designating two TAIs, one responsible for R&D&I policies and the other for the management of ERDF funds. The mission of the TAIs is to ensure the integration of the regional strategies on innovation with the existing policies and funding instruments at the supraregional level. The technical secretariat of the Network is supported by the Spanish Foundation for Science, Technology, and Innovation (FECYT), a body of MINECO.

In the last 3 years, REDIDI has had a very relevant role by providing support for the development of the regional smart specialization strategies (RIS3), preventing potential overlaps and promoting synergies, while ensuring coherence with the National Strategy on Science Technology and Innovation. It provides the forum for disseminating good practices and finding synergies across the different administrations on the implementation of regional R&D&I policies, and the use of ERDF funds.

Since 2014, it has also been active in providing guidance for RIS3 implementation by organizing thematic interterritorial forums devoted to specific items related to innovation, covered on a variable geometry basis by the TAIs designated by the different regions. To date, the following issues have been covered: interregional cooperation on agriculture and innovation, design as a leveraging tool for innovation, innovation on tourism, follow-up and evaluation of RIS3 regional strategies, water and innovation, energy and innovation, and health and innovation.

The European Commission has acknowledged the Spanish Network on R&D&I Public Policies as a case of good practices in coordinating public policies (EC 2012, 2014f).

5   Conclusion

Efforts are underway to improve the European Union innovation ecosystem, aiming to enhance an efficient and effective transfer of the wealth of knowledge it generates into the market. Public administrations play a crucial role in this regard, as their R&D policies may contribute to create the right environment to achieve this goal.

Fragmentation in innovation policy through EU institutions, among member states, and between them and EU authorities has been identified. Therefore, increasing R&D policy coherence is a most desirable objective. However, the EU innovation system is actually composed of a series of national and regional subsystems that present great dissimilarities in terms of size and robustness. Those contrasting differences determine different approaches of public policies in each territorial domain, making it unfeasible to reach a completely coherent innovation policy across Europe.

Nevertheless, the EU innovation system would highly benefit from increasing the internal coherence within each administration level (i.e., EU, national, and regional) in regards to the policies and instruments that may have an impact on R&D&I issues. While an overarching

R&D&I authority coordinating all those policies would probably be the best option to achieve this goal, more realistic coordination instruments have been already implemented in some countries, such as high-level, interdepartmental bodies.

The EU innovation system would also largely benefit from a better alignment of the direct and indirect funding instruments provided by the EU, and the national and regional authorities to promote R&D&I activities. The establishment of a network of national and regional public administration officers responsible of launching relevant policies and managing those instruments has proven to be effective in this regard, not only helping to design those policies but also providing the appropriate forum to exchange visions, experiences, and cases of good practices.

References

European Commission. 2010. Europe 2020. A strategy for smart, sustainable and inclusive growth. Communication from the Commission, COM (2010) 2020.

———. 2011. Europe 2020 flagship initiative innovation union. Communication from the Commission to the European Parliament, the Council, the European Economic and Social Committee and the Committee of the Regions. SEC (2010) 1161.

———. 2012. New practical guide to EU funding opportunities for research and innovation: Competitive European regions through research and innovation. http://ec.europa.eu/research/participants/data/ref/fp7/204008/practical-guide-rev3_en.pdf.

———. 2014a. State of innovation union. Taking stock 2010–2014.

———. 2014b. An investment plan for Europe. Communication from the Commission to the European Parliament, the Council, the European Economic and Social Committee and the Committee of the Regions COM (2014) 903 final.

———. 2014c. Research and innovation as sources of renewed growth. Communication from the Commission to the European Parliament, the Council, the European Economic and Social Committee and the Committee of the Regions COM (2014) 339 final.

———. 2014d. Regional innovation scoreboard.

————. 2014e. EU industrial R&D investment scoreboard.

————. 2014f. ERAWATCH country reports 2013: Spain. https://ec.europa.eu/jrc/sites/default/files/formcr2013_es_final.pdf.

————. 2015. Innovation union scoreboard.

Eurostat. 2014. *Eurostat regional yearbook 2014*. ISBN 9789279389061.

FECYT–ICONO. 2014. Indicadores del Sistema Español de Ciencia, Tecnología e Innovación 2014.

High Level Group on Innovation Policy Management 2013. *Report & recommendations*. ISBN: 978902089301.

OECD. 2011. Multi-level governance of innovation policy. In *Regions and innovation policy*. OECD Publishing. http://dx.doi.org/10.1787/9789264097803-7-en.

————. 2014. Science, technology and industry outlook 2014. OECD Publishing. http://dx.doi.org/10.787/sti_outlook-2014-en.

————. 2015.

6

Funding and Financing: Fresh Thinking Required

Morten Rasmussen and Nicola Redi

Although prudent first steps were taken to promote financing of innovation and R&D at the EU level, problems persist today concerning a fragmentation of funding and financing approaches, the coordination of innovation financing strategies, reduced R&D budgets, and the way funding is channeled into a real market context. This chapter seeks to discuss the context of financing innovation uptake, the steps taken at the EU level, including present-day barriers and inconsistencies that limits or prevents innovation financing efforts, and finally new and innovative ways of financing innovation at the EU level and among the member states.

The chapter provides further evidence for and elaborates on the innovation funding and financing-related recommendations of the High Level Group on Innovation Policy Management (HLG-IPM). See http://www.highlevelgroup.eu/en for more information.

M. Rasmussen (✉)
Innovation Consultant – CARSA, UK
e-mail: morten.ter@gmail.com

N. Redi
Investment Director – Vertis SGR, UK
e-mail: redi@vertis.it

115

The chapter argues that too much fragmentation exists among innovation funding/financing approaches in a multilayered Europe Union and that the way funding is channeled into markets and innovative activities must be improved. European cooperation is, on average, not yet investing sufficiently in R&D and has not fully adopted an open innovation approach. Moreover, there is a need to develop new ways of financing innovation and to broaden the public funding approach. The options to achieve this include: more coordination/cooperation on R&D investments; a broadening of the traditional R&D funding approach; a portfolio approach and "big projects"; innovation bonds; innovation taxation strategies; new mechanisms for incubator and seed capital; funding for PPPs and BUPs; and unorthodox ways of raising venture capital.

1 Explaining Financing Needs and Sources: Innovation Financing/Funding Models and the Emergence of Open Innovation

Before turning to present EU innovation funding and financing[1] endeavors, including their shortcomings and innovative solutions to address the gaps and bottlenecks, this chapter will offer thoughts on the need for innovation financing, the different sources of funding for innovation, innovation models, the importance of R&D expenditures, and the conversion of knowledge into growth as well as the emerging role of open innovation processes.

There seems to be a broad agreement among academia, business, and policy makers alike regarding the potential of innovation policy to strengthen competitiveness, economic growth, and job opportunities. But since innovation in businesses and public sectors are rooted in constantly changing and evolving environments, requiring complex and adaptive policy and financing models, while also taking regional differences into account, there is a general uncertainty in decision-making circles concerning how innovation is best promoted. While recognizing the contextual and geographic variance in innovation performance and

---

[1] The distinction between funding and financing is bold, and often used interchangeably, since both contribute to creating efficient investments for innovative activities. Yet, funding is related to providing sources/resources/revenue streams for projects in particular, while financing to a greater extent relates to financial arrangements related to debt (bonds and loans) and equity.

business specialization and needs, it requires a greater understanding of how innovation support strategies can be developed and implemented, and under which circumstances, including from policy management and funding/financing perspectives. This set of challenges and critical questions are the focal points of this chapter.

From a policy viewpoint, innovation financing and funding should first and foremost be oriented toward the sectors and the types of companies that offer the most promising future forecasts for growth and employment creation in Europe. Industrial conglomerates and large national champions have had since the post-World War II era a very dominating role in the European economy (Eichengreen 2006). Rooted in and facilitated by the economic and social institutions of the Golden Age of Industrial Capitalism, including government support and favorable investment conditions, they have been critical to Europe's economic performance, employment, and GDP. Small and medium-sized enterprises (SMEs) have similarly accounted for a disproportionally large share of value added and jobs, in particular SMEs in Europe's private sector (European Commission 2012b). SMEs were however hard hit during the financial crisis, subject to rising costs of credit and limited access to financing. On this background, SMEs have received priority from European governments, seeking to ease access to financing, address regulatory burdens, and improve SME investments.

While recognizing the fundamental role of large companies and SMEs for future growth and job creation, experiences from the USA offer an interesting perspective in this respect. Here, job creation, one of the key objectives of any growth policy, was increasingly driven by young, leaner, and more innovative firms. In 2010, Thomas Friedman, Pulitzer-prize-winning journalist, analyzed the root causes for US job creation between 1980 and 2005; he reported the Kaufman Foundation's data, noting that "virtually all net jobs created in the US were created by firms that were 5 years old or less. [...] That is about 40 million jobs" (Friedman 2010). According to this analysis, the key ingredient of the US entrepreneurial system is the availability of "smart, creative, inspired risk-takers" who are either grown in the USA or are highly skilled immigrants attracted by America's "vibrant and meritocratic university system" (http://www.nytimes.com/2010/04/04/opinion/04friedman.html). OECD research further supports this by highlighting that age, rather than size, best

accounts for the overall variation in employment creation and job reloca-
tion, when comparing firms with similar characteristics (OECD 2009).
In particular technology-driven start-ups—enabled by online and web
technologies, which have taken advantage of the many new and promising
ways of adding value, reducing costs, and entering markets—are playing
an increasing role in driving growth, jobs, and innovation (Mettler and
Williams 2012).

Using a business life cycle approach to further contextualize and identify funding and financing needs and opportunities, the investments
work in diverse ways during the different stages of a given business, such
as through the research stage, development stage, start-up stage, and
growth/exploitation stage, with the funding or financing itself coming
from the public sector (such as the European Commission and national
and regional authorities), banks, and/or private sources of financing. This
distinction between phases are important for the design of well-targeted
innovation financing schemes and policies, since they have a defining role
for actual financing needs, types of funding sources, and providers accessible. In this context, some major financing instruments for promoting
innovation include bank loans, grants, subsidies, business angel investing,
venture capital, corporate venturing, crowd funding, and tax incentives
(OECD 2011). Grants, subsidies, business angel investing, and crowd
funding are important at the early stages in order to raise capital and seed
funding for innovative start-ups and SMEs.

During the late expansion stages, venture capital and corporate venture
capital become increasingly important, focusing on a more lengthy time
span for investing. A key characteristic of venture capital investments is
their concentration in rather limited geographical areas. Analyzing data
from Ernst and Young (2014) and CBInsights (2015a, 2015b), we see
how more than half of global venture capital investments take place in
California (mainly in Silicon Valley and San Diego). Second and third
ranked, respectively, are the Greater New York area (close to 9 %) and
Massachusetts (slightly more than 8 %). In other words, the closer innovations come to the market, the more localized their financing sources
are—usually at the regional level, not at a national or continental one.
Innovation is increasingly more strongly related to regional innovation ecosystems (Cooke 2005, p. 1131). This is the spatial dimension that better fits

the needs of open innovation strategies: regional innovation systems are networks "capable of supporting numerous clustered and non-clustered industries" (Cooke 2005). They enable global companies to bypass their internal knowledge asymmetries; here, multinational firms establish strong links through controlled, but autonomous, research institutions, located in strategic regions where the most advanced knowledge required for their business is available. The combined presence of innovative firms and leading research institutions—and active collaboration within them—in a region or in a metropolitan area, was recognized as one of the drivers of US employment (Moretti 2012). Again, the role of universities and research institutions as catalysts of employment through innovation emerges; the University of California is a good example: its economic impact was estimated in $46.3 billion every year, compared with public investments of only $3.5 billion (University of California 2012).

To put innovation funding and financing in perspective, and with a view to understand how and when funding matters, the range of innovation modeling processes portrayed in the literature requires a brief introduction. The traditional innovation model takes a point of departure in scientific research as the basis for innovation. It suggests that technical change occurs through a linear process following, research, invention, innovation, diffusion, and marketing (Godin 2005). From this perspective, innovation can be understood as the conversion of knowledge into economic growth. According to an old debate, the linear innovation model can be steered by a "technology push" where new technological advances—enabled by scientific discovery or R&D—leads to innovation in products and services and their successful commercialization and by "demand pull," which has market demand as the starting point, since it subsequently encourages innovative endeavors.

The rather simplified linear account on innovation processes is widely recognized as failing to fully account for the complexity and variety of innovation advancements, which has led to newer innovation models, such as the phased and coupling/cyclical innovation models. Whereas the phased innovation model is based on the fact that innovation projects go through sequential phases, facing many "gates" or challenges that must be addressed during the process, the coupling/cyclical innovation models incorporate interactions and feedback loops throughout the innovation value chain between developers, researchers, manufacturers, etc., which require the developers to reevaluate, even sometimes repeat, the previous steps in the process, potentially requiring new research and development. Innovation ecosystems, such as the regional innovation systems previously mentioned, are the most appropriate environments to successfully host cyclical innovation models.

Innovation funding should therefore be coherent with the diverse variables of innovation processes. First, concerning private versus public R&D, industry-led R&D has a stronger impact on economic growth than government-led R&D. According to the OECD and Eurostat data on 16 Western European countries plus South Korea and the USA during 2005–2013, we found a higher correlation between the average business R&D investments (as a percentage of GDP) and the average yearly GDP growth in the same period, compared to government R&D investments. Second, in terms of knowledge- versus market-driven R&D, corporate R&D investments are performed for a multiple set of purposes; for example, the decision to open a new R&D subsidiary can be both technology and knowledge driven, or based on market proximity purposes (Keummerle 1997). Third, turning to the innovativeness of businesses, SMEs are usually more innovative than the bigger ones (Hamel 2000), and in some industries, like pharmaceuticals, they proved to be more effective in successfully deploying R&D to the market (Deloitte 2014). Last, the geographical scope of funding: regional, national and transnational.

Science and scientific knowledge not only provide a source of inspiration and discovery for business models, but also evidence that guides and supports policy making. Modes of R&D funding, excellence in research, and public–private partnerships are, together with commercialization of new know-how, some key impediments to achieving top innovation performance (European Commission 2015b). As the Innovation Union Scoreboard 2015 also provides evidence for, a robust innovation economy requires national innovation systems with strengths in all dimensions. In this context, R&D expenditure and well-targeted business accelerators can, for example, have a profound impact on firms' innovation and employment performance as well as research output and quality. One example, referring to US practices for accelerators, data show how the success rate of innovative start-ups accelerated in programs like Y-Combinator or Tech Stars, is up to 75 % higher than average Silicon Valley data (Kula 2013). In addition, R&D figures for Europe suggest that the efforts that countries make in terms of input are paid back through improved innovation outputs creating added value. The countries who invest the most on R&D expenditures also have some of the best performances in innovation and competitiveness (European Commission 2015b).

Innovation policy is however not only about R&D expenditures or R&D policy—far from it. This is just the start of a long and complex process involving a wide range of factors and actors that need to be supported and incorporated into the innovation funding and policy framework. Crucially, innovation, funding, financing, and investments must be transformed into the market context. This view has gained increased acceptance, and international and national Western policy regimes no longer consider innovation policy solely as a function of money spent on research activities and related programs. As a matter of fact, innovation is "the successful exploitation of new ideas," p. 143. The successful exploitation of a new ideas relates to different forms of innovation—product, process, organizational, or marketing innovations (Pittaway et al. 2004), a definition that goes far beyond R&D. This explains what we previously mentioned about R&D funding: corporations are investing in R&D not just as a means of new knowledge acquisition but as the opportunity to develop new products and services that meet the needs of specific markets. However, although R&D does not automatically lead to innovation in markets, and nonfinancial means of supporting innovation are equally important, it nonetheless performs an important and rather crucial role in the innovation process.

The traditional R&D-centered approach for innovation has shown its limits in terms of both efficiency and effectiveness. In terms of efficiency, research shows that only a limited number of patents are transformed into successful products or services (some companies have up to 90 % of unexploited patents in their portfolios) (Chesbrough 2003). Patent production is also getting less efficient. Dividing the annual R&D budget by the number of PCT patent application of some leading Western countries, we noticed an average increase of 27 % between 2006 and 2011. Looking at the pharmaceutical sector, data show an 86 % decrease of successful registrations of new drugs out of the R&D pipelines between 1990 and 2004 (Pamolli et al. 2011). Open innovation is the new strategic approach that overcomes the decreasing performances of the traditional, R&D-centered one. Through this model "a company commercializes both its own ideas as well as innovations from other firms and seeks ways to bring its in-house ideas to market by deploying pathways outside its current businesses." Corporate internal R&D is therefore part of a wider, networked set of players, both internal and external, of a specific firm that generates new ideas, carries out prototyping, and brings them into the market; such networks include universities, other public and private research institutions, start-up companies, and venture capitalists, etc. Such networks or *ecosystems* are much more localized and, at the same time, able to attract the best talents and the majority of investments on a global range. For example, this is the case of life science innovations in Basel, Switzerland, or Massachusetts in the USA (Cooke 2005).

Against this background, there is a need to move away from linear thinking toward a more holistic approach to innovation financing, taking into account the interactions of the various actors and factors in the innovation environment. Indeed, innovation poses very complex governance challenges that call for complex management processes and at the same time rigorous planning, while keeping in mind that innovation is not fully manageable. Innovation funding also requires looking at the entire value chain, from research to market, including crossfertilization between sectors.

2 A Prudent First Step: R&D Target Setting, Collaboration, and Close-to-Market Activities

During the last 20 years the EU has developed an R&D policy, while also been trying to align it with the innovation and research-related activities at member state level. Commitments have been made to stimulate and promote innovation and knowledge investments. The EU budget's innovation funds have multiplied during the previous decades and have been supplemented with the use of quantitative target setting for R&D investments (such as the 3 % objective for R&D spending). A wide range of crosscutting initiatives and policies have been designed and implemented by the European

Commission to support and provide funding and financing for innovation activities throughout Europe. These include, but are by far not limited to, Europe 2020, Innovation Union, Horizon 2020, European Research Area (ERA), COSME, and the SME Instrument. They have been complimented with efforts to improve the monitoring, evaluation, and sharing of best practices on innovation policy and performance (at international, national, and regional levels) with a view to broaden the knowledge base and to better assess and develop the most suitable innovation systems at the various scales. Before we address respectively the challenges to innovation funding/financing in Europe, the shortcomings and bottlenecks of existing policy efforts, which hinders Europe from taking full advantage of innovation activities, as well as forward-looking measures to correct them, we will shed light on some of the main EU financing/funding-related initiatives.

As a broad and encompassing 10-year strategy, Europe 2020 seeks to boost and strengthen the economic performance of the member states through greater coordination, ambitious target setting, and flagship initiatives. The Innovation Union is one of the three flagship initiatives for smart growth envisaged by the Europe 2020 strategy. The strategy's objectives are to help Europe develop world-class science, to remove obstacles to innovation, and to further support public and private cooperation (European Commission 2014). A tool specifically concentrating on collaboration within the EU 2020 Innovation Union is the European Innovation Partnerships (EIPs), which bring together public and private actors in EU, national, and regional innovation, and R&D activities, as a strategic tool to "break down silos" and "capture new cross-sectoral value chains" (Independent Expert Group 2014). According to the review of the Independent Expert Group, while the EIPs lack a clear strategy for prioritization and an ecosystem approach to delivery, the tool has a significant potential to align priorities and leverage existing investments by bringing partners together (Independent Expert Group 2014). Furthermore, the Innovation Union is implemented through different action points and instruments, including in particular the Horizon 2020 framework program. The Horizon 2020 research and innovation program has a budget of almost €80 billion over a 7-year period (2014–2020), the largest of its kind adopted by the EU, and accounts for a budget increase from €50 billion in the previous program to €80 billion.

The Horizon 2020 program rightly emphasizes research and innovation as integral to achieving growth, employment, and sound macroeconomic performance.[2] As a financial instrument, Horizon 2020 seeks to promote excellence in science, to develop capacity to deal with societal challenges, and to enhance industrial performance, for example, through investments in key enabling technologies.

Horizon 2020 is further supported by the Structural Funds. The funds' main objectives are to reduce regional disparities between EU member states, but increasingly they have also been oriented toward developing regional innovation and research capacity. A reform of the funds has attempted to streamline the focus areas toward fewer investment objectives—aligned with the Europe 2020—such as innovation, entrepreneurship, ICT development, and human capital (European Commission 2012a). The European Regional Development Fund, together with the European Social Fund, is responsible for the allocation of the financial assistance. The Investment Plan for Europe is another recent development at the EU level through which the European Investment Bank, a major provider of risk capital in Europe, has taken a more prominent role in the European innovation landscape. As part of the measure, the European Fund for Strategic Investments (EFSI), established on the basis of joint cooperation and funding between the European Commission and EIB, seeks to address present investment gaps and market failures in risk taking. Specifically, it seeks to mobilize private financing for strategic investments in such areas as strategic innovation, infrastructure, energy, and SMEs. The EFSI is supported with €16 billion from the EU budget and €5 billion from EIB, and is estimated to be able to yield around €315 billion extra, due to a mobilization of additional financing from private sources and member states and a multiplier effect of real investment in the economy (European Commission 2015a).

The SME instrument[3] has been set up under Horizon 2020, with funds dedicated for high-potential SMEs for close-to-market activities in terms of product, process, or service innovations. Three billion Euros in funding is available from 2014 to 2020. Through the instrument, SMEs have

---

[2] See also R. Frietsch, C. Rammer, and T. Schubert, "Heterogeneity of Innovation Systems in Europe and Horizon 2020," in *Intereconomics*, Vol. 50 (1), January/February 2015, pp. 4–30.

[3] For more about the relation between the SME Instrument and Horizon 2020, see https://ec.europa.eu/programmes/horizon2020/en/h2020-section/sme-instrument.

access to business innovation grants (related to feasibility assessment, innovation development, and demonstration purposes), business mentoring, and a range of innovation support services. In the growing role that SMEs have in Horizon 2020, while also keeping in mind complementary programs such as, in particular, the Program for the Competitiveness of SMEs 2014–2020 (COSME), which has its own SME funding tools, the creation of the SME instrument is part of general tendency, observed during the last decades, for the European Commission to give SMEs—whether cash-strapped or in need of a boost for breakthrough innovation—a solid helping hand with financing and funding. The move is coupled to SMEs' high share of employment and the curtailed bank funding supply for SMEs which, after the financial crisis, still remains fragile (Muller et al. 2014). But it can partly also be explained by SMEs' aptitude to deliver innovations, for example, in relation to ICT-based, EU-funded research and innovation projects (De Prato et al. 2015). The SME Instrument has been drawing inspiration from the US SBIR program, which equally attempts to address the funding shortage for early-stage and high-risk research. According to C. Wessner's SBIR review (2015), some lessons learned from the US SBIR program include that just 2–3 % of funded SMEs are big hits and that continuity of policy action and a clear understanding of what makes up success are important for the commercialization rate of the solutions developed. In a nutshell, and with a view to summing up, many positive steps have been taken at the EU level to develop and redefine innovation financing/funding instruments, also in terms of deepening and widening the mechanisms available for supporting innovative activities in the European business world and among public sectors.

3   Persistent Innovation Funding and Financing Problems: Fragmentation and Need for Prioritization

Although a number of prudent steps have been taken to improve the funding and financing of innovation, a number of problems exists today. Following our previous considerations on the evolution of innovation models, we might notice how innovation financing can be improved in terms of resources availability but, more important, we need to make a shift in the paradigms used to allocate resources.

The EU's quantitative target of investing 3 % of its GDP into R&D has not been achieved, save one member state. The present situation—a situation of budgetary scarcity—in many member states also hardly allows for any significant increase in R&D spending. The financial crisis has led to a decline in R&D spending within most member states, albeit with significant differences between countries, sectors, and actors (European Commission 2013a). Recognizing the constraints on public budgets, any viable and long-term solution requires finding alternative ways to access additional public spending. In this context, the European Commission has acknowledged the many problems linked to a declining innovation spending for future competitiveness and that public and private R&D investments are key for economic performance (Ibid), although R&D investments must be converted into market value.

There is an overall need to increase R&D funding to keep European competitiveness: the share of global R&D investments of 34 European countries dropped by 6 % between 2012 and 2014 (Batelle 2013), representing a potential threat for European economic growth forecasts. But it is not just a question of total investments: the 3 % target should also be carefully analyzed into its main components, increasing those more linked to economic growth. As a matter of fact, the impact of R&D investments varies based on who is driving them. The correlation between average R&D investments in percentage of GDP and average GDP growth between 2005 and 2013, performed on 16 Western European countries plus South Korea and the USA, gives us some interesting indications[4]; business R&D investments have a higher impact than government ones, while foreign business R&D investments are even more correlated to economic growth. Therefore, countries willing to grow should have a higher presence of corporate investments in R&D and should be able to create an attractive environment for foreign firms to create and develop

---

[4] Analysis based on Eurostat and OECD data for the following countries: Austria, Belgium, Denmark, EU-28 average, Finland, France, Germany, Greece, Ireland, Italy, the Netherlands, Norway, Portugal, South Korea, Spain, Sweden, Switzerland, the UK, the USA. Eastern European countries were not included as economic growth was considered to be biased by their inclusion in the single market.

local R&D units. Another interesting finding from the analysis[5] concerns the EU Commission's funding of R&D: this variable was found to have a negative yet limited correlation. In other words, the higher EU Commission R&D financing, in percentage of GDP, the less GDP grew. This finding is partial and biased by the fact that the economic impact of any R&D funding policy is expected to be delayed, given the significant amount time required to develop and bring new ideas into the market. However, it indicates the need to rethink and reshape European R&D funding models.

The financing of innovation is challenged by a risk propensity, fiscal disincentives, discontinuity, and absence of perseverance in R&D and innovation policy making. The EU must continue its agenda to eliminate obstacles for innovation funding. Improved cooperation is needed between actors in the public and private spheres, which necessitates finding new ways to promote closer cooperation between stakeholder agendas, in particular between public policy objectives and commercial business models. Financing mechanisms such as Horizon 2020 and the Structural Funds also require further coordination to overcome a high degree of fragmentation, in order to take full advantage of research and innovation processes. This is a challenging task, given institutional complexity and requires cooperation between EU, national, and regional actors within their own areas of competence. An efficient cooperation will help to ensure a more rapid market use and effective knowledge transfer; it would also help to focus resources in the most promising projects and not merely distributing them without any critical selection and review. Data collected by the ERA (ERA) indicate that government R&D funding in European countries lacks alignment with key principles of European funding policies: just 1 % of national resources are provided to transnational R&D projects within EU countries and only 0.7 % is offered for non-EU ones (ERA 2014). Moreover, only 2 % of government R&D funding is dedicated to project-based R&D with peer review selection carried out by foreign reviewers.[6] Put differently, European national governments are too self-referring in their R&D funding, which leads to a

---

[5] Our analysis of CBInsights data. See www.cbinsights.com.

[6] Eurostat data analysis.

significant waste of resources, in particular with respect to bigger countries like the USA or China that can focus their funding in a more efficient way, making their R&D policies more effective, vis-à-vis European ones.

The need for more coordination in funding is not only limited between EU and member state institutions. Open Innovation is a networked model that works only if all partners are cooperating in bringing new ideas to the end markets. From this perspective, Europe has a significant gap with Japan and the USA: the EU recorded 36.2 public–private copublications between two or more sectors (universities, research institutes, industries) per million (population) against 56.3 in Japan and 70.2 in the USA (European Commission and Deloitte 2013). Increased incentives could thus be given to universities for spending a larger part of their public research funding on public–private partnerships or on business–university partnerships. The need for public–private partnerships, including crossborder cooperation between research centers, also needs to be driven more by needs and benefits than artificial funding requirements at the EU level.

To focus innovation policy mainly on SMEs overlooks the role of the corporate "locomotives" and their leverage in the supply and distribution chains. SMEs are indeed important for innovative activities, since they create new knowledge. We previously mentioned how innovative SMEs have been the main driver of US employment (Friedman 2010) and their leadership in bringing radical innovation to the market (Hamel 2010). However, data from CBInsights indicate that only a very limited number of European SMEs were able to become global leaders: that Europe accounts for only 11 % of global start-up firms valued more than $1 billion (and thus part of the "unicorns' club," i.e., companies that achieve a valuation of at least $1 billion), compared with 64 % of the USA and 19 % of China.[7] In terms of initial public offerings (IPOs) of innovative start-up firms supported by venture capital funds, Europe accounted for 55 operations versus 61 in China and 105 in the USA (Ernst and Young 2015). Only a very limited group of innovative SMEs are able to reach dimensions suitable for the stock exchange market: in the majority of

---

[7] Analysis on Volans Venture, CBInsight, E&Y, and World Bank data.

cases, such companies are acquired by bigger corporations that can further boost the market success of these innovations. This happens in 77 % of cases in Europe and in 82 % of cases in the USA. Eventually, innovative start-up firms and venture capital are tools of corporate open innovation processes: without their investments, the process of innovation will not successfully reach the market in three-quarter of cases.

We previously highlighted the relevance of business-driven R&D for economic growth, especially foreign investments. Here we noticed that corporations are the main driver of innovation's successful market exploitation through the acquisition of innovative, venture-capital-backed, SMEs. Corporations are also becoming more and more engaged in direct investments in innovative SMEs through their corporate venture capital arms. In all these three activities of open innovation (R&D, acquisition, and corporate venture capital), Europe is far below the levels of the USA and other comparable competitors. Business R&D expenditures, in percentage of GDP, are 60 % higher in the USA than in the EU-28. Moreover, South Korean corporations invest, in percentage of GDP, 240 % more than average European ones.[8]

Acquisitions in Europe are also lower, both in number and value, compared to the USA: 181 against 483 operations with an average value of €70 million in Europe compared with nearly €200 million in the USA (Ernst and Young 2015). European corporate venture capital is far behind the US levels: total investments as a percentage of GDP are nearly 470 % higher in the USA than in Europe. The limited acquisition and corporate venture capital markets do not only hinder corporate innovation, but also represent a threat for the European venture capital industry and the overall European innovation policies too. First, without a market for acquisitions, European venture capitalists cannot have the same financial performances relative to their US or Chinese competitors: the lower the exit opportunities and values the lower the average internal return rate. Consequently, European venture capitalists are less attractive for foreign investors. Second, in order to bypass the constraints of the European acqui-

---

[8] See also High Level Group on Innovation Policy Management (2014): *The way forward to improve people's lives: Inspiring and Completing European Innovation Ecosystems*, August 2014, for a discussion on the potential of defence R&D to support innovation in Europe.

sition market, venture funds are looking for exits in the USA. To put it slightly differently, European ideas, founded by European money (including public money from the European Investment Fund and from national funds of funds are funds investing in other funds), become a competitive asset for non-European corporations. Third, the limited presence of corporate venture capital makes it harder for innovative SMEs to grow in Europe. Corporate venture capitalists do not only bring money but they provide industrial support to their portfolio companies, and always operate in syndication with other venture capitalists (McMillan et al. 2010). A small corporate venture capital market means lower industrial mentoring of innovative SMEs and limited co-investment opportunities for European venture capitalists. In summary, European corporations need to invest more in direct R&D, acquisitions, and corporate venture capital operations, and specific European incentives and funding schemes could be designed and implemented.

Lastly, we should notice the role of R&D funding for defense purposes. California and Israel, the global areas with the highest innovation density, have been driven by government support for defense R&D. The percentage of government budget appropriations or outlays for R&D dedicated to defense is 4.41 in Europe against 52.71 in the USA and 14.78 in South Korea.[9] A significant number of civil technologies, even consumer technologies, derive from defense ones. Furthermore, the boundary between defense and civil technologies are often weak: cryptography (used for cyber security), drones, and navigation systems are just a sample of them. Developing technologies for defense applications often requires capacity to operate in highly hostile and extreme environments: their design must therefore be so robust that their application for civil purposes requires few investments. The differences in defense policies and strategies among European member states, and the lack of a common defense system in the European Union, prevents the development of a common defense R&D funding program that could prove very beneficial to the overall innovation performance of the EU.

---

[9] OECD data.

4   Therefore, New and Alternative Models for Financing Innovations Need to Be Developed—A Broadening of the Public Financing Approach

European Institutions have recognized open innovation models as a promising strategy for economic growth. In a recent speech, Carlos Moedas, the EU Commissioner for Research, Science and Innovation, gave a clear vision of the European strategy for innovation:

> Open innovation is about involving far more actors in the innovation process, from researchers, to entrepreneurs, to users, to governments and civil society. We need open innovation to capitalize on the results of European research and innovation. This means creating the right ecosystems, increasing investment, and bringing more companies and regions into the knowledge economy. I would like to go further and faster toward open innovation (Moedas 2015).

The path toward an open innovation strategy for Europe needs a redesign of innovation policy management. Innovation funding should be coherent with the multiple perspectives of an innovation ecosystem and, in order to be effective and efficient, it should address them in a holistic way. Horizon 2020 and its SME program, the development of the ERA and other recent programs represent a significant step forward, but further evolution of these and other tools is needed. It's time to move from a traditional, government-funded, R&D financing tool to a wider spectrum of actions: coherence and focus of such actions at all levels (European, national, and regional) will be mandatory to overcome today's lack of efficiency and effectiveness.

Following the US experience (Friedman 2010), Europe needs to become a more attractive place in the world for the smartest people. European universities could offer not only great learning opportunities but also transparent and meritocratic academic careers. Recent ERA data tell us that 40 % of European researchers are not satisfied by OTM (Open, Transparent, and Merit-based) recruitment strategies, with a pick of 69 % in the case of Italian ones (European Commission and Deloitte 2013). Specific funding policies could be focused on those universities and research institutions that offer the best career opportunities to global talents: ERA could become the standard and auditing body valuing universities' performances and driving specific resources on those meeting the highest standards of talent attraction and retention. Without a strong pool of talented people, any further innovation policy will lose much of its effectiveness.

A second area of funding improvement is related to corporations. We need to have higher cooperative research between the corporate world and academia and a stronger embedding in innovation ecosystems. The contamination of universities by market-driven research could make basic research more aligned to the needs of an open innovation model. Furthermore, the proximity of corporations with universities could offer greater mentoring and collaboration opportunities for academic spin-off companies. Specific funding programs could also be designed to support corporations in their corporate venture capital activities and in acquiring innovative SMEs. The driving element of any funding policy for corporations should be their joint investment: public funding or incentives should be provided only in the presence of a parallel investment by the final beneficiary.

A few words could be spent on defense R&D programs. While they proved to be an important ignition opportunity for innovation in Israel and in the USA, any related policy goes beyond the scope of this book and should be analyzed under the perspectives of national strategies and their integration at the European level. Still, the fast growth and presence of hostile entities near the boundaries of the EU, the direct consequences many member states are facing in terms of refugees and terrorist threats, the instability of proximity countries located at the eastern border of the Union, could stimulate a debate on a common defense strategy among member states. A common European defense strategy seems certain to be beneficial for innovation and growth, although it is a political decision, whether it should become part of a renewed European vision.

Last, but not least, coherence and focalization of resources is a must for any innovation funding policy. Coherence in terms of ultimate objectives and, more important, in terms of selection criteria and openness of funding opportunities: financing opportunities should be focused on transnational, project-oriented, and internationally peer reviewed projects.

5 Exploration of New Options for Innovation Funding and Financing: Specific Recommendations

Against this background, we suggest a series of recommendations, either oriented toward adjusting existing funding and financing mechanisms or creating new ones with a view to better unleash innovative activities in Europe. In line with the remaining chapters of the book, the recommendations draw inspiration from open innovation 2.0 and innovation-ecosystem-building approaches, thus aspiring to the encouragement of user involvement, integrated collaboration, and co-creation and design, from financing and funding perspectives. To better commercialize know-how and to drive innovation into markets, recommendations are presented about the coordination of R&D investments, a broadening of the traditional R&D funding approach, innovation bonds, innovative taxation strategies, mechanisms for incubator and seed capital, public–private partnerships and business-university partnerships, and new unorthodox ways of raising venture capital and increasing corporate venture capital.

5.1 More Coordination and Cooperation in R&D: Within the Commission, Between the Commission and Member States, and Between the Member States Themselves

Fragmentation of and systemic problems with funding and financing mechanisms, sources, and approaches—alongside bureaucratic procedures—are main challenges that hinder innovation and research results reaching markets in Europe. The prerequisite for any reform to innovation funding/financing tools: to address and connect many stakeholders and needs in a dynamic and open innovation environment, further driven by change, is no easy task from an innovation policy management perspective. The fact that innovations not only happen in sectors, but also at the edges of or interfaces between sectors, further complicates reform. Yet, efforts to address the fragmentation, duplication—sometimes even contraction of R&D and funding/financing initiatives—and implementation as well as the varying degree of integration into national innovation ecosystems, must become priority actions.

Some member states have since 2011 cut back direct R&D spending because of fiscal consolidation efforts, also influenced by the low levels of business R&D investments (addressed in the recommendations below), while some also lack a full deployment of Horizon 2020 (Special Task Force (Member States, Commission, EIB) on Investment in the EU. 2014). The fragmentation and duplication of work within the Commission and between the Commission and member states not only limits the efficiency of public research and innovation budgets, but is an obstacle for innovation-oriented research in general.[10] Therefore, to avoid national governments from operating in isolation from each other and the EU research program, more coordination and cooperation is needed on R&D investment. Previously, this was also an appeal in the Aho Report, "Creating an Innovative Europe," from 2006 (Aho et al. 2006). This requires, in particular, a shared, overarching focus and vision about funding/financing instruments, better targeting setting, and a stronger alignment between EU and national research agendas, but potentially also a portfolio approach and big project(s), allowing EU member states to take better advantage of research and innovation processes. A portfolio approach could be focused on digital and energy sectors, re-industrialization, but also the space and health sectors offer some scope for it. A more efficient cooperation will not only help to ensure a more rapid market use and effective knowledge transfer, it would also help to focus resources in the most promising projects and avoid the risk of technologies that are developed in Europe that get commercialized elsewhere.

Following the analysis of this chapter, while the Horizon 2020 represent a big leap forward though providing the biggest EU budget yet for innovation and research, better coverage of the entire value and collaborative integration of public/private stakeholders, it still suffers from a high degree of fragmentation among the various support instruments. While the different funding programs have become more aligned, including between Horizon 2020 and the Structural Funds, synergy is still lacking, with implications for prioritization of the most promising sectors. In this con-

---

[10] Ibid.

text, a stronger thematic focus would be of the upmost help, for example, targeting the outlined sectors for the above portfolio approach. The thematic focus should replace existing tendencies toward dispersive spending methods, which aim to offer something for everyone, an inefficient way of using public resources. Furthermore, Horizon 2020 would also benefit from a more experimental approach (Nesta and the Lisbon Council 2013) to innovation funding, due to an uncertainty of how innovation is best supported in specific policy and market contexts. Finally, Horizon 2020 needs to better integrate the Internet of Things, Big Data, and cloud approaches, with an aim to help Europe develop the Digital Single Market and achieve a global lead in the field, and also internationalization to better facilitate scouting for ideas at the global level and more export-led growth.

5.2   A Broadening of the Traditional R&D Funding to Products, Services, Processes, and Intangibles, as well as Focus on the Entire Value Chain

A wide-ranging coverage of innovations is key, as innovation comes in a wide variety of forms, which in addition to product, service, and process innovations, for example, also include social, organizational, marketing, and methodological and intangible product and process innovations, jointly contributing to firms' competitive advantage, productivity, and growth. Following the widening of the innovation concept in the *Oslo Manual*, the role of innovation policy—and the financing and funding models to support it—still need to better reflect the conceptual broadening, in a way that neither takes an overemphasized technological view on innovation nor simply follows R&D approaches. A study by SOM et al. (2012), for example, highlighted the importance of integrating both nontechnological (such as concerning organization and marketing innovations) and technological innovation activities as a strategy to foster innovation and growth.[11]

While positive steps were taken with EU instruments and programs, innovation funding/financing mechanisms nevertheless still require a

---

[11] Ibid.

broadening of the traditional R&D funding approach toward a higher extent covering products, processes, and intangible innovations (e.g., design), including industries and services. The Horizon 2020 approach, which foresees funding along the entire value chain and from fundamental research to market introduction, needs to be further expanded into all funding schemes and strategies by the EU and member states. The business environment has undergone transformation since the industrial area, illustrated with a shift from tangible products toward intangible ones in the new operating environment for knowledge-intensive businesses, for example. The scope of the type of business supported, the available R&D funding instruments, and innovative financing models therefore need to be widened and also further integration with enterprise policy. Finally, it should target business models and management as well as public governance.

5.3   Offer Innovation Bonds by Expert Bodies and Innovation Financing Agencies

Corporate R&D investments and innovative SME acquisitions are two fundamental activities for a successful open innovation process. Few firms in the world have the significant financial reserves needed to support a continuous stream of research projects and technology insourcing, and the recent "credit crunch" limits the opportunities for funding these projects through conventional bank loans. Furthermore, specific guarantees and loan products issued by public institutions, such as the European Investment Bank, as an opportunity for corporate growth investments, are offered only if used for the acquisition of tangible assets. European corporations do not have the opportunity to finance their innovation-driven growth, as this is mainly based on intangible assets, either intellectual property or SME acquisition and ownership. The crisis of European banking system and the reduction of credit availability recently lead to the growth of private debt and "mini-bond" (corporate bonds issued by SMEs not listed in stock exchanges) markets. These financial products are managed by specialist operators, often in the shape of alternative investment funds, and are regulated by specific national laws that define the mechanisms for the issue, rating and subscription of corporate bonds outside the retail exchange markets. The specialization and competences of private debt and "mini-bond" fund managers and specific rating agencies guarantees the appropriate degree of selection, evaluation, and management of these financial products.

The development and support of private debt and "mini-bond" products dedicated to innovation projects will require the identification and support of specialized operators, in order to ensure the appropriate level of professional management. They would also be more effective if issued by venture-capital-backed SMEs, as issuers would have gone already through the highly selective process of venture capital investments. The use of innovation bonds in parallel with venture capital equity investments could also represent an important financial support for the European venture capital industry: indeed, average total investment of European venture capital from seed to later stage in each company is about €14 million, compared with nearly $24 million of US funds.[12]

Specific financial tools for SME acquisitions by big corporations could strengthen the impact of private debt and innovation bonds. While innovation bonds would be in the range of some million Euro for each issuer, acquisitions can easily go up to dozens of millions. A specific guarantee fund, enabling European corporations to leverage the acquisition of innovative, venture-backed European SMEs, could be established by European Investment Bank, leveraging the experience of the European Investment Fund in analyzing intangible assets through innovative projects and technology transfer. This financial tool would offer European corporations to become more competitive via technology insourcing, would prevent European innovations from being exploited by non-European corporations, and could boost our venture capital industry, attracting more foreign investors in European funds.

---

[12] Our analysis on Ernst and Young (2015) data.

5.4   Adjust Taxation Strategies to Ensure Sufficient Capital Allocation for Productive Investments and Innovative Activities

The role of national tax policy systems to fund welfare and public services, public utilities, and economic infrastructure, etc., must be complemented with a stronger focus on innovation promotion. Tax policy is a very powerful tool to reduce investment costs, ensure capital allocation, and productive investments, and thereby facilitate research results and innovation in markets. Specifically, tax policy has a significant potential to reduce the cost side of innovation, for example, through tax benefits coupled to the expenses of experimentation in development, basis and applied research, and a range of other support activities. Most EU countries, including innovation leaders such as the USA and Japan, make use of tax incentives, for example, in the form of R&D tax credits, accelerated depreciated schemes, and reduced labor taxes for researchers and scientists, to incentives for businesses to invest in R&D, which further has a positive effect on growth and labor productivity growth (OECD 2013). Efforts to address tax arrangements for innovation must consider the type of businesses that qualify, the scope of R&D, and the attitude toward large R&D performers, while also being tailored according to the project and firm specificities (such as growth phases), including being used in combination with other innovation support measures. Coverage, design, and implementation dimensions are not only important because of variations concerning the effects of tax policy on innovation, but also because tax incentives might turn out to be more expensive than expected, since the cost of a tax relief is not always fully transparent.

While continuing the work on closing escape routes and tax loopholes in Europe, tax instruments have a potential for promoting innovation concerns—for example, accelerated depreciation schemes and lower corporate tax rates for innovation-related capital and reduced value-added tax (VAT) rates or even zero rate. Tax policies need, on one hand, to favor long-term investments in innovation to encourage European companies to engage in long-term planning, rather than more short-term or speculative investments, in order to avoid short-termism.

This could, for example, be carried out through R&D tax incentives targeting large companies, high-tech sectors, and the more R&D intensive industries. But, on the other hand, as outlined in the analysis, the lack of access to finance for young innovative companies and start-ups in Europe requires orienting tax strategies and incentives also toward these businesses. Tax relief for young innovative firms—or potentially a lowering of their social contributions—would help target young firms' weak investment rates in innovation and the funding shortage during the first years of development (Wilson and Silva 2013). It would be particularly helpful to decrease or even cancel VAT on any good purchased by start-up companies: in their early stages, start-ups have very limited sales if any at all, while goods and services purchased could be relevant, leading to a potentially high level of VAT credit. Research on SMEs shows no clear picture on the effects of tax incentives for R&D, rendering it difficult yet to draw conclusions (Moncada-Paterno-Castello et al. 2014). However, evidence suggests that while SMEs compared to large firms are likely to increase their R&D investments more in response to tax incentives, they offer lower knowledge spillover effects than larger companies (CPB 2014). Inspiration could also be drawn from Singapore's Productivity and Innovation Credit, which refunds tax to those businesses that make other intangible investments necessary to bring innovations to markets, including training, design, IP acquisition, and other investments in innovative machinery and plants (Rae and Westlake 2014). Last, the global issue of taxation on IPR is a shared concern of all member states, and a level European playing field is important to avoid leaking out IPR from Europe for tax reasons.

5.5 Create New Mechanism for Incubator and Seed Capital

Innovation ecosystems are local networks connecting research, industry, finance, and the public sector. Cooperation among all these actors is fundamental for a successful innovation process that should be market driven; industry-specific competences are required even in early stages of technology transfer, especially in the first steps of start-up creation. This is a significant difference between today's open, collaborative innovation models and the previous linear one, where the role of corporations emerged in later stages. The trend toward an earlier stage involvement of corporations is clearly visible in the USA, where the number of corporate venture capital firms operating in early stage investments grew by 540 % between 2010 and 2014 (CBInsights 2015a, 2015b). Early stage investments are those with the higher risk (this phase is called the "*valley of death*"), and newly established companies require appropriate support and facilities to grow; this is the phase where incubators are playing a relevant role, too. Incubators are facilities hosting start-up companies and offering shared services and infrastructures in order to minimize their initial cash consumption and provide the industrial and managerial advisory services needed to let them grow from a technological and a market point of view. The need for maximizing the effectiveness of incubators has lead the most advanced ones to focus on specific industrial sectors: health care, ICT, clean tech, etc. The Israeli government identified the potential of industry-focused incubators, run by corporate venture capital firms and supported, in early stage investments, by a government, nonguaranteed loan, that covers up to 85 % of the total financial need.[13] The Israeli Government, through the State of Israel - Ministry of Economy and Industry (2015) (OCS Note: not within the Minister of Science and Technology, but within the Industry, Trade, and Labor one), deployed a technological incubator program. OCS is responsible for the initial selection of incubators' management firms: they are chosen among corporate venture firms and venture capital funds based on their business plans, expertise in the selected industry, and additional private financial resources collected for seed investments. Once an incubator management company is selected, any of its seed-invested company is eligible to receive up to 85 % of financial needs in the shape of a long-term, nonguaranteed loan; only 15 % of high-risk seed investments are therefore made in equity by the venture firm running the incubator that can therefore reserve its resources for follow-up on investments on the most promising portfolio

---

[13] Data from the Office of the Chief Scientist, Technological Incubator Program, Israeli Minister of Industry, Trade, and Labor.

companies. Nowadays, the majority of Israeli incubators selected by the OCS program are managed by foreign corporations.

Europe could carefully evaluate the implementation of a similar seed and incubator programs that would definitely boost the appropriate ecosystems for making newly established technological start-ups growth. European Investment Fund, with its experience in technology transfer, incubators, and venture capital, could be the appropriate institution running such a program.

5.6   Provide Supporting Funding for Public–Private Partnerships (PPPs) and Business–University Partnerships (BUPs)

The fragmentation in R&D and innovation policy making necessitates efforts to further build up cooperation between public, private, and academic sectors, as well as citizens. Europe must also take better advantage of and capitalize on its existing scientific output, which is higher than in the USA, although falling behind in papers in the top 1 % most cited. Under these conditions, PPPs and BUPs serve as "key vehicles" for addressing the commercialization of know-how and Europe's investment problems through leveraging private finance (Dhéret et al. 2012). Existing efforts (European Commission 2013b) need to be continued to further promote PPPs and BUPs, which would help align contracting stakeholders' agendas, such as commercial and public policy objectives, in order to jointly collaborate to promote innovation, research, and industrial performance in Europe's many national innovation ecosystems. In line with open innovation, they are capable of contributing as collaborative innovation platforms supportive of co-creative innovation and research activities in Europe (European Commission 2012c).

The EU and member states have a role to incentivize universities to spend a more significant part of allocated public research funding on public–private partnerships and university–businesses partnerships to help facilitate effective knowledge transfer and a more rapid commercialization. But private companies, in particular emerging new innovators and SMEs, must similarly be actively encouraged to participate more in the ERA through

PPPs and in cooperation with research centers. New funding should also be considered for innovative forms of national and business–university cooperation, for example, in the form of joint strategic knowledge sectors that enable a stronger crosssector engagement. Since more innovations are developed in a crossborder context, more emphasis on funding and financing support for transnational PPPs and crossborder cooperation between research centers is also desired. Yet, attention must remain on exploring best practices for public–private partnerships, and in particular the challenges and problems they face now and in the future. In addition, the role and integration of financing and funding public–private–people partnerships (PPPPs), which seek to involve citizens as stakeholders and thereby enable user-driven open innovation, also require further exploration.

6   Unorthodox Ways of Raising Venture Capital and Increasing Corporate Venture Capital

Venture capital and corporate venture capital are two fundamental financial (and industrial) tools for the open innovation model. They often operate together, as corporate venture firms do not always have the financial and business skills of venture capital operators, while the presence of a corporate venture investor is often coupled with industrial partnerships and cooperation opportunities between the invested company and the investing corporation. For example, in the USA, 98 % of corporate venture firms investing with other partners and R&D partnerships are established in 75 % of cases (McMillan et al. 2010). Financial and corporate venture capitalists are therefore complement each other well; however, there are significant differences between these two investment tools. Only 4 % of US corporate venture capital funds are managing third-party money together with the parent company one, and they do not have to comply with the rules of alternative investment funds.

Financial venture capital funds manage third-party money only; to do this, they comply with specific regulations of financial authorities (like the recently released Alternative Investment Fund Management Directive or AIFMD) and with the market standards of equity-closed-end funds. And here a trade-off comes: from a financial perspective, venture capital funds are illiquid, high-risk, long-term investments; but from an industrial point of view they represent a short-term and limited source of innovation funding. The market standard for the duration of a venture fund is 10 years, of which the first five can only be used for new investments (the so-called investment period). The reasons for the presence of a 5-year "investment period" is the common belief that portfolio companies require between 3–5 years from the first investment to be exited. This 3–5 years (or even shorter) time frame was very common in years of financial speculation, at the end of the 1990s, but today's reality is significantly different. The average time to exit in Europe exceeds 6 years (Ernst and Young 2014); in the USA, while the time to receive the first seed round has remained stable around 1.5 years since start-up, later-stage investments (D round onward) moved from 6.3 years in 2005 up to 8.5 years in 2014.[14] Overall, the time to successfully exploit an innovative SME is getting longer while funds' life has been kept stable, becoming inadequate to support the complete path to an exit: this could also explain why running out of cash (no further financial support by present investors) is the second most common cause for start-up failure (CBInsights 2014). The present model of financial venture capital needs therefore to be redesigned: it poorly satisfies the needs of both financial investors and portfolio companies.

Corporate venture capital firms do not have the limitations of financial closed-end funds. Managing the cash provided by their parent company only, they are usually investment companies or even just a budget allocation of the corporation. The 10-year rule do not apply, and they can better follow their invested companies on a longer term. Still, apart from a few cases, corporate venture capital lacks the decision-making speed and the transversal competencies of financial venture capital fund teams: this is also explained by the fact that key people in corporate venture capital are hired from outside the parent company (McMillan et al. 2010). As previously explained, corporate venture capitals are almost always looking for a syndicate investment with a financial venture capital fund.

---

[14] Our analysis on PitchBook (2015), "Venture Capital Valuations and Trends," available on www. pitchbook.com.

A new model for venture capital is therefore needed, to attract more institutional financial investors (banks, funds of funds, pension funds, etc.) while offering a longer term support to portfolio companies. Stock-exchange-listed venture capital companies could be an option. Initial capitalization could be collected through private placements based on a specific investment strategy (a process close to a Special Purpose Acquisition Company or SPAC) and managed by an authorized Alternative Investment Fund Manager (AIFM) company. After the private placement with institutional investors, the venture capital company is listed on a regulated stock market, where further funds could be collected. With respect to a closed-end fund that distributes all returns and is usually not allowed to use them for further investments, the venture capital company could act as an evergreen investor. This new venture capital model should comply with the AIMFD directive (it will be managed by an authorized AIFM) and would be more attractive to investors, due to its liquidity, and could be a better tool for exploiting the value of portfolio companies. It would not be a complete novelty in the European scenario: Imperial Innovation, a London Stock Exchange, AIM-listed company, is eventually a seed fund and a technology transfer company. Other venture investment companies have also been recently listed, like LVentures in Italy.

Europe could therefore innovate the way venture capital funds are designed and support this new model through a specific European Investment Fund financing scheme (as for the present venture capital fund of funds). This measure would enhance the attractiveness for financial investors to bid on European innovation and, in the meantime, it would represent a more effective financial tool in supporting it.

In parallel to this new venture model, a new guarantee system could be designed to support corporate venture capital. As for the case of corporate acquisitions, previously described, the European Investment Bank could guarantee equity investments by selected corporate venture firms in European innovative SMEs. Enhancing corporate venture investments would represent a perfect complement to the new model of venture capital firm that we previously introduced.

References

Aho, E., J. Cornu, L. Georghiou, and A. Subira. 2006. Creating an innovative Europe. Report of the Independent Expert Group on R&D and Innovation.

Batelle; R&D Magazine. 2013, December. 2014 Global R&D Funding Forecast. www.batelle.org: https://www.battelle.org/docs/tpp/2014_global_rd_funding_forecast.pdf.

CBInsights. 2014. The top 20 reasons why start-ups fail. www.cbinsights.com.

———. 2015a. Corporate venture capital year in review. www.cbinsights.com.

———. 2015b. The 2014 US venture capital year in review. New York.

Chesbrough, H. W. 2003. The era of open innovation. *Mit Sloan Management Review*.

Cooke, P. 2005. Regionally asymmetric knowledge capabilities and open innovation exploring 'Globalisation 2'—A new model of industry organisation. *Research Policy* 34(8): 1128–1149.

CPB Netherlands Bureau for Economic Policy Analysis et al. 2014. A study on R&D tax incentives. Final report.

De Prato, G., D. Nepelski, and G. Piroli. 2015. Innovation radar: Identifying innovations and innovators with high potential in ICT FP7, CIP & H2020 projects. JRC Scientific and Policy Reports – EUR 273145 EN. Seville: JRC-IPTS. http://publications.jrc.ec.europa.eu/repository/bitstream/JRC96339/jrc96339.pdf.

Deloitte. 2014. Measuring the return from Pharmaceutical innovation. Deloitte: www2.deloitte.com/content/dam/Deloitte/uk/Documents/life-sciences-health-care/measuring-the-return-from-pharmaceutical-innovation-2014.pdf

Dhéret, C., H. Martens, and F. Zuleeg. 2012. Can Public Private Partnerships (PPPs) lever investment to get Europe out of the economic crisis? EPC Issue Paper, No. 71. Final report of a European Policy Centre (EPC) project with support from the European Investment Bank (EIB).

Eichengreen, B. 2006. *The European Economy since 1945: Coordinated capitalism and beyond*. Princeton: Princeton University Press.

Ernst and Young. 2014. Adapting and evolving. Global venture capital insights and trends 2014. London.

———. 2015. Venture capital insights Q4-2014. www.ey.com.

European Commission—DG Research and Innovation and Deloitte. 2013. Researchers' report 2013. http://ec.europa.eu/euraxess/index.cfm/general/researchPolicies.

European Commission. 2012a. One trillion euro to invest in Europe´s future—the EU's budget framework 2014–2020. Press release IP/13/1096. http://europa.eu/rapid/press-release_IP-13-1096_en.htm.

European Commission. 2014, May 26. European Research Area Facts and Figures 2014. ec.europa.eu: ec.europa.eu/research/era/pdf/era…/era_facts& figures_2014.pdf

Eurostat. 2015, September 15. Eurostat Database. Eurostat: ec.europa.eu/eurostat/data/database

———. 2012b. Small companies create 85 % of new jobs. Press release IP-12-20, 16.

———. 2012c. Open innovation 2012. Open Innovation Strategy and Policy Group (OISPG).

———. 2013a. Innovation union scoreboard 2013. Brussels.

———. 2013b. EU industrial leadership gets boost through eight new research partnerships. Press release IP/13/1261. http://europa.eu/rapid/press-release_IP-13-1261_en.htm.

———. 2014. State of the innovation union—Taking stock 2010–2014. http://ec.europa.eu/research/innovation-union/pdf/state-of-the-union/2013/state_of_the_innovation_union_report_2013.pdf#view=fit&pagemode=none.

———. 2015a. Investment plan for Europe: European fund for strategic investments ready for take-off in autumn. Press release IP/15/5420. http://europa.eu/rapid/press-release_IP-15-5420_en.htm.

———. 2015b. Innovation union scoreboard 2015. http://ec.europa.eu/growth/industry/innovation/facts-figures/scoreboards/files/ius-2015_en.pdf.

———. 2015c. European research area—Facts and figures 2014. http://ec.europa.eu/research/era/pdf/era_progress_report2014/era_facts&figures_2014.pdf.

Friedman, T. 2010. Start-ups not bailouts. *New York Times*, 3 April 2010.

Frietsch, R., C. Rammer, and T. Schubert. 2015. Heterogeneity of innovation systems in Europe and Horizon 2020. *Intereconomics* 50(1): 4–30.

Godin, B. 2005. The linear model of innovation: The historical construction of an analytical framework. *Science, Technology & Human Values* 31: 639–667.

Hamel, G. 2010. *Leading the revolution*. Boston: Harvard Business School Press.

High Level Group on Innovation Policy Management. 2014. The way forward to improve people´s lives: Inspiring and completing European innovation ecosystems, August 2014.

Independent Expert Group. 2014. Outriders for European competitiveness: European Innovation Partnerships (EIPs) as a tool for systemic change. Report of the Independent Expert Group.

Kuemmerle, W. 1997. Building effective R&D capabilities abroad. *Harvard Business Review* 75(2): 61–70.

Kula, H. 2013. *Your accelerator: Worth the hype?* Toronto: MaRS Discovery District Web Site.

McMillan, I. et al. 2010. Corporate venture capital. NIST, US Department of Commerce.

Mettler, A. and A. D. Williams. 2012. The rise of the micro-multinational: How freelancers and technology-savvy start-ups are driving growth, jobs and innovation.

Moedas, C. 2015. Open innovation, open science, open to the world, keynote speech. A new start for Europe: Opening up to an ERA of innovation conference, Brussels, June 22.

Moncada-Paterno-Castello, P., A. Vezzani, F. Hervas, and S. Montresor 2014. Financing R&D and innovation for corporate growth: What new evidence should policymakers know. Policy Brief. European Commission, Joint Research Centre—Institute for Prospective Technological Studies.

Moretti, E. 2012. *The new geography of jobs.* New York: Houghton Mifflin Harcourt.

Muller, P., D. Gagliardi, C. Caliandro, N.-U. Bohn, and D. Klitou. 2014. Annual report on European SMEs 2013/2014—A partial and fragile recovery. Final report.

Nesta and the Lisbon Council. 2013. Plan I—Innovation for Europe—Delivering innovation-led digitally-powered growth.

OECD. 2009. How do industry, firm and worker characteristics shape job and worker flows. Employment Outlook 2009. Tacking the Jobs Crisis. Paris.

OECD. 2011. OECD science, technology and industry scoreboard.

———. 2013. New sources of growth: knowledge-based capital.

Office of the Chief Scientist. 2014. State of Israel - Ministry of Economy and Industry. (2015, 09 15). R&D Incentive Programs. Retrieved from Ministry of Economy and Industry: www.economy.gov.il/RnD/pages/default.aspx.

Pamolli, F., et al. 2011. The productivity crisis in pharmaceutical R&D. *Nature Reviews Drug Discovery* 10: 428–438.

PitchBook. 2015. Venture capital valuations and trends. www.pitchbook.com.

Pittaway, L., M. Robertson, K. Munir, D. Denyer, and A. Neely. 2004. Networking and innovation: A systematic review of the evidence. *International Journal of Management Reviews* 5–6(3–4): 137–168.

Rae, J., and S. Westlake 2014. When small is beautiful: Lessons from highly innovative smaller countries. NESTA.

Som, O., J. Diekmann, E. Solberg, E. Schricke, T. Schubert, P. Jung-Erceg, T. Stehnken, S. Daimer. 2012. Organisational and marketing innovation—Promises and pitfalls? PRO INNO Europe: INNO-Grips II report, Brussels: European Commission, DG Enterprise and Industry.

Special Task Force (Member States, Commission, EIB) on Investment in the EU. 2014. Final task force report

State of Israel—Ministry of Economy and Industry. 2015, September 15. R&D Incentive Programs. Ministry of Economy and Industry: www.economy.gov.il/RnD/pages/default.aspx

University of California. 2012. Economic impact. University of California website. http://universityofcalifornia.edu/economicimpact.

Wessner, C. 2015. Charles Wessner at EASME presenting U.S. SBIR programme. Presentation at EASME, Brussels, 13 June. https://ec.europa.eu/easme/en/news/charles-wessner-easme-presenting-us-sbir-programme.

WiFo, Fraunhofer ISI, Greenovate!, NIFU Step, UNI-Merit and MCI Innsbruck. 2012. Analysis of innovation drivers and barriers in support of better policies—Economic and market intelligence on innovation: Organisational and marketing innovation: Premises and pitfalls. Final Report.

Wilson, K., and F. Silva 2013. Policies for seed and early stage finance: Findings from the 2012 OECD financing questionnaire. OECD Science, Technology and Industry Policy Papers, No. 9. OECD Publishing.

7

Collaborative Governance: A Promising Method for Innovation

Stefan Schepers

This chapter discusses the nature and past reform efforts of the European Union governance system and its predecessors. In addition, it looks at the need for far-reaching innovation in the system, its culture, and operational methods to deal more effectively with new challenges, such as the development of comprehensive innovation ecosystems that can simultaneously bring more economic growth and employment and more ecological and social sustainability. Incremental reforms from the past or ongoing ones will need to lead to more radical reforms to achieve an efficacious and legitimate governance system for the digital economy and society in Europe.

S. Schepers (✉)
Director, European Public Policy Advisors (EPPA), Brussels
Henley Business School, UK
e-mail: stefan.schepers@eppa.com

© The Editor(s) (if applicable) and The Author(s) 2016
K. Gretschmann, S. Schepers (eds.), *Revolutionising EU Innovation Policy*,
DOI 10.1057/978-1-137-55554-0_7

149

1   A Successful Supranational Experiment

The supranational governance model (World Bank 1991)[1] of the European Coal and Steel Community (ECSC) in 1952, followed by the European Economic Community (EEC), which would evolve into the current European Union (EU), was once a fundamental innovation in the European order of states and their governance. Instead of the slow and rigid cooperation procedures of international public law based on full respect of state sovereignty, and therefore requiring their formal ratification to become national law and thus applicable, the new supranational model pooled parts of sovereignty and set up a system for their joint management whose decisions became directly applicable. Legally, it is not a classic state, nor a federation, but a *sui generis* model (Héraud 1961).

This governance innovation opened a new era of managing the Common Good in line with the citizens' expectations of the postwar period and the need for opening hitherto protected markets in order to deal with the new economic paradigm emerging, increasingly based on interdependent scientific developments and rapid technological change, on growing trade and globalization. It was at the origin of Europe's economic recovery and innovation in the second half of the previous century, which in turn led to the unprecedented levels of social protection thanks to its social redistribution mechanisms. It helped to shift the cultural paradigm from a narrow focus on national identity, with all its potential dangers, to a multi-identity concept, more in line with the cultural requirements of the new economic age and with Europe's spiritual heritage. It has served as a model wherever countries tried to develop a more efficient system of interstate cooperation and economic cooperation and integration, though the EU system still stands alone as the most sophisticated one, also generating some of the most innovative and forward-thinking ones in the world (Rifkin 2004).

---

[1] *Governance* is defined here as a system of elected, appointed, and co-opted actors with the power and responsibility for public policy and law making, following formal procedures, and for monitoring its implementation, with the purpose of ensuring the Common Good. World Bank (1991) *Managing Development–the Governance Dimension.*

The governance mechanisms and tools designed to realize a common market, followed by a single market, worked well to achieve the goal of deconstructing national markets, which were no longer in tune with the needs of the shifting economic realities and societal needs. However, its dualistic nature also carried the embryo of later governance gridlock (Hix 2008).

1.1   The Limit of a Legalistic Concept

In fact, the ECSC/EEC is a form of experimentalist and collaborative governance. However neither concept existed at the time; they emerged more recently in scientific literature to replace hierarchical, authoritarian, and legalistic modes of public policy making and implementation dating from the industrial age. Experimentalist governance refers to a multilayered system of policy and rule making (Sabel and Zeitlin 2010). Collaborative governance refers to state and nonstate actors engaging together in a collective forum for consensus-oriented decision making (Ansell and Gash 2008). Just as new management methods in the private sector are required to deal with continuous technological changes, shifting consumer attitudes and new competitive conditions, partly resulting from public policies and regulations, so governance innovation is needed to appropriately manage new market conditions, to deal with new challenges (such as climate change or the multiple consequences of scientific discoveries) and with new citizen expectations, resulting from these scientific and technological developments and the ecological, social, and cultural innovations that they produce.

This poses a particular problem for the EU: it is a formalistic legal construction between sovereign states, not just a voluntary system for cooperation and joint management of selected collective issues. Yet, the outcome of their negotiations is directly applicable; in practice the governance system affects citizens immediately, whether private or corporate, as a national government does under the control of its parliament. But it cannot evolve as smoothly and timely as a national governance system.

Thus the European supranational model incorporates the legalistic concepts and interstate operational procedures and diplomatic culture taken from international public law and the traditional hierarchical, legalistic, and bureaucratic model of national policy and rule making, as it developed during the Industrial Revolution, mainly during the nineteenth century, inspired by its technology, market needs, and management concepts, and, importantly, its slower speed of innovation than at present in the emerging digital age.

To add to its complexity, its member states are not recent constructions, but century-old nations, each with their own distinct history, interests, and cultural identity, depriving the supranational system of the sociological basis that even recent federal constructions have. Only the Swiss confederal governance system bears some resemblance to the EU, though it has grown together over much more time.

Making the challenges even more daunting, the system was expanded in a relatively short period of time (from 1973 to 2007) with another 22 countries, multiplying its diversity, but largely disregarding the potential governance consequences. As if this were not enough, its remit was equally expanded, partly as a consequence of the successful realization of a common market and a (still incomplete) single market and their spillover effects, to include nearly all market-relevant policies, partly as a result of its federalist pretensions. The 2007 Lisbon Treaty was more about trying to repair the system than innovating it. A year later, the financial crisis erupted on Wall Street with dire consequences worldwide.

1.2   The Need of a More Inclusive Concept

The legal perspective of a supranational, multilayered model of public policy making does not capture the reality of political management in the EU, which shows an activist model of public policy making, forever legislating toward goals determined by itself, not merely content with coaching the social and economic actors within its domain. Though it was established after the Second World War, it takes inspiration from technocratic governance models that had emerged in the USA and in Europe in the early part of the twentieth century, either to force mercilessly rapid economic and social modernization (as in Russia since the communist coup in 1917) or to manage, with more respect for civic rights, the consequences of parliamentary and government oversight and regulatory failures that led to the Great Depression in the 1930s (as in the USA and the rest of Europe). Prime among these was the French Bureau National du Plan (national planning office), which increased the role of the state in the industrial market economy, as Jean Monnet had seen it functioning successfully in the USA and whose influence in the early design of the supranational model was significant (Diebold 1959). In essence, this is what the steering agency of the EU supranational system, the Commission, is modeled on. The successful realizations of the EU without doubt go back to the effectiveness of this governance system to deal with the key issues of that time.

Later, the EU systemic problems worsened because one side of the qualification from a legal perspective, supranationalism, came to dominate the minds, not least because it allowed a large fraction of Europe's class of intellectuals, politicians, and officials to present it as an intermediate step toward a fully federal state. They base themselves on the "ever closer Union" written into the constituent treaties to justify ever more centralization, political reach, and power, disregarding that the complexity of a supranational governance system, forever expanding into new policy areas and increasing its economic and sociological diversity with a host of new member states, could reach a point of diminishing returns for the societies locked into it. It overlooks that a "union" can take different operational structures and methods, that outcomes matter more to people than form.[2] It also ignores that the European supranational system does not rest on a coherent social-cultural context and society, as is the case with all successfully functioning federal states, though after several centuries the Swiss model successfully combines them. And it overlooks the potential frictions that can infiltrate a legal structure as consequence of its management culture, and weaken the acquiescence of its members and their citizens.

Therefore, a qualification from a political management perspective is more useful to bear in mind than a purely legalistic one: the EC/EU as

---

[2] European opinion polls are the clearest indication; declining participation in European Parliament elections since 1979 are another.

an experimental governance system.[3] Within the objectives set by and according to the procedural methods of the supranational policy making system, national ministries and regulatory bodies are left some space to interpret and implement these decisions in order to adapt them to national conditions. But this autonomy requires regular peer review of the methods used in the various member states to pursue collective goals. The system itself becomes the subject of regular reviews, too, setting new policy objectives, modifying procedural methods, letting in new member states, and seeking cooperation with nonstate actors. But in the EU, the supranational review of national implementation became seen too much as legalistic compliance, while national political and administrative practices led to a lack of loyal implementation early on in its existence (Siedentopf and Ziller 1988).

Experimental systems need permanent adaptation, and the capabilities for it. In the early years, there was regular attention paid to new policy ideas and for the governance capabilities of the system, but this seems to have declined since the Laeken Declaration (2001), with its grandiose vision of a European Constitution, based again on a one-sided interpretation of the supranational model; after its rejection in French and Dutch referendums, it ended as the Lisbon Treaty (2007), which tried to solve some governance problems and definitively created new ones. It introduced a series of reforms that in fact upset the delicate search for reality-based compromises between the member states and left them, their individual and corporate citizens, vulnerable to policy making driven by the holy purpose of ever closer union and on a "one size fits all" mentality. Perhaps more worrisome, it failed to make a proper link between EU economic and monetary policy making and national welfare and social protection systems (Ferrera 2009).

The Lisbon Treaty also disregards the governance implications of the new complexity resulting from previous integration process and/or from deep technological and economic shifts, not to mention societal support in a more diverse group of member states than before. It simply pursues the same governance trajectory launched half a century ago in a very

---

[3] Sabel, Zeitlin, op. cit.

different context without considering the fundamental innovation that was already required before the financial crisis increased its urgency.

Though the need for well-targeted and appropriately managed European integration and cooperation processes is beyond reasonable doubt, the present system's functioning, its procedures and management culture, are increasingly questioned, while the earlier attention to permanent reform has faded and ossification lurks around the corner. After a lost decade in terms of governance efficacy, the new Commission under President Juncker seems to recognize the need for reforms again, though it may be more wary of experiments than some of its illustrious predecessors, and it probably also has less political space because of many national governments' own reform fatigue and the European Parliament's single-minded pursuit of ever closer union, regardless of the cost and the form.

The EU managed its first double definition of the Common Good well, namely to stabilize peace and bring back prosperity. In the eyes of its peoples, the system deals less well with present threats to security and prosperity. Though one should be careful of idolizing its past problem analysis and solution finding, or to judge its present one without the benefit of hindsight, the facts prove that the EU today is challenged to develop new forms of responsible and efficient public management and to redefine the Common Good, not least in the face of its flirtation with Chicago School liberalism and its dangerous consequences for European societies (Gretschmann 2013).

2 Incremental Reform Attempts and Successes

The history of the EC/EU is full of proposals of reform, aimed to deepen and widen its policy making reach, but some were oriented toward its better functioning. They all mixed European vision with the continuously changing needs of public governance and of the economy, ideology with pragmatism. They brought advantages and created new problems. Broadly speaking, these proposals fall into three groups: those primarily aimed at political cooperation and those aimed at deepening economic integration and its methods, and those mixing both.

2.1   Seeking Political Expansion

Soon after the Treaty of Rome (1957), the Fouchet Plans (1961) sought to develop political cooperation in addition to the emerging common market. It proposed the establishment of a Council of Heads of State or Government, which would meet three times a year and adopt decisions on the basis of unanimity; a council of foreign ministers would cover the interim period. The plan drew an interesting distinction between the powers and responsibilities of the Community, based on supranational integration, and those of a future political union, based on intergovernmental cooperation. After its rejection, a new version also failed to reach agreement. However, some of its ideas would inspire later reforms (such as the present European Council of Heads of State and Government).

It is the first of many examples of the longevity of political ideas, in line with the supranational or federal single trajectory on which the member states are presumed to have embarked forever, or on the contrary to infuse a new dose of traditional intergovernmental methods. Both result from a political ideological approach, while full recognition of the rapidly shifting economic and social realities could have inspired more innovative thinking and experimenting. By not focusing enough on the appropriate governance methodology each time, the EU institutions are in fact themselves an important source of resistance from the member states' governments. Of course, political expediency and national electoral calculations also bear responsibility.

A few years later, the more pragmatic *Davignon Report* (1970) proposed half-yearly meetings of foreign ministers and quarterly meetings of their political advisers. Its approach facilitated coordination, beyond any legal constraints, between the six, later the nine, on international issues and gave an embryonic Community dimension to the foreign policy of the member states. It formed the basis for the later European Political Cooperation (EPC), which would evolve into the European External Action Service (EEAS), provided for in the Lisbon Treaty.

The newly elected European Parliament waded in the political brainstorming with the Spinelli report (1984), which sought to establish a federal Europe by proposing a new treaty directly to national parliaments, but none of them even debated it, except the Italian one, which did not vote on it either. It was, however, the beginning of the parliament's drive toward centralization of power at supranational level, based on the ideological but never proven view that this was the only method to solve Europe's existing, emerging, or imagined problems. The Spinelli report, based on federalist theory developed on an island during the Second World War, instilled a centralist federalist virus in the EP, which became one of the principal causes of the later popular malaise about the EU.

The hitherto most significant development in that line of thought came in 2001, when the Convention on the Future of Europe was established with 102 members nominated by the European Council in December. Officially inspired by the Philadelphia Convention that led to the adoption of the US Constitution, but ignoring completely its different historic, political, cultural, and economic context, its purpose was to draft a constitution for the European Union. The supranational system's ultimate attempt to strengthen itself would hit waning popular support and outright resistance when offered a chance (the Dutch and French referendums rejecting it in 2005). Although the EU had suffered crisis before, none would be as existential as the one now emerging (Zielonka 2014).

2.2   Seeking Economic Innovation

The successful realization of the common market and the emerging economic shifts through research and technology developments brought reform proposals from mainly two other perspectives: the common market required more monetary stability than political or defense cooperation, and there was a gradual realization that Europe risked lagging behind in key industrial sectors. The talk of the day was the American— and Japanese—challenges (Servan-Schreiber 1967). In essence, it sounded not unlike the discussions today: increased competition in an ever more globally connected economy required more fundamental innovations, economically and socially, and these in turn required governance adaptation.

Thus, in April 1965, the Commission tried to launch a common research and technology policy for the first time. It was considered necessary to better face the competition from US companies, in particular in high-tech sectors (aerospace and electronics), where large R&D investments were required. However, it stayed within the supranational logic, involving a higher degree of centralization and was therefore unacceptable to member states at the time.

What was a first opportunity to start a comprehensive innovation policy was lost due to lack of innovative governance thinking, in line with the intrinsic nature of proposed new policies. Different policies require different governance methods, not a "one size fits all" approach. Unfortunately, it would not be the first time that the EC/EU would lose valuable time for reform because of its interpretation of the dualistic nature of the supranational system, well suited to deconstruct national markets and to develop common industry standards, much less suitable for other policy areas. But while increased cooperation was definitively necessary, even unavoidable due to new market requirements, the centralizing federalist dream in Brussels and soon in Strasbourg would remain an obstacle. The other one was the surviving traditional legalistic and political sovereignty thinking in the member states, summarized nicely by the Belgian foreign minister Paul-Henri Spaak: "All countries in the EC are small, but there are those who know it and those who don't."

Apparently, the time was nevertheless ripe for political reflection and initiatives concerning innovation and competitiveness, however modest. Commissioner for Industry Collona di Paliano developed two memorandums calling for the elimination of technical barriers to trade and the liberalization of public procurement; the harmonization of the legal fiscal and financial frameworks in order to promote transnational activities, industrial restructuring notably through European crossborder mergers, measures to facilitate change, and adjustment, such as industrial exploitation of scientific research; and solidarity in external economic relations. The industrial policy thinking behind it was insufficiently innovative and based on old industrial thinking, though recognizing the need to focus on those sectors driving innovation. Indeed, the memorandums emphasized the importance of advanced technological sectors and singled out again electronuclear, aerospace, and information technology.

The Collonna memorandum on industrial policy represents a failed attempt by the Commission to claim a role in general macroeconomics and industrial planning. The Commission's vision was largely right, but its attempt to accommodate prevalent old industrial thinking in some member states created an inherent contradiction with the requirements of research and technology development and innovation in markets. In fact, it goes back to the fault lines in the system itself and the lack of governance innovation to deal with them when new policies are clearly needed.

A decade was lost before many of the economic goals came back in the white paper on the single market. The supranational system's methods and culture seemed to have become one of the obstacles for the innovative policy objectives themselves. The attempt to use the implied powers theory from international law into the different legal-political context of a supranational system only made it worse; it is centralization through the back door and creates a national backlash.

Some progress toward economic innovation was nevertheless made after the first enlargement (1973), when Ralf Dahrendorf, the commissioner responsible for industry, research, and technology, proposed a more pragmatic approach, which led to the creation of a new framework in the form of the European Cooperation in the Field of Scientific and Technical Research (COST) and the funding of some large collaborative research projects by the member states together with the Commission.

Meanwhile, Raymond Barre, vice president of the Commission, focused on the monetary aspects and tabled proposals in 1969 for a mechanism designed to prevent currency crises and to support currencies in trouble. The Barre Plan called for the coordination of member states' economic policies and regular consultation on budgetary policy and fiscal measures directly affecting external trade.

It led to a new proposal one year later, by the Luxembourg prime minister Pierre Werner, seeking a compromise between the conflicting economic policy and monetarist views. His three-stage plan proposed gradual, institutional reform leading to the irrevocable fixing of exchange rates and the adoption of a single currency within a decade, though it did not recommend the establishment of a central bank. The plan was not implemented, but some ideas would survive in the EMS and the EMU.

In 1972 the Commission prematurely tried to mix the political and economic perspectives and submitted a report on the conversion of the existing relations among member states into a "European Union," proposing new common policies and institutional changes. Nothing came of it, but the first oil crisis brought a quick rethink and, in 1974, Leo Tindemans, the Belgian prime minister, was requested to report on how the term "European Union" might be interpreted.

2.3   Mixing Political and Economic Policy Goals

The Tindemans proposals mixed extension of supranational powers with proposals for better governance of the system and extension of the EC into new policy areas. It proposed consolidation of the existing institutions and the development of common policies, a commission president appointed by the Council and approved by the European Parliament, strengthening its powers and electing its members by universal suffrage (before the end of 1978), conferring on the Parliament the right to propose legislation, extending qualified majority voting in the Council and changing the period when each member state held the Council presidency from the current 6 months to 1 year. He sought to expand the policy-making powers by extending the authority of the European Community to include monetary issues, energy, social, and regional policies, to introduce a European education policy, enhance protection for the environment, and the rights of consumers.

No action was taken because, except in times of crisis, political ideas need to mature and require sufficiently widespread support and appropriate management of the interdependent consequences, a process that is more complex and time-consuming in a multilayered governance system such as the EC/EU. However, many of the ideas of the Tindemans report would be realized later, such as direct elections for the European Parliament (1979) and by the extension of competences in the Amsterdam Treaty (1997). Both would also introduce new problems into the system; like other changes before, they prove the need for its permanent evolution and for infusing a large dose of a public management approach into a too rigid legalistic one (Schepers 2014). But given the system's inevitable foundation on sovereign states, adaptation is precisely one of its main governance challenges and a reason for much loss of time and efficacy, with dire economic and welfare consequences.

The aftermath of the oil crisis, economic stagnation, and high unemployment forced the reconsideration of a number of earlier ideas and proposals. The white paper on the single market was agreed (1984), proposing the abolition of barriers to the free circulation of goods and services, people and capital, with a precise 7-year schedule, and proposing about 310 directives and regulations to be adopted with that purpose by the Council of Ministers. It became the most ambitious economic reform project since the establishment of the common market itself and fully in line with one of the two key objectives of the supranational system, namely to create the framework conditions for prosperity.

In 1989 the Delors report took the logical next step and proposed an economic and monetary union (not unlike what had already been in the Werner report in 1970). Four conditions had to be fulfilled: full and irreversible convertibility of currencies, the establishment of the free movement of capital, irrevocably fixed exchange rates between European currencies and, finally, the adoption of a single currency. The Delors report outlined three stages for the achievement of an economic and monetary union: first, completion of the single market, closer coordination of economic policy and cooperation in monetary matters, and participation of all currencies in the exchange rate mechanism of the EMS; second, implementation of a new European system of central banks, which would coexist with the national monetary authorities, and with a supranational monetary institute paving the way for joint decision making; finally, economic authority could be handed over to the Union institutions, and the transition could be made to irrevocably fixed exchange rate parities and, if possible, to a single currency to replace national currencies.

2.4   Seeking Better Management

The continuing economic crisis in the 1970s would also spur a search for innovating the system of policy and rule making. In September 1978 the Commission asked an independent group of experts, chaired by Dirk Spierenburg, for a report on its management approach, and in December 1978 the Heads of State and Government tasked a committee of three eminent politicians to draw up specific proposals to improve the mechanisms and procedures of the Community institutions, particularly with a view to the Community's future enlargement. Finally, an important aspect of modern governance that had hitherto been undervalued was starting to be considered.

The Spierenburg report called for the appointment of a vice president to be responsible for coordinating the Commission's work, and for a reduction in the number of Commissioners to one per member state, in order to increase the efficiency and coordination of the work of the Commission; the number of directorates-general (DGs) should be reduced to ten and the status of Europe's international civil servants and human resources management within the Commission should be modernized. The recommendations in the report were implemented somewhat haphazardly; many were ignored, yet some of its proposals came into practice later.

The Three Wise Men Report (Barend Biesheuvel, Edmund Dell, and Robert Marjolin) called for majority voting to become standard practice and it specified the responsibilities that the Presidency of the Council of Ministers should assume. It emphasized the European Commission's right to propose legislation and capacity for action and proposed that there should be no more than one commissioner per country and that the president of the Commission should enjoy enhanced powers and authority. They repeated a number of management recommendations of the Spierenburg report. They advocated stepping up cooperation between the Commission and the European Parliament, which had recently been elected by direct universal suffrage. An attempt was made to revitalize the role of the Economic and Social Committee, though it would in fact become even more marginal in the system. Finally, the Three Wise Men called for the jointly adopted policies to be applied in a nonuniform manner, which took into account the situation of new and of prospective member states.

Despite the moderate and pragmatic nature of the proposals, their conclusions remained a dead letter at first, though years later many of them would be implemented. However, at the summit in March 1981, the attention to modernization of the European public management and of policy making led the Dutch presidency to launch the establishment of the European Institute of Public Administration (EIPA) in Maastricht, of which former Dutch prime minister Barend Biesheuvel became the first chairman of the board (Schepers 2006). The public management approach also led to some attention now to the role of national administrations in European policy preparation and implementation and to their many cultural and operational deficiencies spilling over into the European system. After the realization of the single market, this would become one of the main causes of the regulatory burden on everyone.

Awareness that not everything worked as well as it should fortunately increased, and the Commission itself spent years in various guises discussing how to achieve better regulation and, on many occasions, showed a dose of pragmatism that helped the system to function. But this is insufficient for systemic change. All these committees and reports remained within the supranational logic and did not question aspects of the system itself. Hence very little substantial improvement was achieved, except the introduction of better methods of prepolicy impact assessment. Despite all these systemic weaknesses and fault lines, one cannot ignore that the supranational system delivered many benefits, as evidenced by the economic and welfare growth in these decades. But much time and efficacy was lost also, for which the price is now being paid.

An exception to this is an attempt made in 2001, when the Lisbon Pact for Growth and Competitiveness introduced the Open Method for Coordination (OMC).[4] This was a half-hearted attempt to innovative the supranational governance system by introducing another method of cooperation. Europe's declining growth and competitiveness today shows that it was largely a failure, and the half-baked innovation attempts of the OMC never became an efficient instrument due to the prevalent political culture and legalistic and managerial weaknesses at its conception. It did, however, point in the right direction of a more collaborative, complementary form of governance for the EU.

3   Inefficacies Mushrooming

Since the realization of the common market and a (still incomplete) single market, there has been a gradual shift of attention away from efficient functioning of the supranational system toward enlargement and grand political designs.

---

[4] Introduced by the European Council of Lisbon in 2000, it was a cooperation method designed to help member states progress jointly in the necessary reforms in order to complete the Lisbon agenda.

This growing lack of societal connection was most apparent in a self-inflicted mini-crisis. The directly elected European Parliament used a relatively minor disfunctioning, compared to the financial waste in some EU programs or in its own operations, to assert its overseeing powers and forced the entire Commission to resign. The so-called Cresson affair is thought to have strengthened the role of the Parliament (Priestley 2008). However, conversely it was also the beginning of the weakening of the hitherto undisputed standing of the Commission as the competent initiator of European policy, as determined by the treaty. This in turn would open the way for the cacophony coming out of member states' capitals and Strasbourg, the seat of the Parliament. Despite the absence at the time of proper impact assessment of new policy initiatives, these others did not make up for the careful preparatory work of the Commission, its often visionary and always high technocratic competence, and its search for European inclusiveness.

The culmination of this trend was the launch of a convention to draft a European constitution, which aimed to find a new balance in the inherently dualistic nature of the system, but in fact sought only to strengthen the supranational layer, and which thus overlooked the key functions of the member states in capital allocation and social protection; it also failed to do much about the focus of the supranational system itself on rule making and control, neglecting the equally important public governance function of coaching and mentoring. While the supranational system became ever more self-absorbed, despite the direct election of the European Parliament, indeed because of its integrationist and regulatory zeal, a new generation arrived for whom the old postwar narrative had little meaning and new ideas about economy and society were penetrating citizens' minds, influenced by the very success of European integration and the cultural effects of new technologies. In parallel, with peace seemingly assured, the only other existential reason for the supranational system, prosperity for all, started to flounder because of so-called neoliberal thinking, which misses the ethical dimension of classical liberalism of Adam Smith and others.

3.1   A Missing Link

In reality, from the very beginning theory and practice did not match. Decision making was based on deal making between the governments of the member states in order to find, as in traditional interstate relations, a *juste retour* for what they were giving up. The focus on the European common interest was entrusted to the Commission with its sole right of initiative. Often decried as egoistic self-interest, governments are in fact doing what they are elected for, namely the management of their long- and short-term competitive interests, the basis for their welfare state provisions. However, the EU system lacks a method to properly include the latter in its economic thinking, because it falls under the competences of the member states and not its own. This creates a politically dangerous fault line, in addition to the weakness or even absence of first defining an up-to-date and visionary European Common Good as an overarching policy framework, not as the sum of individual national interests.[5]

It would be a truly significant reform to include, even before an innovation and a precautionary principle, a Common Good principle, and a method to define it. It would facilitate the much needed shift from debt-driven toward innovation-driven economic growth and help to reduce the growing gaps within societies. But it should not be based on a rear mirror view, but on a future-oriented one, focusing on societal demand and not just on industrial supply, on emerging new forms of living and working together, of social cohesion and cultural diversity. To initiate such a process alone would already help to counter the poison of resurgent backward-oriented nationalism, on the left and right of the political spectrum, in many member states. However, it will not be enough. Fundamental governance reforms are needed to define and work effectively toward a new European Common Good; they concern two key functions of governance: mentoring and regulating.

3.2   An Overemphasis on Regulation

The most effective governance tool to achieve economic integration between states is regulation, as is also proven in other interstate cooperation systems, such as the World Trade Organization (WTO). In the EC/EU it is complemented with a mechanism to alleviate adjustment costs

---

[5] K. Gretschmann, op. cit.

in weaker economies, the so-called structural funds, whose efficacy are a matter for concern. European rules are directly applicable and do not need ratification by national parliaments as is the case with traditional interstate (international) rule making.

The treaties envisaged two sorts of rules: those which allowed member states some discretion in their application (directives) and those which did not. Originally, the EC made more use of the former, but because of abuse by member states (application distorting the purpose, heaping additional rules upon it, etc.), the EU moved toward preferring regulations, not least because the single market requires a level playing field for companies both large and small.

Rule making results from long thought- and consensus-building processes among political decision makers that must align the interests of various stakeholders and the common (public) interest. It is based on the need to establish stable framework conditions for markets to function fairly and competitively, and/or to deal with the negative external costs caused by economic activities, which may either become too high or which can no longer be loaded on the public budget, sometimes openly, because they are deemed a public good, often in a hidden way to maximize profitability. Regulatory intervention follows or leads to shifts in the framework conditions for competitiveness, offering, in particular, new opportunities to those with a strong research basis, strategic agility, and innovative business models. Good and timely (de)regulation is part of the creative destruction processes lauded by Schumpeter, the basis for economic and social innovation.

However, today rapid scientific discovery and technological innovation in the market can make existing regulation sometimes less efficacious or even obsolete, either in its prescription and/or in its application. This results not only from the fact that regulation is mostly post-fact, but also because it leads to adaptation by the addressees. Unfortunately, one regulation is often followed by others, based on the same concepts that meanwhile may have become (partly) bypassed by adaptation of production processes or other industrial activity or in social behavior, in practice reducing or eliminating the needs which led to the original regulation.

Once a regulatory trajectory is opened up, new (public and private) interests grow upon it that prevent timely regulatory innovation, including simply pausing or definitively halting. Rigidity of purpose is often linked to a public good, but it should not necessarily be accompanied by rigidity of methods, in particular not when dealing with such diverse contextual conditions as in the EU. Just continuing a particular regulatory trajectory without regular checks of its impact and costs, and without reexamination of the objectives themselves, is the main cause of excessive regulatory burden and costs. In the end, there is little or no benefit left, and citizens increasingly consider the system illegitimate. It even starts to show authoritarianism, which may later spread, endangering liberal democracy and citizens' freedoms.

To bring innovative thinking to regulatory reform processes, the cognitive assumptions that have led to the introduction of the original regulation must be externalized and compared with scientific advances which have happened in the meantime. An innovative analytical approach, independent pre- and regular postregulation impact assessment can expose inherent weakness in the regulatory methodology and can help to promote improvements. This requires innovation in governance culture and methods.

In governance and management science too there are regular break-throughs and new concepts and methods, such as the concepts of experimentalist and of collaborative governance, the most relevant for the EU today. They allow to complex systems such as the EU as a whole to be analyzed and permit focus on nonlinear dynamics, inter-actions, and feedback, and taking into account known unknowns, to preserve strategic agility, within interdependent economic, political, and social systems.

A pioneer of systems thinking, Russell Achoff, formulated it succinctly: "The righter we try to do the wrong thing, the more wrong it becomes. It is therefore better to do the right thing wrong, learn from mistakes, and correct them." Therefore Commission and Council should rediscover the benefits of experiments; the Parliament should aim to become one for the twenty-first century, not a parliamentary model of the bygone industrial age. Eurozone management has shown that reform is not impossible, but it is better to experiment with governance models in quieter times than during crisis.

3.3   Governance for the Digital Age

The EU has arrived in the digital age. Earlier reform proposals inscribed themselves within the established supranational, legalistic governance paradigm, but today, with deep economic and societal paradigm shifts, the EU is in need of system change, ultimately requiring treaty change; meanwhile, much can be done within the confines of the present one. The traditional functions of public governance, monitoring (establishing and controlling regulatory architectures), mentoring (coaching and incentives for desired outcomes), and capital allocation to ensure social justice and economic and ecological resilience, cannot escape, within less than a decade, a transformation as profound as at the time of the establishment of the first supranational system (the ECSC in 1952).

Legal science, the basis of regulation, assumes a linear dynamic and therefore has often a reductionist outcome in the reality of economic, social, or environmental conditions, even if this was not the intention of decision makers. In the EU, the heavy reliance on regulations results from the need to integrate markets between hitherto sovereign states. If it is applied beyond the pure integration mechanics, in other policy areas requiring different methodologies and tools, there is a real risk of causing unintended collateral effects in the economy or in social systems. This is all the more the case because of the rigid procedural mechanics, resulting from the interstate aspect of supranationalism, and used between decision-making institutions with often a strong silo approach and related defense of own interest.

But one cannot govern the rapidly emerging postindustrial society with the concepts of the preindustrial one. The great transformation in Europe's economy and societies triggered by globalization and digitalization is accompanied by a great stagnation in public governance systems. National governance systems pay the price for their own rigid attachment to outdated legalistic concepts: it leads to declining effectiveness of public policy with negative effects on competitiveness and budgets, on sustainability and social cohesion and, finally, on legitimacy. Regretfully, dominant political behavior and culture in the supranational system often fuels their reactions. The hierarchical, legalistic governance concepts, culture, and methods of the EU system date from the 1950s, and originated even earlier, and are as up to date as a typewriter. Fortunately, system rigidities have been amended a bit, occasionally, by pragmatism of those laboring in it.

Technology development has always led to profound change in societies as much as in markets, and in turn both are changing the political order and the required governance methodology. The competitiveness of nations, or groupings of nations such as the EU, is dependent on the competitiveness of their economies and the adaptability of their societies (Acemogly and Robinson 2012). The key challenge therefore is how to gain advantage out of the potential convergence between the various issues. This also requires a modernization of governance systems and methodology, including its basic concepts.

A radical innovation of the supranational system would be to reconstruct its operation starting from the evidence of the complexity of issues it deals with, and inspired more by management than by legal science. The latter remains important because no system can function without rules, and certainly not a governance system based on sovereign member states, where the absence of rules would quickly degenerate into pure power politics with inevitable disintegrating consequences for the system as a whole. But complexity management demands the active involvement of relevant and accountable stakeholders because of the often existing knowledge asymmetries and the need to develop alignment in order to serve the Common Good.

Complexity is used extensively in the fields of strategic management and organizational studies to understand how organizations adapt to their environments (Von Hayek 1967). It seeks to understand the nature of a system, its constraints and interactions of its parts and generally takes an evolutionary approach to strategy and a flexible one to rule implementation, for there is not one reality but, rather, many circumstantial realities. Several theories have arisen from various sciences studying complex systems; by comparison with the natural sciences, there is relatively little work on developing a theory of complex social or political systems. Nevertheless, it can provide an innovative way of thinking about the EU and could change its strategic thinking, the structure, culture, and operations. It is already penetrating the most intelligent minds in the Commission or governments, but as an almost subterranean correction of the system's persistent legalistic rigidities or political foibles.

The principles of emergence, connectivity, interdependence, and feedback are familiar from systems theory. Complexity builds on them and enriches it by articulating additional characteristics of complex systems and by emphasizing their interrelationship and interdependence. To reach a deeper understanding of complex systems, multiple characteristics must be studied and a rich interrelationship picture built. Complex systems are able to adapt and evolve and thus create new order and coherence. Entities in complex adaptive systems can change their interaction, acting on limited local knowledge, without doing what the system as a whole is doing, and they can also be self-repairing and self-maintaining. The EU is a complex governance system like no other.

Complexity approach to European policy making and management would facilitate the development and inclusion of the Common Good as an overriding objective for all citizens in all member states. It would also provide a basis for evidence-based policy making, for innovative application of the existing precautionary, and the urgently needed innovation principle as key tests for decision making in all the institutions and for their practical implementation management. It is a basis for a new overall governance approach. It will be an important step to help the Commission fully recapture the intellectual policy making leadership in Europe, in collaboration with its key partners, national governments. They together have the accountability to citizens.

4   Collaborative Governance

Within an experimental, multilayered governance system, the challenges of the present times require that hierarchical and legalistic approaches be complemented, if not replaced, by a collaborative governance culture and methodology.

The concept of collaborative governance emerged precisely because of increasing policy failures in traditional hierarchical, normative governance systems, resulting from inevitable knowledge asymmetries in complex systems. These cannot be mastered by a single authority, they can only be distributed among stakeholders and coached toward a Common

Good. To outline a Common Good itself today requires a process of collaborative governance, because it needs to go beyond a mere economic definition of competitiveness, employment, or sustainability to include all aspects that can make the vast majority of people prosperous and content. It thus also implies an ethical dimension, probably the most import glue in society (Sandel 1982).

Partly because of globalization and the ongoing change in the way information and communication is used, and sometimes abused, in traditional or new media, partly because of strategic uncertainty caused by this asymmetric, incomplete, and rapidly outdated information about technology and markets, and about their societal effects, ex ante static law making is increasingly no longer an efficient tool for government to produce value and to move toward a Common Good. Collaborative governance can be applied at every layer of governance, but the focus here is on the supranational one and its interaction with the national governance systems. Even strategic planning has become hazardous, because of the uncertainties about feedbacks in complex systems, and it would be better replaced by the concept of strategic agility (Doz and Kosonen 2014).

The key characteristic of collaborative governance is that it brings together public stakeholders, from the two principal layers (supranational and national), and private stakeholders in a collective forum to engage in consensus-oriented decision making. Its classic definition involves six criteria: (1) the forum is initiated by public institutions, (2) participants in the forum include nonstate actors, (3) participants engage directly in decision making and are not merely "consulted" by public institutions, (4) the forum is formally organized and meets collectively, (5) the forum aims to take decisions by consensus (even if consensus is not achieved in practice), and (6) the focus of collaboration is on public policy or public management (Ansell and Gash 2008).

Supranationalism itself was an innovative, experimentalist form of governance that managed to install systemic collaboration between sovereign states, far more suited to the economic restructuring required at the time than classic international cooperation could ever be. But it does not respond to the criteria just outlined. Today, more than 60 years of advances in the integration process and new requirements resulting from technological, economic, and societal shifts demand new and radical innovations in governance systems, in particular to overcome the key inefficacies in the EU mentioned before. It needs a strong dose of innovation again, and collaborative governance can provide this.

The realization of its first grand political objective, to stabilize political and economic relations between Europe's sovereign states through joint economic policy making, needs to be complemented in order to find a new, attractive leading narrative: it needs integration with the maintenance and modernization of national welfare systems and it needs to become their prime guarantor, without seeking to centralize what belongs to the core identities and societal realities of the member states. All its internal and external policies need to be regularly checked against their impact on citizens' welfare. This is as important today as achieving a resource efficient economy and ecological resilience, which can be useful, perhaps necessary tools, but not prime objectives.

Therefore, the present EU system needs to leap beyond the concepts and methods inherited from a different economic age, toward more collaborative forms of governance, with national governments and with other stakeholders to deliver innovative, postindustrial economic growth needed to maintain but modernize national welfare societies, and to contribute to global stability (Fuchs 2013). This goal is incompatible with continuing regulatory overstretch and rigidities and with an ideological pursuit of "ever more Europe," no matter what for or how. It is also incompatible with linear, top-down hierarchical approaches that fail to grasp the complexities and interdependencies of economic competitiveness, ecological resilience, and scientific and technological progress.

The EU has elements of collaborative governance already in embryonic, experimental, or even emerging form, and no legal barriers should prevent their further development, until the next treaty change brings a more radical governance redesign in line with the requirements of the ongoing science- and technology-driven economic shifts. In order to deal with the rigidities of the system, a healthy dose of pragmatism has been there for a long time, it can now serve as one input for proper reforms, but slow, informal adaptations are not the same as system change and insufficient to remedy the negative effects of its dualist nature and limited governance toolbox.

4.1   Public Initiation

The treaty provides the Commission the sole right of initiative; thus, it implicitly has the right to decide how to exercise it within the confines of the treaty and guidelines given by the European Council of Heads of State and Government. This institution is one of the few well-thought-out innovations of the Lisbon Treaty; in fact, it has more democratic legitimacy than many like to think, and it is potentially a highly useful partner for the Commission.

The most important starting inputs for effective collaborative governance are considerations of foresight and of public value, that is, the contribution to the Common Good. It was foresight that stimulated the Founding Fathers to launch the supranational, experimentalist model of European integration. It will be foresight that will help today's leaders align the multiple visions of its future in the very different and more complex global context of today.

Professional foresight is a transdisciplinary approach that seeks to improve the ability to anticipate, create, and manage change in a variety of domains (scientific, technological, environmental, economic, cultural, and societal), on a variety of scales (personal, organizational, societal, local, national, and global) and through a variety of methods. The overarching objective is to permanently and comprehensively establish anticipatory thinking and a reflective handling of uncertainty in government institutions. This requires changes in the culture of organization and the processes of communication (Buehler and Dorn 2013).

All too often, policy makers think in terms of legislative periods rather than a future, long-term view and act in ways that are, as a consequence, both short-range and reactive. By contrast, government foresight aims to improve political decision making by taking into account long-term and uncertain developments and derive strategies for governments from the acquired knowledge and insights. It can be particularly useful to ensure policy focus and coherence and strategy planning in the Commission because of its stable 5-year mandate. Perhaps it is no coincidence that the decline of interest in foresight, once prominently present in the Cellule de Prospective under Commission president Jacques Delors, happened at a time when thinking in EU institutions became more inward-looking and silo based. It is a hopeful sign that the new Commission president Jean-Claude Juncker has given new importance to foresight through the establishment of the European Policy Strategy Center. However, foresight and strategy are not identical. The former is the basis for the latter, which requires its own, often scenario-based, methodology and which should be part of the next phase in the process.

Foresight studies provide a solid launching platform for reform processes, in particular in settings where uncertainty resulting from complexity must be coped with and where a kaleidoscope of views and multiple, open and hidden, interests among different governance layers and nonstate actors make the setting of policy direction very difficult. They greatly facilitate the development of a common framework of thinking and ultimately of alignment of policy vision. This is all the more important at a time when the traditional narratives for European integration and cooperation have waned and a new one, attractive to the generation for whom all the previous realizations are self-evident, has not yet been formulated nor percolated in their minds. An aligned vision and a common narrative can also help politicians to counterbalance the negative effects of the media on politics, whereby mass media and/or the new social media create, sometimes deliberately so, a view on reality which does not correspond to its real complex nature, which in turn can hinder effective policy making (Schudson 2002).

Equally important is the public value of the policy or rule intended. Originally intended as a yardstick in governance, it is an equally important concept for business, as Peter Drucker famously said: "The business of business is society" (not just markets). In order to be credible and accountable in the hearts and minds of Europe's citizens, any Commission initiative should explain the potential public value, its specific contribution to the Common Good, in terms of its positive effects on innovation and consequently on economic growth and competitiveness, in terms of prosperity for all and social cohesion and of respect for Europe's diverse identities, and in a language that is intelligible for all. Public value thinking goes beyond the underlying self-interest approach of public institutions, as analyzed already by Max Weber, and beyond the focus on shareholder value regardless of other considerations and society's interests (O'Flynn 2007). The public value of a policy or rule determines its contribution to the Common Good and it is in particular important at the concluding phase of collaborative governance processes.

It will be no less a change for corporations, which only hesitantly start to open up for new thinking about their role in the market and in society but which is still far away from applying it, driven as it is by short-term financial interests, often purely transactional in the financial services sector itself. Also the world of often righteous management of nongovernmental organizations (NGOs) is in for change if it wants to play a constructive role in the search for public value, because their often single issue, single study approach, frequently with a considerable dose of manipulation because of their lack of legal accountability, which corporations do have, does not fit with complex realities and ignores collateral effects on communities and in the economy.

The benefits of the adoption of public value as the principal, overarching objective of policy making is its positive effect on credibility and accountability, while simultaneously improving efficiency.[6] Both approaches would greatly enrich the existing practice of Commission impact studies and take them beyond technocratic analysis. Foresight and public value allow governments and individual citizens, and civic groupings with an economic purpose, corporations, or others such as noneconomic issue organizations, to set their sights first on what is needed for the long-term, common interest. It is very helpful to look beyond the silos.

They thus contribute to finding a much needed new narrative for the European Union and they act as a motivational force for the many who do not dwell on the past. Thereafter, when elaborating flexible, strategic scenarios to achieve optimum outcomes, follows the discussion of how to overcome temporary, but often understandable, obstacles on the way forward and how they can be managed in order to minimize transition costs. However, this requires innovation in the traditional patterns of consultation as managed by the Commission and governments, and of advocacy by interest groups of all denominations.

---

[6] Stoker, op. cit.

4.2   Nonstate Actors

The innovation of consultation in the EU is the most practical and useful step toward (more) collaborative governance in the short term, given the fact that a revision of the Treaty to bring more radical governance reforms in line with collaborative governance principles is unlikely soon for political reasons. This seems to be recognized by the Commission in its communication on better regulation.

Real consultation is organized skepticism. It is not a cosmetic exercise, a benign one-off opportunity for stakeholders to vent their views when in fact the direction of policy and much of its elaboration is already decided, as was all too often the case in the past. If properly executed, it can greatly contribute to the development of a common vision, the alignment of different interests and the legitimacy of policy. It is a key ingredient in the accountability of decision makers. It can provide useful inputs in the definition of public value and the development of flexible strategic scenarios to achieve it. This can only be achieved if it is a permanent, dynamic process of deliberation (Karpowitz and Mansbridge 2005). It can positively affect the strengthening of dual European-national identity, alignment, and consensus and a joint vision of the Common Good. All this is much needed in the EU and will undoubtedly improve its legitimacy.

These desirable outcomes will not come automatically; they require careful preparation by the Commission as initiator. However well intentioned and prepared the Commission may be, if the other stakeholders are not, the process of consultation is unlikely to produce the desired outcomes for anyone. Here the EU has a problem which is truly not of its own making: the unpreparedness of those which it sees as its principal stakeholders to consult, after national governments. It goes deeper than the fact that the relatively small Brussels-based bureaucracies of corporate or other civic groupings (confusingly labeled nongovernmental, or civic society organizations, as if business does not, or should not, belong to society) may themselves lack the capacity to fully appreciate the task at hand or the consensual methods to execute it. The origin of this general problem is different for corporate and nongovernmental organizations and it is rooted in their respective models to pursue their own goals.

Today's new challenges require bringing societal and public policy issues from the periphery to the core and developing a corporate strategy that serves the public interest in a responsible way (Zadek 2007). Unfortunately, in stock-market-listed corporations this is difficult because of short-termism of some institutional investors or speculative practices—a fundamental problem of today's market functioning which intervention by a strong enough global market regulatory power, such as the EU, should correct in the interest of everyone.

In the European model of separation between the board of directors and CEO, the general view is that the chairman of the board is responsible for the long-term interests of the company and for its forward and outward looking, while the CEO looks after day-to-day operations. Obviously, their cooperation is an important ingredient in the success of the company (Kakabadse et al. 2010).

As the key task of the board is setting the corporate strategy, this now definitively requires the development of an inclusive vision of the role of the corporation in society and of its interaction with that society. While the stock markets may still be at the stage of shareholder value before everything, in practice corporations have to consider their public value, too (Gomez and Meynhardt 2014). Failing to do so can lead to at least reputational damage resulting in a weaker (stock) market position, and in due time also political and regulatory risk. Developing a vision corresponds to the need for building a collective view inside and outside the company about its contributions to society. It is far more demanding than fashionable mission statements or some corporate social responsibility action to plaster over more serious gaps. For the vision to be understood and accepted, it needs to start from the prevalent societal paradigms and policy makers' challenges resulting from foresight, technological, economic, geopolitical developments and other inputs, not from the products or services themselves (Schepers 2010).

Such an inclusive vision is a form of humanizing the corporation; embedding it in its global, regional, and national societal contexts requires considering not just the market context but a territorial one, that is in a social structure, which is more complex to deal with (Thoenig and Waldman 2007). This requires profound understanding of paradigm changes, as much so as public decision makers. Engaging with politics and society helps to acquire this and ultimately gives back insights to steer corporate strategy and improve competitiveness.

An additional, specifically European, problem is the coordination between the role of headquarters, European trade associations, and company subsidiaries in a multilayered governance system. Policy making in the EU is a continuous trade-off between the collective European economic interest and the national interests of the member states (Gretschmann 2001). It is therefore essential to smoothly manage the corporation involvement between the supranational and national level of decision making and to understand the role, interests, and procedure of each institution involved in order to avoid the likelihood that the best possible business approach ultimately does not deliver results.

Inappropriate strategy development and internal management gaps are the main causes for corporations that are insufficiently prepared for mutually useful engagement in the public policy making process, even if the authorities offer the opportunity. Even if they were prepared, one would have to watch out for incumbents trying to defend their existing business model against innovators. Due to the lack of autonomous growth possibilities, many promising start-up companies are an easy acquisition target for cash-rich corporations. They may do so in order to innovate their product or service range and in that case there is a public value resulting from it; but every so often they do so to bury a competing technology, which produces an economic and socially negative effect.

Therefore, the identification of innovative challengers to take part in consultation processes is highly important, together with the advice of scientists who have a good, peer reviewed standing and who can provide deep insight in scientific and technological developments. The Commission's own Joint Research Center does play a useful role in impact assessment preparation, but it is embedded in the system and thus its independence cannot be guaranteed. The simplest and most efficient way to do so is consultation with multiple stakeholders based on continuous dialogue and solid trust.

Internal innovation could bring corporations' dearest wishes for better market regulation rapidly closer. But the experiences show that they are ill prepared to deliver their part of what they ask from the Commission and governments. Following repeated demands to alleviate the regulatory burden, the Barroso Commission launched a program (REFIT) aimed at evaluating the implementation of regulations. It combines two objectives: simplification (easier to understand) and reduction of regulatory burden (less monitoring, reporting and other requirements). It soon became apparent that the business side does not have the capabilities to deliver on time all the relevant inputs in impact assessment (such as comprehensive social-economic analysis and others) nor the legal and regulatory expertise, nor the political insights in all 28 member states' interests and public administration operability, to be able to make a meaningful contribution to the EU co-decision-making system.

The problem from the perspective of NGOs is partly similar. Even more so than companies, which are subject to the strict rules of corporate law, stock markets, and of legal transparency requirements, there is a management issue, though of a different nature. The lack of legal requirements about their structure, governance, and operational and financial transparency has facilitated the emergence of opaque structures and de facto oligarchic management.

The business model of the nonphilanthropic, political NGOs is based mostly on actions relating to single issues, driven by single studies, seldom or never peer reviewed; this assures their growth in membership and income. It is supported by effective media coverage, in the traditional press and through new social media, which combine to create simple visions ignoring the systemic complexity in which these issues are embedded. NGOs, and policy makers under their spell or experiencing information asymmetries, often assume the inevitability of economic, ecological, and social trade-offs, and this leads to a push for even more restrictions, regulations, and controls (Kramer and Porter 2011). This is partly the result of their own silo approach, partly of a preference for doom-and-gloom thinking and for moral grandstanding, popular among environmental organizations and researchers since the first report of the Club of Rome, *Limits to Growth*, and useful since it helps to bring in funding. Yet, it acquired a perhaps disproportionate influence. And it is a source of resurgent authoritarianism.

While the identification of issues by NGOs is often very useful and a real contribution to the democratic debate, their solutions mostly are not. Both would have been better served with an inclusive approach, based on resilience thinking and leading to public–private collaboration for research and technology developments designed to overcome the problems resulting from the first and second industrial revolutions and from population growth. This is starting to be recognized.

However, the policy making deviation resulting from the present situation is more serious in Europe, because of particular characteristics of the supranational decision-making system. Due to the lack of democratic legitimacy, the EU Commission and Parliament prefer to rely on NGOs as presumed representatives of European citizens, which of course they are not; they have never been tested in an election. However, companies, as producers of goods and services, have a tangible public value, whereas NGOs have mainly an intangible one, quite a difference when it comes to ensuring people's prosperity. Thus they not only generously subsidize them, but use them as objective allies in their struggle for "ever more Europe" as the panacea to solve all problems. The cornerstone of the welfare states, competitiveness, has come under stress as a result, and people blame the EU for failing to deliver what is its core task, namely creating the framework conditions for innovation in growth, employment, and welfare.

While at the moment industry or NGOs are generally ill prepared to become truly useful and accountable partners for the Commission and governments in innovated consultation mechanisms, a natural and key democratic partner is almost completely overlooked: national parliaments.

Despite the existence of a European Parliament, real democratic legitimacy and accountability still lies with the age old parliaments of the member states, deeply rooted in societal consciousness. They are supposed to control not only the national governments, and thus their decision making in the Council and strategic steering in the European Council, they are also responsible for spending national taxation incomes and the maintenance and modernization of welfare and social protection mechanisms. While their role in European policy making is mostly limited to scrutiny of Commission proposals before the Council agrees on a common position, there is no obstacle in the treaty that prevents the extension of their role to the preproposal consultation processes of the Commission and indeed to the feedback evaluations.

It is surprising that this has not yet become a systemic part of supranational decision making, and another indication of the outdated, legalistic thinking that today is so much an obstacle to governance innovation, EU legitimacy, and democratic accountability. National parliaments are overlooked because of the traditional interstate dimension of supranationalism, but on the other hand it produces regulations directly, applied often with far-reaching impacts in societies, so at the very least all national parliaments should be consulted at the dawn of major new policy developments (such as an energy union, a digital union, a resilience-based circular economy, and others).

It would be quite feasible for the Commission to meet the relevant committee(s) of national parliaments and to engage in a discussion with them based on its foresight and impact studies, possible scenarios and intended proposal(s). This would quickly lead to increased democratic legitimacy, to better alignment of the proposal with the member states before the technocratic discussions and negotiations in the Council working groups and before the first reading in the European Parliament. It would merely add a couple of extra months and a bit of travel for a small delegation of senior Commission officials, in principle the same team for all the capitals, in order to create a common framework in their minds. It would not change the role of the European Parliament in the formal codecision process.

In order to come to up-to-date forms of consultation processes, it is important to not only focus on the process methodology, but also on the participating stakeholders, which have some serious homework to do first, whether they be industry or nongovernmental organizations. But the most significant innovation would be to add a second, well-organized, and timely consultation path with all the national parliaments. No doubt legalistic traditionalists, fetishists of sovereignty theories, or federalist diehards will unite to oppose such innovation, but the future belongs to innovators.

4.3   Engaging in Decision Making

The EU is still far away from codecision as envisaged by collaborative governance, yet much more can be achieved with an innovative approach, leaving intact the formalistic decision making in the institutions.

A meaningful start to the consultation process with relevant stakeholders and national parliaments requires an assessment, as accurately as possible, of the various interests and conflicts among key stakeholders, both public and private ones. When this is not done, the consultation process may not only produce a flawed consensus, and as a consequence a high risk of policy failure or rule ineffectiveness, it will also increase dissatisfaction with the process itself and those who steer it. It will also fail to explain the potential contribution to the European Common Good and become quickly bogged down in technocratic discussions; these are necessary at a later stage, not when determining a vision, policy direction, and potential, alternative outcomes.

This key characteristic of collaborative governance is largely beyond the reach of Europeans today given the legal constraints of the present treaty, the prevalent sovereignty thinking in capitals, and the centralizing focus of a traditional parliament in Strasbourg. None of them responds to the needs of the digital age, which is rapidly weakening the traditional role of parliamentary representative democracy and bureaucratic control systems of the industrial age. In fact, the very technologies used to exercise hierarchical control are now increasingly being used against it, thanks to increased education, access to information, and easier means of communication (Karvalics 2012).

It is inevitable that the supranational system moves from a hierarchical one toward a heterarchical system, far more suited to preparation and decision making in complex conditions in multilayered experimental governance systems. This will imply also that the move from directives, which leave member states some application space, to regulations, based on a "one size fits all" approach, need to be reversed in many instances. But the reason for this move, the undoing of the single market because of a national lack of proper application or of so-called gold-plating European regulations, will become obsolete when in a more collaborative system stakeholders are involved in every stage of a policy process.

Therefore, the pre-decision-making phase of impact assessment based on analysis of complex, interdependent systems, on innovation and precautionary principles, and on the desired outcomes for European citizens, is all the more important to achieve decisions that are aligned with the Common Good. Not the procedures themselves, but the transparent, evidence-based inputs, and the open and fair engagement with national parliaments, offering a national perspective, and of incumbent companies and challengers, reformed nongovernmental organizations, and independent scientists, all offering a common European perspective.

However, one should not overlook the limitations of scientific inputs. Science can play just as much a role in legitimizing political authority as in criticizing it, or it can even serve as a lightning rod for decision makers to shift their responsibility in the face of contentious decisions. This seems to be happening quite often with European agencies, whose original advisory role has extended in practice, further weakening democratic legitimacy of the system. Science and technology are not static, nor are societies, even less so in an economy based on rapidly evolving technologies. This provides another reason why the legalistic approach is insufficient because it starts from an erroneous belief that there are linear relations between quantifiable variables, whereas the reality of complex system analysis shows that they are in constant interaction and change. Real stakeholder engagement and exchanges can help to overcome scientific limitations as well as their own individual tunnel visions, creating a real added value for the Commission as policy initiator. Rather than being a prisoner of national experts offering their own approach and being forced to aggregate them, the Commission will more easily find the way toward a European Common Good and effective mentoring and regulating in the variety of inputs and feedback during the consultation processes.

Governance cannot be entirely top-down or bottom-up. Efficient governance in the public interest requires a balanced mixture of both. This can make the supranational system, provided it is reformed fundamentally, including its political-administrative culture, well suited to the current and future economic, ecological, and societal challenges of Europe.[7] In practice it will be necessary to preserve a (smaller than today) dose of traditional legal and hierarchical characteristics, but to complement them with an equally large dose of new governance characteristics, such as reflexive and open coordination, stimulating peer review (and not just corrective), soft-law-style self-regulation or specific incentives, transparency as a rule with limited but supervised exceptions,

---

[7] See chapter on foresight.

experimentation and alignment building through deliberations, using evidence-based arguments based on analysis of issue and system complexity (Poul 2010).

Effective deliberation among the stakeholders requires that parties are willing, even forced to share relevant information, even though transparency may be reduced by accepting that participants are not quoted outside meetings or that certain sensitive information remains privy to the Commission. However, one should realize that too much transparency can have adverse effects, too, such as increasing misunderstandings or undermining trust (Maucher 2011).

This in turn raises the question of accountability of all the actors in the process. The legalistic approach of accountability in the supranational limits it to formalistic types, such as political (toward the Council and Parliament), financial (toward the Court of Auditors and other auditing bodies), managerial (in the case of agencies), or the Court of Justice and the Ombudsman (Busuioc 2013).

This is too restrictive a view of accountability. When the Commission opens a consultation process using the inputs described before, all actors must either amend their analysis of the European Common Good or subscribe to it and focus on finding the least burdensome way for all stakeholders (companies, public administrations, citizens) to achieve it. The efficacy for the Common Good of any institution and its normative frameworks depend on the context and (at least partly) on specific goals. It implies not only evidence-based operation of the system, but also that for all participants in such a deliberative process there must be a set of shared principles of justice, a set of ethical and legal norms without which they cannot function (Rawls 1972). Given the current deficiencies indicated with corporate and nongovernmental actors, an effort to remedy these is required; without this, accountability will remain limited to the consultation results with national parliaments.

4.4   Formal Organization and Collective Meetings

Collaborative governance needs formal organization, ensuring that all stakeholders take part on equal footing and that there is clear progress toward a concrete outcome, being the setting of policy objectives, the outline of a regulatory architecture, or simply solving the practicalities in the invariably diverse realities.

This is easy enough to achieve, but the final, decisive step of collaborative governance, collective decision making, is impossible in the European supranational system because of the current institutional setup and division of powers. It is even the question of whether it is desirable, the experience of the Constitutional Convention and the treaty that ultimately came out of it should give pause for thought. Considering the complex nature of any multilayered system, it may not be a disadvantage, certainly at the experimental phase, to have an informal part, where accountable stakeholders reach a desired outcome, and then pass it on to the formal, legalistic part, where the institutions move the decision making to its conclusion. This does not have to be an empty last step: the institutions are part of the process from the beginning themselves, only they retreat to formalize it using their ultimate regulatory power. Some people may object that it limits democratic decision making: rightly so, it limits electorally driven, ideologically distorted decisions with little basis in day-to-day, complex economic and social realities, which cause so much damage today. Traditional parliamentary democracy has reached its limits in the new economic, societal, and cultural realities of the digital age, a bit like aristocratic governance came to an end with the emergence of early industrialism and trade. An election is not an anointment by divine right to do whatever, whenever.

In the EU, to be sure, the practice of hearings is a far cry from collaborative governance, because of its one-directional question and answer method. It does not allow for multiperspective analysis and for alignment building toward a shared vision of desired outcomes. Key inputs such as foresight, innovation and precaution, resilience, and public value, which all help to determine the Common Good, are not present or just superficially. The practice of large "consultation conferences" is even less useful.

In a multilayered system, with an inevitably hierarchical dimension between the supranational institutions and the national governments, it is nevertheless possible to develop successful new forms. The EU has already done so with a variety of supportive governance structures, which add a heterarchical dimension (Kjaer 2010). Only the rules of procedure and the management culture of most of these bodies, committees of all kinds, and de facto coregulatory agencies are in dire need of radical innovation if they want to be considered as collaborative by even the most benign of observers.

Given the conceptual poverty and methodological weaknesses of business and nongovernmental actors, it may be desirable to organize, separately from the consultation with each of the national parliaments, a series of consultation groups, each with a diverse, tripartite composition (European and national officials, representatives from diverse business sectors and from NGOs, and academics). In this way one can avoid the danger of ideological guerrilla warfare.

4.5   Consensual Decision Making

Given the required preparatory efforts described earlier to make collaborative governance an effective method, one should assume that the goal, the Common Good or a specific aspect of it, to be pursued are shared by all participants in the process. Cooperation between the actors in the process will hardly be possible if they do not at least have a shared objective, even if they may differ on the ways to achieve it. Therefore, it is so important that the culture of the leader of the consultation process, the Commission, is that of a true and fair "director of the orchestra" (Blauberger and Rittberger 2014).

At this final stage, achieving public value of the final outcome is important. There are a number of prerequisites. Its search in economic matters is more comprehensive, hence more complex, than merely seeking to soften the dominant shareholder approach, as the concept of corporate social responsibility does. One cannot first make money knowingly with ecological destruction and then spend some of that money to set up an animal reserve, or destroying the social harmony and beauty of a city, and then pay for an art museum or a school for deprived children. Public value of some product, service, rule, or any activity requires inputs from a wide range of stakeholders and an open-minded, relational approach by each of them to seek if and how it supports the Common Good in the context of the shifts analyzed by foresight studies. It is a fundamental departure from the traditional top-down approach of governance and in practice demands permanent learning and adaptation, which makes it well suited to the future networked economy and society. It requires equal changes in company strategy and management, or indeed with other actors. A learning collaborative system is one in which cognition is distributed among its participants and used for individual outcomes that together serve the Common Good.

Consensual decision making will also be easier if one tries to focus on sharing opportunities rather than on sharing burdens. This can be facilitated by putting the emphasis on starting innovation cycles based on a new logic adapted to the postindustrial age and the ecological and social challenges resulting from the industrial and the new one. Therefore, a new logic must be based on developing a more resilient economy and society and the tool to achieve this is the so-called circular, or resource-efficient, economy.

Nowadays, the inclusion of the concept of resilience in a public value analysis cannot be overlooked because of its importance to stability or to nondisruptive evolution in complex systems and to ensuring a competitive but resource-efficient economy, inevitably requiring a lot of diversification in methodology by industrial sector. Resilience is the capacity to understand the interacting elements of complex systems and how they self-organize and change over time and can be influenced to maintain a desirable equilibrium (Biggs et al. 2015). Given that the value of strategic planning is quite limited when dealing with complexity, ensuring that a system remains resilient, and thus also adaptable, while avoiding total turbulence, is a major policy goal.

Resilience thinking therefore makes it possible to move away from conservation-based policy, with its narrow focus on regulatory and accessory actions, to ensure that economic-ecological, or social, systems are not disturbed by trying to meet specific, often ad hoc, targets, and which is the source of a large part of the regulatory burden in the EU, of ineffective and costly regulations. This will help to overcome much antagonism in the present system and facilitate consensual outcomes. As discussed earlier, regulation follows a linear and therefore restrictive approach to managing complex systems, often based on a single issue study, lacking interdisciplinary inputs and real world checks. It dominates much of EU thinking on health and the environment, which is based on the Amsterdam Treaty (1999), and on political views and scientific knowledge predating it.

What the EU really needs is a multidisciplinary scientific approach and other governance tools to achieve desired objectives. This can be done through collaborative management between research, industry, and government and by a broad, coherent spectrum of public and private investments in research and innovation. It would help to achieve better regulation and increase sustainability and competitiveness simultaneously and thus build comprehensive public value, not just ecological value. Perhaps it will also help against the technophobia, which seems to hover over the European Parliament, though its origin may lie as much in its populist search for credibility, given the steady decline of voter turnout since the first direct elections in 1979, as in its capability gap to evaluate new science and technology, due to its own rejection of independent impact assessments.

Consensual decision making is not the same as making a patchwork of individual wish lists, designed to protect existing bureaucratic practices, business models, or the market of NGO actions. It requires all stakeholders to first seek to share the foresight analysis, and then the potential scenarios or impact studies of a given policy proposal. This is as much a mental exercise, requiring openness and transparency about views and interests, as one of evaluating facts, bridging information asymmetries, and exploring potential processes to desired outcomes.

The Commission can mentor this, as it has relevant experiences, such as from the so-called European regulatory networks, which allow informal deliberations and a nonhierarchical approach of problem solving. Also the Open Method of Coordination could provide lessons, despite its relative failure to deliver because of some original design errors. Orchestration is not the same as delegation, or even less a superior–subordinate relationship. It of course requires a culture of seeking a joint objective, creating mutual dependence and interest; if that basic element is missing, perhaps because of a failure of gradual alignment, then one is back to traditional rule making with all its weaknesses and failures.

Consensual decision, at the end of the process of collaborative governance, in many cases still needs to take the form of a directive or regulation, though there is now sufficient experience with other forms of stabilizing agreements reached to include them fully in the EU governance toolbox. One can think of self-regulation by certain groups of actors, of peer review mechanisms, incentives of all kind, and other methods that help to steer individual and collective behavior in a desired direction.

5   Conclusion

The first president of the European Council offered a deep insight in the nature of the European Union by making a distinction between Europe as a space and as a home.[8] Spaces need order, often spontaneously or deliberatively agreed, mostly cultural determined as in families. Order in public spaces is the prime role of any form of governance (Fukuyama 2011). As mentioned before, otherwise there is no social life possible, and without it individuals do not survive at all or barely. The nature of governance determines how much people can feel at home in a space and can pursue their happiness there. Refugees understand this distinction very well.

The local, European, global market is a space where citizens produce the goods and services that they (presume to) need for their survival and material welfare, which allows the development of their personalities and co-influences their happiness. Markets need rules for access, such as product standards and other criteria and rules of operation, such as antitrust rules and others. But a legal-economic structure becomes only a social home when other criteria, often intangible ones, are fulfilled.

In a historic perspective the EC/EU has done very well. But its very successes require continuous innovation of its governance system, culture, and methods; otherwise, the spatial or the homely dimension suffers, and when the feeling of belonging declines, spaces lose their support. This is what has happened in Europe because of the pursuit of a single interpretation (centralizing federalism) of a single legalistic model (supra-nationalism) for Europe. Multiple objectives require multiple forms of public governance; their management needs to be varied depending on inherent policy characteristics and desired outcomes. As a multilayered

---

[8] H. Count Van Rompuy, president of the European Council, on receiving the Charlemagne Prize in Aachen, May 29, 2014.

governance system, the EU has often been pragmatic and experimented with other forms of cooperation, but they never received proper, equal importance.

The present age demands innovation to ensure the unique European, humanistic model, but economic paradigmatic innovation has always gone hand in hand with equally significant governance innovation; each facilitates the other and contributes to the Common Good, providing the framework for the individual pursuit of happiness.

Acknowledgments The author expresses his gratitude to Tristan du Puy and Léonard Tapié for their contributions.

References

Acemogly, D., and J. Robinson. 2012. *Why nations fail: The origin of power, prosperity and poverty*. New York: Crown Publishing Group.

Ansell, C., and A. Gash. 2008. Collaborative governance in theory and practice. *Journal of Public Administration Research and Theory* 18: 543–571.

Biggs, R., M. Schlüter, and M.L. Schoon. 2015. *Principles for building resilience*. Cambridge: Cambridge University Press.

Blauberger, M., and B. Rittberger. 2014. Conceptualising and theorizing EU regulatory networks, Jerusalem Papers in Regulation & Governance, No. 65.

Buehler, I., and J. Dorn. 2013. *Government Foresight in Deutschland, Ansätze, Herausforderungen und Chancen*. Berlin: Stiftung Neue Verantwortung.

Busuioc, E.M. 2013. *Myths of accountability and European agencies*. London: Oxford University Press.

Diebold, W. 1959. *The Schuman plan, a study in economic cooperation*. New York: Praeger.

Doz, Y., and M. Kosonen. 2014. *Governments for the future: Building the strategic and agile state*. Helsinki: SITRA Studies.

European Parliament. 1979. The legal basis for direct election is provided in the Art 223, ex article 190(4) and (5) TEC, TFUE.

Ferrera, M. 2009. National welfare states and European integration: In search of a virtuous nesting (The JCMS annual lecture). *Journal of Common Market Studies* 47(2): 219–233.

Fouchet Plans. 1961 November 2. Draft Treaty on European Political Union

Fuchs, R. 2013. *Intelligent growth—The Green revolution*. Munich: Hanser Verlag.

Fukuyama, F. 2011. *The origins of political order*. New York: Farrar Straus & Giroux.

Gomez, P., and T. Meynhardt. 2014. The public value scorecard: What makes an organisation valuable to society. Performance 6, nr 1.

Gretschmann, K. 2001. Politikgestaltung im Spannungsfeld von Nationaalstaat und Europäische Union, Aus Politik und Zeitgeschichte.

———. 2013. Joint action versus free ride: EU financial crisis management based on a common good? In *Is there a European common good*, eds. S. Puntscher Riekmann, A. Somek, and D. Wydra. Baden-Baden: Nomos Publishers.

Héraud, G. 1961. L'inter-étatique, le supranational et le fédéral. Archives du Philosopie du Droit, 6: 179–191.

Hix, S. 2008. *What's wrong with the European Union and how to fix it*. Cambridge: Polity Press.

Kakabadse, A., N. Kakabadse, and R. Knyght. 2010. The chemistry factor in the Chairman/CEO relationship. *European Management Journal* 28: 285–296.

Karpowitz, C., and J. Mansbridge. 2005. Disagreement and consensus: The need for dynamic updating in public deliberation. *Journal of Public Deliberation* 1(1).

Karvalics, L. 2012. *Transcending knowledge management, shaping knowledge governance*. Hungary: University of Szeged.

Kjaer, P. 2010. Constitutionalizing governing and governance in Europe. In *Rule of law and democracy: Inquiries into internal and external issues*, eds. L. Morlino, and G. Palombella. The Netherlands: Brill.

Kramer, M., and M. Porter. 2011. *How to reinvent capitalism and unleash a wave of innovation and growth*. Watertown, MA: Harvard Business Review.

Maucher, S. 2011. Schattenseiten der Transparenz, Wittenberg Zentrum für Globale Ethik. Discussion paper.

O'Flynn, J. 2007. From public management to public value; paradigmatic change and managerial implications. *Australian Journal of Public Administration* 66(3): 353–366.

Poul, K.F. 2010. The metamorphosis of the functional synthesis: A continental European perspective on governance, law and the political in the transnational space. *Wisconsin Law Review* 2010(2): 489.

Priestley, J. 2008. *Six battles that shaped Europe's Parliament*. London: John Harper Publishing.

Rawls, J. 1972. *A theory of justice*. Cambridge: Harvard University Press.

Rifkin, J. 2004. *The European dream*. New York: Jeremy P. Tarcher Inc.

Sabel, C., and J. Zeitlin. 2010. *Experimentalist governance in the European Union*. London: Oxford University Press.

Sandel, M. 1982. *Liberalism and the limits of justice*. Cambridge: Harvard University Press.

Schepers, S. 2006. The convergence of European, national and regional interests and the establishment of EIPA. In EIPA Scope, 25th Anniversary issue.

———. 2010. Business-government relations beyond lobbying. *Journal for Corporate Governance* 10(4).

———. 2014. New governance for new challenges in the EU. In *Rethinking the future of Europe*, eds. S. Schepers, and A. Kakabadse. New York: Palgrave Macmillan.

Schudson, M. 2002. The News media as political institutions. *Annual Review of Political Science* 5: 249–269.

Servan-Schreiber, J.-J. 1967. *Le défi Américain*. France: Denoël.

Siedentopf, H., and J. Ziller, eds. 1988. *L'Europe des Administrations*. Bruxelles: Bruylant and European Institute of Public Administration.

The Davignon Report. 1970, October 27. Report on the problems of political unification, Luxembourg.

The Future of the European Union, Laeken Declaration, Laeken (Belgium). 2001, December 15.

Thoenig, J.-C., and C. Waldman. 2007. *Marking enterprises, business success and societal embedding*. New York: Palgrave MacMillan.

Treaty of Rome. 1957. Treaty establishing the European Economic Community and Related Instruments (EEC Treaty).

Treaty of Amsterdam amending the Treaty on European Union. 1997. The Treaties establishing the European Communities and certain related acts.

Treaty of Lisbon amending the Treaty on European Union and the Treaty establishing the European Community, signed at Lisbon. 2007, December 13.

Von Hayek, F. 1967. *Theory of complex phenomena*. London: Routledge & Kegan Paul.

Zadek, S. 2007. *The civil corporation*. London: Earthscan Routledge.

Zielonka, J. 2014. *Is the EU doomed?* Cambridge, UK: Cambridge Polity.

8

Governance of the Alignment as a Basis for Renewing Innovation Policy

Andrew Kakabadsea and Nada Korac-Kakabadse

The recommendations of the HLG on Innovation Policy Management (HLG Secretariat 2013) assert that a radical new approach to innovation policy is needed. This vision, based on an innovation ecosystem (ideas, institutions, policies, regulation) can only be achieved through all-encompassing, collaborative governance that is interactive and value generating. This chapter pinpoints the crucial role of institutional arrangements

A. Kakabadse (✉)
Professor of Policy, Governance and Ethics Room 500,
Engine House Greenlands Campus Henley Business School,
UoR Henley on Thames Oxfordshire, RG9 3AU, UK
e-mail: andrew.kakabadse@henley.ak.uk

N. Korac-Kakabadse (✉)
Lecturer in Governance, Policy and Leadership Room 500,
Engine House Greenlands Campus Henley Business School,
UoR Henley on Thames Oxfordshire, RG9 3AU, UK
e-mail: nada.kakabadse@henley.ak.uk

© The Editor(s) (if applicable) and The Author(s) 2016   **193**
K. Gretschmann, S. Schepers (eds.), *Revolutionising EU Innovation Policy*,
DOI 10.1057/978-1-137-55554-0_8

as the driving force for achieving such radical change. Redesign for collaborative governance needs regional political cohesion, dynamic interactions, and cooperative, broader stakeholder engagements.

1   Introduction

The Innovation Union Scoreboard (IUS) and INNO policy Trendchart have charted innovation performance of member states within the European Union (EU). The IUS measures innovation across 25 indicators as enablers, firm activities, and outputs. Trendchart[1] (2013) captures the growth in EU-level funding (Fig. 8.1), along with more than 2,000 policy measures[2] that have been launched at the national

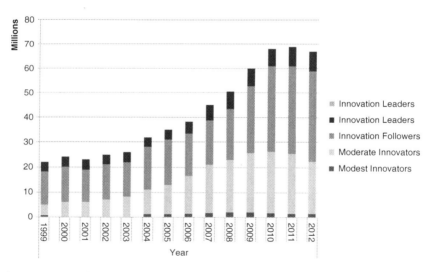

Fig. 8.1   Growth in EU research and innovation funding (1999–2012)
Source: Adapted from Izsak et al. (2013)

[1] http://ec.europa.eu/DocsRoom/documents/5220/attachments/1/translations/en/renditions/native

[2] Measure that mobilizes resources (financial, organizational, or human) through publically funded research and innovation.

level. Innovation league table leaders are Denmark, Finland, Germany, and Sweden. The combined motivations underpinning such initiatives, programs and their instruments,[3] asserts innovation is the supranational competitive driver, and its renewal is to address the many "grand societal challenges" ahead, such as climate change, energy, health, and agro-food (Geels 2014). Thus, policy makers and firms must radically reorient their alignments for this new wave of innovation. The problems are as follows: (1) the existing innovation frameworks are more often industry or firm-centric; (2) measurement data capture is designed to be narrow, where it differentiates the richer from poorer states (modest countries may not have sufficient infrastructures to get the data or it may be very expensive); and (3) governmental institutions seem not to be well suited in their current form, unless it is in their interests to really facilitate or solve the societal/ social challenges. Further, the isolated transactional interest-based decision-making process is impacted mostly, but pays little attention to civil society and real public opinions.

In the post-World War II era (1945–1973), European social and economic institutional arrangements (DiMaggio and Powell 1983) had helped triple the average citizen's buying power and reduced typical working hours by one-third (Eichengreen 2008). In the latter part of the twentieth century, intentional design by the group of elitist oligopolistic governments was for greater collaboration between member states. Governance design, such as the Single European Act (SEA) that came into force in 1987, was the basis for building the single market. The Delors report (1989) set out three stages of monetary and economic union whereby in 1999 the single currency, the Euro, was introduced, along with a single monetary policy under the authority of European Central Bank (ECB). The regulatory golden age (Levi-Faur 2011, p. 814) had cut down the barriers between member states, opened up the common market, and allowed for the free movement of goods, capital, services, and people.

Innovation transited into technological cooperations (scientific, research, knowledge) focusing supranational (EU)—government (national)—business (corporate) tripart relations on industry-science

---

[3] Europe 2020; EC 2013, 2015).

linkages for dominant benefit. Then new diverse partnerships, that were encouraged through policy mechanisms, fostered public–private partnerships as knowledge transfers, advisory services, joint ventures, spin-offs, and innovation networks. But again, governance design selective processes ensured lucrative contracts went to the preferred few, in an otherwise supposedly merit based system. Thus the typical linear vertical systems (research, invention, innovation, diffusion) served industry and industrial developments' leading firms. Consequently, governance policy pathways have supported more incremental innovation streams, through the technoscientific programs' (3–7 years) renewable funding. In essence, the institutional process has benefited and given preference to narrower stable known relationships within life cycles. Critical to institutional arrangement have been the few, increasingly specialized and experienced growing private corporate sector organizations as the value creators.

At EU level, evidence-led learning from institutional innovation governance of the last 10 years (Fig. 8.1 above) highlights that regional innovation policy implementation has supported to a greater extent the more technologically advanced countries, which in turn have dominated economically. The same member states consistently lead the league tables. A widening governance/ innovation gap has extended between the different member states (followers/ modest innovators—see Table 8.1 below). Further, each member state owns national innovation approaches and has been and is influenced by the protectionist supranational-level competitive processes and their effects, that is, EU-level grants and funding procedures, an ever growing range of rational measurements, sociopolitics,

Table 8.1   Policy governance framework

Level	Policy process	Structure/system
Supranational		Decentralization
	Implementation ↑↓	
National		Cooperation
	Integration ↑↓	
Regional[a]		Diversity and autonomy
	Formulation ↑↓	
Local		Engagement
	Idea generation ↑↓	

Source: Designed by authors
[a]This region is within the Nation

sophisticated selection criteria, lobbying for access, and special interest groups, etc., causing invisible limitations as formal (constitution, laws, regulations, rights) and informal (customs, traditions, cultures, networks) constraints. Thus, governance impact has emerged as complex and over-stringent, not effectively addressing each country's specific conditions and requirements, as part of an EU coherent policy design and its regulatory methods of cooperation between member states. Public society participation remains missing in what should be a tetra-relationship of inclusive public governance. Policy social impacts reflect differences as salaries, living standards, skills development, growth, job opportunities, and health risks, where exploitation and diversity serves elitist agendas. Consequently, this leads to further mistrust and disunity with a supra-national body that is then perceived unfavorably by the less affluent and greater controlled member states.

The impact of the financial crisis (2007–2008) in Europe exposed differences to such an extent where certain national governance systems failed and resilience risks at the supranational and national levels emerged. The rhetoric of the Lisbon Strategy goal (2000; 2010) "to make the EU the most dynamic and competitive knowledge-based economy in the world, capable of sustainable economic growth with more and better jobs and greater social cohesion" was not achieved. The great transformation in Europe's economy and societies triggered by technology developments has instead been accompanied by a stagnation in public governance systems. This has led, together with insufficient evidence-based policy making, to declining effectiveness of public policy (Gieve and Provost 2012), accompanied by a growing political protectionism and regulatory burden, resulting in negative effects on competitiveness, social equality, and sustainability. European governance today is in urgent need of change, as the embedded nature of current governance "regimes" is serving the old "divide and rule" mentality, with a reluctance to change, as it is working well for certain interest groups.

The EU governance system and structures are professionally formalized (constitution, treaties), but in practice the supranational and national interests remain conflicted. There are growing challenges to alignment. The Europe 2020 Horizon work program rhetoric, offering €80 billion in funding for projects, reflects many of the problems that divide Europe today. But, if the intention is to equally balance Europe's 28 member nations, how long and expensive was the German reunification process alone? What happened to Yugoslavia in 1991? What is happening in Greece in 2015? The rise and fall, as integration of older and newer member states, exemplified by the Ukraine, is at a critical juncture, as the existing regulative, normative, and cognitive pillars of institution (Scott 2001) that historically served economic and technological competitiveness must now serve wider social challenges. But your neighbor's problem is these days your problem, too! The underlying pattern suggests that within supranational institutions, there is a struggle between two opposing worldviews (the US transactional debt-based mode and the European social model). What is Europe's own philosophical value? How does it understand Solidarity? And where is its foreign policy?

2   Contrasting Philosophical Foundations of European Governance

Modern-day Western institutional and corporate governance systems have emerged from the Roman Empire (27 BC–AD 476) and the Christian crusades. Pope Innocent IV (1252) charged the institutions of the day, that is, townships, universities, guilds, and liveries, with the dual responsibilities of wealth creation and equitable redistribution. The religiously informed "social" model of institutional governance dominated in Europe for approximately 250 years.

Theologically parting, Henry VIII's adoption of the Protestant Reformation (1529–1537) gave him increased monarchist rights. English royalty was in desperate need of funds and the Royal Charter was used to attract wealth creators. For a fee, the monarch gave privileged and exclusive right to trade and undertake business activities in a particular locality or sector. Depending on the success of the venture, the monarch then shared the profit with the individual/ institutional holder of the Royal Charter. Thus was introduced the counter-model of corporate governance, that of *shareholder* privilege or value.

The more mature and ethically informed "social" shareholder model and the English royalty shareholder model of corporate governance sat side by side in Europe until the rise of America as a global power.

In America during the 1910/1920s, a transition of dominant wealth creators from being managers to investors occurred. The question arose: how can the funds of the shareholder could be protected from "unscrupulous" managers? On the basis of a deficiency of trust, in contrast to the European social model, Harvard Business School experimented with the drafting of protocols and regulations that channeled managers' activities to invest shareholder funds in an honest, transparent, and appropriate way. In the drafting of these protocols, Harvard Law School challenged Harvard Business School by stating that the monitoring of the enterprise was insufficient to both protect and effectively capitalize shareholder funds. Without an understanding of context (internal and external to the organization) managers would pursue whatever goals they had in mind. What was required was effective mentoring of management by the board, bearing in mind the challenges faced in that context.

Thus emerges the longstanding debate on how the twin and contrasting functions of governance: monitoring and mentoring could be aligned (Berle and Means 1932; Jensen and Meckling 1976; Fama and Jensen 1983; Donaldson and Davis 1991). The perspective of Harvard Business School took precedence; board attention was and has become more preoccupied with the monitoring of procedures.

The institutional response to the financial crisis (2007–2008) was regulatory and procedural intervention. However, monitoring without mentoring reflects inefficient governance. A culture of monitoring alone leads to mistrust and constant interrogation, the cause of dysfunctionality. There is in practice, a continuous sharing of control and trust between owners and managers— it is a matter of adapting the inter- "monitoring-mentoring" relationship to align with the context, and of owner-manager appetites to be engaged for risk taking. In the case of the EU, member state relations, power agendas, political views, and reelection motivations often feature in policy formulation (Khan and Kakabadse 2014). Over the years there has been a considerable growth in lobbying practices within Europe, where lobbying itself has limited regulation. Further, these days the role of media and social media have become a platform and mechanism for shaping the agenda. Media ownership remains largely in the control of a few people; it is easier to direct editors and their journalists' biases to reflect the power play between groups. It seems odd that the current Syrian refugee crisis is a headline, yet what is actually happening in Syria remains less reported. Thus, the public engage social media and mobile communications more and more to raise awareness and truth of the issues, but these interactions are also increasingly being closely monitored.

There will always be different national governance systems within a supranational region. State systems themselves may change direction with each newly elected government. The cohesion challenge is for collaboration to offer a set of structural and systemic mechanisms that are overarching and, at the same time, flexible, enabling adoption by different national frameworks (state/ liberal/ coordinated) and collective markets successfully. Concurrently, politicians and leaders of Europe face the bigger challenge of establishing and practicing governance values that truly reflect the "European Ideal" that they actually are striving for. The unwelcome reality is that Europe has been designed to be as it is at present, and the challenge is for those in a position to do so, to radically alter the nature of collaborations—as this is leads toward a self-destructive European trajectory. Majone (1997) explained many years ago that global competitiveness is where innovation rewards regulatory institutions that are depending on their strategic choices.

3 Value Delivery for Governance

The nature and culture of organization, whether institutional or privately governed, is bound to an understanding of value. This maybe explicit, but more often remains implicit within practices. It can be discretely observed as purpose, motivation, and success. During the 1990s, technology supported internationalization and the focus of organization was on shareholder value, that is, making money. In the early twentieth century, the Harvard school of thought turned the attention toward stakeholders (Freeman 2010), those with direct interests in organization, or in our case institutional, success or failure. Kakabadse's (2015) findings of a 5-year study into stakeholder engagement[4] articulate that sustained success is focused on value delivery. First, there has to be a consensus about value. Second, the focus is on getting a view on engagement and

---

[4] Research carried out across 14 countries, including 80 interviews with private, public, and third sectors.

alignment, that is, the context. Then and only then, strategy (S) can be formulated, which is a good fit to the context (E × A):

Strategy + (Engagement × Alignment) = Value delivery

(Kakabadse 2015, p. 20).

However, the research found that in 82 % of cases, value creation was strategy[5] led by leadership (internal dependency on knowledge/capability/resources/sensemaking), but ignored engagement concerns, derailing the strategy. Actually longer term sustainable success depends on "getting the realities of engagement and realities of structure and systems alignment right, to make things happen now, where strategic thinking shapes the future" (Kakabadse 2015, p. 17). This explanation not only challenges old school leadership strategy-led thinking, advocated by many business schools, but explains leadership's critical role in testing and retesting value propositions to the context.

Holistic appreciation of this simplified formula offers explanation relevant not only to corporate failures, growth of organizations, turnaround strategies of firms to their markets, new market entry, but also in this case institutional governance of the European Union. Where the context has radically changed toward volatility, uncertainty, complexity, and ambiguity (VUCA), EU institutional governance policies and instruments (strategy) for innovation need to be radically restructured to the new context. The question is whether the renewal of governance structures and systems are to be designed for the real "common good" of Europe, or to serve the interests of the same elites of today but in a new context. What is the value proposition? The problem is Europe is entangled in a power struggle between those that want a "common good" and those that want to preserve the status quo arrangement (resistance).

While there is a need to make the distinction between institutional (state/ supranational) and corporate governance, at the same the question arises whether today's state or supranational region is and can be run more and more like a corporate entity? The historic development of and crises within EU governance is subject to similar agency and stewardship concerns. Further, where engagement and alignment are intertwined, the evidence suggests institutional arrangements are actually disengaged and

---

[5] Leadership often create and implement strategy alone, based on their own perceptions.

misaligned. EU current governance innovation systems and people appear to be following the corporate Harvard shareholder approach more, at a time when the context has changed.

Let us consider the issues of present-day corporate entities. Evidence from global studies of over 12,500 organizations across 21 countries and over 5,000 boards across 14 countries (Kakabadse 2015), identifies that dissention and an incapacity to engage are the norm with damaging consequences for the enterprise. It is not uncommon that less than 30 % of employees within an organization are fully engaged and delivering value to the business. This can be perceived in two ways. First, employees are not themselves engaging in the workplace. Second, current corporate culture does not allow diverse opinions and ideas to flourish, restricting only those that fit the profile to fully engage within the organization.

Even within top teams, 34 % find themselves unable to agree on the mission, vision, and strategy and regularly enter into unproductive interactions that lead to a misalignment of thinking and ill usage of resources. This suggests self-interest above common interest. Another issue is that of open and transparent communication, as 65 % of top teams are inhibited to raise the relevant and uncomfortable issues and, through inaction, allow the organization to deteriorate. Corporate crises rarely happen overnight and without prior knowledge. The question here is what is the type and nature of leadership that is resulting in such team dynamics?

In terms of value delivery, perceptions vary within organizations at different levels. Boards are down rated by their management by more than 55 %, and are often considered to be out of touch with the challenges facing the enterprise. In terms of monitoring, 80 % of the boards were found to be out of touch with the reality of the organization. The information flows and communication interactions are partial and incomplete, which affects decision making and motivations. Considering the EU, career politicians interests seem distinct to the rhetoric of the European Ideal (i.e., intelligent manipulation), or it may be that a good personal life overrides the ground realties of ordinary people of Europe.

Ultimately, talking about the truth is pr oblematic (Kakabadse 2015) the higher up the organization you go. Many if not all of these findings are likely to exist within institutional environments.

4 Toward Collaborative Governance

EU governance has and continues to engage both Open Method of Coordination (OMC) and Community Method (CM). OMC (the Amsterdam Treaty, 1997) rests on soft law mechanisms as guidelines. First, the Council of Ministers agree on broad policy goals. Then member states shape their national and regional policies. Next, benchmarks and indicators are agreed for best practice. The criticisms of this approach are that of significant variations in policy interpretation at the different national levels; a regionally slower pace of development where each nation progresses at its own pace; lack of legitimacy if there is limited participation; the fact that it is not legally binding (hard law); risk of redundant policies with little impact; possible conflict with the CM method; and it is experimentalist. However, this approach softly emphasizes intergovernmental cooperation and imposes no sanctions. The more traditional CM method presses supranational powers of the EU bodies (Commission, Parliament, Court of Justice, Council) as the supreme decision-making authority. Its legislative procedure is codecisional between these bodies, but each body's procedural culture, role, breadth, team makeup, and quality of information remains unclear, and their interactions between each other can be a time-consuming; CM seems a priori and unduly influenced by elites. Is there opportunity to improve the pace and dynamic interactions where the different bodies' committees convene at similar times and remain independent to each other, but can also formally interact better and quicker in decision making?

OMC did not include the full four-stage governance architecture defined at Lisbon, but only fragmentary elements such as European Action Plans, objectives, targets, scoreboards, indicators, peer review, or exchange of good practices. From its inception, the OMC was widely hailed as a "third way" for EU governance between regulatory competition and harmonization, capable of opening a sustainable path for the Union between fragmentation and a European Supra-state (Larsson 2002). Many academic and political commentators embraced the OMC as a suitable instrument for identifying and pursuing common European concerns while respecting legitimate national diversity, because it commits member states to work together in reaching shared objectives and performance targets, without seeking to homogenize their inherited policy regimes and institutional arrangements (Hemerijck and Berghman 2004). Many likewise view the OMC as a promising mechanism for promoting experimental learning and deliberative problem solving, because it systematically and continuously obliges member states to pool information, compare themselves to one another, and reassess current policies against their relative performance (Zeitlin 2010; Cohen and Sabel 2003; Telò 2002). But no one questions the justification of so many indices, benchmarks, and measures and what they serve? Are academics and researchers benefitting from or reinventing the wheels for the sake of EU agencies and their research funds?

The criticism of democratic deficit in the EU needs to be far more nuanced. European Council heads of government and Council ministers are all operating under national parliament scrutiny, so if there is a problem it is their presumed lack of oversight. The Commission does not take decisions: it only has a right of initiative. The European Parliament however has a low level of legitimacy with citizens and is captured by consumer and green interest groups, mostly opposing economic reforms and radical innovations (technophobia is widespread). The system is dysfunctional, but for many complex reasons.

Noting that effective governance needs both "monitoring and mentoring," there seems to be an opportunity for these two methods to be combined and integrated (hard and soft) into an optimal single policy developmental framework (Fig. 8.2 below). The focus at higher levels should be on cohesion and clear agenda setting, while the lower levels need broader inclusion and participation within process (Gieve and Provost 2012).

At present, the current EU governance system prioritizes strategy (S). This is internal to political leaderships' own judgments, and even the

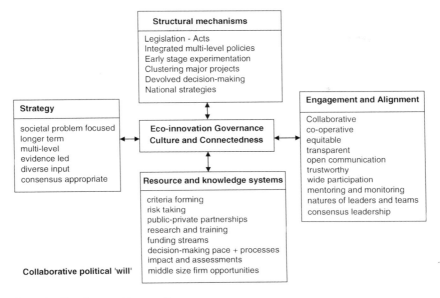

Fig. 8.2 Eco-innovation policy governance

current OMC method has limited stakeholder engagements (experts, regulators, industry leaders, panels, round tables) which emerges top-down. It is clear that top-down-only governance is short-term, high-cost, and politically oriented. More worrisome, it is out of touch with public opinion and is not addressing societal issues.

In contrast, a more integrated collaborative governance (CG) structure and its systems need to give greater priority to not just direct organizational stakeholders, but to a much broader societal participation (policy open forums[6]) and public input at the lower levels. Societal problems exist locally and their ideas as solutions need to emerge widely allowing for bottom-up contributions. The framework must radically change to seek contextual contributions (E × A) where the agenda must be evidence led rather than politically motivated. Donahue (2004) asserts that CG is

---

[6]Tetra relations—inclusive of public opinion.

problem-focused, seeking solution or improvement as opposed to simply being opportunistic. The structure is designed to bring public, private, and societal participation together in collective forums with public agencies to engage in consensus-oriented decision making:

> A governing arrangement where one or more public agencies directly engage non-state stakeholders in a collective decision-making process that is formal, consensus-oriented, and deliberative and that aims to make or implement public policy or manage public programs or assets (Ansell and Gash 2008).

It has developed as an alternative to the adversarial and managerial modes of policy making which promote interest group pluralism and accountability failures (especially as the authority of experts is challenged). Collaboration reflects maturity in governance design where growth of knowledge and institutional capacity become increasingly specialized and distributed. As institutional infrastructures become more complex and interdependent, demand for collaboration increases.

This brings to attention the natures of peoples that shape and lead innovation policy development at different levels. This approach is suited to more "cosmopolitan" mindsets as opposed to current political protectionist agendas that are in play. At the higher levels, politicians may benefit from collaborative training and professional development programs. Collaboration encourages positive challenging and openmindedness as part of consensus-building. Further, inclusive process includes potentially troublesome stakeholders which is important to the legitimization of outcomes. This is different to current approaches that seek to appoint people of likemindedness, and informal networks are used to preserve the status quo.

Although public agencies are typically the initiators or instigators of collaborative governance, there is need for active participation by non-state stakeholders. This includes citizens as individuals and as representing variety of organized groups. Currently, EU engagement below the national level, at the regional and local levels, is very low. Thus, there is opportunity for the framework to adopt a more locally visible presence and interaction in policy development.

Critical to collaboration is the flow and openness of communication. At each level, there is opportunity for dialogue as opposed to discussion and for forums to influence above and below levels. Meeting approaches should be deliberative and multilateral with all participants directly engaged in decision making. Collaboration is distinct to consultative engagements as participants need to take and have direct interest in the outcomes and impacts; it is about having collective joint responsibilities.

5   Institutional Resilience

An exemplification case, the latest crisis unfolding in European governance can be seen in the divergent and uncollaborative responses of member states to the Syrian refugee situation that has evolved during the last 3 years. Never mind that the phenomena is not new: the Huguenots (1685); The French Revolution (1789); The Russian Revolution (1917–1921); the Jewish escape from Germany (1939); 7 million people have been forcibly moved (4.5 million IDPs; 2.5 million refugees). Act 1A of 1951 Convention provided the first universal definition of a refugee regime where current embodiment is in post-Cold War UNHCR definition (Barnett 2002). There are 2.3 million refugees in bordering countries of Syria, yet within the Europe Union, consensus has not been reached on how to deal with this humanitarian issue. Further still, what happens to those born or dying during the journey?

Hendrick and Struggles (2015) research on Europe has coined the phrase "dynamic-governance" as what is required know. Governance is a means of driving and enabling institutional performance. Dynamic governance has to respond quickly and adapt to the ever changing context. Resilience demands proactive action rather than characteristically being defensive and bureaucratic. The pace of response depends on a cohesive leadership and the ability to engage and align the appropriate knowledge and resources, finances, human skills, and technologies. Bartlett and Ghosall (1989) posit that in nonhierarchical structures, the networking and culture of organization, become critical to success. More recently, Koza et al. (2011) Global Multi Business Firm (GMBF) model refers to "strategic assembly/ disassembly" as constructing organization in a calculated, forward-looking manner with the intention of competitive advantage under dynamic environments. This requires complex competency and capability (Klijn 2008) in acquisition and deployment.

Thus, the focus is on varied flexible assets; exploiting characteristic differences of location and societies; having access to high-value resources, but not necessarily ownership of them; and adopting a wide global perspective on strategy and innovation. In these types of structures, skills and teamwork become critical for fast-paced decision making. Teams are brought together for specific projects based upon the context. As such, disassembly at the end of a project enables resources to be deployed elsewhere.

This institutional arrangement maybe suited to the European Union, which consists of 28 member states with different political approaches and structures, wide geographical locations, and diverse customs and societal cultures, within which are unique institutional arrangements. Thus governance for innovation has to be robust and resilient to be sustainable for the longer term. Leadership needs to have better understanding of structure and system complexities as social, cultural, economic, and political impacts of ecological interactions and feedback in the application of EU policy making and functioning.

Primarily, policy makers have a role in building resilient systems. Resilience theory assumes highly complex interactions between subsystems in the economy and the ecology and it suggests that it is difficult to make policy as a deliberate intervention that produces anticipated results. Rather policy should be seen as an experiment and a continuous collaborative effort between key stakeholders (governments, corporations, academia, public) and as an effort to structure social institutions (from the legal system to the market) in order to encourage the emergence of innovation. Policy can also help to build cultures of continuous innovation that can also strengthen social systems and build general resilience. Conversely, the risk is from overcomplexity, overregulation, and inadequate performance appraisals that all may require leadership to simplify and clarify the issue and address the issue as less complicated.

6   Eco-innovation Governance Model

Policy makers alone cannot change the market. This occurs through a combination of regulatory and market forces working together toward goals. There have been a number of examples where policies have had an impact: zero-emission cars, carbon taxing, renewable energy projects, and health and safety. The problem for the EU is to bring all the different elements of "policy idea generation" to "policy implementation" (Table 8.1) into an all-encompassing framework that has flexibility in meeting the needs of different member states. Figure 8.2 above captures the different mechanisms and systems that need to work together. Each element can be tailored to suit member state circumstances. These are supported by getting the $S + (E \times A)$ right for the eco-innovation agenda.

In Fig. 8.2, the culture and connectedness is what binds the success of policy outcomes. How the "success formula" is used at different levels can vary. Thus each item in Fig. 8.2 can be stringently or partially applied, but must feed back into the adjoining levels. This framework is flexible, but dependent on support at the top from an all-encompassing, value-driven collaborative leadership and engagement. Thus, at the heart of the current dilemma in Europe is whether the collaborative political will establish clear independent regional identity—distinct to external political wills.

7   Conclusion

The upcoming fourth industrial revolution, Industry 4.0, will indeed bring about highly digitalized and connected industrial processes and renewed global corporate firm structures. Collaborative advantages will shape the industrial, energy, digital, biological, telecommunication, transportation, and robotic infrastructures in novel combinations. Tomorrow's academics and researchers will claim and counterclaim theories and their hypotheses to the new structures and systems. In keeping with this, institutional governance of the EU and its member nations has to radically change to remain useful and relevant. National governments have weakened and the EU is the only region to face major unique challenges to its core existence. Without integral collaborative coherence, it will collapse and fail.

The simple truth is there are only two possible future states of Europe: (1) continue to serve interests of elitist agendas, which was originally not the case as exemplified by the welfare growth from around 1950 to

2007, and (2) genuinely appeal to the European Common Good. For the last 60 years the first item outlined above has prevailed, behind a façade of false promises and hopes for public appeasement (the second truth). Actually, history informs us that true radical shifts have only come about as revolutions, wars, natural disasters, and economic crises, that is, major shocks to the system, where victors and survivors explain one-sided versions of events as gospel. If the transactional and damaging nature of European politics practiced by the elites to serve their purposes continues against the European Common Good, it will rely on more shocks.

If research were undertaken to explore "the will to practice collaborative governance," what would be discovered? Would the findings among those in power, that is, the "political class," reflect findings from "electoral voters" of European democracy or autocracy? Because for collaborative governance to work, it is important to establish what genuinely exists today. Would European elites be willing to open up to this truth?

Either Europe should genuinely make a tectonic shift toward the European Common Good, or it should accept that it is a weakly governed football to be kicked around. Sometimes, academics and politicians can over-engineer the problem. To our minds, governance structures and systems for innovation policy are simply frameworks. Any framework can work, given the chance. Ultimately, governance is a people issue. Where there are people, it comes down to ethics. The radical change needed is toward ethical collaboration. The social model needs to rebuild trust and bridge mentoring-monitoring fractures for alignment. The dominant shareholder value model monitoring (Business) is missing "mentoring" (coaching, guidance, face-to-face interactions, ethics).

Europe's social model of putting people first has always been there. Only it has not been principally enforced and therefore has been subject to external influences as the causes of many of the problems Europe faces.

Overlooking governance organization always comes at a high price: deteriorating framework conditions for competitiveness and weakening social fabric. How will the EU governance framework function in a digitalized, global economy driven by an interacting range of new scientific developments and their opportunities and risks, and in the more slowly evolving, culturally different, and internally fragmented societies of Europe? Without deep thinking and experimenting, European and national governance systems are drifting further apart, with serious ecological fallout for business. We are already in the age of human micro-chipping and cashless economics, thus the textbooks or online resources are being rewritten.

The ongoing economic and monetary crisis and refugee crisis are the precursor signals of a failing misaligned governance model inherited from the previous century—the industrial age—that no longer suffices. The European system needs to move away from linear models focused on regulation and control to (try to) achieve desirable social and economic outcomes, an aim toward more collaborative government models involving relevant stakeholders and based on foresight and impact assessment toward a future state. It is essential to align the wider stakeholder views and interests and engage public input in process. Cocreation of desirable economic and social outcomes in the digital economy invites cogovernment alignment, leaving behind old hierarchical mindsets and operations.

In Europe, this requires innovation and completing the EU supranational methodology, which has proven its use for other purposes, but not for innovation and competitiveness in a science- and technology-driven global economy and not for dealing with the emerging new cultural and social paradigms. The EU is often unpopular because it tries to do the right things in the wrong ways, an indication of the current systemic problem.

In conclusion, radical innovation to the EU's governance system has been discussed as the most promising way forward for policy innovation: collaborative governance. It was argued that through direct and formal engagement of nonstate actors in political decision making, the EU would considerably increase its democratic legitimacy and transparency. Jointly sharing not only information, know-how, and experience, but also ownership and responsibility for processes, concrete policy outcomes, and the management of risk would prove enormously valuable to relaxation the EU's current regulatory stringency and make it more flexible, agile, and resilient to manage the transition to societal grand challenges. By relieving the pressure on public agencies, Europe's risk aversion could be mitigated for the sake of providing innovation the necessary space to unfold, which at the end of the day would increase Europe's global competitiveness and actually help realize the ambitious goals of the Lisbon and Europe 2020 agendas.

References

Ansell, C., and A. Gash. 2008. Collaborative governance in theory and practice. *Journal of Public Administration Research and Theory* 18(4): 543–571.

Barnett, L. 2002. Global governance and the evolution of the international refugee regime. *International Journal of Refugee Law* 14: 238.

Bartlett, C.A., and S. Ghoshal. 1989. *Managing across borders: The transnational solution*. Boston: Harvard Business School Press.

Berle, A., and G. Means. 1932. *The modern corporation and private property*. New York: Macmillan.

Cohen, J., and C.F. Sabel. 2003. Sovereignty and solidarity: EU and US. In *Governing work and welfare in a new economy: European and American experiments*, eds. J. Zeitlin, and D.M. Trubek, 691–750. Oxford: Oxford University Press.

DiMaggio, J., and W. Powell. 1983. The iron cage revisited: Institutional isomorphism and collective rationality in organizational fields. *American Sociological Review* 48: 147–160.

Donahue, J. 2004. On collaborative governance. Corporate social responsibility initiative. Working paper no. 2, John F Kennedy School of Government Harvard University, Cambridge. http://www.ksg.harvard.edu/mrcbg/CSRI/publications/workingpaper_2_donahue.pdf. Accessed 22 Sep 2015.

Donaldson, L., and J.H. Davis. 1991. Stewardship theory or agency theory: CEO governance and shareholder returns. *Australian Journal of Management* 16: 49–65.

Eichengreen, B. 2008. *The European economy since 1945: Co-ordinated capitalism and beyond*. Oxford: Princeton University Press.

European Commission. 2013. Horizon 2020. http://ec.europa.eu/programmes/horizon2020/en/what-horizon-2020. Accessed 21 Sep 2015.

Euopean Commission. 2015. Innovation Union Scoreboard report. 14th Edition. http://ec.europa.eu/growth/industry/innovation/facts-figures/scoreboards/files/ius-2015_en.pdf. Accessed 21 Sep 2015.

Fama, E.F., and M.C. Jensen. 1983. Separation of ownership and control. *Journal of Law and Economics* 26: 301–325.

Freeman, R.E. 2010. *Strategic management: A stakeholder approach*. New York: Cambridge University Press.

Geels, F.W. 2014. Reconceptualising the co-evolution of firms-in-industries and their environments: Developing an inter-disciplinary triple embeddedness framework. *Research Policy* 43(2): 261–277.

Gieve, J., and C. Provost. 2012. Ideas and coordination in policymaking: The financial crisis of 2007–2009. *Governance. An International Journal of Policy, AdministrationandInstitution*25(1):61–77.doi:10.1111/j.1468-0491.2011.01558.

Hemerijck, A., and J. Berghman. 2004. The European social patrimony: Deepening social europe through legitimate diversity. In *Connecting welfare diversity within the European social model*, eds. T. Sakellaropoulos, and J. Berghman, 9–54. Antwerp: Intersentia.

Hendrick and Struggles. 2015. research in A. Kakakbadse (2015) The success formula: How smart leaders deliver outstanding value. London: Bloomsbury.

Izsak, K., P. Markianidouu, and S. Radosavic. 2013. Lessons from a decade of innovation policy what can be learnt from the INNO policy. TrendChart and The Innovation Union Scoreboard. file:///C:/Users/User/Downloads/ReportLessons%20from%20Decade%20of%20Innovation%20Policy-June%202013.pdf. Accessed 21 Sep 2015.

Jensen, M.C., and W.H. Meckling. 1976. Theory of the firm: Managerial behavior, agency costs, and ownership structure. *Journal of Financial Economics* 3: 305–360.

Kakakbadse, A. 2015. *The success formula: How smart leaders deliver outstanding value*. London: Bloomsbury.

Khan, N., and N.K. Kakabadse. 2014. Shaping the European mindset: A governance design and policy innovation agenda. Chapter 3. In *Rethinking the future of Europe, A challenge of governance*, eds. S. Schepers, and A. Kakabadse, 42–76. Basingstoke: Palgrave Macmillan.

Klijn, E.-H. 2008. Complexity theory and public administration: What's new? *Public Management Review* 10(3): 299–317.

Koza, M.P., S. Tallman, and A. Ataay. 2011. The strategic assembly of global firms: A microstructural analysis of local learning and global adaptation. *Global Strategy Journal* 1(1–2): 27–46.

Larsson, A. 2002. The new open method of co-ordination: A sustainable way between a fragmented europe and a European Supra State? Lecture presented to the Uppsala University, 4 March.

Levi-Faur, D. 2011. Regulatory networks and regulatory agentification: Towards a single European regulatory space. *Journal of European Public Policy* 18(6): 810–829.

Majone, G. 1997. From the positive to the regulatory state: causes and consequences of changes in the mode of governance. *Journal for Public Policy* 17(2): 139–167.

Sabel, C., and J. Zeitlin. 2010. *Experimentalist governance in the European Union*. Oxford: Oxford University Press.

Scott, W.R. 2001. *Institutions and organizations*, 2nd edn. Thousand Oaks, CA: Sage Publications.

Telo, M. 2002. Governance and Government in the European Union: The open method of co-ordination. In *The new knowledge economy in Europe: A strategy for international competitiveness and social cohesion*, ed. M.J. Rodrigues, 242–272. Cheltenham: Edward Elgar.

Zeitlin, J. (2010) Towards a stronger OMC in a more social Europe 2020: A new governance architecture for EU policy co-ordination. Chapter 11, pg253-272 in (Eds) Marlier, E and Natali, D with Van Dam, R., Europe 2020 - Towards a More Social EU? Peter Land, Brussels. Available at https://books.google.co.uk/books?hl=en&lr=&id=YipIKAwcSeYC&oi=fnd&pg=PA253&dq=zeitlin+eu&ots=UK30HEOlU5&sig=367Q3iHG9od4pt-LviAJuesNcYE#v=onepage&q=zeitlin%20eu&f=false.242–272.

9

Toward True Regulatory Reform: How to Make EU Governance Innovation Fit

Christoph J. Bausch

1 Introduction

The European Union is a complex adaptive system constituted by a myriad of different actors with often discordant political agendas and interests. The central aim of EU governance therefore is to reconcile and align this divergence and translate it into compromise solutions that serve the common European good.

Since the European Commission's 1985 White Paper and Single European Act (SEA), regulation has been the EU's most notorious tool to this end. It helped cutting down trade barriers, creating a common market and allowing for the free movement of people, goods, capital, and services. Given its great success in so doing, it soon advanced to become the EU's primary governance choice in promoting and managing the European integration process all across an ever-growing number of policy areas.

C.J. Bausch (✉)
Senior Consultant EPPA / Project Director High Level Group
on Innovation Policy Management, Brussels
e-mail: christoph.bausch@eppa.com

© The Editor(s) (if applicable) and The Author(s) 2016
K. Gretschmann, S. Schepers (eds.), *Revolutionising EU Innovation Policy*,
DOI 10.1057/978-1-137-55554-0_9

However, after more than five decades of continuous enlargement and integration, in both territorial and political terms, the EU's governance system has hit the brick wall and is today no longer able to cope with the challenges it faces in the postindustrial, digital age. The technological progress of the new millennium has triggered large-scale political and socioeconomic developments that outrange, in their scope and complexity, by far what the EU's regulatory system can account for, resulting in the chronic political and economic stagnation that has paralyzed Europe for almost one decade now.

During its more than 2 years of work, the High Level Group on Innovation Policy Management (HLG) has discussed this problem specifically for Europe's innovation policies, which by the EU institutions and numerous member state governments are considered key to modernize Europe's economies and lead them back to competitiveness and growth. The HLG has shown in its two reports (2013, 2014) that in precisely those policy areas where the EU does not have exclusive competencies such as in R&D&I, or the economic, employment, and social policies, the governance instruments chosen to develop common solutions have to be innovative themselves to account for the complexity and ecosystemic nature of the phenomena they aim to manage.

Governing innovation requires innovative governance; this means that to get added value of its innovation initiatives, such as the Horizon 2020 program, the EU has to adapt its governance system, and above all its regulatory regime, to new realities. The legalistic-procedural, top-down regulatory mechanisms developed in the 1950s and 1960s to create common markets that still characterize Europe's governance system today are inadequate to transform Europe into an "Innovation Union." This is because its most notorious policy instruments, EU Regulations and Directives, seldom adequately reflect the multidimensional character of such a union and often fail to align the diversity that constitutes it, resulting in systemic exclusion of stakeholders and ultimately in low-quality regulation and policies.

This chapter seeks to rethink EU governance from the perspective of a theory that can offer substantial new insights into our understanding of the EU as complex system, of systemic change and how this change can be managed: complexity theory. In applying this theory together with its concept of transition management as proposed governance method to the realm of EU governance, we will work under the notion of the EU as *complex adaptive system* in a state of disequilibrium (crisis) and transition, trying to restore a stable order but relying on inadequate and outdated strategies and governance methods thereof. Despite the many efforts made to reform these methods, we will conclude that the EU has to date failed to bring about a true modernization of its governance system because these efforts have largely bypassed the core of the problem, which lies in the very nature of its regulatory regime and its overreliance on regulation as the *sine qua non* means of governance.

Europe's regulatory regime requires a general overhaul, and we will argue that neither the Community Method (CM) nor its proposed alternative, the Open Method of Coordination (OMC), are alone capable to bring about such a modernization. Where the CM is too static, legalistic-procedural, and exclusive, the OMC is too flexible, tentative, and without the necessary regulatory effect. We therefore suggest walking along a middle way: collaborative governance, which we believe can bridge between these two governance paradigms and support the EU in transforming its regulatory regime from one defined by control and overregulation toward one built on facilitation, management and stewardship.

2   The "Golden Era" of Regulation in the European Union

When in 1985 the Delors Commission issued its famous White Paper on "Completing the Internal Market," it heralded what some later would call the "golden era of regulation" in Europe (Levi-Faur 2011, p. 817). The ambitious objective of the paper was to create a more favorable environment for stimulating enterprise, competition, and trade through the establishment of a common European market within only 5 years (COM 1985, 310: 6). To this end, the Commission provided that all kinds of national trade barriers should be abolished; rules harmonized and legislation and tax structures approximated; and monetary cooperation established as well as the necessary flanking methods put in place to encourage European business to work together (COM 1985).

The Delors Commission sought to implement these objectives by combining methods of positive and negative integration, that is by creating common institutions and regulatory standards on the one hand while eliminating all obstacles to free trade and competition on the other (cf. Scharpf 1999). Though, because both positive and negative integration presupposes the transfer of sovereignty and political decision-making powers from the national to a higher level, member states had to equip the EU with an appropriate governance instrument awarding it sufficient leverage and legitimacy to interfere in member states' markets, policies, and legal constructions. Regulation soon proved the most efficient governance tool for this purpose, most notably in form of EU regulations, directives, and EU court decisions by means of which the common market and institutions could be regulated into being.

This process was accompanied and conditioned by structural changes in the governance systems of the member states. As Majone (1997) explains, in the age of increased global integration and interaction, economic competition of industries and businesses takes place not merely among producers of goods and services, but also, increasingly, among *regulatory regimes* at the global level, in which businesses operate. Accordingly, international competition rewards regimes in which institutional innovations do not lag behind to so-called "new strategic choices" and which provide for their economies enabling framework conditions to innovate in (Majone 1997). Regimes that have adapted to these new strategic choices underwent a transition from "positive" (or interventionist) systems to "regulatory" systems, in which regulation replaced the classic instruments of state governance, that is taxing (borrowing) and spending (Majone 1997). All European states have passed through this process and have transformed into "regulatory states"—a constitution they have maintained until today but have not always sufficiently adapted to changing socioeconomic realities.

Among the most important of the new strategic choices to which member states adapted is the Europeanization of national policy making (Majone 1997). This refers to the increasing interdependence of national and supranational policies within the EU. This highlights, on the one hand, the central role of regulation in EU policy making, and on the other the impact of EU decisions on regulatory developments in the member states. This trend can be accounted for both in quantitative and qualitative terms, in the increasing number of legal acts issued by the European institutions every year, and the effect this legislation has at member state level.

In 1990, for instance, the EU issued a total of 1,485 legislative acts, of which 1,067 were regulations, 59 directives, and 359 decisions. Within the following decade, this number almost doubled: in 2000, the European institutions adopted a total of 3,011 legislative acts, 2,433 regulations, 35 directives and 543 decisions. After 2000, the amount of acts issued by Brussels then halved again to 1,550 in total in 2010, after most objectives of the White Paper and Single European Act have been implemented.[1]

For about two decades, EU regulation translated into national law has started to exceed rules made by the member states themselves. Majone has demonstrated this for the case of France, where already in 1991 the vast majority of laws were established at the EU level with only 20–25 originating in Paris. Hoppe (2009) has shown the same for the German case, where the ratio between EU law transposed into German federal law and law issued by Berlin is almost exactly 80:20, with 10,279 legislative acts for the year 2008 (treaties, regulations, directives) originating in Brussels (81 %) and 2,391 in Berlin (19 %).

The second important strategic choice that Majone outlines is the emergence of new actors in the political realm and the rise of so-called third-party government. Third-party government refers to the shift from direct to indirect or proxy governance via administrative decentralization, in particular the delegation of policy-making authority to independent or semi-independent regulatory agencies (Hoppe 2009). Since the early 1990s, this gradual shift has resulted in the development of what Levi-Faur (2011) has called the "Single European Regulatory Space," a multi-layered and multispatial regulatory realm composed of a myriad of actors such as Commission directorate-generals (DGs); regulatory committees; decentralized agencies; the European Parliament and its committees, and forums; and working, expert, and advisory groups. All these actors are, in one way or the other, involved in policy designing, decision making, and implementation at different levels.

While administrative decentralization can also be understood as an attempt to more efficiently accommodate business' needs for operating in a growing single market by including a greater number of specialized actors

---

[1] Overview developed according to statistics on EU legislation, EUR-Lex: http://eur-lex.europa.eu/en/statistics/index.html.

for problems that have grown too complex to be dealt with by policy makers alone, the EU system of decentralized agencies has become an enormous and cumbersome structure and source of increasing regulatory burden and costs. This is because its main purpose is still the production of regulation in the tradition of positive and negative integration, that is, the production of law and rules that primarily aim at abolishing trade barriers and completing the single market rather than *managing* the markets already created and policies put in place.

But the EU of today looks fundamentally different than the EEC of 1985. Not only has the Union substantially grown, territorially and politically, also is it faced with entirely different political and socio-economic challenges, which by far outrange those of the 1980s. At the supranational level, the Community has continuously extended its powers and influences over the member states in a growing number of policy areas, while the member states underwent large-scale socio-economic and politico-institutional transformations. Most European countries have developed into postindustrial societies and have tried to account for this transformation with according reforms and modernization. The EU, in contrast, its political-institutional constitution and in particular its regulatory regime, have remained largely the same as 30 years ago.

The 2000 Lisbon Strategy and 2009 Lisbon Treaty have made a considerable attempt to modernize Europe's governance structures and have set in motion a number of initiatives to reform the EU toward a "Europe of innovation and knowledge" (Lisbon Strategy 2000). However, in so doing, they have fallen gravely short of expectations because the treaty and its strategy have left the regulatory nature of the Union largely unquestioned. The EU is still a regulatory command-and-control actor whose preferred governance method is the production of regulation. However, a competitive, dynamic, and knowledge-based Innovation Union cannot be regulated into force. The abolishment of trade barriers and creation of an innovation arena is but the first step in this endeavor; what however is required is governance strategies that *enable* and *manage* such an arena and capitalize on methods such as the promotion of coordination and cooperation, stewardship, smart interventions, and regulatory modernization rather than legal control.

3   The First Steps Toward Reform: The EU's Better Regulation Initiatives

Probably the two most significant attempts to reform EU governance and implement the Lisbon 2000 and Europe 2020 strategies have been the EU's better regulation initiative and the introduction of the Open Method of Coordination (OMC) as alternative political decision-making mechanism vis-à-vis the traditional Community Method (CM). We will first discuss the Better Regulation initiative while the OMC will be discussed in the second part of this chapter.

3.1   The Better Regulation Reform(s)

The Better Regulation initiative was adopted under the Baroso Commission and aims at "designing EU policies and laws so that they achieve their objectives at minimum cost. It ensures that policy is prepared, implemented, and reviewed in an open, transparent manner, informed by the best available evidence and backed up by involving stakeholders."[2] In order to ensure that EU action is effective, the Commission seeks to "assesses the expected and actual impacts of policies, legislation, and other important measures at every stage of the policy cycle—from planning to implementation, to review and subsequent revision" (Lisbon Strategy 2000).

Contextually, the EU's better regulation initiative, which has been revived under the Juncker Commission, is founded upon three principles, which Löfstedt (2004) has identified as key for driving the EU regulatory regime: competitiveness, sustainable development, and good governance. From the very outset of its existence, the European Community has placed competitiveness at the very heart of the European integration process so to create for its businesses framework conditions that would allow them to uphold Europe's economic power in a rapidly coalescing global arena, while maintaining strong welfare societies.

---

[2] See http://ec.europa.eu/smart-regulation/index_en.htm.

Good governance in turn comprises elements such as effective and efficient political institutions, democratic participation, transparency in political decision making and implementation, and the credibility and accountability of the EU's political institutions. And finally, sustainable development refers to the EU's goal to establish the highest public health and environmental standards across all industry sectors and promote these internationally.

These three mutually interdependent principles have over the past two decades decisively influenced the need of what the Commission now calls better (or smarter) regulation: because without regulatory reform, EU economies cannot maintain their competitiveness, without which welfare states cannot be financed, and without which neither governments nor industry can remain innovative to develop new solutions for sustainability.

Since the mid-1980s these principles have induced the Commission to embark on a comprehensive review and evaluation of the state of its regulatory affairs. In the following regulatory reform and modernization have been flagged by more and more member states as key policy priority. It was then the Commission's 2001 White Paper on European Governance that initiated the reform process by setting up a comprehensive agenda for the establishment of better regulation standards (COM 2001, p. 428). Concomitantly, a high-level group of experts on regulatory matters was installed, the Mandelkern Group on Better Regulation. This group was commissioned to elaborate on a strategy for how to improve the EU regulatory regime. In its final report, it proposed as core element of regulatory modernization, the introduction of a *new impact assessment model*, calling for its adoption by 2002 and its application to all Commission proposals with possible regulatory effect.

In addition to regulatory impact assessment (RIA), the Mandelkern report also highlighted the need of enhanced *consultation* as a means of open governance that allows stakeholders to contribute to the development and implementation of policy. The report furthermore called for a simplification of regulation at the Community and member state levels through a Commission-led systematic, targeted, and rolling program of review and simplification of existing EU legislation. Finally, the report stressed the importance of improving the implementation of law by taking into account the consequences of proposed legislation on those having to ultimately enforce and comply with it.

And indeed, 2 years later in 2002/2003, the Commission launched a package of measures commonly referred to as the Better Regulation Agenda, comprising eight targeted communications (COM 2002: pp. 704, 713, 276, 278, 719, 718, 709, and 725) all aimed at simplifying and improving the EU's regulatory regime by streamlining EU legislative procedures, cutting down red tape, and modernizing and enhancing the quality of regulation through improved consultation processes (COM 2006).

The Commission's aim was to look at both the "stock" of past EU legislation and the "flow" of new policies. To this end, it introduced a horizontal system to assess the impact of legislation (RIA) and improve the process and design of legislative proposals. In detail, this included a rolling program of simplification of existing legislation; a "testing" of Commission proposals still being looked at by the Council and European Parliament; factoring consultation into all Commission initiatives; reducing paperwork and administrative costs; and looking at alternatives to laws and regulations (such as self-regulation or co-regulation).

In 2007 the Commission then gave a new boost to this initiative and adopted the Action Program for Reducing Administrative Burdens in the EU. This program established common goals for the EU and member states to reduce administrative burdens on EU businesses with which the Commission sought to increase the EU's GDP by 1.4 % (€150 billion) and boost job creation and growth. A relatively large number of initiatives went hand in hand, such as the European Parliament and the Council's inter-institutional agreement on a "common approach to impact assessment" in 2005; the establishment of a Commission-appointed Impact Assessment Board (IAB); a strategic revision of the better regulation policy together with a review of the consultation system of external stakeholders; or the expansion of the better regulation principles to the whole policy cycle (COM 2010, p. 543).

However, only very few of these initiatives have translated into actual results and still fall short of expectations. Despite its reform efforts over the last two decades, the EU has not succeeded in bringing about a *true* reform of its regulatory system, and has largely not even succeeded in properly implementing the individual reform measures, such as the RIA or the consultation system for external stakeholders. Although often stated, we would like to argue that this is not necessarily due to a lack of political will in the

EU institutions and member state governments. Rather, it is because all these reform attempts have concentrated on individual components of the regulatory system rather than a reform of the system itself.

4   Shortcomings and Main Bottlenecks of the EU Regulatory Reform

Despite will and efforts invested into regulatory reform, a real modernization of the Community's regulatory system is still pending. This is because in all these initiatives, past and ongoing, the Commission has too narrowly framed the reform debate and has failed to consider the *functioning* of the regulatory system itself. Essentially all envisaged reforms take place accepting the *logic* of the EU as *regulating polity* with the Community Method as overarching governance paradigm. In this understanding, the main purpose of EU governance is the production of law rather than *managing* the markets and policies created to ensure that they function well. This has resulted in the paradox situation where the EU tries to modernize a system without modernizing the system itself.

Probably the most evident reason for this dilemma is that the *functioning* of the EU regulatory system is anchored in the treaties, which means that the necessary reform competencies go beyond the Commission's mandate and would require a political debate at the highest member state level. However, such debate would not only require an enormous political effort from member states and EU institutions, but could eventually result in significant power shifts (or even cuts) between the EU institutions and between them and the member states, with redefined missions and tasks, and a redistribution of influences. It should not be surprising that such discussion has to date not yet taken place and will be very difficult to be launched in future.

In any case, such debate would need to address, *inter alia*, four main problems that can be identified as the main problem areas and bottlenecks to a true reform of the EU regulatory system: (1) the EU's multilevel governance system; (2) the EU's co-decision making system; (3) "comitology" and the EU's system of regulatory committees; and (4) the lack of coherence and accountability of the EU's system of decentralized agencies.

4.1   The EU's Multilevel Regulatory System

According to the OECD, regulatory policies in a multilevel context can only be effective if they reflect the diversity of needs and interest and encourage horizontal and vertical coordination and cooperation mechanisms across the different governance levels (OECD 2009). The current institutional and governance system of the EU does not yet provide for such an umbrella set of coordination mechanisms, though several efforts have been made to improve such coordination within the institutions themselves, such as the creation of the seven Commission vice presidents with overarching function by the Juncker administration.

In 2007 the Commission appointed a High Level Group of Independent Stakeholders on Administrative Burdens, which produced a report on best practices in member states to implement EU legislation in the least burdensome way (2011). In this report, the group points out that despite a number of ongoing efforts, a large part of the burden generated by EU rules derives from the way member states implement legislation. The systematic use of EU directives is identified as central source of regulatory incoherence because it facilitates non-coordination in implementation. Directives only provide guidelines and define certain results to be achieved without however defining how they ought to be achieved.

When transposing directives into national law, member states subject the implementation of these guidelines to their own legislative procedures and interpretations, often resulting in so-called "gold plating" of rules at the expense of regulatory harmonization. In particular businesses are then faced with a situation where they, despite operating in one single market, have to comply with different national rule sets. This not only undermines the logic of the single market, but also creates considerable regulatory burden and costs.

The progressive enlargement of the EU to 28 member states has exacerbated this problem as the process of finding agreement between 28 parties in the Council, and between the Council and Parliament as co-legislator, has become very complicated and time-consuming. Consequently, the working groups in the Council and the European Parliament committees often produce regulatory add-ons and amendments instead of simplifying and harmonizing existing legislation (see the subsequent chapter). Furthermore, these legislative add-ons are not subjected to the same regulatory impact assessment so that member states therefore tend to protect their established national regulatory approaches.

As the OECD (2009) states, among the core elements that need to be assessed for higher quality regulation are: the misalignment to reduce burdens and improve synergies, improving compliance and inspections, regulatory impact analysis also at the lower levels of government (national, regional), strengthening transparent mechanisms in the regulatory process, and encouraging the use of alternatives to classical regulation. It is necessary to more strongly promote these quality principles throughout the EU and its different governance levels to improve the regulatory management at the different levels. However, the establishment of such vertical coordination and cooperation mechanisms is impeded by a lack of political will and sufficient financing in many member states.

4.2 The EU's Co-decision-making System: The Problems of the Ordinary Legislative Procedure

Despite the Commission's efforts to institutionalize regulatory impact assessment in all of its legislative proposals with regulatory effect, and despite some initial work done by the European Parliament to develop its own RIA, the ordinary legislative procedure (co-decision) remains a central source of regulatory incoherence and poor quality legislation. This is because Commission proposals are often being altered and amended throughout this process, sometimes beyond recognition, without a real assessment of the legal and socioeconomic consequences these changes will bring. Moreover, the legislative procedure is very slow and time-consuming to an extent that more and more legislation is already obsolete before it has even been adopted and implemented.

For a long time, amendments added to Commission proposals during co-decision have not been subject to any RIA. Only recently has the European Parliament made some efforts to establish its own in-service impact assessment by creating a Directorate for Impact Assessment and

European Added Value in early 2012. This body is composed of two units, one dealing with the assessment of new initiatives, and one with the "costs of non-Europe," that is, the estimated costs of not completing the economic and political union.

The concrete tasks carried out by this directorate are the screening of Commission road maps, initial appraisal and detailed assessment of Commission impact assessments, impact assessments on substantive amendments being considered by Parliament, and the development of briefing notes or studies analyzing all or part of a Commission IA.

However, parliamentary impact assessment has so far failed to deliver on its objectives and responsibilities. The IA directorate is not equipped with the necessary resources and capacities such as the required technical, scientific, and socioeconomic expertise to undertake a proper impact assessment of the amendments tabled by Parliament. It furthermore remains unclear what exactly is meant by "substantive amendments" as there is no legal definition. As the European Parliament's own impact assessment handbook (2013) states: "It is up to the parliamentary committee(s) responsible to determine whether one or more of the amendments tabled during its consideration of a Commission proposal is 'substantive' and, if appropriate, whether it or they should be the subject of an impact assessment" (p. 6). This means that the initiation of a RIA lies within Parliament's own discretion.

As concerns the Council, the member states have so far taken no initiative to establish its own body dealing with regulatory impact assessment of the many amendments produced in the working groups. Given the lack of methodology to conduct such an assessment, as well as the alleged lack of funding for such a body, impact assessment is essentially left to member states' own discretions, capacities, and methods.

Only in May 2015b have the European Parliament and the Council issued a draft Inter-Institutional Agreement on Better Regulation, which calls upon both institutions to better coordinate impact assessment—a call that has already been made 10 years earlier in the 2005 Common Approach to Impact Assessment. According to the proposed agreement, European Parliament and the Council shall carry out an impact assessment of any substantial amendment made to a Commission proposal at any stage of the legislative process (art. 10).

However, the agreement neither defines "substantial amendment" nor does is provide in any detail how exactly this impact assessment should look like in practice. The only guideline provided on RIAs in the Council can be found in a briefing by the European Parliamentary Research Service (EPRS) of February 2015, where it says,

> Council working parties should now, at an early stage of the debate on specific legislative proposals, consider the relevant Commission IA on the basis of an *indicative checklist*. However, pressure from at least a third of member states for the Council secretariat to go further and to install a small impact assessment unit *has so far been resisted*. (Collovà and EPRS 2015: p. 3, emphasis added).

From this it becomes clear why the many reform efforts could not deliver on objectives they set: Parliament and the Council still lack awareness of the burdens and costs they cause through the changes and amendments they impose on Commission proposals during co-decision and during the inter-institutional negotiations. The reality is that once the Commission issues a proposal, it can be changed and amended in a seemingly arbitrary fashion without any serious assessment of the consequences these changes may bring at the other end of the policy cycle, which also makes the Commission's ex ante assessment obsolete. The result is that during the informal inter-institutional trilogue negotiations, where the three institutions discuss their respective positions, only the initial Commission proposal has undergone an assessment. This means that two-thirds of the final legislative outcome have not been systematically assessed or commented on by stakeholders. This not only raises questions of democratic legitimacy, but is a practice that decisively undermines the quality of legislation in the EU.

4.3   Comitology and the EU's System of Regulatory Committees

Comitology, today known under the term *delegated and implemented acts*, refers to the system in EU rule making in which committees composed of member state representatives and the Commission assist the Commission in implementing legal acts. Every year, the Council of Ministers and the European Parliament confer to the Commission implementing power to issue implementing rules and give effect to legislation. Once a legal act is adopted, the Commission is assigned to develop measures to implement it. In this process, it works with committees to obtain their opinion and approval. Comitology is therefore also referred to as "non-legislative rule making" with the committees acting as a "mini-Council of Ministers" (Blom-Hansen 2008).

The first comitology committees were created in the early 1960s in order to assist member states in dealing with the technicalities of implementing the Common Agricultural Policy. Their number grew considerably over time, today amounting so something between 2,800 and 3,200. It is argued that they have been created because member states sought to delegate complex and time-consuming decision-making tasks for secondary legislation to the Commission without losing control over it (Blom-Hansen 2008; Hardacre and Damen 2009). As the development of implementing measures is a complicated act that requires a great deal of technical expertise, time, and coordination to ensure consistent application and enforcement, the Commission is considered to be better qualified to handle this task while member states can maintain a "mechanism of oversight" (Hardacre and Damen 2009).

With the European regulatory regime significantly expanding over the past decades, the need for committees has increased as well as the policy areas they are involved in. Today, there is virtually no European policy without comitology. However, the evolution of this system is characterized by inter-institutional tensions and power struggles over the control of EU executive rule making (Hardacre and Damen 2009). In particular the European Parliament and the EU's decentralized agencies have continuously sought to expand their influence in the decision-making process.

The legal basis for comitology is laid down in Council Decision 1999/468/EC, amended and modified through Decision 2006/512/EC 7 years later. The most important feature of the 2006 decision was to introduce the Regulatory Procedure with Scrutiny (RPS). The RPS was added to existing comitology procedures to explicitly account for Parliament's demand of greater involvement in this procedure. The RPS granted Parliament powers over comitology that more accurately reflect its power in co-decision, thus increasing its democratic control over decisions concerning the implementation of Community legislation. Concretely, Parliament received the right of ex post vetoes on implementing measures of general scope that amend a legal act which was adopted under co-decision (Hardacre and Damen 2009).

The 2009 Lisbon Treaty then introduced further modifications and gentrified the role of Parliament. Most notably, the Treaty introduced a two-track system for implementing measures, separating all comitology decisions into delegated (art. 290) and implementing acts (art. 291). According to the legal text, delegated acts refer to "non-legislative acts of general application," supplementing or amending laws in their "non-essential elements," whereas article 291 applies when a "legally binding Union act…identifies the need for uniform conditions of implementation."

With this, the Treaty sought to simplify and clean up the "comitology jungle …both in terms of a more comprehensive comitology system and a more straightforward delegation process for participating actors" (Stratulat and Molino 2011). Furthermore, Lisbon sought to increase the democratic legitimacy of comitology by upgrading the role of the European Parliament. For instance, the procedure for delegated acts is now more streamlined and transparent in that the Commission now drafts its measures directly and simultaneously to Parliament and the Council, instead of first having to ask the committees' opinion (Stratulat and Molino 2011). Furthermore, Parliament is now an equal co-delegator vis-à-vis the Council where co-decision applies.

However, despite the progress made in 2006 and 2009 and through the establishment of the European Commission's Comitology Register[3] that lists the different committees and their meeting agendas, minutes, and the draft implementing acts, EU comitology remains an extremely complex, opaque, and cumbersome mechanism of EU rule making.

The committees, of which the exact number is still unknown, work behind closed doors; the names of the member state representatives participating are not made public until the conclusion of discussions, of which in turn only very superficial summaries are provided. This hardly allows any insights in the debates and the different positions at stake.

---

[3] See http://ec.europa.eu/transparency/regcomitology/index.cfm?CLX=en.

Furthermore, comitology systematically excludes stakeholders, which means that those directly concerned with implementing decisions are given no opportunity to be heard. This is particularly problematic as many of the implementing measures require a great deal of technical expertise and experience to be effective—know-how that national ministries and the Commission alone do not have. The technical input of industry especially is therefore crucial to ensure that drafted measures are of high quality and work in practice. Hence, stakeholders have repeatedly stressed that there should be a streamlined consultation and contribution process that allows for providing reasonable feedback on the drafted measures. This would bring comitology better in line with the Community's principle of proportionality that provides that implementing measures must be appropriate to achieve the aim defined, and must be reasonable in accounting for the diversity of interests and needs involved.

Furthermore, there is so far no comprehensive control and assessment mechanism of the quality and potential impacts of comitology decisions, and the question of political accountability remains unclear. Even though impact assessment is currently in the course of being introduced for secondary legislation, RIA for comitology decisions is still only in its infancy, leaving the large majority of non-legislative acts without any critical review (Alemanno and Meuwese 2013). If implementing acts are to be of the highest quality and democratically legitimized, comitology has to be opened to the public, stakeholders have to be involved in this process, and decisions taken have to be subject to a regulatory assessment.

4.4   The Lack of Coherence and Accountability of the EU's System of Decentralized Agencies

As outlined above, agencies and networks have started to play an increasingly important role in EU policy making and implementation. Even though administrative decentralization has the potential to create decentralized, informal, and even experimental governance niches and better engage stakeholders, the EU's system of decentralized agencies has become a structural bottleneck to regulatory reform. EU agencies have been created on a case-by-case basis in successive waves through various mixes of political interests over the last two to three decades, resulting in a confusing and incoherent system where agencies are not held accountable for their decisions despite the growing influence they have on key regulatory decisions (cf. Evaluation of EU Decentralized Agencies 2009). This can be observed in a number of policy areas where agencies regularly exceed their defined missions and tasks in a quest to expand their own power and influence. This results in political trench battles between the European Commission, the member states, and the various agencies, paralyzing the regulatory process and not infrequently leading to legal challenging.

The general structure of the EU's agency system is problematic in that there is neither an overarching rationale cutting across the agencies nor an assessment of their pertinence. Only the recently created agencies were subject to an impact analysis and cost–benefit analysis, and there is missing clarity on why many of these agencies were created in the first place and whether other regulatory methods would have been more appropriate. Furthermore, EU agencies' accountability methods are questionable, as many agencies seem to understand accountability as obligation to report on their accomplishments and incurring risks only if these accomplishments are considered unsatisfactory. According to the 2009 evaluation report, this accountability and reporting obligation was unsatisfactory and information was scarce. In practice, performance reporting is almost nonexistent, or does not take place in an accurate enough form that could serve as basis for the discharge procedure, as agencies have an obvious self-interest in protecting their own continuity.

The EU has started to recognize these problems and has made an attempt to "rectify" them by adopting in 2012 the so-called Common Approach on EU Decentralized Agencies. This aims to make the agencies more coherent, effective, and accountable. According to the European Commission, this common approach foresees a range of improvements, including "the need for an objective impact assessment before deciding to create a new agency, criteria for the choice of the seat and headquarters arrangements, regular overall evaluations (every 5 years), and the introduction of sunset or review clauses foreseeing the option of merging or closing down agencies, ex ante and ex post evaluations of the agencies' programs/activities, the development of key performance indicators, a multiannual programming to be linked with multiannual resource planning, a stronger link between actions performed by the agency and human and financial resources, a streamlined governance structure and making it clear who does what."[4]

It however remains to be seen to which extent the Common Approach will and can be implemented in practice. According to the Commission progress evaluation reports published in December 2013[5] and April 2015 (COM 2015, p. 179 final), several important improvements could be achieved, such as the adoption of guidelines on the prevention and management of conflicts of interests between agencies and between Agencies and the European Commission, to avoid the above-mentioned trench battles. But practice shows that these trench battles continue and that further efforts will be necessary.

4.5   Summary

Despite important reform efforts made, the European regulatory system remains an overly bureaucratic, opaque, and time-consuming machine increasingly incapable of delivering on its key objective: the alignment of diverging interests and agendas and their translation into common rules.

On the micro level, this is because several individual components of the regulatory system, in particular its political decision-making mechanisms such as co-decision, comitology, or the system of EU agencies, do not work in practice and increase the EU's immobility to respond rapidly and efficiently to complex new problems. At this level, it is the system's overly bureaucratic nature, its awkwardness, and its systematic exclusion of stakeholders that hampers the agility a regulatory system today needs to maintain its managing capacities.

On the macro level, EU governance is at its core still driven by the traditional Community method that (mis)understands its main purpose as controlling and producing regulation. Though, as long as regulatory reform leaves this method as an overarching EU governance rationale

---

[4] See http://europa.eu/rapid/press-release_IP-12-604_en.htm.
[5] See http://europa.eu/agencies/documents/2013-12. 10_progress_report_on_the_implementation_of_the_common_approach_en.pdf

unquestioned, reform attempts are likely bound to fail. This is because the EU can today no longer be governed by means of political command and control, nor can an Innovation Union be regulated into being. A new approach is required; one that appreciates the EU as system of complexity with constantly changing nonlinear relationships that can only be managed by distributing the growing complexity rather than trying to control it.

In the following section we will discuss this concept of complexity, which we believe can bring substantial insight into our understanding of the EU as system, of systemic change, and how to manage it.

5   The EU as Complex System in Transformation

In times of increasing global integration and interdependence, understanding the nature of systems, their relations and interconnections, and of systemic change, becomes a key for policy makers to manage large-scale systemic phenomena that affect societies. The citizens of Europe today face a number of these transformational phenomena, be it globalization, climate change, or the rapidly progressing digitalization of almost all areas of private and professional life, that provoke fundamental changes in the way people live, organize themselves, and interact, work, and play.

These phenomena and the changes they induce occur at such speed, depth, and magnitude that they have started to erode in its very core the established governance system that seeks to manage them and increasingly render its key regulatory instruments useless. Policy makers in the EU today face the dilemma of applying previous solutions to new problems; in other words, EU governance today appears as a simple 1960s integrated circuit computer trying to process a complex Windows 10 operating system.

A concept that has been attracting increasing attention in academic literature, but also among increasingly more policy makers and offers new insights to the way we understand social systems and systemic change, is *complexity theory*. Developed in the early 1980s and rooted largely in the work of the biologist Ludwig van Bertalanyff, modern complexity theory is an "interdisciplinary field of science that studies the nature of complex systems in society, nature, science, and technology... and provides a framework by which *groups of interrelated components* that influence each other can be analyzed" (Rotmans and Loorbach 2009, emphasis added, p. 185). This group can be a biological organism, a company, a city, or even a whole society or group of societies such as the European Union.

Though complexity theory was first primarily confined to sciences with relatively little consideration in social and political sciences, it soon started to find application to problems in sociology, political science, and international relations by "offering a new set of conceptual tools to help explain the diversity of and changes in contemporary modernities undergoing globalization" (Walby 2003). In sociology and related disciplines, the key objective of complexity theory today is to understand and explain the behavior of societies as complex systems that run through different cycles: relatively long periods of stability and order (so-called *equilibrium* phases), interrupted by those of change, instability and even chaos, and then adaptation to their internal and external changes and restore a stable status (Rotmans and Loorbach 2009). Simply put, complexity theory tries to understand societal systems in transition in order to manage this transition toward a more stable setting.

Complexity theory understands societies as systems composed by *interrelated components* that periodically face so-called "persistent problems" (Rotmans and Loorbach 2009). These persistent problems are related to "system failures" that sneak into the system (the society) or are produced by the system itself and cannot be corrected by the market or policies alone. These persistent problems, or in other words systemic phenomena, are highly complex, because they are multidimensional and deeply embedded in the societal, institutional and other constituent structures of the system and involve a myriad of different actors.

According to Rotmans and Loorbach, a transition is a "radical structural change of a societal (sub)system that is the result of a co-evolution of economic, cultural, technological, ecological, and institutional developments at different scale levels." In order to deal with system failures and manage such a transition, a sound understanding of the system is therefore indispensable.

A first important consideration that follows for how to manage societal transitions is that these transitional developments take place at different scale levels so that they can hardly, if at all, be managed by classical political command and control strategies. Or in other words, societal transition cannot be *controlled* and *regulated*, but needs to be *managed*. Such management is possible through smart and strategic *influencing* of a system transition into a more stable and sustainable direction as opposed to controlling the transition. In complexity theory, such smart influencing is called "transitional management" (Rotmans et al. 2001).

Before discussing the concept of transition management in more depth, it is first necessary to elaborate on what constitutes a complex system and how it is characterized. According to Rotmans and Loorbach (2009), complex systems

* are *open* systems that interact with their environment and constantly evolve and unfold over time. They contain many diverse components which are in constant, nonlinear interaction with each other;
* have a *history* and are *path dependent*: Prior states of the system have an influence on present states, which again have an influence on future states;
* encompass various organizational levels. They have *emergent properties*, that is, higher level structures from interaction between lower level components; and
* have *multiple attractors*: an attractor is a preferred steady system state set, to which a complex system evolves after a significant amount of time.

We like to argue that the European Union exhibits all of these features: it is an *open* system in constant interaction with its environments, inner and outer, social, political or economic, in an interconnected global context. Through this interaction with other systems, it evolves, unfolds, and changes over time. It contains many diverse components in constant interaction with each other that are nonlinear, such as between the local, regional, national, supranational, and international level or between the different political, economic, and societal governance systems that together constitute it. This interaction influences the constitution and development of the individual components, in both a vertical and horizontal way, in that effects at one level (e.g., the national) affects the other levels (e.g., the supranational), which again influence back thereby producing a constant cause and effect loop.

The European Union has a history, and it appears that it is perhaps too much path dependent on previous states in the sense that strategies from previous decades continue to have a disproportionate effect on the Union's current and future designing. The EU encompasses various organizational levels, from decisions taken at the level of the European institutions that themselves are a product of underlying organizational levels to the national and regional political structures, agencies, networks, courts, and so on. The interaction between the lower components of the system constitutes and structures the higher levels, like for instance national policies directly influence, and sometimes even determine, policy making at the European level.

Lastly, the EU has multiple attractors, and we like to argue that its current preferred state set is a governance system built on the Community method and regulation as its main instrument of power to govern both the system as a whole and its components. The EU governance system evolved to this condition over the past two to three decades because it proved the most successful and efficient way to create a union of societies with a common market and promote its integration process during continuous enlargement.

However, EU integration today has reached its capacities and the Union seems to be standing at the brink of collapse: it is caught in a paralyzing struggle between national politics and the strive for "more Europe"; it suffers from a lack of democratic legitimacy and declining trust from its citizens, businesses, and increasingly even its political elites as the gap between national welfare systems and EU neoliberal policy making grows while overly rigid or poor quality regulation suffocates innovation in the private sector. It overly relies on regulation and bureaucratic procedure with which it tries to manage phenomena that require entirely different, novel strategies; and it is losing its competitiveness and influence in the global context. In other words, the EU is in a state of critical instability trying to cope with a transition for which it relies on inadequate and outdated strategies.

5.1   Complex Adaptive Systems

A special case of complex systems are complex *adaptive* systems. These kind of systems are adaptive in that they have the ability to learn from experience, adapt, and change. Hence, they are able to respond to and adjust themselves to changes in their environment and within themselves. They constantly create variety and diversity by developing new components and relations, which provides a source of innovation and renewal (Rotmans and Loorbach 2009, p. 187). From this diversity and variety, which can come both from the inside and as stimuli from external sources, the system then choses a so-called *predominant selection,* which "maintains the system in a dynamic equilibrium by preventing variation or by pushing it into a certain direction" (Rotmans and Loorbach 2009). And finally, complex adaptive systems have two important features: they *co-evolve* with their components and can *self-organize* themselves (Rotmans and Loorbach 2009).

By self-organization, Rotmans and Lorbach refer to a complex system's capacity to develop an internal self-management without interference from outside. Whereas there can be external impetus and stimuli that can trigger processes of change in the system by adding variety and diversity and thereby challenging the predominant selection, a complex system will eventually push the system to a "predominant selection" and thereby create stability.

Co-evolution, in turn, means a process where "interaction between different societal subsystems influences the dynamics of the individual societal subsystem, leading to irreversible patterns of change" (Kemp et al. 2009). This rejects the notion that in a complex system, one entity or player has a single impact on another entity or player—for example, if the European integration would take place merely vertically, as a top-down from EU institutions to the member states. Since complex systems are understood to take all other systems as their environment, systems co-evolve through *adaptation* to their environment. In this sense, complex systems are *ecosystems* and co-evolution means that "the evolution of one domain or entity is partially dependent on the evolution of other related domains or entities… or that one domain or entity changes in the context of the other(s). The notion of co-evolution places the emphasis on the evolution of interactions and of reciprocal evolution" (Mitleton-Kelly 2003).

The EU co-evolved with its member states and other systems in its environment, just as its governance system co-evolved with that of its member states and other systems in its environment over time. Both the member states and the environment have added to the European Union's diversity and variety, from which the system developed a predominant selection and was consolidated. Regarding EU governance, the two key elements of this selection have been *positive and negative integration* of which regulation is the most manifest policy tool. However, whereas the EU's system components (its societies inside as well as its environment[s]) have continued evolving and changing, most notably at the economic and societal level in co-evolution with technological progress and socioeconomic transitions, the EU's predominant governance selection still has not.

In other words, while facing a complex new variety and diversity, the EU forcefully preserves a previous predominant selection against co-evolution with and adaptation to new realities; thereby it prevents itself to move to reestablish equilibrium. Even though being an adaptive system, the EU has failed to overcome its path dependency on previous strategic choices and clings to governance tools and mechanisms developed 50 years ago. But the realization of the Lisbon strategy, the Horizon 2020 agenda, or the creation of an Innovation Union cannot succeed if the governance instruments do not co-evolve with what they aim to manage.

5.2 Managing Complex Adaptive Systems: Managing the European Transition

If we agree with the above information, that the EU is a complex adaptive system currently in a state of disequilibrium trying to manage the transition into a more stable, sustainable setting, then we shall now discuss how managing this transition can take place in practice.

Since co-evolution is not instantaneous but a process that takes place over time, internal processes of complex adaptive systems have to adjust to external changes (Walby 2003). Twenty years ago, Stuart Kauffmann (1993, 1995) has illustrated this adaptation via the concept of so-called "fitness landscapes." The concept of fitness landscapes assumes that the landscape of a system, that is, its environment, changes as a result of changes in the constitution of the landscape, that is, in its components. In this sense, Kauffmann argues that, "as one system evolves, it changes the landscape for others, changing their opportunities, and thereby their potential for success or weakness. The landscape can be adapted or deformed by systems, with complex consequences for their development" (Walby 2003, p. 9).

However, as we have argued above, this adaptation process of a complex system and its internal processes to external changes can be *influenced*. For this, Rotmans and Loorbach provide the concept of transition management. Transition management is based on three principle guidelines with which a complex adaptive system can be "directed":

1. Encouraging frontrunners. Rotmans and Loorbach argue that managing transition requires to create "quasi-protected" niches for frontrunners: so-called "transition areas." Frontrunners are understood as "agents with peculiar competencies and qualities: creative minds, strategists, and visionaries" that have the capacity to create new and innovative structures. In order to unfold their full potential, these agents have to be allowed niches with sufficient independence from the regime and resources (knowledge funding, possibly even exemptions from laws) to experiment. These frontrunners can then build coalitions and networks and develop so-called "transition agendas."

An example for how to implement this idea is the High Level Group on Innovation Policy Management.[6] Initiated under the Polish presidency of the European Council in 2011, the HLG successfully created as a niche (transition arena) in which its members were able to develop politically bold recommendations for how to better manage the transition of the EU into an innovation union. Its success was due to the following characteristics:

* It brought together a high-level group of agents with special competencies and qualities: creative minds from the EU institutions (EU Council and Commission), member state governments, innovative businesses, and academia. This inclusive, *tripartite structure* of the group allowed discussions from the various standpoints of innovation and gave the group a special democratic legitimacy;

---

[6] See http://www.highlevelgroup.eu/en.

* Even though affiliated with the organizations that they were sent from, the participation of its members took place in a *personal capacity*. This independence made the group a quasi-protected niche that allowed for frank and open discussions that would otherwise, in case members would have formally represented their organization, not have been possible;
* The group was *self-funded* and *self-organized* and had its own secretariat and research team. This allowed the group to be fully independent from the regime while yet being directly embedded in it;
* The discussions between the members took place during regular, general meetings as well as informal bilateral exchanges under respect of the *Chatham House rule*, that is, under anonymity. Decisions were based on *consensus,* which means that the final outcome, the two reports and their policy recommendations, are the result of a consensual agreement between the parties that take common ownership of what they have jointly negotiated; and
* Finally, the group was a *temporary* initiative and not formally institutionalized so as to avoid creating yet another advisory body and adding further to the already heavy institutional complexity of EU governance.

The HLG's *transformation agenda* in the form of its two reports and recommendations was then presented to the EU ministers at the formal and informal Competitiveness Council in May 2013 and December 2014. Since then, the two publications provide policy makers in the EU institutions and member state governments with guidance and reference.

2. Allow for *guided variation and selection*. The second guideline highlights the importance of diversity in preventing rigidity and maintaining flexibility of the system. As we have argued above with reference to Rotmans and Lorbach, in the equilibrium phase of a system, there is continuous variation and selection, but with a predominant selection that maintains the system. However, as soon as a system "settles," the dominant selection tries to decreases diversity. This situation must be avoided by maintaining diversity in the system as it is otherwise not sufficiently agile to respond to systemic changes which will ultimately result in paralysis or even system failure.

As discussed above, this situation can be seen in the European Union where regulation has emerged as dominant selection. However, by making regulation the *sine qua non* EU governance tool, regulatory diversity is being inhibited, and the EU's regulatory regime is no longer able to co-evolve with its internal and external dynamics and respond to systemic changes.

3. Anticipate *future trends and developments*. As Rotmans and Loorbach explain, this means to take into account weak signals and seeds of change that can act as "harbingers of the future" and serve as key condition of a proactive, long-term strategy for managing transitions. The future orientation is thereby accompanied by a *strategy of adoption*.

A concept that in this context has already established itself as useful methodology to develop strategies of adoption is *strategic foresight*. Professional foresight is a trans-disciplinary approach that seeks to improve the ability to anticipate, create, and manage change in a variety of domains (scientific, technological, environmental, economic, and societal), on a variety of scales (personal, organizational, societal, global, universal) and using a variety of theories and methods. Foresight thereby serves as instrument for future-oriented thinking and is an indispensable instrument for policy makers in a context of rapid socioeconomic and technological changes.

Foresight is already an established policy tool in the USA and a number of Asian countries, and increasingly also in the European Union, though in the EU in a less prominent way. Examples for foresight institutions or those relying on it are the US National Intelligence Council; the Organization for Economic Cooperation and Development (OECD); the EU Institute for Security Studies (ISS); the European Strategy and Policy Analysis System (ESPAS); the Centre for European Policy Studies (CEPS); the Research and Development Corporation (RAND); or the Stiftung Neue Verantwortung that advises the German government, to list only a few.

Policy making in times of rapid change will increasingly rely on its ability to anticipate future trends and prepare itself as much as possible for eventualities. Despite its natural limitations in providing predictions of the future, professional strategic foresight can provide useful *indications* of key future trends and challenges and help policy makers prepare strategies of adoption.

These three guidelines represent an important first starting point toward building a more adaptive and agile EU governance system fit to cope with transition and societal change. The EU and national policy makers should create and proactively support innovation niches to allow frontrunners to independently develop transition agendas. However, providing niches alone will not suffice; these transformation agendas have to be recognized and implemented, even if they propose radical political changes. Too often have we seen innovative thinking developed independently or semi-independently from the regime that have ultimately led to nothing but paper waste. A new, strong commitment is needed, both in the EU institutions and in the capitals that appreciates and supports the existential role of frontrunners in ensuring diversity and renewal of the system and prevents systemic paralysis.

Policy makers can take inspiration not only from the work of the High Level Group on Innovation Policy Management, but also from the private sector where so-called collaborative entrepreneurship is already a well-established practice to generate wealth through exploiting underutilized innovative ideas in collaboration (Miles et al. 2005; Hekscher and Adler 2006).

Collaborative entrepreneurship according to Miles, Miles, and Snow refers to a practice where firms come together in collaborative networks where they match underutilized resources with unexplored market opportunities to commercialize a constant stream of innovations by sharing resources while trusting in the equitable distribution of resulting wealth. These networks can be regional, national, transnational or even global. The members of the network operate independently in their markets, but share ideas in an "innovation catalogue" to alert potential allies to opportunities for collaboration. The boundaries of the network are dynamic and the relationships between the operating units are multidirectional and informal, so that the restraints of planned innovation and inter-unit rivalry can be overcome and innovative ideas become a common resource that can be exploited collaboratively.

If understood as units in a complex system, EU member states could profit greatly from this model of cooperation. States could form collaborative networks for defined policy challenges where each member state operates autonomously, but shares innovative ideas in a joint catalogue as a common pool of ideas to be exploited collaboratively. This catalogue could be for instance in form of a database managed by the European Commission, and could allow the participating states to exchange knowledge, information, and experience. Being a union committed to solidarity, cooperation, and the common wealth of its citizens, sharing knowledge and information and mutual learning would not only benefit the individual countries but the Union as a whole through establishing trust and solidarity.

To a certain extent, this mechanism of open coordination, knowledge and information exchange between member states already exists in the European Union in form of the so-called Open Method of Coordination (OMC). The OMC is a fairly new governance tool that was introduced at the Lisbon Council in March 2000 and is often described as "third way" of European integration "between regulatory competition and harmonization, [as] an alternative to both intergovernmentalism and supranationalism" (Zeitlin 2005). Tucker (2003), in turn, has referred to the OMC as "experimental mode of soft governance."

The OMC has its roots in previous soft governance tools, especially the Broad Economic Policy Guidelines (BEPG) and the European Employment Strategy (EES). But unlike the BEPG and EES, which are limited to individual policies, the OMC can cover a wider range of policy areas, from social protection and pensions, education and training, research, innovation, and SMEs, to an information society and e-Europe. These policies are at the heart of the national welfare state where member states tend to resent intervention from the European Commission and Parliament and seek to keep decision-making authority under their control. The OMC is therefore a method that allows the Community to achieve common policy objectives in areas that lie outside the regulatory competencies conceded by primary legislation.

5.3   Characteristics of the OMC and Its Shortcomings

In its Presidency Conclusions of the Lisbon Council, the Portuguese government that headed the summit officially defined the OMC as follows: "Implementation of the strategic goal will be facilitated by applying new open method of coordination as the means of spreading best practice and achieving greater convergence toward the main EU goals" (European

Council 2000). It further said that "a fully decentralized approach will be applied in line with the principle of subsidiarity in which the Union, the member states, the regional and local levels, as well as the social partners and civil society, will be actively involved, using variable forms of partnership. A method of benchmarking best practices on managing change will be devised by the European Commission networking with different providers and users, namely the social partners, companies, and NGOs."

Even though this term is not officially used, the OMC presents an experimental approach to governance and political decision making that, as Szyszczak (2006) explains, however, "does not entail a systemic change to the underlying constitutional settlement of 1957." In this respect, "firm boundaries [are] drawn between 'old' governance, or the Community method, and 'new governance,' which may exist outside the legal constitutional structured of the EU" (Szyszczak 2006). The OMC in this sense is conceptualized as a method of European integration that relies on coordination, flexibility, participation, and mutual learning rather than the methods of positive and negative integration. As such, it is probably the most radical attempt the EU has made to reform the established Community method to date.

However, while the OMC is an innovative governance method to develop common solutions in policy areas where the EU lacks exclusive competencies, the question whether it brought any tangible results in its now 15 years of existence is subject to controversial debate. Sandra Kröger (2009) for instance argues that the answer to this question depends on which side of the debate between the "soft" and "hard" law approach one stands. Defenders of the classical hard law approach would argue that soft law "leads to uneven integration while it cannot assure compliance; that it cannot prevent a race-to-the bottom of social standards; that it cannot compensate 'negative integration' and instead favors the adoption of market-making policies; and that it opens the door for blame avoidance strategies as well as for legitimizing discourses which are not democratically backed" (Kröger 2009).

Proponents of the soft law approach, in turn, argue that the OMC "respects subsidiarity; that it better accommodates existing structural diversity; that it responds better to strategic uncertainty due to its flexibility and revisability; that it involves lower transaction costs than hard law; that it helps to avoid political deadlock; that its effects may be longer lasting than hard law which it could eventually bring about; and that it is more open in terms of stakeholder participation" (Kröger 2009).

Indeed, from the perspective of EU governance, the OMC must be welcomed as an important attempt to provide member states with an alternative to the more static and legal-procedural Community method. As such, the OMC combines a number of elements presented above in the context of transition management and collaborative entrepreneurship. Member states can forge cooperations and network-type alliances to share knowledge and develop policy solutions without giving up their sovereignty. The OMC therefore provides much more opportunities than the Community method to develop transformation agendas such as the Europe 2020, which is the OMC's most notorious outcome so far.

However, after initial euphoria, the OMC has evidently fallen short of expectations. Its greatest deficit remains its informal and unbinding nature: it fails to adhere member states to agreed measures and provides no enforcing mechanism to ensure implementation. The main criticism is that member states will easily agree on setting any kinds of objectives and benchmarks, but without sanction mechanisms most initiatives will probably lead to nothing. This has led to much criticism about the OMC's lack of ability in delivering tangible political results with some questioning the OMC's *raison d'être* altogether and even suggesting its abandonment (cf. *i.a.* Sapir 2003; Kok 2004; Hatzopoulos 2006; Tamtik 2012; EPRS 2014).

However, without disregard to the OMC's limited success so far, this criticism is not entirely appropriate as it a) applies upon the OMC the logic of the Community method with its focus on hard law to an approach which *per definitionem* is framed as an alternative to the Community method, and b) misjudges its ability to encourage information exchange and mutual learning between member states. Even though this cooperation does not translate into hard policy at the Community level (and is therefore not quantifiable for statistical purposes), the OMC has contributed substantially to mutual learning among member states and the exchange of best practices, which often serve as impetus for their own national initiatives. Member states predominantly consider the OMC as idea pool from which they can fish inspiration and ideas. In this sense the OMC has indeed already created considerable added value for those participating in it.

6   Building the Link: Collaborative Governance and Regulatory Co-creation

When the OMC is too loose to translate member states' cooperation into hard policies, and the Community Method is too static and exclusive to account for the diversity of interests concerned, collaborative governance and its notion of regulatory co-creation is a concept that offers solutions for bridging between the these two EU governance paradigms.

Collaborative governance is a relatively new concept and refers to "a governing arrangement where one or more public agencies directly engage non-state stakeholders in a collective decision-making process that is formal, consensus-oriented, and deliberative and that aims to make or implement public policy or manage public programs or assets" (Ansell and Alison 2008[7]). Collaborative governance differs from related concepts such as collaborative public management (cf., e.g., McGuire 2006) or network approaches in that the engagement of the public actors with non-state stakeholders is *direct* and *formal* as opposed to advisory and consultative. This means that the desired outcome of this collaboration, such as law or policy, is produced *jointly*, so that the non-state actors participating take ownership of the outcome and responsibility for their implementation.

Collaborative governance also differs from public–private partnerships as these primarily seek to achieve communication and coordination. Collaborative governance goes a step further and aims directly at making decisions, materialized in form of law and policy. As Ansell and Alison (2008) put it, "A public–private partnership may simply represent an agreement between public and private actors to deliver certain services or perform certain tasks. Collective decision-making is therefore secondary to the definition of public–private partnerships."

Even though collaborative governance calls for direct and formal engagement of non-state stakeholders, it does emphasize the role of the "public manager" as enabler and steward. Ansell and Alison (2008) for instance argue that public agencies "have a distinctive leadership role" in collaborative governance, responsible for bringing parties to the table and

---

[7] In introducing the concept of collaborative governance we rely to a large extent on the work of Ansell and Alison 2008 and their meta-analytical study of the existing literature on this issue.

"steer[ing]…them through rough patches of the collaborative process," thereby ensuring the integrity of the consensus-building process itself. Leadership is therefore crucial for "setting and maintaining clear ground rules, building trust, facilitating dialogue, and exploring mutual gains" of the collaboration (Ansell and Alison 2008).

During the work of the High Level Group on Innovation Policy Management, the important role of the HLG secretariat as coordinator and steward became evident. The secretariat brought together the members; organized their meetings and handled the communication with and between them; guided through the meetings in a consensus-oriented process; launched bilateral meetings with all members to obtain individual viewpoints and inputs; and aligned the different positions into draft reports then presented to the plenum for discussion and approval. Without the secretariat as central contact and management point, the HLG could not have functioned in practice, and neither could it have developed a joint report that aligned the many different positions at stake.

The concept of leadership is also found in complexity theory approaches to administration. Klijn (2008), for instance, sees the leader (or manager/steward) of a complex system as having to fulfill three major tasks: (1) "managing the unmanageable"; (2) undertaking "smart interventions"; and (3) "riding the fitness landscape." As complex systems are considered unmanageable in the sense of uncontrollability due to their complexity, unpredictability and their multiple emergent and quickly changing properties, "adjusting to changes is often a wiser strategy than trying to get a grip on them," says Klijn.

In this situation, a manager adjusts and adapts to developments rather than directing them. What follows from this is the concept of smart interventions. As we have already outlined above, smart influencing is an integral part of transition management. If complex systems are unpredictable and uncontrollable, as Klijn further states, "then interventions should be aimed very specifically at a system's characteristics…[trying to] establish interactions between agents that realize interaction patterns and/or outcomes that are in the desired direction." Therefore, the manager fulfills a facilitating role: his task is to "connect actors with the elaborate content of proposals, and explore whether this content matches the preferences of the involved stakeholders and the organizational arrangements for interactions" (Klijn 2008).

Connecting actors and involving stakeholders then automatically increases the knowledge available and allows for more targeted interventions into the system's characteristics (Klijn 2008).

The benefits of this approach for the EU regulatory system are obvious: facing ever more complex problems, a regulator system needs to bring together the relevant actors concerned with this problem. This includes the traditional public actors (Council, Parliament, Commission) as well as non-state stakeholders such as enterprises, scientific research institutions, and civil society organizations as these can bring in knowledge that the regime would otherwise lack. Their involvement—even if merely informal at this stage—therefore automatically increases the available knowledge and understanding of the system and the problem that needs to be dealt with. This is important both at the designing stage of policy but even more for implementing regulation, which requires specific technical knowledge and operational experience to draft measures that intervene in the system in a smart way.

Through the provision of this information from the different actors in the policy chain, smart interventions can be launched, be it in the form of regulatory or non-regulatory measures, depending on what the specificities of the problem require. Though, the non-state stakeholders have to be formally and directly engaged in the process of deciding on these interventions, as otherwise a joint ownership of the collaborative outcome is not guaranteed and proper implementation is impossible. The process toward this outcome has to be facilitated and coordinated by a manager—which can be the European Commission—which has to connect the actors with each other and with the problem, organize their interaction, and negotiate toward an alignment of the different positions. As Klijn puts it, the manager has to be "aware of the opportunities in [the] landscape, as well as the positions of the actors, and use them to realize interesting policy proposals or to adapt proposals and actor coalitions, in such a way that fit the landscape" (Klijn 2008).

The success of a collaborative policy undertaking however not only depends on the role of the manager. Equally important is the readiness of non-state stakeholders to participate in such collaborations and ultimately share the ownership and responsibility of the negotiated outcomes. Stakeholder inclusion is thereby not the sole responsibility of the manager, but relies on joint initiative. This however leads to the question of which incentives non-state stakeholders and in particular companies may have to participate, in particular why they should accept political ownership and responsibilities that go beyond their usual understanding of corporate social responsibility.

Generally speaking, the main incentive lies in the relationship between participating and achieving concrete, tangible effectual policy outcomes through direct, face-to-face interaction with policy makers (Ansell and Alison 2008). This incentive however considerably declines if stakeholders see their engagement merely consultative or ceremonial. This is predominantly the case in Europe where stakeholder engagement takes place in form of public consultations as part of the impact assessment process, usually ex ante and after legislation has been adopted and implementing measures are developed.

The incentive to participate is also low if alternative options exist where stakeholders can achieve their objectives unilaterally, for example, in courts or through allies in legislature. Participation therefore depends mainly on two factors: (1) whether the collaboration is the exclusive forum for decision making, and (2) whether stakeholders perceive their goals to be dependent on cooperation from other stakeholders—in other words, if there is interdependence (Ansell and Alison 2008). If one of these two, or both, criteria are met, the success or failure of collaboration depends to a large extent on the commitment of the participating parties. Commitment in turn depends on a range of factors, including good leadership (management), expectations of the collaboration, and transparency but, most importantly, on *ownership* of the process and its outcome.

In the EU, engagement of non-state stakeholders in political decision making is predominantly consultative; very seldom can stakeholders take direct responsibility for the outcome of the decisions made. This results in the dilemma that they often have to seek other—informal—ways to influence the decision making, mostly in form of lobbying or campaigning. Decision makers, in turn, are held ultimately responsible for policy outcomes and are unilaterally exposed to the public when policies fail to deliver. Collaborative governance, in contrast, shifts ownership of decision making from the public agent to the engaged stakeholders, or apportions it (Ansell and Alison 2008). The sharing of the responsibility is therefore key for collaborative governance but presupposes the will on the public side to share the responsibility for regulatory outcomes with non-state actors and on the private side, the readiness to accept this responsibility.

In summary, collaborative governance increases democratic legitimacy and transparency of EU decision making as it engages non-state stakeholders in political decision making through direct and formal participation in designing and implementing policy; it relaxes regulatory stringency, increases the quality of legislation and makes the EU's regulatory system more agile and internationally competitive in responding to complex new challenges; and it distributes ownership and political accountability between the public and private, thereby forcing a new commitment from enterprises to deliver on their corporate social responsibility.

However, applying collaborative governance in practice will be difficult. The current legal situation does not allow for such collaborative undertakings in the ordinary legislative procedures as stakeholder participation is clearly defined in the regulations and foreseen only via the specifically dedicated routes such as the public consultation mechanism. Working collaboratively with non-state actors in the open method of coordination in turn may bring participants considerable added value in terms of knowledge exchange but will unlikely result in hard law. Therefore, a legal anchoring of collaborative governance in the treaties would be necessary, which however would require a considerable political push from the EU institutions and member states alike, which currently seems far out of reach.

7   Conclusion

Thirty years after the Delors Commission issued its famous White Paper on completing the single market, the EU's political priorities have remained essentially unchanged. What Delors committed to in 1985 are the same objectives Jean-Claude Juncker has placed at the heart of his working program: completing the single market; enhancing Europe's economic competitiveness; creating of jobs and generating growth for the well-being of Europe's citizens.

What however has substantially changed is the *context* in which these objectives are to be realized. The EEC of 1985 was a community of ten industrial, mainly western European societies whose primary objective *ex vi termini* was the development of an economic community through the abolishment of trade barriers and the creation of common political institutions. The EU of today, in contrast, is a highly integrated union of 28 postindustrial societies with a solid politico-institutional structure and a legislative architecture of several million pages, which are embedded in a strongly interdependent and globalized world and face highly complex, large-scale, socioeconomic challenges that outrange those of the 1980s and 1990s by far.

What this chapter has tried to demonstrate is that such a Union can no longer be *controlled*, but needs to be *managed*. The methods and instruments the EU relies on to this end are, however, no longer adequate and in urgent need of overhaul. This is because EU governance's purpose is no longer primarily the creation of a single market; despite remaining gaps, this market has largely been realized today. Its primary purpose is to manage the market created and the regulatory system put in place to govern it.

However, as we have argued, this regulatory system is no longer able to respond to the challenges of our time and has become incapable of managing the EU in its present complexity. Important reform efforts were made, but none of these have met the expectations and have failed to bring about a true modernization. This is largely because the reform debate has been too narrowly framed and has targeted merely individual system components rather than discussing the system itself and its purpose in a changed context.

Before this chapter went to discussing complexity theory and transition management as a way to rethink EU governance, it outlined what we believe can be considered the main bottlenecks to a true regulatory reform. It concluded that the European regulatory system is in its essence a cumbersome, legalistic-bureaucratic, opaque, and exclusive system that misconceives its purpose as producing regulation that to an increasing extent is of poor quality or altogether obsolete before it has even been adopted. In forcefully preserving this system, the EU obstructs its own natural capacities of adaptation and self-organization, and impedes on itself to co-evolve with changing environments, both outside and within.

However, the alternative to the traditional Community Method, provided for in form of the Open Method of Coordination, is in turn equally incapable of managing Europe alone. Its unbinding and informal character, despite the value it doubtlessly generates through information exchange and mutual learning, only maintains the old problem of member states protecting their national interests and established politico-institutional and legal structures. Experience has shown that without any form of sanction, Europe's political capitals will hardly assign sovereignty and decision-making powers for the sake of "more Europe."

We therefore suggested collaborative governance as possible bridge between these two governance paradigms. When embedded in a more comprehensive regulatory reform, this concept can allow Europe's regulatory system to transform from a regulating command-and-control apparatus into a more agile regime better able to respond to the challenges of our time and manage Europe through transition back into equilibrium and stability.

However, realistically, a true reform of EU governance will require modifications of Community legislation. This can only be achieved if there is political will, and eventually political agreement at highest political level. We should not be too optimistic to expect radical changes soon, but we can place hope in the power crises have in sparking reform and change.

Acknowledgments The author would like thank Eduardo Mulas for his research that contributed to this chapter.

References

Alemanno, A., and A. Meuwese. 2013. Impact assessment of EU non-legislative rulemaking: The missing link in 'Comitology'. *European Law Journal* 19(1): 76–92.

Ansell, C., and G. Alison. 2008. Collaborative governance in theory and practice. *Journal of Public Administration Research and Theory* 18(4): 543–571.

Blom-Hansen, J. 2008. The EU comitology system: Who guards the guardian? Paper presented at the Fourth Pan-European Conference on EU Politics organised by the ECPR's standing group on the European Union, Riga, Latvia, September 25–27, 2008.

Collovà, C., and European Parliamentary Research Service. 2015. How does ex-ante impact assessment work in the EU? European Parliament-PE 528.809.

Lisbon European Council. 2000. Presidency conclusions (Lisbon Strategy). http://www.europarl.europa.eu/summits/lis1_en.htm.

European Commission. 1985. Completing the internal market. White paper from the commission to the European council. Brussels, COM(85) 310 final.

———. 2001. European governance: A white paper. Brussels, COM(2001) 428 final.

———. 2002a. A framework for target-based tripartite contracts and agreements between the community, the states and regional and local authorities. Brussels 11.12.2002, COM(2002)709 final.

———. 2002b. Action plan "Simplifying and improving the regulatory environment". Brussels 5.6.2002, COM(2002)278 final.

———. 2002c. Better monitoring of the application of community law. Brussels 16.5.2003, COM(2002)725 final.

———. 2002d. Impact assessment. Brussels 5.6.2002, COM(2002)276 final.

———. 2002e. On the collection and use of expertise by the Commission: Principles and guidelines. Improving the knowledge base for better policies. Brussels 11.12.2002, COM(2002)713 final.

———. 2002f. Proposal for a council decision amending decision 1999/468/EC laying down the procedures for the exercise of implementing powers conferred on the commission. Brussels 11.12.2002, COM(2002)719 final.

———. 2002g. The operating framework for the European regulatory agencies. Brussels 11.12.2002, COM(2002)718 final.

———. 2002h. Towards a reinforced culture of consultation and dialogue— General principles and minimum standards for consultation of interested parties by the Commission. Brussels 11.12.2002, COM(2002) 704 final.

———. 2006. Better regulation—Simply explained. Brussels.

———. 2010. Smart regulation in the European Union. Brussels, 8.10.2010, COM(2010)543.

———. 2015a. Progress report on the implementation of the common approach on EU decentralized agencies. Brussels, 24.04.2015, COM(2015)179 final.

———. 2015b. Proposal for an interinstitutional agreement on better regulation. Strasbourg 19.05.2015, COM(2015) 216 final.

European Parliament. 2013. Impact assessment handbook. Guideline for committees. http://www.europarl.europa.eu/EPRS/impact_assesement_handbook_en.pdf.

European Parliament and European Council. 2005. Inter-institutional agreement on impact assessment. Common approach. http://ec.europa.eu/smart-regulation/better_regulation/documents/ii_common_approach_to_ia_en.pdf.

———. 2012. Joint statement on decentralised agencies. http://europa.eu/agencies/documents/joint_statement_and_common_approach_2012_en.pdf.

European Parliament Research Centre (EPRS). 2014. The open method of coordination. Brussels, European Parliament PE 542.142: http://www.europarl.europa.eu/EPRS/EPRS-AaG-542142-Open-Method-of-Coordination-FINAL.pdf.

Hardacre, A., and M. Damen. 2009. The European Parliament and comitology: PRAC in practice. EIPASCOPE 2009/1.

Hatzopoulos, V. 2006. Why the open method of coordination (OMC) is bad for you. *European Law Journal* 13(2): 309–342.

Hekscher, C., and P. Adler, eds. 2006. *The firm as collaborative community: The reconstruction of trust in the knowledge economy.* Oxford: Oxford University Press.

High Level Group of Independent Stakeholders on Administrative Burdens. 2011. Europe can do better. Report on best practice in member states to implement EU legislation in the least burdensome way. Warsaw.

High Level Group on Innovation Policy Management. 2013. Report and recommendations June 2013. http://www.highlevelgroup.eu/sites/default/files/download/file/130088%20EPPA_HLG%20REPORT.pdf.

———. 2014. The way forward to improves people's lives. Inspiring and completing European innovation ecosystems.

Hoppe, T. 2009. Die Europäisierung der Gesetzgebung: Der 80-Prozent Mythos lebt. In *EuZW*, Heft No. 6. http://www.highlevelgroup.eu/sites/default/files/company/HLG_report2014_V9_web.pdf.

Kauffmann, S. 1993. *The origins of order.* Oxford: Oxford Univ. Press.

——— 1995. *At home in the universe: The search for laws of complexity.* Oxford: Oxford Univ. Press.

Kemp, R., D. Loorbach, and J. Rotmans. 2009. Transition management as a model for managing Processes of co-evolution towards sustainable development. *International Journal of Sustainable Development & World Ecology* 14(1): 78–91.

Klijn, E.-H. 2008. Complexity theory and public administration: What's new? *Public Management Review* 10(3): 299–317.

Kok, W. 2004. Facing the challenge: The lisbon strategy for growth and employment. Report from the High Level Group chaired by Wim Kok. Luxembourg: Office for Official publications of the European Communities.

Kröger, S. 2009. The open method of coordination: Under-conceptualisation, overdetermination, de-politicisation and beyond. *European Integration online Papers* 13(1): 5.

Levi-Faur, D. 2011. Regulatory networks and regulatory agentification: Towards a single European regulatory space. *Journal of European Public Policy* 18(6): 810–829.

Löfstedt, R.E. 2004. The swing of the regulatory pendulum in Europe: From precautionary principle to (regulatory) impact analysis. *The Journal of Risk and Uncertainty* 28(3): 237–260.

Majone, G. 1997. From the positive to the regulatory state: Causes and consequences of changes in the mode of governance. *Journal for Public Policy* 17(2): 139–167.

McGuire, M. 2006. Collaborative public management: Assessing what we know and how we know it. Public Administration Review Special Issue December 2008.

Miles, R.E., G. Miles, and C.C. Snow. 2005. *Collaborative entrepreneurship: How communities of networked forms use continuous innovation to create economic welath*. Palo Alto, CA: Stanford University Press.

Mitleton-Kelly, E. 2003. Ten principles of complexity & enabling infrastructures, London School of Economics. http://psych.lse.ac.uk/complexity/papers/ch2final.pdf.

OECD. 2009. Multi-level regulatory governance: Policies, institutions and tools for regulatory quality and policy coherence.

Ramboll-Management-Euréval-Matrix. 2009. Evaluation of the EU decentralised agencies. Final Report Volume II, http://europa.eu/agencies/documents/conclusions_at_system_level_en.pdf.

Rotmans, J., and D. Loorbach. 2009. Complexity theory and transition management. *Journal of Industrial Ecology* 13(2): 184–196.

Rotmans, J., R. Kemp, and M. van Asselt. 2001. More evolution than revolution: Transition management in public policy. *Foresight* 3(1): 15–31.

Sapir, A. 2003. *Report of an independent high-level study group established on the initiative of the president of the European Commission*. Brussels: European Commission.

Scharpf, F. 1999. *Governing in Europe. Effective and democratic?* Oxford: Oxford University Press.

Stratulat, C., and E. Molino. 2011. Implementing Lisbon: What's new in comitology? Brussels: EPC Policy Brief April 2011.

Szyszczack, E. 2006. Experimental governance: The open method of coordination. *European Law Journal* 12(4): 486–502.

Tamtik, M. 2012. Rethinking the open method of coordination: Mutual learning initiatives shaping the European Research Enterprise. *Review of European and Russian Affairs* 7(2): 1–24.

Tucker, C.M. 2003. The Lisbon strategy and the open method of coordination. A new vision and the revolutionary potential of soft governance in the European Union. Prepared for delivery at the 2003 Annual Meeting of the American Political Science Association, August 28–31, 2003.

Walby, S. 2003. Complexity theory, globalisation and diversity. Paper presented to conference of the British Sociological Association, University of York.

Zeitlin, J. 2005. Conclusion: The open method of coordination in action: Theoretical promise, empirical realities, reform strategy. In *The open method of coordination in action: The European employment and social inclusion strategies*, eds. J. Zeitlin, P. Pochet, and L. Magnusson, 447–503. Brussels: P.I.E. Peter Lang.

10

Developing Top Academic Institutions to Support Innovation

Jean-Claude Thoenig

1   Introduction

Any competitive innovation ecosystem requires a stimulating higher education and research environment. Academic institutions are key contributors and stakeholders to fuel such economic and societal dynamics.

Such a statement is obvious at local levels. Regional technology innovation ecosystems such as Silicon Valley in California; Boston; Tech City in London; Paris-Saclay, or the Beijing ecosystem are rated by the MIT Technology Review (2012) as being the most promising worldwide for the years to come. Each benefits from the collaboration with an academic fabric located in its area, which includes at least one if not more research universities supported by several colleges and vocational schools.

Identical configurations are at work when considering countries or regions of the world. An obvious case is provided by the USA. Its dynamic leadership

J.-C. Thoenig (✉)
Centre National de la Recherche Scientifique University
Paris-Dauphine, France
e-mail: jeanclaude.thoenig@free.fr

© The Editor(s) (if applicable) and The Author(s) 2016
K. Gretschmann, S. Schepers (eds.), *Revolutionising EU Innovation Policy*,
DOI 10.1057/978-1-137-55554-0_10

is dependent on a sophisticated blend of business entrepreneurship, federal funding, and a skilled labor force, a key contextual factor being the existence of a dense network of universities. While in 2013 the members of the European Union (EU) had an estimate of more or less 3,300 active higher education institutions (HEIs), the number reached an estimated 4,500 universities and colleges granting degrees across the various states of the USA. Quantity per se does not really make the whole difference, at least not as much as quality. The world leadership of the US innovation ecosystem relies first of all on the quality of its academic production both in higher education and in research.

US HEIs are overrepresented among the best of the best universities worldwide as measured by metrics of excellence. For instance 22 of its universities are ranked in the top 30 segments of the world league as defined by the 2015 Annual Ranking of World Universities, better known as the Shanghai ranking. By comparison only four HEIs located in EU member states—all four being British—join this segment.[1] The leadership of US HEIs covers fields such as emergent technologies, just to name one. It is also the case for most academic areas, from life and earth sciences to humanities and social sciences where their colleges and vocational schools are persistently positioned as world benchmarks. Academic contribution to innovation ecosystems does not mean an overspecialization in a few niches while dropping any attention for general education and for research in basic science as well as in social sciences and humanities. Cutting-edge innovation production requires intellectual agility and cognitive openness of the labor force. Its educational background matters as much as its professional expertise. Size as such does not by itself make a difference. For instance the California Institute of Technology includes 300 faculty members and enrolls 2,130 students, 55 % being postgraduates.

Universities and institutes of technology acting as knowledge hubs inside performing innovation clusters look similar in the USA as well as in other regions of the world. They cover a wide spectrum of academic domains. Their classrooms provide at the same time excellent teaching to high-caliber students, and their research labs provide outstanding knowledge that might be in one way or another of relevance for societal needs and economic progress. Leading research universities set benchmarks not

---

[1] Another university based in Europe is ranked in this segment: the Swiss Federal Institute of Technology at Zurich.

only inside their national environment but also for universities located in other regions of the world (Thoenig and Paradeise 2014). They define new academic knowledge agendas others would later imitate. They operate at the forefront of innovation. They definitely are research universities but of a special kind. In the USA they are part of a class of HEIs that, comparatively speaking, are running so-called very high research activity.[2] While metrics-based ranking approaches have been welcomed by many EU member state policy makers, no classification has ever been developed at the levels of the EU and of most of its member states as such, as if all HEIs would be equal—a principle crystallized into their legal frame—and even much more equal than the US stratified system, this is not the case in terms of quality production and support by steering agencies.

A collateral strength of the US academic fabric relates to its density. Should two or three leading domestic HEIs start to underperform, their decline would not induce major damages for the whole innovation ecosystem capacity competitiveness as such, at least less than what would be the case inside an EU-based ecosystem today. This presents to a large extent the robustness of the US innovation ecosystem for many years. Ferocious competition is at work between HEIs to attract talent and deliver knowledge. The same happens in receiving successful access to federal grants and donors such as companies. For private as well as for public research universities, such revenues are a matter of financial survival. For instance one-fifth of the operating revenues of the University of California–Berkeley are federal grants and contracts.[3] But for Washington policy makers this is less a worry than a resource: should one HEI fail, many other substitutes are accessible to play the game.

The People's Republic of China, while still lagging behind the USA, has in the last few years also paved the road to high competition dynamics in building a national ecosystem based on two main pillars: the academic excellence of some of its HEIs and close linkages with innovative firms and emergent markets, for instance associated inside a local or a national cluster.

---

[2] The Carnegie Classification of Institutions of Higher Education is a framework for classifying US colleges and universities in terms of missions. HEIs classified at the top in terms of academic quality grant at least 20 doctorate awards per year. Their research activities are assessed by research expenditures, the number of research doctorates awarded, the size of research-focused faculty, and other factors.

[3] See http://opa.berkeley.edu/campus-statistics/financial-and-research-data.

Therefore, to develop a competitive innovation ecosystem at national, and a fortiori at regional levels such as the EU, requires a web of strong academic institutions that play the role of knowledge hub in research and education. They have to provide an actual strategic capacity of their own, enabling them to get their projects funded by private donors, companies, as well as by public grants, to allocate a great deal of attention to evolving societal needs as well as to new economic opportunities. They should also contribute to overcome mental and practical obstacles to business-university cooperation—such as preferences for subsidies because of presumed academic freedom—that may still survive in some countries such as France and new EU member states. In any case such academic institutions will have to play a major role in defining new horizons for knowledge development, as is the case today for multidisciplinary issues. Their performance has to be rather consistent across time and domains. Scientific merits are considered the main criterion of success in a competitive environment.

2   Where Is the EU Academic Landscape Heading To?

Building a stronger academic capacity inside the EU is an ambition often considered as a geopolitical and socioeconomic priority for the years to come. Though a dozen or so of its universities may compete with their US counterparts, the EU has not yet reached a critical mass that builds up a competitive innovation ecosystem of its own. It may even be lagging behind upcoming Asian ecosystems like China and India. While time goes by, many obstacles have yet to be overcome by the EU and by its member states before giving birth to relevant achievements.

Reforming academic institutions is often considered to be a desperate cause when not a nightmare to avoid. Inside the EU the landscape remains highly scattered when it is not heterogeneous at the local level—HEIs operating according to a variety of statutes and constitutive rules—and at the level of the member states—higher education and research affairs being steered with very different approaches.

A series of initiatives have already been launched to decrease the fragmentation of the European academic fabric. For instance, some common standards such as the Bologna agreement about education diplomas have been defined and implemented by member states. Specific programs funding student exchanges and supporting R&D projects have also been launched in the EU budget. In the last 20 years new ideas have spread around to handle the challenges raised by evolving societal expectations. A worldwide massive wave of enrolled students has gone hand in hand with a commodification of higher education—students being more and more mobile internationally—and a corollary globalization of world standards—world league ranking being a major reference. Higher education and research are supposed to contribute increasingly as the vehicles that build a knowledge society, as defined by the EU Lisbon agenda of 2001. At the same time taxpayer money has become scarcer and policy makers less generous. Some concepts prescribed by the OECD and the World Bank have for better or worse been supported by policy makers in most member states: quality benchmarks such as the ideal of the so-called World Class University, ranking metrics to assess academic performances, increasing attention allocated to cost rationalization and new public management principles (Thoenig and Paradeise 2015).

To some extent the structural opposition between three models of higher education and research—the Anglo-Saxon, the German Humboldtian, and the French Napoleonic model—is slowly fading away (Paradeise et al. 2009).[4] Relevant steps forward have already decreased heterogeneity in the world of European academia. Agreeing to share common standards or joining intergovernmental research programs generates positive incremental achievements, even if sometimes they may require patience and compromises. Nevertheless much remains to be achieved. The legacy of the past still remains an influential source of heterogeneity.

---

[4] Differences between the three models refer among other things to the degree of proximity between the universities, the state, and the referential community (local or national), the status of the universities (whether similar or different in the same country), the ties between education and research activities, and inner institutional and organizational structures of universities. See G. Neave,"The Bologna Declaration: Some of the Historic Dilemmas Posed by the Reconstruction of the Community in Europe's Systems of Higher Education," in *Educational Policy*, 2003, 17 (1): pp. 141–164.

One fundamental reason is that national steering of higher education and research affairs remains very active, even more than in previous times. A de facto quasi-hegemony of member state policy makers is not per se to be considered as a good or bad principle on the road to building an EU innovation ecosystem. What is at stake is a pragmatic question: do the ways member state public authorities actually steer the domain of higher education and research facilitate the capacity of the EU—not to be restricted to the sole EU policy makers—to build such an ecosystem? Facts may suggest that this may not be the case, at least within the very near future. To a large extent this delay is the consequence of many fault lines in the EU policy-making system. For some issues are handled at the EU level and many others remain member state competence, while at the same time the economy is more and more conforming to a single market. No effective governance system has been implemented until now to overcome these fault lines. For instance the Open Method of Cooperation (OMC), as defined in Lisbon in 2001, has clearly failed. Traditional cooperation styles remain much too slow to cope with rapid technology progress and ongoing market evolutions.

It is often mentioned that national policy makers are not spontaneously eager to welcome initiatives that might open the door to third parties—other member states, the EU Commission, etc.—to have a say how to steer their own national jurisdiction. Apart from obtaining financial opportunities, foreign interference in my own backyard is not really welcome. I as a member state want to have the final say about exclusive control in my academic affairs including the steering of the HEIs located on my territory. Even when common principles are shared that may harmonize the EU academic landscape they actually induce more heterogeneity across countries. This is what happens most of the time with the autonomy of HEIs.

Flexibility of local research and education entities is a crucial prerequisite to allow them to be more active contributors to innovative ecosystem building and performance. Autonomy is the name of the game. An HEI should benefit from maneuvering and defining its own strategic capacity, therefore having discretion for instance about its revenues and its expenditures, about which partnerships to build with other parties of its cluster or about the financial vehicles to run joint programs with companies. Policy makers, politicians, and HEI heads claim *urbi et orbi* that autonomy has to be allocated. This does not at all imply that public universities should be privatized. Nevertheless, wide differences exist between countries for instance in terms of the decision-making capacity of their own governing bodies to allocate their budgets, to raise revenues such as tuition fees, to set up institutional arrangements and vehicles such as endowed foundations attracting money from donors, and to deliver specific diplomas.

A comparison between public and nonpublic hubs of regional ecosystems suggests that the former benefit from a high level of strategic capacity despite the fact that they are part of a state system. Constitutional and legal factors may matter but in the end what makes the difference is the way the system is actually steering its HEIs. Such is the case when comparing a private foundation such as the Massachusetts Institute of Technology with a campus such as the University of California–Berkeley that is part of the major public university system in the world. Both research universities operate in very autonomous ways, a slight difference being that Berkeley is not allowed to decide in a discretionary way the level of tuition fees for most of its students (Thoenig and Paradeise 2014). An identical autonomy-based steering method is how the Swiss federal authorities manage their relations with their two very successful institutes of technology at Zurich and Lausanne.

What happens inside the EU? A study made by the European University Association suggests that the autonomy principle does not carry the same meaning and content when comparing how member states and German Länder steer their HEIs (Estermann et al. 2011). Four different components of autonomy are assessed: organizational, financial, human resources, academic. The scorecard suggests major differences. Two countries, the UK and Estonia, score at the top on all four facets. A few other countries such as France and Greece score very low in terms of autonomy of their HEIs. Most of the other countries have moderate autonomy, sometimes high on one or two facets and average or below average on the others. In synthesis the impressively wide spectrum suggests that the flexibility capacity of local HEIs varies dramatically from one country to another, some being agents acting in a highly centralized national system and others being able to act in an entrepreneurial mode in decentralized systems.

Worse, in some cases the right hand of policy makers ignores what their left hand does. The way the authorities apply their policies, far from making the changing environment of academia easier to understand, in fact amplifies uncertainty and even confusion by producing a series of effects, which, although they are not always contradictory, contain their share of ambiguity.

On one hand, policy makers use more or less coercive measures to drive the universities. They force them to rationalize their administration to take on new missions, adopt a rationale based on the quest for excellence, and implement rulings and laws that follow each other at high speed. In France, for instance, three new laws regarding higher education and research were introduced between 2006 and 2013. They concerned a very scattered collection of points, ranging from how to implement the Bologna Declaration or to cooperate, and how local institutions may combine forces or even merge, to defining teachers' responsibilities, languages of instruction, or institutions' accounting systems. Guidelines gush forth with no time for the preceding one to be deployed in the field before the next arrives. The more productive and pushy the policy makers become to try to get results, the less things actually change on the ground and vice versa. These lead the academic institutions to navigate between great caution and opportunism. Public policies also encourage opportunistic tactics, which make use of the tools for purposes other than those they were designed for. In the UK, the Conservative government introduced a ceiling to university tuition fees of £9,000 per year. The idea was to ensure financial protection for all universities. In fact, it is used by some of them to increase the number of students they recruit by maximizing their investments on additional academic personnel recruitment and infrastructure building. More precisely, the top-ranked institutions are the ones that gain the most from the provision, and they do so at the expense of the mid-range institutions, because the latter do not have the same advantages as the former in the competition to attract mobile students. Opportunism is also expressed in several EU countries by HEIs hunting for students from outside Europe, because they pay tuition fees that are significantly higher than the legal cap set for national residents and Europeans.

Another practice of central policy makers is to develop procedures and uniform indicators themselves and impose them top-down, relocating micromanagement into HEIs. Nevertheless, the latter remain closely controlled by the incentives and evaluations to which their performance is henceforward subject. This remote control is a modern version of bureaucratic administration, which combines the invention of common performance or quality criteria with the assignment of financial resources, the formulation of formal structures, and the verification that they are actually applied. In fact, it inflames the paradox of seeking to create autonomy. It makes them more compliance seeking, instead of heightening their local strategic capacity. In fact their dependency on how the resources of public policies are used is increased. The local HEIs that the central officials wanted to make more autonomous by giving them administrative expertise, in fact behave like disciplined agents in the eyes of their principals, who assign resources to them. This happens in countries that also hope to spend less taxpayer money for academia. In the UK, the performance criteria used in universities are defined by the ministry—using categories built with the support of academic peer committees—which implements them via the Research Excellence Framework when assigning financial resources.

The argument underlying the observations listed in this section is that reform dynamics like the ones currently in progress are not by themselves going to facilitate the creation of a competitive academic capacity at the level of an EU innovation ecosystem. Despite some initiatives launched that have member states adopt shared standards or even joint common programs in research and in education, dysfunctional consequences have not made the landscape capable of generating spontaneous prerequisites to harmonize policies so as to build up sufficient academic institutional capacity to back up a European ecosystem. More specifically, the obstacles refer to the strength of national steering approaches. They keep playing a decisive role, in some cases now more than ever. All are trying to address identical issues such as increasing international competition and decreasing public money. But each does it in its own way. Path dependence remains strong. The current landscape, which was diverse, enters a phase of complexity. National policy makers' goodwill is less a problem than the fact that they basically have to care first and foremost so much about their own jurisdiction that they do not share identical cultural and cognitive mind-sets, and still major differences are at work between the constitutive blueprints ruling the various countries. The idea of building up the academic support for a EU ecosystem might be listed by them not as a priority on their agenda, but as a source of distraction. Why should the EU rush to put higher education policy issues on its agenda? It might be a good idea to consider, but not now; later on, in a few years, why not? One should not forget that EU member states are also competitors, higher education and research being major factors of success for national balances of payments.

3   Learning from Change Reforms

To expect that a majority of member states will spontaneously apply much pressure so as to push the EU and its ruling bodies to handle the issue might be a do-gooder wish but has very little chance of occuring. Unfortunately, as time goes by, the delays in catching up with other regional or national ecosystems might become longer; to place the EU among the leading continental competitors worldwide is with the goal to achieve—not just two or three competitive academic poles but at least twenty if not more by 2025. To give birth and develop, academic poles initiatives have to be considered and launched at least 10 if not 20 years in advance. The problem is that a 2025 time horizon is quite short. Three lessons should be kept in my mind by policy makers, whether at the national or at the European level, when considering how HEIs should and could contribute more intensively and actively to allow an EU competitive ecosystem to emerge. They may be listed as three "dont's": do not waste time to launch change processes as soon as possible, do not anticipate immediate relevant outcomes, and do not set up a centralized governance process in the new academic fabric.

First, the time required for changes is quite long. A former president of Harvard University said a century ago that to build another HEI such as Harvard would require at least half a century. Such wisdom remains valid today. The Federal Institute of Technology at Lausanne has been considered since its creation a decent but average local HEI. Nowadays, it is the academic hub of a highly performing local innovation ecosystem, it is ranked in the world league according to Quacquarelli Symonds (QS) and has joined the top 100 segment of the Shanghai ranking world league. It went through a radical change of its research and education strategy, it modified its governance style, and it built up strong partnerships with companies dealing with emergent technologies in numerous fields. This transition period started in the early 1970s. It is still going on according to the blueprint that had been defined half a century ago and was implemented step by step under the leadership of three different presidents. In other words, changing and remodeling academic institutions requires patience and continuity. As social and human organizations, they have to address managerial and strategic challenges such that they attract and retain talented faculty and students, to set up productive and cooperative ways to make different disciplines compatible under the same roof, to upgrade and diffuse cutting-edge R&D production, etc. Running them in a sustainable manner as top-of-the-pile HEIs requires much more than sheer charismatic leadership or business/ firm-inspired strategic capabilities and operational skills (Thoenig and Paradeise 2015). Such ambitions cannot be achieved by decree and require changes that cannot be managed top-down. This may lead to contradictions. For policy makers tend to underestimate the importance of time horizons when launching a reform policy. Sometimes they dream that this or that university would be a good candidate to join the ranks of the elite of the elite. They forget that academic change requires long time horizons that are not compatible with electoral time horizons. They expect positive outcomes to occur in the short term, which often means before the end of their political mandate.

Second, policy makers are sometime willing to allocate plenty of taxpayer money to build a new campus, to buy costly equipment, and to attract top-notch faculty members. Money is not the main effective vehicle or incentive to grow an academic hub, although it is needed. They may also believe that the size of the faculty and the number of registered students are prerequisites for success, which is far from true when considering the quality and status of most world-class universities. A spectacular case is provided by the Paris-Saclay University project. In order to add an academic critical mass to an already promising technological innovation cluster developed in this suburban location by companies, both multinational and local companies, and public research institutes such as the Centre National de la Recherche Scientifique and the Commissariat à l'Énergie Atomique et aux Énergies Alternatives, the French government has spent about €6 billion to build new infrastructures and to fund research programs of such a Greenfield project. The intended ambition is to catch up with the Federal Institute of Technology in Lausanne and with Cambridge, the success criterion being to rank this new institution among the top twenty in the world league. The way is to merge seventeen already established institutions, some more than 200 years old such as the École Polytechnique. They also do not a priori share much in common—a French understatement—as they cover a variety of different domains such as management, engineering, information technology, or agriculture. Some are actually specialized research institutes and others classic universities. Some are elitist *Grandes Ecoles*—for instance the Ecole Polytechnique steered by the ministry of defense, the Ecole Normale Supérieure de Cachan steered by the ministry of higher education, and the business school called HEC Paris (ranked as one of the two top management schools in Europe), which is steered by the Paris Chamber of Commerce. Others are public universities such as the University of Paris-Sud. This project would regroup 300 research laboratories, 15,000 faculty and doctoral students, and spent 15 % of the French public research budget. Will money and size make the difference? This is a question still open considering the internal heterogeneities when they are not open to resistance attitudes to the full merger that have been expressed since its initiation several years ago (Thoenig 2015).

A third lesson derived from scientific observation of higher education steering relates to the unintended consequence of centralization. The more HEIs are parts of centralized systems—the less they are autonomous, and the less they have some form of control on their own resources—the less they compete between themselves but also with HEIs that do not belong to their own system. It would be too easy to blame them and only them. In fact, the steering of centralized systems is a key part of the problem. To develop differentiation and competition means to develop inequality among them. For instance, this is occurring whenever public decision makers refer to a unique model of HEI positioning as it may be discerned in the policy incentives and tools. One best approach requires each university to align its way of doing things according to standards set by world-class academic institutions such as Harvard or Cambridge. The unintended consequence is a classical benchmarking paradox. If all universities were to adopt the same strategic responses to try to align themselves according to the same model, a hierarchy would be generated, which is eventually made visible by rankings benefitting some and disqualifying others while directing a large number of them away from certain necessary missions of higher education. Performance in leading-edge research is one about many missions of HEIs. When each of them focuses its efforts to comply with it, even though it is often unattainable for many, the ability to accomplish other missions such as undergraduate education or contribution to local development can deteriorate. Does it make sense to cut the financial funds allocated to HEIs that are not able to compete with research universities—they are many among small and mid-size institutions—but are more or less performing in preparing students for labor markets, and to pretend that they do not need cutting-edge, knowledge-based education? A similar question may be raised about autonomy. As a principle, decentralization is a good steering approach for academic affairs. But some nuances might be helpful in defining its content. Research universities as academic hubs need even more autonomy than other HEIs to be competitive in achieving their main mission. A cutting-edge research environment refers to a highly competitive international environment—he who runs faster wins—and it becomes even more difficult for policy makers to assess them, research assessment basically requiring academic criteria more than administrative guidelines. A way to give room to competitive games and spirit is that public steering systems do not have a monopoly on higher education: other research universities exist that are not institutionally part of their jurisdiction and even are run as private institutions that are research universities. In that case public HEIs have a stronger capacity to negotiate with their steering bodies.

4 Why Federal Approaches Are More Successful in Generating and Implementing Academic Changes

How do we bring the issue of the academic contribution to European innovation to the EU agenda? As of today the role of Brussels remains associated with the fact that EU governing bodies are basically considered as providers of ways and means to sponsor arenas that set up new research projects and allocate additional funding to academic activities. Their policies are considered as legitimate insofar as they basically remain distributive policies. To suggest that the EU as such might endorse a more constitutive approach raises eyebrows, constitutive meaning that EU policy tools would require institutional capacity to steer and reform academic affairs. The hostile prejudices expressed are many: the fear that it gives birth to a centralized and distant policy making level, political opposition, and ideological resistance to more European integration, etc. How to make an evolution happen is a serious issue not only because member states may be shy to see Brussels leading the game, but also because reforming the institutional academic fabric might imply choices that would not satisfy every state, in particular those that may not acknowledge the existence of an academic hub potential located in their country.

Torn apart between the Charybdis danger of not playing a part at all and the Scylla idea of building up a new institutional academic system of their own from scratch, steered in a centralized and bureaucratic manner, the EU institutions such as the Brussels-based Commission should define a third alternative. One may wonder whether a federalism-based model of policy making should not be considered.

Switzerland provides a fascinating example of a major reform of its institutional academic landscape run in a federal mode. Up to the end of the twentieth century, the Swiss universities were steered and funded by cantons. Local parliaments and executive branches of each of them were in charge, benefitting from some additional funding allocated by the Confederation. The national government steered two HEIs of its own called federal institutes of technology, one located in Zurich and one located in Lausanne, the latter having been set up and steered by the local canton but transferred to the federal policy makers in the early 1970s. Several cantons also had set up by their own initiative undergraduate colleges (*Technicums*) to supply a highly skilled labor force to local companies. The cantons were very proud of their own HEIs, as markers of their identity and as autonomous polities and sources of prestige whether locally or in some cases internationally. The first Shanghai ranking positioned three Swiss HEIs (the universities of Zurich and Basle as well as the Federal Institute of Technology of Zurich) among the 100 top world institutions. The small country called Switzerland was the third highest ranked country in terms of the percentage of its HEI, much lower than the USA but close to the UK, and in absolute terms much higher than any other member state of the EU.

But by the end of the 1990s several issues pushed the executive branch of the Confederation to consider that a reform of the landscape was becoming a must: the increase of student enrollment, whether domestic or foreign, the recession of taxation revenues, and the fear that the Swiss quality of academic production would drop given much tougher international competition. While most cantons were still caring about their own university future and autonomy, Bern put political pressure to put the issue of the reform of the whole national landscape on its agenda. Early on the initiative raised major cantonal resistance from political parties and cantonal policy makers. It became headline news in the media. But in the end a new national law was passed that designed an integrated system including three categories: federal institutes of technology, universities, specialized *Hautes Ecoles* such as the former *Technicums* and other vocational schools from education to art. The process enacted to set up this quasi-revolution is worth considering for it explains to a large extent how this achievement was made possible.

The federal policy makers co-opted the stakeholders involved—academics, heads of HEIs, political party leaders, cantonal policy makers, business associations, etc.—and shared with them intensive analysis, constructive deliberation, and lasting negotiations in order to overcome obstacles and design acceptable but also rational compromises. Horizontal coordination of the Swiss means that stakeholders are respected as expressing relevant arguments, solutions, and ideas. They also share a public common good reference and ideological pragmatism. The national and cantonal levels played win-win games. Since September 2011, the Confederation cares jointly with the cantons about the quality and the competitiveness of the Swiss domain of higher schools. The public status of academic institutions and much of the taxpayer money are pragmatically blended with support to and from private firms. A direct linkage is made between the massive attraction of academic talent from foreign countries and the economic benefits the Swiss economy could derive from it. For instance, the two federal institutes of technology are generously funded by the national parliament so that they may keep charging low tuition fees to foreign students. Policy makers in Bern are also by law committed to allocate the same amount of taxpayer money for the coming 4 years, enabling the two institutes to work with a time horizon that will remain stable. Integration means that the various academic institutions involved are simultaneously cooperating—their heads meet several times per year in Bern, their research laboratories manage joint projects—and competing—for instance to raise funds from private donors or from research grants. Academic quality as controlled by a dedicated body makes the difference for the benefit of the single winners but also for the benefit of the very successful national innovation ecosystem and its strong academic hub.

Though the Swiss case should be considered as a showcase given its major achievement, other countries also address academic affairs using identical approaches. Within the EU this also happens in Germany. What is theorized as *Horizontale Politikverflechtung* (Benz et al. 1992) defines a common way to set up arenas facilitating deliberation and negotiation systems co-opting the various parties and stakeholders, the Bund, the Länder, the academic community associations, and industry, etc.

Federalism also is at work in the USA when considering the steering capacity of academic hubs from a national innovation ecosystem perspective. In the USA the estimated of the number of active institution granting degrees in 2013 was around 4,500. Comparatively speaking, the US number includes a higher proportion of nonpublic institutions operating under a variety of legal and fiscal statuses. Public sector universities and colleges report to state legislatures. The executive branch also steers federal research laboratories in various domains, from energy to health. Such a heterogeneous academic fabric might be very complex to handle at the federal level given its heterogeneity and also the importance of pork barrel practices. Yet Washington plays a decisive role in a persistent manner in the way it allocates differentiated funding to universities in particular in the field of major research and development programs. It defines and operates a policy that supports universities playing a decisive role in R&D and that operate like academic innovation hubs. In fact, the federal policy is in line with a classification—which is not a ranking metric—of higher education institutions according to their actual distinctive mission—for instance, in fields such as research, education, or local development. The Carnegie Foundation for the Advancement of Teaching, an independent not-for-profit body[5] updates this classification every fifth or sixth year. In fact, policy makers trust academics' judgments. Professional and HEIs associations as well as think tanks and foundations have been since the end of the nineteenth century very active and influential actors whenever constitutive policies are at stake to reform the national academic landscape. The National Science Foundation keeps advising top policy makers and evaluating federal research programs. Whenever academic and scientific issues are under consideration, federal policy makers give much credit to stakeholders such as academics, state governors, leading think tanks, and private foundations, just to name a few. Pioneering massive support given to some leading research universities to domains such as nanotechnologies, agronomy, or IT gave birth to leading innovation ecosystems.

The argument of federalism as underlined here should not be understood as implying that only federal states can make it. The purpose is more pragmatic: it refers to an approach that is effective; whenever a common good to deliver has been defined as the rationale—such as upgrading the European competitiveness as well as addressing societal needs—some changes may be required in a field such as the academic landscape reforms, the issue being not yet positioned as a priority for political agendas, the legitimacy of the institutions formally in charge of the future of ecosystems being not yet shared by influential stakeholders. In contexts that a priori seem stalled in terms of change, stakeholders adopt a collaborative approach. Cooptation, negotiation, and cooperation as processes facilitate the way to deal with divergent views. This collaboration culture and the methods are useful in multilayered governance systems such as supranational ones whenever objectives are clear and strategies to achieve them are flexible. Federalism as a style of policy making means polyarchy. The EU Commission should play two roles much more than it is used to: acting as a convener and a coach. It should not govern as a regulator or a standard setter as is the case for policies dealing with markets.

---

[5] Carnegie classification available at http://carnegieclassifications.iu.edu/.

In pluralistic democratic polities, passions, suspicions, and prejudices often play a crucial role and may hinder the construction of new solutions. Therefore, deliberation and aggregation remain poor alternatives. Governance based on agnostic visions may be more adequate (Mouffe 2009). This principle refers to the give and take that occurs between actors or stakeholders who consider each other as adversaries, not enemies. An enemy defines his/her stance in the symbolic death of the other party. The conflict is a zero-sum game. One actor takes it all or loses it all. Though enemies may even respect one another, their purpose is to kill each other. An adversary bases his/her stance on a dynamic of conflict, which is not the same thing. Conflict is resolved through a compromise or a synthesis. For adversaries share enough values or objectives to make negotiations possible such that neither party wins nor loses. It expresses respect for the adversaries.

5   First Steps Matter

The ambition to develop a specific EU innovation ecosystem implies that the EU academic fabric, while evolving by considering good practices at work in other regions of the world, should not just replicate models already existing in the USA, India, or China.

The political leadership of the Commission should help European stakeholders leave the zone of indifference and enter a zone of shared acceptability about required academic evolutions. The scenario to avoid is to subcontract the task mainly to administrative approaches and routines. Setting up arenas and processes keeping stakeholders busy preparing reports but with no access to policy making capacity would not change much. The issue has to be considered as a transversal policy, meaning that it should not be under the sole jurisdiction of one specific general directorate located in Brussels. Federal steering requires know-how and legitimacy that are quite different from administering programs that fund specialized knowledge domains and educational niches to competing institutions. Constitutive policies and the inequalities they may induce require some form of political legitimacy, and not sheer bureaucratic excellence.

How higher education and research should contribute to the building of a highly competitive European Union innovation ecosystem is an issue that cannot be addressed as such independently from all the other policy facets that such an ambition covers. Interfaces between the world of academia and the other stakeholders involved or to be involved are key concerns that have to be addressed straight on to overcome prejudices about academic affairs as long as their contributions make sense for and get appropriated by companies, public service institutions, users, and citizens, just to mention a few.

Therefore, suggestions and ideas as expressed hereunder should be related to reform initiatives made for other innovation policy domains such as property rights, cluster management, or public service delivery. They also imply that the ambition itself of building such an ecosystem within the next 10 years is endorsed and legitimized by the political authorities ruling the European Union. Yet the suggestions made hereunder may seem quite modest. They should be seen with two lenses. They avoid defining right from the beginning major institutional change blueprints related to the roles and jurisdictions of the EU and its member states about a domain, higher education and research, in which the stakeholders involved will have to cooperate anyway. They are first steps that enable the generation of halo effects in the interim.

5.1   Identifying and Assessing Potential European-Level Academic Hubs

A preliminary step would be to identify HEIs having the potential to play the rule of cutting-edge innovation hubs.

This initiative should be launched as soon as possible and supply detailed information within a short time period. Its mission would be to list European-based HEIs from the point of view of several perspectives such as the network of partnerships they are embedded in, the type of domains they are covering, their way of managing and diffusing knowledge downstream, the relevant knowledge developments they may produce in the very coming years, their capacity to cooperate with nonacademic innovation stakeholders, their ability to react to new opportunities and to multidisciplinary requirements, and how they are positioned internationally. This would also cover the quality of their internal management as organizations, their ability to attract talented faculty, researchers, and students, and their funding policies.

A priori not more than two dozen HEIs may qualify for such a study as far as they would fit criteria similar to those used by the Carnegie Foundation to label very high-caliber research universities, but more weight and attention should be given to their role and potential as academic innovation ecosystem hubs.

The presidency of the Commission should mandate this study and fund it. It would be assigned to professionals well acquainted with academic affairs. An independent body would supervise it with the support of outside experts. The High Level Policy Group on Innovation Policy Management might help define which HEIs to observe, which information and data to collect, and how to interpret them. The European Political Strategy Centre as well as the Joint Research Centre of the EU Commission could provide advice and play role as well.

The next step would be to define a classification—and not a ranking—of HEIs as academic innovation hubs.

This should be subcontracted to a dedicated institution that is autonomous enough so as not to be vulnerable to third-party administrative or political interferences.[6] Every fourth of fifth year the classification would be revised in line with possible evolutions having occurred in the meantime at the level of a single HEI. This classification would provide a guidance tool for companies in search of adequate partnership environments and for policy makers in charge of economic development, but also and above all for EU policy initiatives to support HEIs as active and competitive EU-level innovation actors in various ways such as supporting partnerships with companies, other universities and research institutes, as well as public service agencies, cutting-edge innovation initiatives, and programs. They might also deliver some form of quality certification.

It may happen that some member states are not be immediately eligible to have a HEI located in their own country selected or even classified. In any case *saupoudrage* of support should be avoided: academic quality and

---

[6] The US National Science Foundation could provide a reference. Some of its academic members are assigned full-time for 5–7 years to handle such jobs.

contribution potential are the names of the game. At the other extreme one scenario to avoid during the implementation phase of any EU distributive policy is hyper-concentration. For instance a French program of support to set up local competitive clusters launched an initial call to select only twelve of them with a support of €100 million each. This was not feasible facing strong demand and lobbying by local economic and political actors. Yet the task force in charge was powerful enough to drive the government to accept the creation of three categories: world-level clusters, potential world-level clusters, and so-called national clusters. Seventy de facto clusters were selected since the 12 world-level ones received over 3 years nearly €150 million of support each, the "potential" ones—another ten—some €20 million each, and the 50 "national" level €5 million each or less. The lesson was learned, and the criteria applied to a different program aimed at upgrading HEIs' academic excellence, concentrating 75 % of the €7 billion program on the top layer, 15 % on the promising layer, and 10 % on the focused layer.

5.2   A Dedicated Policy Arena

Another initiative for the presidency of the Commission would be to open new avenues to coordinate mid- and long-term development perspectives of the many stakeholders. In line with some principles described in section 4 of this chapter, the purpose would be to set up an arena where various stakeholders would meet a few days per year to debate and share points of view, ideas, and experience.

This could be a dedicated council dealing with specific academic development reforms or a section of a council dealing more broadly with the construction and the governance of the European innovation ecosystem as a whole. Its members might be people in charge of executive functions operating at the European, national, or local levels, steering higher education and research affairs as well as economic development policies, heading HEIs, companies, and professional associations, etc. Such an arena would favor open discussion and informal negotiation opportunities. It would debate, assess, and report about initiatives and opportunities, achievements and obstacles, that are of relevant interest for the linkages between academic, societal, and economic needs, cooperation, flexibility, and shared action logics being at the core of competitive innovation systems. It could get some advice and backup from a pool of European and non-European experts in innovation management, science prospective, or innovation cluster design.

5.3   Articulating Research and Innovation: The Challenge of Transversality

In the coming years policy makers will have to fit the requirement of designing and managing transversal policies.

Articulating research and innovation policies is by far more productive than keeping them separate. Being locked in their unique space paradigm, the risk is that they become too supply oriented and forget demand. They may also be prone to vested-interest capture processes or to routine biases. To build a very performing European innovation ecosystem and therefore to develop high-level academic hubs with the potential to collaborate with economic actors, transversal policies become a decisive requirement for public policy makers at the EU level but also at national and local levels. Policy maker mind-sets make less and less sense when they consider that clear-cut differences exist between normal versus frontier science or between core- versus project-based funding. Though the evolution of technologies, life, and nature sciences should still attract major attention, social sciences and even humanities should also play a relevant part more than they currently do given evolving societal needs and the impacts they may have for users and public authorities who are supposed to appropriate the benefits of innovation. Fostering a broad science base for innovation purposes will more and more remain an old type of science policy approach. Policy making paradigms should evolve. The Commission should give special attention to support such an ambition, which is not the case currently.

The EU budget is far from being irrelevant, at least considered in global terms. Main EU programs are well endowed, to say the least. For instance, the Erasmus program has an overall indicative financial envelope of €16.45 billion for 7 years (2014–2020). Horizon 2020, which is supposed to be the flagship EU program dedicated to research and innovation program, receives funding of nearly €80 billion. Two of its major sections are the Marie Sklodowska-Curie actions with an estimated €6.16 billion to be spent between 2014 and 2020, and the European Research Council with a budget of €13.095 billion for the same period. Apparently, money is not a major obstacle and innovation is considered as an explicit matter of priority. Yet a closer analysis suggests four observations. First, some of the programs support initiatives that are not explicitly focused on innovation; this is the case with Erasmus. Second, though specific programs are labeled as dedicated to projects combining research and innovation, in fact the reference to innovation gets much less attention than the reference to research, in particular for grants funding HEIs projects. Third, innovation-focused sub-programs do not explicitly fund the midterm development of specific HEIs but research projects, each of them being assessed for its own scientific merit. Fourth, some of the programs are in fact run as a set of sub-programs each covering a specific, narrow thematic niche. In other words, silo dynamics is at work between sub-programs, not to mention the fact that the same silo logics may also occur across the various programs when not across from initiatives taken by various units inside the Commission.

To support the ambitions listed above as soon as possible, allocating additional funding from the Commission budget should not be a major obstacle. As important is when the challenge is organizational and administrative: how to successfully run an institutional development-focused project, which means how the various segments of the Commission will actually cooperate to address policies combining research, innovation, and education facets while at the same time fostering economic competitiveness and social welfare by a closer and more fruitful collaboration between academia and industry. The Commission should handle such a project with adequate professional skills and innovative operational processes. For the institutional development of HEIs requires not only the allocation of more funds but also and above all to coach and convene a multilayer action arena. A dedicated task force reporting to its presidential level could be seriously considered as a way to supervise administratively an unusual but decisive ambition such as the contribution of its academic landscape to the new EU innovation ecosystem.

Acknowledgments Catherine Paradeise, Philippe Laredo, and Ronan Stéphan have expressed comments and made suggestions that have been very stimulating. My special gratitude also goes to Stefan Schepers.

References

Benz, A., F.W. Scharpf, and R. Zintl. 1992. *Horizontale Politikverflechtung. Zur Theorie von Verhandlungssytemen*. Frankfurt: Campus Verlag.

Estermann, T., T. Nokkala, and M. Steinel. 2011. University autonomy in Europe, vol. II, The Scorecard. Brussels: European University Association.

MIT Technology Review. 2012. World innovation clusters. http://www.technologyreview.com/news/517626/infographic-the-worlds-technology-hubs/.

Mouffe, C. 1999. Deliberative democracy or agonistic pluralism? *Social Research*. 66: 745–758.

Paradeise, C., E. Ferlie, I. Bleiklie, and E. Reale (eds.). 2009. *University governance: Western European comparative perspectives*. Dordrecht: Springer.

Paradeise, C. and J.-C. Thoenig. 2015. *In search of academic quality*. London: Palgrave Macmillan.

Thoenig, J.-C., and C. Paradeise. 2014. Organizational governance and the production of academic quality: Lessons from two top U.S. research universities. *Minerva* 52(4): 381–417.

Thoenig, J.-C.. 2015. Why France is building a mega-university at Paris-Saclay to rival Silicon Valley. The Conversation portal article. http://theconversation.com/why-france-is-building-a-mega-university-at-paris-saclay-to-rival-silicon-valley-41786.

11

Cultural Diversity and Political Unity in the Innovation Ecosystem

Michel Praet and Tristan du Puy

Culture transcends nature, or more precisely, it transforms it continuously. When Cicero would address the notion of culture as "*excolere animum*," he would point at our ability to farm and to render nature habitable. Culture is also a process of transformation at the societal and individual scale. From it, we draw our goals, our methodologies of thinking and often our perceptions of belonging. However, this process is not one-sided; it is rather built as a feedback loop. Culture brings societies to life and shapes human becoming, and, in return, we make it evolve by challenging its basic values and hierarchies. Scientific progress also embodies challenges and opportunities for culture: mass societies and their cultural industries, the development of the internet and Information and Communication Technologies (ICT) with which the notions of ancestry and territoriality loose meaning.

M. Praet (✉)
Head of the ESA Brussels Office Belgium
e-mail: Michel.Praet@esa.int, BE

T. du Puy
Master student in International Economic Policy,
Sciences Po Paris, France

Culture and politics are two sides of the same token. Always confronted with relativity and the magnetic attractiveness of the absurd, they are facing the burden of creating meaning while refusing the easiness of ignoring diversity in order to achieve unity. For Arendt (1968), culture and politics are based on the same grounds as neither of them aims for truth or knowledge, but for judgment and choice, for the exchange of opinions and perceptions from which unity can be reached. They make decisions and influence the world we live in, the way we change it and the way we perceive its future. However, it would be wise to note that if in politics, a form of unity is needed in order for society to move forward, even if the content of this unity is in constant transformation, culture does not and must not aim for such unity. On the contrary, culture thrive in diversity, challenged; it becomes more dynamic and richer.

Cultural diversity and political unity in Europe are two challenges strongly intertwined and they need to be faced together. European integration requires a common vision of the future, while accepting the diversities of our cultural inheritances. Furthermore, they both need creativity and innovation as the environment that surrounds them is experiencing disruptive technological and societal modifications. Thus they also need to be disruptive in order to remain able to tackle the questions set by them.

Cultural diversity and political unity: in such a short phrase might lie the biggest challenge European integration will face. Without having the arrogance of trying to bring a final answer to this intellectual conundrum, this chapter will however pursue the goal of refining its outline.

1   Political Unity Comes from Culture and Cultural Diversity

Culture and civilization are two parallel dynamics, similar in their principles and outcomes, only different in their objects. Man is cultivated once he has made the effort of humanization explains Raphael Neira, to which he adds, "Each time man focuses his efforts on himself, one talks about culture; every time he modifies the world, one talks about civilization" (Jean Laloup and Jean Nélis 1963).

Thus is underlined the transformative power of culture and civilization. Bridging the gap between culture and civilization, we obtain a sense of belonging at the individual level; bringing together the diversities of culture, we obtain a sense of unity at the societal level. It is thus via these two mechanisms, culture and civilization, that political unity is reached.

The dynamics of culture can be split into two distinct ones, its normative effect and its transformative one.

1.1 Culture Has Normative and Transformative Values Through Which It Brings Social Cohesion

> Suppose the art of viticulture, whose function is to bring the vine with all its parts into the most thriving condition—at least let us assume it to be so (for we may invent an imaginary case, as you are fond of doing, for purposes of illustration), suppose that the art of viticulture were a faculty residing in the vine itself, this faculty would doubtless desire every condition requisite for the health of the vine as before, but would rank itself above all the other parts of the vine, and would consider itself the noblest element of the vine's organism. (De Finibus Bonorum et Malorum, Cicero, -45)

The metaphor of the vine is at the center of Cicero's explanations of auto-culture as a means to achieve a higher form of human nature, drawing from its "basic nature." This ability has been inscribed in Man since his origin, as the "faculty residing in the vine itself" and is a dynamic ability, allowing a constant becoming of Man, a perpetual process of humanization as is the perpetual evolution of the vine he describes. On the contrary, *sine cultura*, the accomplishment of the being cannot be achieved "as a field, although it may be naturally fruitful, cannot produce a crop without dressing, so neither can the mind without education" (Cicero, -45). This *cultura animi* set as a requirement by Cicero is seen by Arendt (Arendt 1961) as an ability to observe and draw from the world in order to grow, or as Martin Buber (1938) wrote, "I become I in saying You." Accepting diversity, one will however not hesitate to affirm its tastes among others, remaining aware that this statement remains a matter of choice. For Arendt, Cicero builds the notion of *humanitas* on the one of *cultura animi*, this capacity of eventually refusing constraints to assert one's choices. In terms more adapted to a societal context, the *humanitas* would be the ability to claim values and create hierarchies while knowing they only stand as such because of our personal taste. As Cicero writes, "I would rather, so help me Hercules! be mistaken with Plato, whom I know how much you esteem, and whom I admire myself, from what you say of him, that be in the right with those others" (Tusculan Disputations, Cicero, -45).

Cicero envisions a choice made while being aware of diversity; for Christina Schachtner it is an aggregate of diversity or a "conglomerate of interconnected meaning contexts" (Schachtner 2014). Both definitions do not stand in opposition but the second one might be more practical to understand the normative value of culture.

As a source of transcendence at the individual and societal levels, culture and civilization infuse our values and as a consequence moral systems and legal frameworks. These legal frameworks are full of principles whose interpretations lead to important jurisprudential debates. These principles are to gain or lose importance according to cultural and civilizational evolutions. The ever-increasing influence of the European Court of Human Rights at national and European levels illustrates very well how human rights became a major component of modern law considerations. This role of human rights can itself be linked to the promotion of the concept of the individual during the Enlightenment. The development of administrative law as a means to control state power in France may also be perceived as a cultural, or civilizational, change and the search for an equilibrium between private and public interests.

Lay and law states in Europe are the result of a long cultural evolution, from the recreation of a public power with the Roman Catholic Church imposing peace, sometimes against the will of feudal lords, to the building of absolute monarchies during the seventeenth century and a new relation between the religious absolute and sovereignty, to the "Age of revolutions" as coined by Eric Hobsbawm promoted by such notions as the one of the individual. Carl Schmitt would write that our institutions, meaning our legal and political concepts, are copied on our theological concepts (Schmitt 1985).

Culture, being the source of values also embodies them through another of its virtues, which is symbolism.

In symbolism, too, we find a normative and a transformative aspect. Embodying values and beliefs, artistic and cultural creations influence their spectators. De Botton will say that one does not feel the same, that we are not the same person, according to the place where one stands.

"In both early Christianity and Islam, theologians made a claim about architecture likely to sound so peculiar to modern ears as to be worthy of sustained examination: they proposed that beautiful buildings had the power to improve us morally and spiritually. They believed that, rather than corrupting us, rather than being an idle indulgence for the decadent, exquisite surroundings could edge us toward perfection. A beautiful building can reinforce our resolve to be good" (De Botton 2006).

Though we may choose to ignore these, and remain free to interpret them in our own manner, they always set frames of reference. Should we choose Plato's side or the others, he will remain a point of comparison and an influence. Ignorance or distortion would be the only means to exit this dualistic frame, though one might argue that culture influencing culture, we are never truly ignorant of such a cultural inheritance.

Culture and civilization appear at every stage of the becoming of values, at the foundation, as well as in representation and becoming. At the individual as well as the societal level, they bring transcendence and their coordinated actions have social cohesion for consequence.

1.2　As a Consequence, Culture Defines Our Goals

Culture, both at the individual and societal level, brings meaning or, going further, purpose. Allowing us to set a specific hierarchy of values, culture also helps us define more precisely our spiritual objectives. Via cultural symbolism, one gets a clearer perception of notions such as beauty or happiness; drawing from cultural diversity, it is also easier to identify more accurate definitions of them. Finally, political symbolism, which can be considered as a specific sort of cultural symbolism, strengthens a sense of belonging and common destiny in society.

"What, will you leave me when you have raised my expectations so high? I would rather, so help me Hercules! be mistaken with Plato, whom I know how much you esteem and whom I admire myself, from what you say of him, than be in the right with those others.

"I commend you; for, indeed, I would myself willingly be mistaken in his company." As suggested before, *humanitas* for Cicero is a matter of choice and assertion of one's preferences regarding values. This ability to choose derives from the *cultura animi*, or "an attitude able to take care, preserve, and admire the things of the world," as Arendt defines it (1968). Thus, culture can be understood as a tool giving the ability to choose and assert one's tastes. It helps us accept diversity and gives us the liberty to choose from this diversity.

De Botton (2006) confronts two definitions of beauty in architecture as he asks himself how true beauty can be defined. The first one is that of the Doge's palace in Venice, and the second is Le Corbusier's, the two of them being completely opposed in all their aspects. Le Corbusier perceived beauty as the consequence of the efficiency of the building, its proficiency to fulfill its role. For a house, beauty would be based on the house's ability to provide "(1) a shelter for light against heat, cold, rain, thieves, and the inquisitive; (2) a receptacle for light and sun; (3) a certain number of cells appropriated to cooking, work, and personal life." On the other side, the Doge's palace beauty had nothing to do with the building's efficiency but rather with its "sported carvings on its roof, a dedicated arrangement of white and pink bricks on its façades, and deliberately slender, tapering, pointed arches throughout." De Botton later concludes that this notion of architectural beauty resided on the functionally unnecessarily. Different values are expressed and different purposes are implied in these architectural styles. Drawing from them both, one is able to assert his preferences, his chosen meaning of the word "beauty." As Arendt would say, it is by drawing from both that one can express his *humanitas*.

Allowing us to refine our perceptions of spiritual goals, meaning what we look for in notions such as happiness, beauty, or truth, culture shapes and transforms what we crave for. Such an ability can be added to the normative one: culture shapes and transforms who we are and where we evolve, as well as where we crave to go and where the society we evolve in craves to go. A more societal analysis of this phenomenon is the one made by Max Weber in *The Protestant Ethic and the Spirit of Capitalism*, or how the foundations of the Protestant Ethic pushes individuals to look for the accumulation of capital in their lives.

Political symbolism is the society-wide version of the phenomenon described above. "The supreme role of politics is to give community a sense of mastering its destiny," Marcel Gauchet (2002) would say.

Political symbolism draws from culture and from its diversity. Symbolism lies as well in the appearances given to the political institutions, as in the nature of the goals given to the state, or in the manner public power is used and represented. We can only make a reference to the work of Ernst Kantorowicz on the subject and his description of the second, immortal body of the king, the embodiment of the royal crown, and also a representation of the people of the kingdom, which pushed Louis IX to declare at the Mansourah battle after the conquest of Damiette in 1249, "Beware of thinking the fate of the state lies in my person. You are yourself the state" (Picq and Descoings 2009).

From a sense of belonging, deeply infused in the ideas of kingdoms or nation-states, political symbolism also brings a sense of common destiny. One would speak about "manifest destiny" in the USA, and during the unification of Germany, the notion of "*sonderweg*" was used. If these are more abstract notions, symbolism can also lie in the setting of very specific goals for the community, as going to the moon was for both the USA and the USSR.

Symbolism is a powerful tool, a cultural unification of a kind, which however does not necessitate forgetting the diverse nature of culture. It is a means to give a dynamic to societies. Here, as at the individual scale, culture gives purpose and refines purposes. Joseph Campbell (1972) tackles the subject precisely, in a strongly metaphorical manner, when writing, "It is not this simulacrum that the world needs, rather a transmutation of the whole social order, so as that with every detail, every act of the secular life, the vivifying image of the universal god-man, immanent and affecting everyone of us, is awoken in our conscience."

1.3   And Culture Shapes the Way We Think

Culture, if it influences the way we act via goal setting and a normative action, also shapes the way we think. Culture plays a big role in the subjectivity residing in our perception of the world and our analysis of it. Heisenberg's principle of uncertainty shows how our decisions determine our perception; Noam Chomsky's work describes how our language determines our reflection. Drawing some conclusions, one could advocate that culture is a major source of innovation via the fostering of serendipity.

According to De Botton, our environment, meaning architectural environment, influences our behaviors. Werner Heisenberg, when setting the principle of uncertainty, set a complementary principle: the fact that there is a limit to the precision in the simultaneous measure of the speed and position of a particle forces us to make choices in what we wish to measure, in how we wish to perceive our environment. He concludes, "…we decide, in our selection of the type of observatory tool employed, which aspects of nature will be determined and which will be let in the shadows" (Arendt 1968). Scientific knowledge and knowledge in general are marked by subjectivity, or "the relative tendency to invoke personal, irrelevant, or extrinsic factors as opposed to more intrinsic criteria in the evaluation of persons and objects" as Blass defined it while crafting his Blass Objectivity-Subjectivity Scale (BOSS). And this mark borne by knowledge is likely to be repeatedly accentuated at every step of the measurement and analysis process. For Muckler and Seven (1992), the following stages are concerned by the subjectivity "stain": selecting measures, collecting data, analyzing data, and interpreting data, and this list covers most of the measurement and interpretation process. Setting aside the fallibilities of the "human instrument," the source of these "personal, irrelevant, or extrinsic factors" is to be seen as culture.

However, this intrinsic subjectivity of knowledge needs not to be perceived as something fully negative. First of all, modern techniques such as inferential statistics bring more objectivity in the analytical process. Second, without being as radical as Protagoras' "Man is the measure of all things," Muckler and Seven highlight that in some fields of research, "objectivity seems to mean consensus of subjective opinion" and that proceeding to both subjective and objective measures and comparing their results can be an important source of information if these results differ." Third, they advocate for the development of a detailed analytical model, which could determine the accuracy of the human measurements, as the accuracy of other measuring tools is frequently analyzed.

Culture understood as a source of subjectivity transforms our perception of the world, our analysis of it, and as a consequence the way we think it and the way we evolve in it. Via a more abstract route, Noam Chomsky's work also shows how culture, through languages, shapes our way of thinking.

Language, which can undoubtedly be understood as a part of culture, also influences the way we think, or the way we associate stimuli to percepts, sounds to meanings.

Using a bio-linguistic definition, a language is a state of the faculty of language. Following Noam Chomsky's demonstrations, genetic factors or the universal grammar, which might be the result of genetic mutations and is thought to be identical for the whole human species, interprets our environment as a linguistic experience and produces deep structures. At this stage personal experiences and memory might play a transformative role. And finally, generative grammar, specific to a language and consisting in a set of transformative rules, transforms the deep structures into surface structures, which are the sentences and chains of words we pronounce and write (for the specific case of speech, phonological rules determine the way surface structures are pronounced). It is the role of this generative grammar that can be isolated as the role of languages in the way we express ourselves. Chomsky explains it in the following manner: "In the case of language, the technical term for the underlying belief systems is 'grammar' or 'generative grammar.' A grammar is a set of rules which generates an infinite class of 'potential percept,' each of them being matched with its phonetic, semantic, syntax aspects, and classes of structures which form the language itself" (Chomsky 2006).

The language, more than influencing the way we think and express ourselves, structures our thinking. In the study of human development, François Jacob, quoted by Noam Chomsky, observed that "the role of language as a communication system between individuals would only have appeared in a second time" (Chomsky 2007). Jacob goes further and explains that according to him, the main quality of language, rendering it unique, is its "role in the symbolization and the evocation of cognitive images," allowing "a mental creation of the possible worlds. Jacob (1977)"

If we earlier focused on the influence of culture caused by its hierarchies of values and general content and then its role in perception, it is here the role of culture as a structural framework for thinking that is highlighted. Regarding the specific influence of culture on the way we think, we have also tackled the two aspects of the process of acquiring knowledge, the empirical aspect and the rationalist one.

If innovation is understood as the overrunning of a set dialectic framework, and creation as the act of bringing into existence, thus focusing on the sheer newness of the result and having a larger, less determined meaning than innovation which is purpose oriented, the structural role of culture is to be major in both processes. Creation draws from the environment but rearranges it, transforms, and processes it. The subjectivity brought by culture in perception and the rationality, based on cultural structures, used to process this perception are two important sides of creativity.

Finally, drawing from the functioning of the Weizmann Institute of Science, where meetings between researchers is encouraged as well as publishing in order to favor cross-silo thinking, we can advocate that cultural diversity is a great source of creativity via serendipity. The thirst for knowledge, the acknowledgment of the advantages and drawbacks of every research field, and the mind-set of fundamental research where the means but not the goals are determined, are keys to creation. This can all be brought by cultural diversity, Daniel Zajfman, president of the Weizmann Institute, would also add, "There is no good research without aesthetic emotion" (Rompuy 2011).

To conclude this first part, we advocate that culture and cultural diversity shape the way one as well as society behave, determine our goals and structure our thoughts. Drawing from this multidimensional action, one can assert that culture brings political unity, and as culture can only survive and strive in diversity, cultural diversity is the source of political unity.

2   Culture Is in Constant Becoming, as Our Societies Are

Culture is based on diversity. Through diversity, culture is challenged and remains in constant becoming and in a perpetual adaptation process. Such values as acceptance and moderation are vital for this. Fraser, bringing a more systemic approach, underlined the necessity of the multiplicity of cultural spheres in a society.

However, cultures are not the only challengers of culture, and technological as well as societal changes are raising new issues such as the disruption of the notions of territoriality and ancestry (Schachtner 2014) on which culture relied; the magnetic transformative power of the consumption society, making consumption goods out of culture; or the search for absolute objectivity in scientific research.

Culture is challenged, both in its unity and diversity, and politics are deeply needed to foster cultural innovation and adaptation.

2.1 Culture Is Based on Diversity, It Needs Diversity

Culture needs to be challenged through diversity. If there are some universal values and basic human rights, there also needs to be acceptance for diversity. Cioran would declare, "There is no intolerance or proselytism that does not show the bestial nature of enthusiasm" (Cioran 1975). Some of this diversity can be found in language diversity, particularly in Europe as was described in the Maalouf report. Finally, exchanges between cultural spheres have to be encouraged, particularly in a Union where transnationality is so strong.

"In itself, every idea is neutral, or should be; but man animates ideas, projects his flames and flaws into them; impure, transformed into beliefs, ideas take their place in time, take shape as *events:* the trajectory is complete, from logic to epilepsy… whence the birth of ideologies, doctrines, deadly games" (Cioran 1975). If societies bring cultures to life via a process that requires a certain agreement on the values inserted in these cultures, the strength of this agreement should never be as strong as to lead to the refusal of other cultures and values. Apart from certain rights recognized as necessary for the respect of the intrinsic value of Man and the functioning of societies, moderation and acceptance should be the principles on which relations between different cultural spheres are based.

Montesquieu illustrated this need for tolerance in his famous *Lettres Persannes*, fighting the renewed intolerance to Protestantism in France, which followed the revocation of the Nantes edict in 1685. Adopting the point of view of two Persians, he would expose the dangers of proselytism. The sprout of intolerance can be found everywhere but only man can be held responsible for his germination: "I admit that histories are full of religious wars: however, we should be cautious, it is not the multiplicity of religions which produces wars, but the spirit of intolerance which animates the one that believed it was dominant" (Waddicor 1977).

Tolerance is a requirement, and as Levinas underlined it, it is a necessity that needs to be respected by everyone even if reciprocity is not guaranteed. "I am responsible for the Other without waiting for reciprocity, were I to die for it. Reciprocity is his affair. It is precisely insofar as the relation between the Other and me is not reciprocal that I am subjection to the Other; and I am 'subject' essentially in this sense. It is I who support all.... I am responsible for a total responsibility, which answers for all the others and for all in the others, even for their responsibility. The I always has one responsibility more than all the others" (Lévinas 1982).

In such a sense, tolerance and moderation are prerequisites for cultural diversity. In regard to the other, acceptance and not understanding are required. The "*Bekanntschaft Instinkt*" is seen by Nietzsche as a means to achieve an instinct of appropriation and conquest (Nietzsche 1901).[1] Thus cultures should accept other cultures, and the relations between the different cultural spheres is what allows systems to adapt and evolve. Embracing diversity, cultural imperialism is to be rejected. In such a union as the European Union, cultural diversity partly takes its origin in language diversity as shown by the Maalouf report.

The Maalouf report, published by the end of 2008, highlighted the need for language diversity in Europe. The European Union, created by a diverse group of countries, which became even more diverse throughout the several enlargements, should craft its identity drawing from this diversity. "We even believe that it can offer the whole of humanity a model for an identity based on diversity," states Amin Maalouf.

Creating an identity based on diversity can sound very vague a project, but Mr. Maalouf gives specific recommendations in his report. In fact, he isolates two particular propositions: we should make sure that the bilateral relations between people in the EU involve their two languages rather than a third language; all Europeans should learn a "language of international cooperation," de facto English, as a means to communicate efficiently with everyone, and a second language which he calls the "language of identity." This language would be learned for its cultural aspect. It would also give each person a competitive advantage in specific areas.

---

[1] "Ramener ce que l'on appelle l'instinct de la connaissance à un instinct d'appropriation et de conquête," *La Volonté de Puissance*, I.365, Nietzsche

Learning this second "language of identity" would facilitate following of the first recommendation, as every country would have citizens proficient in a second specific language. Mr. Maalouf explains, "Using this approach, we would hope to overcome the current rivalry between English and the other languages, a rivalry which results in the weakening of the other and which is also detrimental to the English language itself and its speakers."

Such a system would efficiently encourage linguistic diversity in Europe, and would also reinforce the bilateral relations between each EU country, thus strengthening the European cohesion, which cannot be solely based on relations between individual countries and Brussels-based entities. Finally, as language is one of the most personal aspects of one's culture (as suggested above, it even changes the way one thinks), it needs to be respected above all other cultural aspects. As Amin Maalouf stated, "The European ideal is founded on two inseparable conditions: the universality of shared moral values and the diversity of cultural expression."

Cultural diversity is both an aim and a reality in our modern societies. For Christina Schachtner, culture is in itself based on "a conglomerate of interconnected meaning-contexts," thus grounded in diversity. More importantly, cultural spheres interact because individuals no longer belong to one unique sphere. Jacques Généreux, in his book *L'Autre société*, highlights the importance for individuals to be able to be part of different communities in society, as such reinforcing their own identity. This diversity, undoubtedly reinforced by globalization and tools such as the internet, leads to a transformation of cultural and public spheres. "The idea of culture as a 'self-contained sphere' has become obsolete in an age of digital media," states Christina Schachtner. This transformation brings strong positive changes, as public life can now fully accept diversity when fulfilling its normative role.

However, if such diversity can lead to a strong political unity, it must be well managed to fully benefit society. Marcel Gauchet (1998) warns us of what he names "the democracy of identities," in which a perverted conception of representativeness dominates. The representative democracy used to aim at bridging the cultural differences between the individuals in order to isolate a form of common will, and make sure that these differences remained visible in the public sphere and played a role in the political process. The emerging conception of the representative democracy focuses only on a continuous representation of the differences, leaving aside the synthesis necessary to craft policies and act. "The local and temporary chases the global," states Gauchet. The issue is not the one of over-representation, which would not make sense in a democratic context, but that of forgetting the notions of common good and collective unity. "By wanting to give an exact image of itself, aiming at granting the requests of the totality of its elements, it comes to slipping away from its own nature. In the name of democracy, it turns its back to the supreme democratic requirement, that of governing itself (Gauchet 1998)."

2.2   Culture Is Faced with Technological and Societal Challenges

Culture is nowadays faced with the need to adapt to the changes brought by technological innovation, societal transformations, and scientific progress.

Globalization and the IT revolution disrupted the very notion of territoriality with which culture was profoundly bounded. Mass culture and the consumption society are another kind of challenge as they might lead to a loss of meaning of cultural objects, transformed in sole entertainment goods. Finally, the search for scientific objectivity carries interrogation regarding the upkeep of the human dimension, as Hannah Arendt calls it.

> In most countries, citizenship rests on the three principles of territoriality, ancestry, and consensus (Benhabib 1997). In view of our increasingly networked world, territoriality and ancestry seem to have become anachronistic criteria for belonging, based on the fiction of a chosen society (Schachtner 2014).

The two dynamics of globalization and the development of the internet and communication tools have challenged the way we perceive space. As a consequence, our relationship with notions such as the land or the territory on which political belonging are based have also changed. If there is no corresponding, Westphalian definition of culture, cultural belonging also used to be deeply bound to a spatial demarcation. Alain Guerreau (1996), a French medievalist, analyzes the role of space as such during the twelfth and thirteenth centuries in Europe: "We can make the hypothesis that, if these variables were not functional, the system was, leading to the bestowing on all individuals belonging to the same micro-space of the same distinctive habitus. This structural particularization, emphasizing the heterogeneity of the social space, was probably quite efficient as a soft method to settle men." This role of space in the determination of political and cultural belonging was maintained throughout and after the modern era in Europe as the notions of nation-state rose.

Nowadays, and particularly in Europe with the development of the European Union which frontiers change with the successive enlargements, the relation between cultural and political belonging and territoriality tend to distend, as analyzed by Christina Schachtner and Seyla Benhabib quoted above. In this European Union, EU citizens can vote and run for elections at the local and European level. The system of attribution of social benefits depends on long-term residency and not citizenship. A guide drafted by a regulation passed in 2004 gives the definitions of the separate notions of "habitual residence," "temporary residence," and "stay."

Such important changes could lead to the transformation of citizenship and personal culture from given into acquired characteristics, but the modern threat of uprooting is also a consequence of this disruption of our perception of space. At the state and societal level, Poul Kjaer (2010) analyzes this movement as a definitive abandonment of the link between territory and sovereignty, arguing that the development process of the European Union is but the materialization of globalization. "Expansion is limited only by the level of globalization and the borders of Europe therefore remain a contingent phenomenon. Any attempt to achieve a 'final' definition of the borders of Europe, as is often demanded in relation to the debate on potential Turkish membership, is therefore futile."

However, this detachment process is far from complete and territory and nation-states remain a reality on which culture and citizenship still depend. Benhabib (2005) would write the following lines in 2005, which have become more relevant than ever in 2015: "Undocumented migrants, by contrast, are cut off from rights and benefits and mostly live and work in clandestine ways. The conflict between sovereignty and hospitality has weakened in intensity but has by no means been eliminated. The EU is caught among contradictory currents which move it toward norms of cosmopolitan justice in the treatment of those who are within its boundaries, while leading it to act in accordance with outmoded Westphalian conceptions of unbridled sovereignty toward those who are on the outside."

The detachment of the notions of citizenship and culture from territoriality, though not complete, sets new challenges in regard to the building of individual identity, social cohesion, and the management of people's rights in the international arena.

> Mass society, on the contrary, does not want culture, but entertainment and the articles offered by the entertainment industry are consumed by society as any consumption good. The products necessary for entertainment serve the biological process of society itself, even if they are not as necessary to its life as bread and meat are.... The free time which leisure is meant to fill in is a hiatus in the biological cycle conditioned by work in the metabolism of men with nature (Arendt 1968).

Hannah Arendt gives a very precise analysis of the consumption society which she considers in itself less of a threat to culture, as the prior use of culture as a means to achieve social recognition was. However, she highlights the tendency of the entertainment industry to use culture to produce entertainment goods, emptying in this process culture out of its content. A good example for this process would be Bruno Bettelheim's description (1976) of how the Disney interpretations of classical fairy tales, keep the main narrative elements but suppress the deeper symbolic and psychological aspects, which were of upmost importance for the personal development of children.

The difference between cultural objects and entertainment goods is that cultural goods have an immanence and permanency that entertainment goods cannot attain because of their sheer functional aspect. Hannah Arendt describes this functionality as the fact that entertainment goods are only created in order to maintain the vital cycle of society, that is they are only created to entertain. This "reductio ad functionality" can also be seen in a totally different context, which are the Google search engine and a larger development tendency of the internet. If we agree that the search engine only fulfills its role by presenting the web pages related to the keywords used, one aspect of the algorithms used has to be high-lighted, and is analyzed by Eli Pariser (2011). One of the methods used to render the results of the research process more precise, and more importantly more relevant for the person searching, is the personalization of Google results according to a set of factors going from the type of internet browser used to the previous researches made. Marc Zuckerberg (2011) illustrated the aim of this mechanism, which is in fact implemented by most web-related algorithms, as follows: "A squirrel dying in front of your house may be more relevant to your interests right now than people dying in Africa." This disruption of the results of personal research on the web, steered by sheer functionality, can be linked to Arendt's critique of the entertainment industry, and seen as a threat for the diversity of culture.

Finally, Hannah Arendt had warned of the search for perfect objectivity in science, and though her conclusions need not to be agreed upon, they should be reminded, as they are meaningful debate setters. She takes the example of the astronaut as a metaphor of the Heisenberg's man trapped in the search of an impossible objectivity, because only encountering the reality of space through his measuring instruments and analysis. Applied to the observation of nature, this quest for an Archimedean point remains noble, however, applied to the observation of man, it becomes a danger-ous approach, one leading to a new perception of technology, not "as the result of a conscious effort of man to increase its material power, but as a large-scale biological process" (Arendt 1968).

Such a perception could be a threat to the very human dimension as she names it.

2.3   As a Consequence, Politics Needs to Foster Cultural Innovation

Faced with these challenges, we advocate that cultural innovation is needed, as well as the adaptation of corresponding values. Our cultural and political inheritances remain relevant, however not fit for a world where the technological and scientific progress and the societal transfor-mations have given birth to new doctrines such as transhumanism. The evolution of culture could act as a trailblazer for institutional and political changes, and this cultural evolution should be favored by states and politics. If true innovation in these domains cannot be expected to come from institutional sources, public incentives and education policies (such as the development of transversal study programs) can however be drivers for creative thinking. Hava Tirosh-Samuelson (2007) highlights how these changes, of major importance for the evolution of society, are not accompanied with according critical thinking. "Focusing on self-fulfillment, transhumanists do not take the notion of virtue seriously enough nor do they explain how the values of the authentic Self promote human flourishing.… A more rigorous analysis of the meaning of happiness which lies at the foundation of the transhumanist project is needed."

Culture needs to follow the evolution of these questions because societies are rooted in intertwined cultural contexts and evolve along with them. Such cultural innovation needs to be accompanied with the promotion of symbolism, which will allow continuity and the upkeep of a sense of belonging of individuals to their societies. In the face of the important technological changes and consequential societal changes, Yehezkel Dror (2015) advocates for the promotion of "*raison d'humanité*," values which would assure that, whatever the consequences of progress might be, human oneness will always prevail, as well as the fundamental value of human life. "What is needed is a constantly growing sense of human communality combined with the readiness for efforts and also pain now in order to assure a good future for generations to come. Many agencies can help build up and diffuse such a sense, for instance writers and artists producing emblems on human oneness. But most important of all are spiritual leaders leading toward wide acceptance of *d'humanité*, as an increasingly dominant hyper-value and meta-ethical basis."

Culture is challenged by social and technological changes, and as a response it must change to, evolve in order to remain able to fulfill its role of goal-setter and source of political unity. The different actors influencing the evolution of culture need to coordinate their actions; states needs to encourage creators and make sure that the state of the cultural market does not lead to a reduction of cultural diversity. On the other side, the cultural industry needs to reject short-termism and the lone search to maximize its profits.

The symbolic value of culture is needed more than ever.

3   The Consequences for States and the EU

Facing strong challenges, culture is in need of political action and innovation. This part will focus on how European actors, from all sectors, can react to protect the diversity of culture and improve the access to culture, by addressing market failures and bias set up by technological innovation and globalization.

3.1   Cross-Sectoral Innovation, Collaboration Based on the Idea of Diversity

The cultural industry market is a very specific one due to the characteristics of cultural goods. The production process is very long and costly, as it is associated with irreversible costs (especially for the audio-visual industry). It leads to the creation of an intellectual property, which can be stored and transferred for a very low cost. Marginal costs intervening after the creation of the intellectual property are low, too. Regarding the market itself, the demand is difficult to predict as Richard Caves's "nobody knows" principle states, and this demand drops brutally when a new cultural good enters the market and replaces older ones. This evolution of demand leads to the implementation of discriminatory prices: in the movie industry, prices vary strongly between seeing a movie at the cinema or on cable TV a few years later. All these products have a very low substitutability as every creation is unique and kept unique via the management of the intellectual property rights (IPR). Finally, the presence of gatekeepers limits the price-setting power of consumers and reinforces the need for strong and costly marketing campaigns at the launch of a new cultural good.

In this very specific industry, Smithian principles of free market cannot be solely applied. Structurally, the rules of IPR management and the presence of gatekeepers lead to consolidation and the restriction of competition. Only the most important companies can afford to play the "nobody knows" roulette in the film industry, only the biggest firms taking advantage of media cross-ownership can exploit franchises to their maximum by developing corresponding products for all available cultural markets. As Nicholas Johnson would state, "At the global scale, the overbidding of manufactured super-productions and superstars replaces diversity, quality, and new talents" (Grand and Wood 2004). Cultural innovation and creation comes from individuals and companies, but public actors need to intervene on the market, either by some competition regulation, or via incentives, in order to favor cultural diversity and to make sure that the structural mechanisms of the market do not lead to a decrease in cultural diversity.

The cultural industry and the cultural sphere are areas where private and public actors, academia, and producers need to align their strategies and act together. If in the USA, the Motion Picture Association of America and the government seem to have found common ground in the advocacy for the development of bilateral free trade agreements (FTAs) encompassing cultural industries, in Europe the public and private sectors cooperation is yet to be developed.

Such collaboration needs to be based on diversity. The multiplicity of cultures in Europe needs to be protected in the reinforcing of the industry. Culture is a common good, which benefits society far more than just by leading to job creation and innovation as shown in the first two parts. This makes a second argument for state intervention in the cultural sector, as well as for the industry to adopt a longer-term vision than an exclusive maximization of profit.

If the toolkit for state intervention is already quite developed, the collaboration methods need to be crafted.

3.2   Advocating for the Development of Integrated and Collaborative Methods in the Cultural Industry

In Europe, the cultural industry market is not a unified one. Broadcasting networks are nation-based and geoblocking prevents an efficient dissemination of content. This fragmented state favors the domination of US cultural products. The low marginal production prices and transfer prices in the cultural industry facilitates exports. Benefiting from a naturally dynamic and large market at home, American production companies are extremely competitive when entering foreign markets, as the costs associated with entering the market are very low and the previous producing costs already matched. Peter S. Grant and Chris Wood wrote that in 2001, although India was producing more movies than the US and was exporting them successfully, however not on the US market, the revenues from selling American movies' intellectual property rights abroad was equal to 750 times the revenues made by India. "The American cinema industry benefits, by itself, from a trade surplus in its trade relations with every country in the world. No other American company can present such results," declared Jack Valenti in front of the US Congress in 2002.

To compete with such giants, the European companies need to gain scale and have access to more efficient broadcasting networks, as well as to have an easier access to financial means. However, Europe should also refrain from creating a similarly unified industry where the favorite tool to bypass the "nobody knows" principle is the copy of previous successful creations, thus inhibiting true creation.

In their action with cultural industries, governments have the ability to use positive and negative actions, incentives, or regulation.

Competition regulation is a complex topic in the cultural industry, as some mechanisms first appear as counterintuitive. Due to the characteristics of the market and industry stated above, acting in the sole aim of establishing perfect competition on the market can lead to a decrease in cultural diversity. Permitting some consolidation can be more favorable, provided that the rightful incentives and regulations are set to make it support creation diversity. On the contrary, giving more pricing power to retailers via the resale-price-maintenance mechanism in Canada has encouraged the diversity of the offer on the book market by preventing over-competition between bookstores and following consolidation.

Regarding incentives, a quite comprehensive toolbox exists. States can establish broadcasting quota, cap the possible private expenses for certain industries, limit the power of gatekeepers and control cross-media ownership,[2] sponsor creation in underrepresented art forms via subsidies or fiscal incentives or even control the broadcasting ratios of foreign versus national products.

---

[2] See the *Elephant Next Door,* for a survey of different media ownership regulations, http://www.mediareform.org.uk/wp-content/uploads/2013/02/The-Elephant-Next-Door.pdf.

To be efficient, these policies need to share objectives with the industry, and vice versa. Collaborative models, to be set up by all stakeholders involved, should guarantee this efficiency.

Cooperation between these two parties can also take the form of public-private partnerships (PPPs) in the building of ICT infrastructures. The development of transnational broadcasting networks is also to be privileged. Arte, created in 1992, is the illustration of an efficient collaboration between two national broadcasting networks, encouraged by public actors. Since 2006, Arte is also broadcasted in Belgium, under the specific Arte Belgique label. Transnational by nature, it favors diversity and creativity while also being a material representation of the common cultural ground shared by European countries.

Cultural industries are very specific industries, entertaining sometimes contentious, sometimes positive relations with culture and cultural diversity. If there is no easy way to encourage creativity, governments have tools to regulate the market and make up for the market failures. They also need to cooperate with the industry and harmonize their long-term goals.

Being aware that culture benefits society and individuals more than in the classic economic ways, it is by acting together that the private and public actors can face the challenges set by technological and societal progress.

3.3   Curiosity: The Search for Beauty and Happiness

Creativity however keeps a mysterious aspect, as true creation mostly remains the result of serendipity. As quoted above, Daniel Zajfman, president of the Weizmann Institute, would say, "There is no good research without aesthetic emotion." The search for happiness and beauty should be an ever-present goal of cultural industries and cultural public policies.

The sources of sheer newness of thinking and making remaining for the most part unknown, one should follow his curiosity as Aristotle stated in *Metaphysics*, "Now he who wonders and is perplexed feels that he is ignorant…therefore if it was to escape ignorance that men studied philosophy, it is obvious that they pursued science for the sake of knowledge, and not for any practical utility…. Clearly then it is for no extrinsic advantage that we seek this knowledge; for just as we call a man independent who exists for himself and not for another, so we call this the only independent science, since it alone exists for itself" (Aristotle and Warrington 1956).

Symbolism is the medium linking cultural objects and their creation with such meanings and principles. Of major importance to achieve political unity, it is of similar importance to foster creativity and as a consequence cultural diversity. "Conscience cannot invent a symbol or predict its efficiency as well as it cannot predict or steer the dream we will make tonight" (Campbell 1972).

Culture is a concept encompassing a diversity of meanings depending on the context surrounding its use: from a hierarchy of values and a system organizing individual and societal goals, to specific structures of thinking and the subjective part of every empirical and analytical process. Finally, culture may be best understood as a catalyst, a symbolic force that can bring societal and political cohesion via the definition of a common future and shared purpose. Transformative and normative, culture strives in diversity. Challenged, it grows stronger. In an ever-changing environment, culture needs to constantly evolve and adapt in order to keep fulfilling its role. Such a process needs to be favored by all relevant actors, be they private or public, individuals or institutions, and by all relevant means.

The power of symbol and culture should not be undermined. True creation is always backed by a cultural inheritance, and shaped by abstract symbolic goals such as the search for knowledge, beauty, or the pursuit of happiness. Arthur Schopenhauer (1818) argued that art, leaving aside the unnecessary, and independent from the influence of the will, allows a true comprehension of the world and a true apprehension of Ideas.

> If poets sing of the blithe morning, the beautiful evening, the still moonlight night, and many such things, the real object of their praise is, unknown to themselves, the pure subject of knowledge which is called forth by those beauties of nature, and on the appearance of which the will vanishes from consciousness, and so that peace of heart enters which, apart from this, is unattainable in the world. How otherwise, for example, could the verse—
> "*Nox erat, at cœlo fulgebat luna sereno, Inter minora sidera,*" affect us so beneficently, nay, so magically?

References

Arendt, H. 1968. *Between past and future*. New York: Viking Press.

Aristotle, and J. Warrington. 1956. *Metaphysics*. London: Dent.

Benhabib, S. 2005. Borders, boundaries, and citizenship. *Political Science & Politics* 38(4): 673–677.

Bettelheim, B. 1976. *The uses of enchantment*. New York: Knopf.

Buber, M. 1938. *Je et tu*. Paris: Fernand Aubier.

Campbell, J. 1972. *The hero with a thousand faces*. Princeton, NJ: Princeton University Press.

Chomsky, N. 2006. *Language and mind*, 3rd ed. Cambridge: Cambridge University Press.

Chomsky, N. 2007. Of minds and language, Biolinguistics.

Chomsky, N. 2012. *Le Langage et la Pensée*, 4th edn. Paris: Payot.

Chomsky quoting Jacob, Jacob, François. 1977. Evolution and tinkering. *Science* 196(1): 161–171.

Cicero, M., and J. King. 1927. *Tusculan disputations*. London: W. Heinemann.

Cicero, M., and C. Moreschini. 2005. *De finibus bonorum et malorum*. Monachii [Munich]: Saur.

Cioran, E. 1975. *A short history of decay*. New York: Viking Press.

De Botton, A. 2006. *The architecture of happiness*. New York: Pantheon Books.

Dror, Y. 2015. Priming political leaders for fateful choices. *ERUDITIO* 1(6): 40–49.

Gauchet, M. 1998. La Religion dans la démocratie, parcours de la laïcité. Paris: Gallimard. p. 174

———. 2002. *La démocratie contre elle-même*. Paris: Gallimard.

Grant, P., and C. Wood. 2004. *Blockbusters and trade wars: Popular culture in a globalized world*. Vancouver: Douglas & MacIntyre.

Jacob, François. 1977. *Evolution and tinkering. Science* 196(1), 161–171.

Kjaer, P. 2010. *Between governing and governance*. Oxford, UK: [Tournai]: CastermanHart.

Laloup, J., and J. Nélis. 1963. *Culture et civilisation: initiation à l'humanisme historique*, 4th ed. Paris: Tournai.

Lévinas, E. 1982. *Ethique et Infini*. Paris: Fayard.

Maalouf, A. 2008. A rewarding challenge: How language diversity could strengthen Europe. Proposals from the Group of Intellectuals for Intercultural Dialogue set up at the initiative of the European Commission, EAC_C5_Rapport_gr_intello_interi1

Muckler, F., and S. Seven. 1992. Selecting performance measures: "Objective" versus "Subjective" measurement. *Human Factors—Special Issue: Measurement in Human Factors* 34(4): 441–455.

Nietzsche, F. 1995. *La Volonté de Puissance*. Paris: Gallimard.

Pariser, E. 2011. Beware online filter bubbles. TED, https://www.ted.com/talks/eli_pariser_beware_online_filter_bubbles?nolanguage=us

Picq, J., and R.D. Descoings. 2009. *Une Histoire de l'Europe: Pouvoir, Justice et Droit du Moyen Age à nos jours*. Paris: Les Presses de Sciences Po.

Van Rompuy, H. 2011. Opening speech for the hundredth anniversary of the first "Conseil de Physique Solvay".

Schachtner, C. 2014. Transculturality in the internet: Culture flows and virtual publics. *Current Sociology* 63(2): 228–243.

Schmitt, C. 1985. *Political theology*. Cambridge, MA: MIT Press.

Schopenhauer, A. 1818. The World as Will and Idea—Supplements to the Third Book. p. Chapter XXX, On the pure subject of knowledge.

Tirosh-Samuelson, H. 2007. Facing the challenges of transhumanism: Philosophical, religious and ethical considerations. *The Global Spire, e-publication of Metanexus institute*.

Waddicor, M. 1977. *Montesquieu, Lettres persanes*. London: Edward Arnold.

Zuckerberg, M. 2011. In E. Pariser, When the internet thinks it knows you. *The New York Times*. http://www.nytimes.com/2011/05/23/opinion/23pariser.html?_r=0. Accessed 22 May 2011.

12

Beyond the Crystal Ball: Foresight

Stefan Schepers

The future of Europe is not singular and linear, but plural and complex. Various "futures" are possible, some of them bringing positive developments, others bringing dramatic, if not catastrophic, changes. Much of what will happen in the decades to come will depend on the strategic agility to manage the various interdependent paradigm shifts and on efficient collaboration between key actors, in the first place, though not exclusively, the EU Commission and national governments. In addition, the role of other stakeholders such as companies large and small, academia, and of course civil society will have an impact on our collective future.

Indeed, whether the future of Europe will be a happy one for all its people or not, will depend in the first place on the steering mechanisms without which social life is impossible, as Claude Lévy-Strauss already observed in small, so-called "primitive" societies (Lévy-Strauss 1955). How much more valid this is in contemporary, technology-driven, complex and continuously evolving, highly populated societies. Europe has

S. Schepers (✉)
Henley Business School, UK
e-mail: stefan.schepers@eppa.com

© The Editor(s) (if applicable) and The Author(s) 2016
K. Gretschmann, S. Schepers (eds.), *Revolutionising EU Innovation Policy*,
DOI 10.1057/978-1-137-55554-0_12

309

experience with sleepwalking into disaster (Clark 2012). Observing national and European idiosyncrasies today, nothing seems to guarantee that it could not happen again. European governance systems date from the 1950s and have not yet been fundamentally adapted to the postindustrial economy and society. They are capable of crisis management, as shown, hesitantly, a couple of times recently, but they also all too often seem to apply Churchill's famous comment (about the North Americans): "They always choose the right solution, after having tried all the others." Other stakeholders are not much better positioned, business being in a trance of neoliberal market thinking and many civil society organizations being absorbed in their single issues. A new failure to manage the Common Good is very well possible.

What will happen if and when the "perfect storm" arrives, as some analysts have defined it? It can take form concretely within the space of a generation, forcing most of us as well as our children to face an array of scenarios (Beddington 2011). Demographic growth disparities; food, energy and water shortages; the effects of climate change not properly and timely dealt with; major health threats resulting from environmental damage or industrial irresponsibility; persistently low economic growth in key economies; concentration of wealth and persistent massive poverty; resurgent intolerant nationalism; increasing governance crises and failed states; and powerless global organizations can all converge to create a never before seen geopolitical, economic crisis leading to uprooted societies and immeasurable human suffering. According to other thinkers, Europe may be well placed to develop and implement the changes required to ensure appropriate technological responses and sustainable economic growth, by which it will serve itself and the world (Rifkin 2004).

However, there is one key condition for this optimistic scenario: Europe must rise immediately to the challenge of innovating its governance and its policies in order to deal with these global challenges and contribute to the development of their solution. This will require more than the usual little steps. It demands a blueprint for radical innovation and a road map for its confident and consistent implementation, a road map which implies, first of all, reacting with agility to the interactions and feedback and not simply pursuing the same trajectories regardless of impact or a changing context (High Level Group 2013).

Europe needs to work toward innovation ecosystems that would make it possible to unleash dynamic cross-fertilizations and feedback between the hitherto insufficiently coherent actions of the EU and national governments, large and small companies, universities and centers of learning across borders and across economic sectors. Europe needs to design up-to-date processes for the generation of policy strategy and leadership capabilities for execution, taking into account its multilayered system and a renewed focus on the Common Good.

A more effective use of Europe's research and innovation capabilities and of its vast intangible assets can create entrepreneurial opportunities with multiple benefits, such as enhancing its overall resilience and global competitiveness, contributing to global problem solving and strengthening its global influence. Last but not least, it could also help Europe to preserve and at the same time innovate its welfare model, for its citizens no doubt the ultimate purpose of the EU, together with helping to ensure sustainable economic growth as the basis with real security in a troublesome world, starting in its nearer neighbors.

1   The Importance of Foresight

Foresight, future-oriented thinking, is an indispensable policy instrument in the context of rapid socioeconomic and technological changes. It is not sufficiently used in the EU, despite the evident foresight of its Founding Fathers. Professional foresight is a transdisciplinary approach that seeks to improve the ability to anticipate, create, and manage change in a variety of domains (scientific, technological, environmental, economic, cultural, and societal), on a variety of scales (personal, organizational, societal, local, national, and global) and through a variety of methods. The overarching objective is to permanently and comprehensively establish anticipatory thinking and a reflective handling of uncertainty in government institutions. This requires changes in the culture of organization and the processes of communication (Freuding et al. 2013).

All too often, policy makers think in terms of legislative periods rather than taking a future-term view and act in ways which are, as a consequence, both short-ranged and reactive. By contrast, government foresight aims to improve political decision making by taking into account long-term and uncertain developments, deriving strategies for governments from the knowledge and insights acquired. It can be particularly useful to ensure policy coherence and strategy planning in the Commission because of its stable 5-year mandate and its important mentoring role, which today is often neglected.

This chapter provides a concise overview of foresight studies relevant to the creation of an innovation ecosystem, particularly for the early identification of issues that can have an impact on it and the ways to deal with them. They include those key characteristics which allowed Europe to overtake the once brilliant Chinese civilization between the fifteenth and twentieth centuries (Ferguson 2012). On the path to this ascent, Europe faced a myriad of obstacles and challenges. Much in the same way, today's Europe faces not one, but several concurrent and fundamental challenges to its values, markets, democratic governance, and welfare societies.

1.1   Science and Technology Developments

Since time immemorial, societal developments have to a large extent, though not exclusively, been influenced by economic conditions, and these are determined by technologies available to solve key problems, be it the provision of food or the effects of climate change (Maddison 2001). Hunting, fishing, and gathering assured the survival of the first hominids, who 2.5 million years ago discovered the use of stone to produce a variety of tools. When hominids migrated from Africa to other continents, this simple technology nevertheless permitted them to settle, at first only for intermittent periods, in somewhat larger communities. These settlements in turn made possible the emergence of the first specialist occupation, that of the potter, to store food and water (Oliver 1999). Technologies continue to bring radical change to social life; pottery and bronze tools once had the same impact as more recent inventions are having in our age. But we do not yet have the hindsight.

We look benignly at the discoveries of the past, of which we know the multiple advantages and how to manage any possible disadvantages. But how can we deal with future discoveries, which carry many unknowns? Europe will be facing challenges because of a myriad of scientific developments and these are affecting the economy and society more rapidly than before. It took over 80 years for the automobile to reach more than half the population, it took the mobile phone, another cause of paradigm shifts, no more than 10 years. Radical innovations spread to and cross-fertilize with other sectors of the economy; this changes the conditions of social life and inevitably of governance (Perez 1998).

The drivers of the present industrial revolution are multiple and have, like before, known and unknown interdependent effects. To name but a selection: the internet (mobile apps, crowdsourcing, crowdfunding, crowd teaching); information technology (quantum computing, new microprocessors, big data, cyber-based assets); automation (advanced robotics, drones, human-machine interfaces, driverless vehicles, decision making); energy (solar, wind, biomass, geothermal, tidal, hydrogen, shale oil and gas, electrical power storage); life sciences (biotechnology, molecular and cellular genetics, neurobiology, bioinformatics, immunology); smart materials (nanotechnologies, graphene, composite materials, bio-materials, use of soft matter such as proteins or polymers).

In fact, the world is entering a new age, the Anthropocene, the age when the capacities for self-destruction and mutations have reached a level that they had never before in the Earth's history. They require deeply innovative governance methods for mentoring and monitoring scientific and economic developments and for creating the framework conditions to ensure that resulting market developments are a force for the Common Good. This in turn demands interdependent systems changes and, very important to avoid new derailments, new value developments (Dror 2015).

Science and technology themselves are not problematic, but their use can be. It demands deep interdisciplinary thinking about potential benefits and about limits to be determined by as yet nonexistent global governance. Europe's precautionary principle can be a useful tool for this, provided that its application is not politicized and that it is based on ecological and social ecosystem analysis, involving all the relevant stakeholders.

1.2   Competition

In economic history, it has forever been the case that competition has been driven by science and technology, but it is innovations in energy sources, communication, and finance systems, which are having the biggest impact and which in turn drive change in other sectors and in societies. The world is now in the early stages of a fourth industrial revolution, but Europe is not leading it as it did the first and second industrial revolution; it could at least strive to remain a key actor.

By 2030, the competitive position of the EU in the global landscape will be more contested than ever. The EU will represent only 6 % of world population and its share in the global GDP will have fallen to 15–17 %, behind the USA and China. Without an overarching drive for innovation, its geopolitical position, its growth and welfare societies cannot be maintained.

New economic powers, such as China, Russia, Brazil, and India, as well as other emerging economies like Mexico, Turkey, and South Africa may reinforce their roles as serious competitors to the EU and the USA in a completely multipolar international system. The latter two will produce less than half of the global GDP, with proportional loss of influence, all the more so because the emerging economies follow a different path to modernity, which is neither wholly nor partially based on the same cultural roots. But interdependence also increases economic and political vulnerability to unexpected events such as internal turmoil in one of these countries, or resulting from research and technology innovations, which may rapidly shift their competitive position. All new economic powers still fail to achieve the social stability that Europe's welfare state models bring, and they are thus prone to sudden and violent upheavals. The ongoing events in the Arab world are but one tragic example, made worse by ill-considered interventions.

The prominent role that trade has played during the past 20 years may be considerably downsized by 2030, further increasing the importance of the single market for Europe's companies, and of an extended European Economic Area, although the single market is in urgent need of completion and of efficient, unhindered functioning (ESPAS 2013). This shift is largely due to emerging economies becoming more mature and diversified, whereas they previously used commodities exports as an important tool for fast economic growth and the growth of their own industry and market. Parallel to this phenomenon, the "cutting up" of value chains will be less frequent, while new technologies may strengthen Europe's manufacturing industries.

Improving trade cooperation with all strategic partners, but also investing in emerging new powers, will help the EU remain a relevant player in global trade and finance. But the growing importance of trade in the Southern hemisphere will unavoidably change the global balance of power. At the same time, this new geopolitical context may bring new security challenges for global trade, 90 % of which travels overseas.

Spurred by growth in GDPs, emerging countries will also be more active on the global financial markets through the increase of their global investments. While Brazil, Russia, India, and Turkey are likely to achieve substantial growth, China will likely spearhead the process, turning into a world leader in foreign direct investments (FDIs).

Breakthroughs in science and technology will continue to shape every aspect of people's lives and will determine the most competitive economies. Internet data flows will grow to unprecedented levels, favoring knowledge sharing and innovation. Consequently, dependence on highly connected electronic and space-based infrastructures will also grow, as will their vulnerability.

In order to be ahead of the many competitors, the EU will have to invest intensely in R&D in order to reach the 3 % threshold by 2020, which must be considered the absolute minimum to remain competitive in R&D with the USA, Japan, and China.

Given its constraints on public budgets, it must develop more effective models of cooperation between public and privately funded research and across all member states before 2020, including having a global view of collaboration tools to exchange practices and find inspiration for innovative practices and ensure rapid market access of outcomes. For key sectors, strategic partnerships will help to ensure maximum benefit from the resources available. Meanwhile, European companies, incumbents, and innovation-spurring start-ups will need to collaborate with each other and with their international equals to be competitive on the global market, for instance through international platforms and networks to exchange views on innovative production and organization practices. New small companies will be more important for creating employment than the large behemoths, which however bring other advantages. Open and fair (reciprocal) cooperation agreements between them will be in the mutual interest and require amended thinking about state aid and competition.

The risks and benefits of new technologies should be assessed early on in order to develop regulatory frameworks appropriate for these new technologies that do not stifle innovation. The uniquely European hazard-based approach must be firmly rejected in favor of innovative risk management, based on collaboration between stakeholders and research. This in turn demands a careful process of nudging (part of) society toward a new realism, avoiding often artificial panic, which is becoming a hallmark of modern Europe (Berger et al. 1991). Corporations will need to seek a renewed focus on their public value, which can probably not be done without a different attitude of investors, brought about if necessary by regulations to force more attention for the Common Good. It may be the only way to restore the social contract and respond to civil society and media criticisms, however unbalanced and manipulated these may sometimes be (Neal and Davis 1998).

1.3   Sustainability

The biosphere, its diversity and interrelationships, provide the basis for our life. Today, we have the capacities to influence it more than ever, but all too often it is overlooked that we are an integral part of it and therefore remain susceptible to the development of the ecosystem in which we live (Biggs et al. 2015).

According to the World Bank, by 2025 climate change will cause significant water and crop scarcity in some 36 countries and affect 1.4 billion people, potentially igniting regional conflicts (Chatham House 2013). Energy and food scarcity might also cause trade disputes and political crises in regions already unstable.

Stress on sustainable development against a backdrop of greater scarcity of resources, like food, water, and traditional energy sources like oil and gas, and persistent widespread poverty, compounded by the consequences of climate change, will create further instability and slow down global growth. The new reliance on unconventional oil and gas is not likely to lead to a relevant boost in growth, but the potential of solar energy remains huge.

Before 2030, in fact even earlier, the EU will need to develop a clear strategy for low-carbon emission and energy and materials efficiency, investing heavily in new technologies and promoting a rule-based governance of energy resources. This is all the more needed as suppliers of raw materials may impose export controls as part of a more interventionist industrial policy.

In general, combining sustainability with competitiveness and managing resilience in natural ecosystems will require a shift from a conservationist toward a more dynamic environmental policy based on research and technology investments and cooperation between stakeholders. Business and ecology can profit from ensuring maximum resource efficiency and adaptation to climate change demands, such as by developing "circular" economic business models, which can also help to reduce dependence on uncertain sources of supply.

Overall, the interdependence between climate change, geopolitical shifts, resource scarcity, and security of supply can bring multiple benefits for Europe's lead in sustainability R&D and implementation as well as value creation.

1.4 Governance

Systems of democratic governance are being challenged by alternative models of delivering economic growth. They are further weakened by the effects of globalization, which undermine the steering capacities of individual governments, by the dysfunctioning of the US political system and the technocratic nature of the EU, with a decreasing legitimacy in the eyes of many.

Public confidence and governance legitimacy are essential prerequisites for developing solid strategic direction and implementing reforms. Therefore, new forms of democratic participation must be experimented with, also using the potential offered by new technologies.

The EU will be challenged even more to overcome the gap between an economically prosperous core and a periphery with significant innovation and competitiveness problems which might eventually lead to social upheaval and weakening or some form of disintegration of the Union itself. It will also have to find a neighborhood policy that is economically attractive for countries to the east and south whose membership cannot be contemplated without risk of internal political backlash and overstretch of its institutional setup. This will require innovative governance methods that allow a balance to be found between the interests of various stakeholders.

In general, a governance gap will likely weaken the legitimacy of national governments and international organizations alike. No single power will be able to play a leading role in the search for shared solutions to global problems. The key to success will be strengthened collaboration between national, regional, and global governance and between state and non-state actors (corporations, nongovernmental organizations) to build a consensus on strategic issues and pathways.

Multilateral institutions may find it very difficult to adapt to a new global power landscape. The system is likely to have the capacity to contain large-scale wars, but not smaller ones that equally bring economic devastation and human suffering, but it will be unable to meet other global challenges during the next two decades and there will be increasing pressure to reform multilateral institutions to reflect shifting power relations, including a drive toward greater inclusiveness.

1.5   Geopolitics

Fragmentation will continue to increase and the world of 2030 will be a mosaic of state and non-state actors, making international consensus and cooperation more difficult to achieve (Chatham House 2013). As such, the risk of international and intrastate conflicts will intensify, particularly in the Middle East, the Caucasus, Southeast Asia, and Africa. Accessibility to potentially dangerous technology will also make room for a growing number of small but destabilizing groups engaging in terrorism, and cyber and bio-war.

No leading actor appears set to achieve global leadership. While the USA will continue to represent the preeminent power in military terms, budgetary limitations and its dysfunctional political system will circumscribe its outreach, while its ideological worldview often alights or worsens conflict situations (as seen in the Middle East). China, whose military budget might well surpass that of the USA by 2030, is likely to face internal issues that prevent it from extending its military influence, or which may conversely lead to adventures. There, and in other countries, nationalism may again become a destabilizing force in international relations. Nationalism on the right and the left may even become problematic for the EU itself. "Coalitions of the committed" formed by a variety of state and non-state actors will address major global issues on a case-by-case basis. In this context, international organizations will have to radically change their approach and rely on small and agile coalitions to fulfill their objectives (Chatham House 2013).

The EU's long tradition as a consensus builder and its experience in rule-based integration will constitute a key asset in an increasingly fragmented world, where soft power, multiple stakeholders' management, and coalition building will likely count much more than sheer military power (Chatham House 2013). With this approach, the EU could become a flexible "super-partner" able to engage with a number of different actors and on a broad range of issues, including trade, conflict prevention, crime, climate change, and the environment or societal reconstruction. This, in turn, will contribute to its economic interests; but it requires carefully managing its own internal destabilizing forces.

Traditional supranational methods, useful for market integration and standardization, cannot be relied upon in other areas of policy making that require a more open, collaborative approach with (groups of) member states and other stakeholders. The EU will be challenged to develop new models of collaborative and democratic governance in order to effectively manage the growing complexity and interdependence of strategic economic and ecological issues it faces. Elections per se do not confer democratic legitimacy if conditions such as participation, collaboration, and public confidence are not fulfilled, which will require a deep re-thinking of the role of national parliaments.

This new approach is particularly needed to manage cross-border flows of trade, investment and services, and cross-border environmental issues. Without governance and regulatory innovation, the framework condi-tions for systemic change cannot be developed, thus hindering both technological innovation and competitiveness. Innovative governance, on the other hand, can reduce or put an end to short-term infighting and wasting resources. Lack of coherence within the EU and among member states is a serious obstacle which must be eliminated through an overarch-ing innovation policy drive and new steering methods.

But the EU's external actions are challenged by a weakness concern-ing its own identity and how its citizens perceive it. Europe is more a cultural identity than a well-defined geographic area, and on this basis it has developed a unique societal system (Duroselle 1965). In particular it raises questions about its relations with key neighboring countries such as Russia or Turkey, which are burdened historically and culturally but which require an innovative vision for the future and one developed in Europe with its own interests at the core.

1.6   Welfare and Social Cohesion

Global competition happens not just to be in the fields of research and economy, but also in governance systems and social models. Bhutan's innovative gross happiness index should be given more attention every-where (Kelly 2012). New technologies pose new challenges for democratic open societies and bring new opportunities to modernize democratic governance and stakeholder engagements. In particular the European open societies and welfare models, though in need of modernization and strengthening in changing times, will remain one of the main assets of Europe's global attraction and influence with people living in more unequal and autocratic systems. It will help to attract the best researchers and entrepreneurs needed to maintain a strong innovation stream in all sectors.

While at global level the middle class is growing, European countries face growing social inequality (and resulting political and social instability). An increased supply of labor could lead to a wider circulation of workers and a surplus of skilled workers, but also create risks for outsiders and vulnerable social groups such as the young, the unskilled, women, or people aged 55 and older.[1] Migration is useful when their skills can match labor market demands, but migration flows may be hampered by the financial crisis, societal resistance, and policy ineffectiveness. Employment of the workable population and employment-friendly welfare state adaptation therefore become central given socioeconomic pressures linked to increased spending on health care and pensions as well as on migrant integration, which all call for the promotion of skill sets and framework settings supportive of innovation.

The growing income and social inequality across the European Union is damaging to economic growth scenarios. Social inequality is correlated with poor health outcomes, variation in citizens' access to education leading to unequal educational outcomes and low productivity, which could put confidence in public institutions and the social consensus required to adjust in the face of shocks at risk. Higher inequality (after taxes and transfers) tends to limit the pace and durability of growth spells, which are important to achieve solid, long-run economic performance (Berg and Ostry 2011). Since inequality impedes growth, it calls for extra redistribution. Redistributive measures and efforts to improve economic opportunities for the poor, and the resulting narrowing of inequality, accordingly help to support faster and more durable growth (Berg and Ostry 2011).

The growing consumer class will affect resources in the EU market, such as energy and water, and will increase the pollution levels unless technology can bring progress. It can be assumed that this will have equally significant effects on migration flows and climate change, suggesting that the uncertainty arising from a new global consumer class is a central challenge the EU should prepare itself for.

Individual empowerment will increase, but so will the risks of a social and political divide. Empowerment refers to basic opportunities becoming

---

[1] For analysis of future social risks, see P. Taylor-Gooby (2005) *New Risks, New Welfare—The Transformation of the European Welfare State* (Oxford University Press).

more available for marginalized people. Education is seen as the main method of bridging the gap between developing and high-income countries as well as promoting equality in general (National Intelligence Council 2012). Education relates to employment, income, and life expectancy and is linked directly to gender equality. As countries like China, Japan, and South Korea attach more and more importance to education, it will further facilitate a stream of high-quality researchers and innovators.

Furthermore, empowerment is strictly linked to access to technology. Technological innovation can have positive effects on the economy and society and can positively influence the political climate, particularly if combined with education initiatives. However, increased global interconnectedness and higher education levels are leading to a need for new methods (IT based and other) of identifying conflicting interests and of transparently building compromises.

On the other hand, decline of trust in political institutions and authorities among large groups which are challenged by rapid change and whose social position is weakened requires appropriate responses to ensure political and social stability. The resurgence of nationalism and its political exploitation on the left and right of the political spectrum, in many countries, is a potentially serious threat to the multiple benefits of the EU. The divide often assumed between the individual and the state or the EU is caused more by specific policy failures, such as a lack of effective responses to the origins of the financial crisis and its aftermath, allowing inequality to continue rising, bureaucratic and political intrusions in citizens' lives pushed by single-interest organizations, and violations of the Copenhagen Principles by the state or civil rights by large corporations.

Poverty and social exclusion still affect a significant proportion of the world population. For all the progress made, weak education systems and the prevalence of disease, both epidemic and non-epidemic, will remain a major burden on human development. Current economic policies and global patterns of development suggest that areas of extreme wealth and dire poverty will continue to coexist.

In general, national social contracts will come under increasing stress if, in the aftermath of the financial crisis, no appropriate regulation is put in place to ensure the productive use of capital. Rising inequality within and between member states will put a heavy price on the Union

(Stiglitz 2012). Well before 2030, national welfare mechanisms will have to be modernized to ensure their continued effectiveness and reduce their overall costs, but they remain essential stability mechanisms in society.

1.7   Demography

By 2030, the world population's growth might have reached a plateau and could gradually start to decline, which may lead to less competition for natural resources, particularly water and energy, and fewer upheavals in formerly tumultuous regions due to the youth bulge (ESPAS 2013). However, there will be growing distress on public finances caused by the need to support a fast-aging population in Europe, Japan, and China.

During the next two decades, a shrinking in the working-age population in Europe will mirror sharp growth in developing countries, a phenomenon which will put high pressure on the European welfare models. European welfare systems need therefore to become more efficient and affordable, especially with regard to health and pensions. Whereas labor demand from employers may be stable or even slightly declining overall, there will be an increased labor demand in sectors such as health, social, and mental care, which may be the ones where a significant part of the labor supply should be channeled in order to reduce unemployment. But this will also require innovation to increase efficiency and affordability.

In addition, Europe may also face increasing immigration from developing countries, posing integration problems but also offering many opportunities on labor markets. Internal and transnational migratory flows, urbanization and birth/aging rates will continue to constitute determinant variables for governments and business.

1.8   Culture

Europe's cultural diversity and wealth of resources offer a unique advantage for creativity and innovation compared to its main competitors. European culture is a synonym for creativity, mixing Greek and Roman, Christian and humanistic contributions, the basis of modern research and industry, civil, and social rights. These past wisdoms can provide useful inputs for creative thinking about today's problems. Together they make up a European worldview that influences its relations with the rest of the world. Its more than five centuries of tangible and intangible assets provide a unique combination and a solid basis for innovation efforts to be made, given appropriate methods. This requires more careful nurturing through education and ICT and avoiding a general debasement of education and culture levels through a lack of proper regulatory frameworks and a misinterpretation of commercial freedom and long-term societal interests. Although Europe is technology friendly on the whole, this is not always the case. For instance, outdated views in universities about research cooperation with business mean that only a few countries manage to emulate the more effective cooperation of the USA or Japan.

The development of innovative tools such as health technologies, alternative energy sources, hi-tech communication devices, and social platforms will enable both states and individuals to exercise greater influence on their own and the global context.

Global networks of nongovernmental organizations, multinational businesses, and research institutions will virtually replace the traditional nation state. Personalized, cutting-edge technologies allow individuals to form ad hoc coalitions and influence decision-making processes, while national governments limit themselves to coordinating such groups. Old hierarchical structures will also decline in favor of a world where reaction speed and strategic agility count more than social position or issues such as poverty and world peace. Indeed, clusters of dynamic entrepreneurs take the lion's share in this fast-paced and highly connected world.

Millions of individuals are being empowered by the social, educational, and technological progress of the last few decades. It is estimated that more than half of the world's population will have internet access. However, new information technologies will remain unavailable to many people because of illiteracy and lack of access to electricity, although in some regions the availability of mobile phones may compensate for limited access.

Finally, the role of the media as an important cultural actor needs to be examined when preparing for future challenges. Media influences or even creates the framework for social and political actions because they are producers and messengers of opinions and symbols; they can ignore or amplify them, depending on their own orientation and interests (Schudson 2002). Images in particular can spur action, and so can social media campaigning, but they make evidence-based policy more difficult and may lead to undesirable outcomes or collateral effects in the long term.

2 Conclusion

In a more globalized world, science and technology, and demographic, cultural, social, and political developments are interacting and driving deep paradigm shifts whose outcomes are uncertain everywhere. They have the potential to contribute to the Common Good, but equally they can slip into the opposite. Moreover, they are not happening in a synchronized way, which in itself is a complicating factor. Economic and political systems, the world over, are at different stages of development and move in different directions.

We have but one way to steer them: through efficient governance, based on foresight and on multidimensional evidence building, involving all stakeholders which can usefully contribute to understanding the complexity of the emerging world. Within this, Europe is but a small part, held together primarily by common beliefs. Governance implies mentoring and monitoring social life, and allocating capital toward the Common Good. But our principal collective governance system, the EU, is in need of repair in order to make it fit for the challenges of the new age.

References

Beddington, J. 2011. Food, energy, water and climate, a perfect storm of global events? Paper archived by the UK Government Office for Science.

Berg, A., and J. Ostry. 2011. Inequality and unsustainable growth: Two sides of the same coin? (IMF Staff Discussion note).

Berger, P., and A. Wildavsky et al. 1991. Health, lifestyle and environment: Countering the panic. (The Social Affairs Unit)..

Biggs, R., M. Schlüter, and M. Schoon. 2015. *Principles for building resilience*. Cambridge: Cambridge University Press.

Chatham House/FRIDE Report. 2013. Empowering Europe's future: Governance, power and options for the EU in a changing world. https://www.chathamhouse.org/sites/files/chathamhouse/public/Research/Europe/Europe_Future.pdf.

Clark, C. 2012. *The sleepwalkers: How Europe went to war in 1914*. New York: Harper Collins.

Dror, Y. 2015. Priming political leaders for fateful choices. *Eruditio* 1(6).

Duroselle, J.-B. 1965. L'idée de l'Europe dans l'histoire (Denoël).

ESPAS Publication. 2013. The global economy in 2030: Trends and strategies for Europe. http://europa.eu/espas/pdf/espas-report-economy.pdf.

Ferguson, N. 2012. *Civilization: The west and the rest*. London: Allen Lane Penguin books.

Freuding, B., J. Fricke, L. Schmertzing, and F. Keisinger. 2013. Government Foresight für Deutschland. Stiftung Neue Verantwortung, 20/13

High Level Group. 2013. Report of the High Level Group on innovation policy management. http://www.highlevelgroup.eu/sites/default/files/download/file/130088%20EPPA_HLG%20REPORT.pdf.

Kelly, A. 2012. Bhutan gross happiness index: A big idea from a tiny state that could change the world. *The Guardian*, December 1, 2012.

Lévy-Strauss, C. 1955. *Tristes Tropiques* (Librairie Plon).

Maddison, A. 2001. *The world economy: A millennial perspective*. Paris: OECD.

National Intelligence Council. 2012. Global trends 2030: Alternative worlds. https://globaltrends2030.files.wordpress.com/2012/11/global-trends-2030-november2012.pdf.

Neal, M., and C. Davis. 1998. The corporation under siege. (The Social Affairs Unit).

Oliver, R. 1999. *The African experience: From Olduvai Gorge to the 21st century*, 2nd edn. Boulder, CO: Westview Press.

Perez, C. 1998. Neue Techologien und sozio-institutioneller Wandel. In *Kondratieffs Zyklen der Wirtschaft*, ed. H. Thomas. Nefiodow, Herford: Busse und Seewald.

Rifkin, J. 2004. *The European dream: How Europe's vision of the future is quietly eclipsing the American dream*. Cambridge: Polity Press.

Schudson, M. 2002. The news media as political institutions. *Annual Review of Political Science* 5: 249–269.

Stiglitz, J. 2012. *The price of inequality.* New York: W.W. Norton & Company.

Taylor-Gooby, P. 2005. *New risks, new welfare: The transformation of the European welfare state.* Oxford: Oxford University Press.

13

Match and Mold: The Crucial Role of Enterprises to Manage Innovation – A Case Study

Egbert S.J. Lox

1 Purpose

A view on the crucial role of enterprises to manage innovation within an innovation ecosystem is given based upon common materials technology industry best practices. These are illustrated at several occasions with experiences made and lessons learned during the transformation of Umicore from a mining to a materials technology company.

The description highlights the value of flexibility in the innovation undertakings. This feature explains for the most part the resilience of industry-driven innovation efforts. The innovation methodology developed is offered as inspiration for innovation processes in other industry sectors and in public bodies.

E.S.J. Lox (✉)
Senior Vice President Government Affairs at Umicore
and Honorary Professor at Karlsruhe Institute of Technology (KIT), Belgium
e-mail: egbert.lox@umicore.com

© The Editor(s) (if applicable) and The Author(s) 2016   **329**
K. Gretschmann, S. Schepers (eds.), *Revolutionising EU Innovation Policy*,
DOI 10.1057/978-1-137-55554-0_13

2   Background on Umicore

Umicore's roots date back to the nineteenth century. The roots of the industrial activities included the mining of zinc in Europe, whereby its license to operate was based upon an innovative process for the primary extraction of zinc from ores. Over the years, many other nonferrous metal activities were added to the portfolio, and through continued innovation in the extraction process technology a business leadership position was reached in many of the areas of business activities. The business model was "linear"; ores were transformed into metals, using the technology competency "metallurgy" (Fig. 13.1). Research and development activities were focused on process innovations, which yielded worldwide technology leadership positions. Strong process engineering competencies—and teams were established and the new processes were even licensed worldwide.

Around the end of the twentieth century, the economic viability of this business model with its strong industrial operations basis in Europe became challenged. This led to a necessity to innovate the business model substantially. The outcome was a "circular" business model, which included a shift in the position in the value chain of product making on the one hand, and a "closing-the-materials-loop" concept on the other hand (Fig. 13.2).

Today, the industrial activities span 29 chemical elements, mostly nonferrous metals. These elements are transformed into products that have a function, also described as "materials solutions." Key examples are materials solutions that enable sustainable mobility, which ranges

Fig. 13.1   Former, linear business model of Umicore predecessor companies

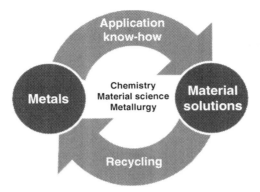

Fig. 13.2   Current, circular business model of Umicore

from catalysts used to minimize the emission of obnoxious components in the exhaust gas of combustion engines up to several products for electrified powertrains. The latter include catalysts for fuel cells, cathode materials for lithium-ion batteries, and crucial parts of the connectors and switches for electrical currents. This is the upper part of the activities circle (Fig. 13.2), and the technological competencies needed now include chemistry and material science, on top of metallurgy. These activities are complemented by the industrial activities for enabling the high-quality recycling of the products that contain the elements out of the portfolio at the end of their functional life. This is the lower part of the activities circle. Knowledge is created and innovations are developed and implemented into the industrial processing plants to enable the re-extraction of the elements from these complex waste streams. The process technology combines several high-tech pyro-metallurgical and hydro-metallurgical processing steps. Doing so an "atomistic" level of re-extraction is established which allows running indefinite times through this circle without negative impact on the quality of the products. This is a unique property of metals. These combined operations, generating materials solutions for clean technologies on the one hand and ensuring keeping the elements used in the industrial loop on the other hand, clearly serve sustainability endeavors.

3   Technology and Competency Needs

In a dynamic global technology competition, there is a need for regular upgrade of the competency portfolio. The challenge usually is to acquire these new competencies in a rapid way and at the same time at a top-class level, while still nurturing the most valuable historical competencies basis. There is no unique or straightforward way to reach this target; usually, several approaches need to be combined. A possible starting point is the acquisition of a few companies that have a strong and complementary technology basis. This acquisition can be done worldwide, whereby a constructive integration process is needed to secure the long-term blossoming of the acquired competencies. This needs international experience of the management to work positively with the cultural diversity. It also needs a well-developed human resource strategy, so that job rotation on an international scale can be applied to make the acquired competencies quickly available within the major divisions of the company. This is a path forward that in practice only private enterprises do on a systematic basis to quickly upgrade their competency portfolio. It is today, in peacetime, rarely applied by governmental research and technology institutions.

Another way to acquire new competencies is to buy intellectual property, such as patents and licenses, on the worldwide market, and then to import this knowledge in the existing internal research, development, and innovation teams. This process is not always easy and requires a solid basis for the acquired competency to be already present within the company. One has to be able to understand the specific technologies and to judge the real value of the acquired knowledge well. Therefore, it is usually applied to grow existing competencies to a higher level quickly rather than to kick-start a new one. A recent development in the possibilities to purchase external knowledge is generated through the internet-based creativity services. There exist several platforms that link together on a virtual and worldwide basis scientific and technical questions on one hand, with answers and solutions on the other hand. One can experiment with these new services on an ad hoc basis. Typical lessons learned comprise the need for a solid internal starting base of the sought-after technology, so that one can both formulate very clearly the relevant questions, as well as understand and judge the value of the answers obtained well. Next to this is of course the important step to accept the externally generated answer and to implement it as a basis for further work. While this might sound straightforward, real-life experience shows that a deep-rooted culture of openness is required to overcome the "not-invented-here" reflex. This comment is also valid within one company for ideas generated in one department to be accepted by another. Sometimes a management process is needed for nurturing this behavior. Companies sometimes install a "not-invented-here award" for the best example of a team adopting an idea from a source outside of its own perimeter. Within private enterprises, such decisions can be taken and installed quickly—no need to compromise with established power structures or politics.

A different path toward the generation of technical competencies is to establish and grow them to a high degree within the company. This path usually starts with an external trigger, for example, by the hiring of an established experienced specialist or by initiating a collaboration with a well-renowned external research and technology institution. In the latter case, topics can be suggested for master's of science degree theses and company funding can be provided for PhD work at the university. In a globalized world, and from a private enterprise viewpoint, these hirings and collaborations are systematically done on a worldwide scope. To do this successfully the company needs both the expertise for international human resource processes and for university collaboration contract negotiations.

No collaboration runs by itself: substantial input is needed on a regular basis to ensure continued focus and to help removing both practical and technical obstacles on the way toward achieving the next collaboration milestone. This intensive interaction is facilitated by the vicinity of the collaboration partner. Helpful is the definition of a vicinity criterion for selecting the collaboration partners. An example of such a criterion is the need to be able to physically meet with the partner within a day of travel, which translated into a first level of partners that can be reached within a radius of about 150 km around the company's own technology centers for enabling trips by cars and into a second level of partners that can be reached within a radius of about 2,000 km around the company technology centers for enabling trips by air travels. The exemplary result of the application of the first-level criterion in the year 2010 for partners of the Umicore corporate Research & Development & Innovation center in Olen (Belgium) is shown in Fig. 13.3.

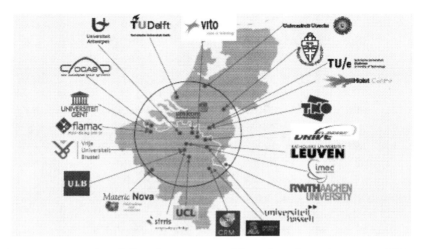

Fig. 13.3 Example of first level partnerships of Umicore in 2010 within a radius of 150 km around the R&D&I center in Olen (Belgium)
Note: Author's graphic account

A key performance indicator can be used to monitor and steer the intensity of reaching out to external partners. This also helps in ensuring a continuity of this undertaking, as reporting is needed when a gradual but systematic change in this context is happening. In materials technology industry, a typical dimension for the intensity of external collaborations is in the order of magnitude of 10 % of the annual R&D&I budget.

A competency is not developed alone by having one top-class expert hired or by establishing one collaboration with a top-class research institution. Around these a company internal "ecosystem"—a team, a scientific service network, and a research infrastructure—needs to be developed. The last of the three is the easiest to reach, as scientific and technical infrastructure can be purchased on a worldwide scale and, thanks to relatively well-developed international standards, also installed with a good degree of straightforwardness in the company local research, development, and innovation centers. Also the scientific service network is developing well on an international basis in the meantime, thanks to the internet and in general modern communication services. For example, high-end electron microscopy analysis can be done by a dedicated service provider several thousand kilometers away—but in the same time zone—while the company researchers observe in real time the results on their internet-connected computer screens and are able to express their wishes through the microphone. Much more difficult however is the setting up of the team of coworkers around the top-class expert. Especially for high-end innovation work a portfolio of dedicated knowledge and skills is needed, which span the conceptual, IT, and practical experimental work levels. Unfortunately, there is no guarantee at all that a sufficient number of dedicated trained human resources is available in a realistic living distance around the location the company research center. In such cases, initiatives should be taken by the company to develop them, in close collaboration with local universities, schools, and vocational training centers.

Doing a research project with a top-level institute somewhere in the world, far away from the company main research center, can be combined by having a compatriote doing post-doctoral-level work there, funded by the company as part of the research collaboration. This compatriot can be linked to a local university or school where he can subsequently built up his own research team and where he can then train there future collaborators for the company research center. A good understanding and collaboration with the local university is mandatory, including their willingness to start a new area of research activity but also including the company's medium-term, continued commitment to co-fund these academic research and teaching activities. Experience shows that this is possible but that it needs several years, thus a strategic-level planning of the competency needs is necessary.

The external purchase of technologies and competencies as well as the identification of the best potential collaboration partners in itself need the skills and procedures to find them on the worldwide market and then to rate them. Companies typically establish "technology scouting" activities for this. A good practice is to give the coordination of this mandate to an experienced research manager that has a solid record of accomplishment of technical and commercial successes, so that he can operate with a high degree of open-mindedness and without suffering from the "not-invented-here" protectionist reflex. The first steps of the technology scouting activities can be done through working with international databases, with investment banks and with start-up funding providers.

In addition, memberships of advisory boards at universities, technology institutions, and governmental funding agencies can be efficient sources. At some point, a mission to visit the potential collaboration partner is needed. At Umicore we have developed and applied dedicated procedures, for example, to scout at universities. This had the format typically of a full-day visit with a team of experienced researchers. Part of the day was dedicated to mutual presentations, in which we described our activities and needs on one hand, and in which the university colleagues described their activities and competencies on the other hand. The other part of the day was dedicated to topical discussions in small bilateral teams and to facility tours. A joint review of potential and/or proposed next steps would conclude the day. This type of interaction was performed with several universities and research institutions worldwide and resulted usually in at least one collaboration project, whereby this sometimes took a substantial delay after the visit. In general, the lessons learned with respect to the topic technology scouting are the value of patience, persistence, and then the need to manage the expectations well.

When developing new competencies at least a medium-term planning horizon is needed, typically spanning a period of 5–10 years. In the world of global business, a lot can change in such a time frame. Reasons for the potential changes comprise the economic cycles, political events, or radical technology innovations. All of these can induce a change of the business focus and thus ultimately lead to a need for a different competency portfolio. Still, some competencies have a kind of universal character, and are needed even despite changes of the business focus. The skill is to identify these "universal" competences well so that the efforts can be focused on them. A tool that proved to be valuable in identifying these universal valid competences is the so-called scenario planning. Good literature exists about this tool. One example of its application is shown in Fig. 13.4.

Starting from a business reality at some point of time, one can develop a scenario that describes an "ideal" world out of the viewpoint of your products and markets, and at the same time generate an opposite scenario, that would describe a "bad" world. Then one could construct a third scenario, in which one key business parameter changes substantially. Each of these scenarios has to be elaborated with some imagination. Possible consequences for the characteristics of the company products and services

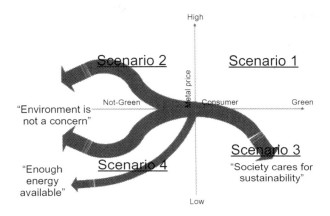

Fig. 13.4 Example of the result of a scenario planning exercise

have to be defined. Then one can come back to the technical level by deriving which technical competencies are needed for being successful in each of these three scenarios. There is a high probability that some competences come back in the three scenarios; they are the ones requiring focus on "must have's," while the other ones could be inscribed on a "watch" list and could be seen as "nice-to-have." The latter ones can be worked on when a good opportunity is available, for example, the invitation to join in a publicly funded research consortium that uses some of these competences.

Finally, to help in the planning of which technology competencies will be needed, it is valuable to define probable technology road maps that span a time horizon of up to 20 years. This definition can be done based on excellent technical understanding of the characteristics of the products and processes, and then applying solid imagination or even just extrapolation. Also, excellent information on technology road maps is available in the public domain, resulting from the top-quality work of the European Commission and/ or of sector trade associations. From these road maps the needed technical competencies can be derived. One ends up with a probable timeline when competence must have reached the needed maturity level within the company. A development action plan can be constructed on this information as well. One example of such a competence road map and of the possible and cost-efficient pathways to generate them is shown in Fig. 13.5.

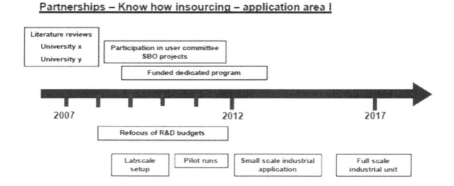

Fig. 13.5 Example of a roadmap for the development of competences

4   Organizing the Innovation Efforts

A common approach to reach innovations in industry is to structure the work as a process of consecutive steps. These steps start at the ideation/ discovery phase and end with a stable and profitable running industrial operation. One really useful tool to enable a common terminology on the position of a technology in this chain is the concept of a "Technology Readiness Level" (TRL). This concept originates from the aeronautics industry and it is in the meantime well applied in industry and in publicly funded projects, such as the current Horizon 2020 research program undertaking in the European Union. A description of the ten TRL levels currently used is given in Fig. 13.6.

It is common practice in industry to structure the innovation process in work programs. Each work program ideally targets raising the maturity of an innovation by one TRL level. Then a work program is subdivided in a collection of work packages, some of which are parallel to each other and others are consecutive. A work package has a pretty detailed description of deliverables, timelines, competencies, and resources needed. Project planning tools can be applied to structure each work package and to identify critical paths. In addition, risk maps can be elaborated and risk mitigation plans can be proposed. This detailed

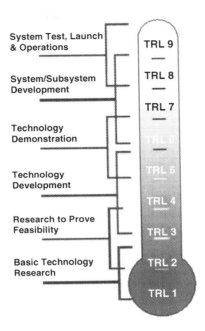

Fig. 13.6 Typical description of Technology Readiness Levels

level of structuring the innovation work is also a good tool in the decision process about which of the work packages has to be assigned to external partners, and which ones must stay within the company perimeter. Eventual needs for additional intellectual property measures can be defined. These can be the protection of in-house inventions by applying for patents and also acquiring "freedom to operate" rights, by purchasing external patents or securing licenses on them. Increasingly, technology companies even develop real strategies around the intellectual property aspect of their innovation work. This includes mapping the existing IP landscape, identifying the remaining gaps, and suggesting research work to address these opportunities.

For the first phase of the innovation, the TRL 1, several approaches are possible, depending on the type of innovation needed. If there is a need for an incremental innovation, usually the ideation is done internally, with company team members only. Structured creativity techniques such as brainstorming, brain-writing, trigger word analysis, morphological tables, etc., are valuable techniques meriting application. If there is a need for a bigger step of innovation, the team can be enlarged with colleagues from other departments, be it within the same business unit from different parts of the business process chain or from other business units. Also reaching out to tacit external sources such as the ones resulting from literature and patent searches can be recommended. Only then when real major innovation steps are needed, would an enterprise look for active external sources. This approach was described above and can serve two important goals. Either one is looking for really different ideas that would not be possible or probable to be generated with the internal competence portfolio. An example of this is the linking of chemistry and materials technology to aspects of the digital economy. Or, one is looking for an external support for ideas that fall outside of the common company culture. An example on how to get this external support has been mentioned above as well: one could use one of the internet-based suppliers of answers to address specific technical questions. If their answers match your own "out-of-the-internal-box" thinking results, this can be very supportive in passing internal juries. Another example to get this outside view is to formulate your innovation need into a research program that is submitted to a good public funding agency. Their evaluation processes are usually very professional and rigid, with the support of external specialists. Again, when the evaluation result is positive solid arguments have been generated to support and prioritize the proposed innovation ideas. When the evaluation is negative, it can be recommended to accept this as serious feedback that indicates that important aspects have not been well covered by the company's internal reflections. Finally, if one is wishing for an innovation completely outside the scope of the company current business perimeter, then a dedicated external approach is needed. In this case one can order an innovation project at a top-level technology provider, such as an Fraunhofer Institute in Germany, the CEA in France, vito or IMEC in Belgium.

In this ideation phase, usually many ideas are created, and practical experience shows that it is more difficult to select and prioritize the ones that should be further developed than to generate them in the first place. This process merits a high degree of attention and professionalism to avoid wrong decisions whose implications become visible only much later in the innovation process. In this selection process, a voting by a jury of company internal specialists can be recommended as a simple way to ensure a broader view on the choices to be made.

But, even with a careful selection procedure, there is no guarantee that the choices made stay the best as time goes on. Indeed, the boundary conditions such as potential applications of the new idea, the relevant legislation and the technology ecosystem in general do evolve quickly even in the field of material technologies. To cope with this reality one can apply the pragmatic concept of a "parking lot of ideas." The success of such a concept involves carefully writing down all the ideas together with the comments about why they are or are not selected at some point of time to be further developed. Then, this list should be reviewed at regular intervals, typically at least once per year in concurrence with the preparation of following year's budget for R&D&I activities. The list can also be used during the discussion of the milestones of the development of the chosen ideas, when they are moved up on the TRL scale and thus when more insights become available on the pros and cons of them. Many examples exist in industry that an unexpected negative performance result of an idea, chosen to be pursued for one application, brings one back to reviewing the original selection criteria. This can trigger the innovative insight that the idea could instead of a failure even be a breakthrough for a different application. This process of inventing is dynamic and thus needs both flexible and rapid decision processes on top of intensive communication. All of this is straightforward for private enterprises; it is a kind of "normal" business practice. Clearly, however, these are not the obvious procedures for public institutions. The strength is to combine the best of these worlds in a respectful way.

With the invested scientific and technical efforts, an idea is moving up the TRL scale to become a new product, a new application, a new production process or a new service. Reaching a higher level on that scale represents an important milestone, which needs again thorough discussions about the insights gained and about the better view on the size and content of the upcoming/ remaining work packages. That review is needed over and over again to make the basic and thorough choice to continue an idea or to stop it at some of these TRL levels. It is clear that also these decisions are difficult, but for different reasons than the ones applied for the first TRL level. Indeed, the achievement of a higher TRL level represents quite an investment of resources such as human resources (skilled researchers) and capital investments (experimental equipment). When stopping a project a substantial amount of financial means will have been consumed and these will not generate a direct return any longer. Beyond that, and usually even worse, precious "time-to-market" is lost. It is a good practice to attach top-level attention to these decision moments. One way to do this is to systematically use the project—or even the work package level steering committee concept. Depending on the corresponding TRL level a different composition of the steering committee can be appropriate. For example, at higher TRL levels the contribution of marketing, applied technology, and production skills will be beneficial, whereas at lower TRL levels colleagues from other R&D&I departments, thus representing the same basic skills but from a different technology angle, can help broadening the horizon.

The scientific work related to the lower TRL levels nowadays has fewer requirements on the location of the laboratory and technology center. Of course, an ecosystem is needed, which enables among other things good scientific exchange and which allows for short "proof-of-concept" types of experiments and/ or computer simulations. Thanks to the modern information technology these types of interactions and these type of services can be organized virtually on a global scale. This is even an advantage for a broad and diverse input to the idea generation process.

For the work on the higher TRL levels usually experiments on various sizes of equipment are needed. This means that laboratory and pilot plant scale facilities must be available. These represent substantial investments that take time to be installed. In this stage of the innovative work, time is a critical factor and even a practical idea killer.

One consequence is that laboratories are increasingly built as multipurpose facilities. They can be modified and adapted rather quickly to various types of experimental work, on the basis of a well-deployed supporting experimental infrastructure.

Another consequence is that public infrastructure such as technology and business incubator centers is generated throughout the European Union. Some of them offer experimental space on a rented basis. One example of this in Belgium is Innotek, a public undertaking that offers on

Fig. 13.7   Technology houses of Innotek in Geel and Mol (Belgium)

a for-rent basis offices and space for experimentation in technology at two locations, see Fig. 13.7. The neighborhood of among others high-quality scientific service providers such as vito and an international school creates a valuable ecosystem.

Multiple examples exist around the concept of public-private partnerships for enabling easy access to experimental facilities. One type of these partnerships is dedicated laboratories that companies embed in a university campus. Several advantages exist for such an approach, of which two are mentioned here, because they proved to have a strong effect in practice.

One advantage is the ease to work with bachelor- and master-level students, offering them a topic of industrial relevance for their theses, providing them with easy access to dedicated and up-to-date experimental equipment and being able to coach them out of an industrial expertise, on top of the academic guidance needed for such thesis-level work. The structured interaction between an academic and an industrial coworker is an inherent element and proves to be an inspiring and valuable side effect. An additional aspect is that one can help educate the students about applying the best practices of safety and of quality assurance while doing the experimental work. Both aspects are common practice in the meantime in industry and large RTOs, but even today they are less explicitly implemented at universities. Finally, reporting directly into the company proper knowledge management system is facilitated.

The second advantage is the possibility to host a team of company researchers away from the interference of day-to-day business-related issues. Experience shows that the pressure from short-term problem-solving needs is difficult to resist. Short-term successes are much more visible and stronger arguments in practice versus the long-term damage caused by regular interruption of basic innovation work. Just the mere fact of allowing a team of company coworkers to deploy their activities a bit outside of the corset of company rules, habits, and culture proves to be refreshing.

Another type of partnership is that companies deploy some of their teams in highly specialized RTO's that offer access to experimental equipment, which is unique in the world and beyond the investment capacity of even large companies. Strong examples are IMEC in Belgium, for microelectronics-related work, and CEA in France, for energy topics.

If the dedicated equipment is not yet easily accessible or not locally available, public-private partnership initiatives were taken in the recent years to generate them. One example of this is the Flanders Materials Center (FLAMAC). This is an initiative that aimed at providing the facilities for doing high-throughput experimental work in the field of material science. A few companies, leaders in the field of material technology but with complementary product portfolios, joined forces with the major industry association and the regional public funding agency to build up an impressive, "open access" type of experimental infrastructure embedded in a university campus. Fig. 13.8 shows schematically the

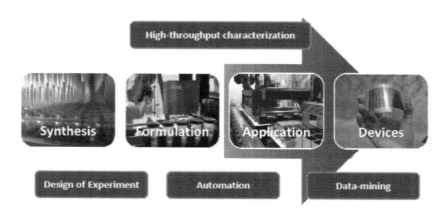

Fig. 13.8 Example of high throughput experimental equipment installed and competencies developed at FLAMAC

high-throughput experimentation competencies developed and some of the experimental equipment installed. The joining of forces included the cofunding of this multimillion-Euro laboratory by the industrial partners and their membership of the advisory board, so that their management expertise and methods were available to the team. A scientific sounding board was installed as well, to include the experience and the needs of various universities in the work program.

A second example is the joint undertaking of a few companies, together with a university and the regional funding agency to develop and build one of the most performant transmission electron microscopes in the world. This tool, called QUANTEM, shown in Fig. 13.9, is a critical asset for top-level materials technology development work, and easy access to it is a strong competitive advantage. The collaboration model had several elements: the co-financing of the investment yielded a multiyear priority access right to the analytical capacity, and dedicated training of company coworkers ensured the development of their skills of scientific interpretation of the results, thus enabling high scientific value to be gained from the experiments.

The above descriptions focused on the laboratory scale of the experimental work. For the other type of experimental work, related to the upscaling of the production processes, typical for the higher TRL scale levels, much larger types of equipment such as pilot plants are needed. As of today, this equipment tends to be custom designed and built on purpose, with limited flexibility with respect to its application. The size of the equipment is usually such that it needs to be built and operated on an industrial site, to benefit from the skilled production workforce and from the utilities and logistics infrastructure. With all these boundary conditions it becomes clear that this activity is almost exclusively done by industrial stakeholders. The role of the public agencies is important on the level of substantial subsidies to the investment. Nevertheless, there is room for the evaluation and discussion of a higher level of public–private partnership for this pilot plant activity. Indeed, this upscaling step, getting the product and the process close to the commercial application proves to be a "valley of death" in too many recent examples in the European Union. Among the many reasons for this, one needs particular attention, and that is the speed of deployment of the pilot scale experiments. The public–private partnership provision of multiple-purpose, flexible

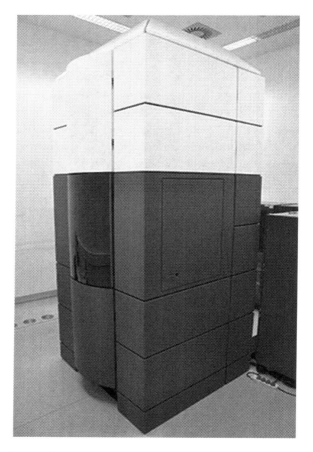

Fig. 13.9 The performant Transmission Electron Microscope (QUANTEM) installed at the University Antwerp (Belgium)

pilot plant scale equipment to perform the most common processing unit operations would help. Having these processing units designed to be mobile and to be able to operate on the basis of a "plug-and-play" principle could allow the faster assembly of a pilot plant experimentation facility. Some limited public—and somewhat more private—initiatives were started, though. For example, some of the large industrial parks of the chemical industry in the European Union have evolved from a single company activity to a multiuser site. Examples exist that the former central process engineering divisions were transformed into pilot plant scale service providers. An EU-wide, coordinated approach to deploy these concepts further has clearly amplified its value.

5   Collaborating in Consortia

The European Union—as well as many other parts of the world—is faced with substantial technological, economical, and societal changes that happen or need to happen. Among these changes are addressing the limited material resources, the need for sustainable energy supply, and clean mobility. Companies operating in these markets need to adapt or even better seize the opportunities generated by these changes. The innovation efforts needed are substantial and far-reaching, and the timing of this need is immediate. This is well understood by the public bodies in the European Union and beyond, and several initiatives are taken. Among the many initiatives, industry increasingly sees particular value in joining, promoting, or even initiating joint public–private undertakings.

One of these public–private undertakings that deserves attention is the Knowledge and Innovation Community (KIC) of the European Institute of Innovation and Technology (EIT). Several of the KICs exist already, each focused on a specific topic. The reasons for their installation are that the classical pathways toward innovations in their respective fields bear the risk of not addressing the most critical needs. The societal acceptance of the need for these innovations and of the need for the different behaviors of the European citizens in dealing with these major societal topics are of the utmost importance. Typically, neither company-driven nor university-driven innovations alone can yield these solutions. That is exactly the unique approach of the EIT: it aims at combining technology innovations with education and with new business. Taking the example of the recent installed EIT-KIC on raw materials, a large consortium was built up, with about 40 private companies, about 40 universities, and about 40 RTOs throughout the whole European Union (see Fig. 13.10). The consortium has a business plan for a time period of about 7 years with an integrated budget of more than €1 billion, of which about 30 % is funded by the European Union. The deliverables are

Fig. 13.10 Example of the members of the consortium of the Knowledge and Innovation Community on Raw Materials of the European Institute of Innovation and Technology

multiple and challenging; they include the training of several thousand master's degree students with a focus on raw materials issues, the development of Massive Open Online Courses (MOOCS) on the topics, the generation of several patented innovations, and the starting up of many new small companies. To that aim, collaborative innovation approaches are structured and regular technology brokerage events foreseen. Venture capital funds are defined as one of the target participants to these events. The management and the advisory board of the consortium combine working experiences in public and academic institutions as well as in private companies.

Another recent example is the Energy Materials Industrial Research Initiative (EMIRI). This association is driving forward research and innovation in the field of advanced materials for low-carbon energy applications. Innovative energy technologies are required to cost-effectively meet Europe's energy and climate change challenges. These technologies will be enabled by the introduction of new, advanced materials.

By bringing together research, industry, and trade organizations, and leveraging Europe's world-class capability in advanced materials, EMIRI aims to contribute to generating tangible growth in economic value and employment opportunities for Europe. About 60 members of this association assemble together in regular technology brokerage events, in which ideas are collected and prioritized, dealing with the scientific needs of the Strategic Energy Technology (SET) plan of the European Union. The results are offered to the stakeholders at the European Commission as possible guidance for the allocation of the public funding support in these areas. For the members, the benefits include the ability to have a voice in long-term priorities, to be informed about EU and member state priorities, and funding opportunities. There is also a benefit from the enhanced visibility of European and national policymakers as well as being part of a proactive, motivated network of potential future consortium partners.

Finally, we would like to share the positive experience we have had in joining public initiatives on the EU level, such as the European Innovation Partnership on Raw Materials (EIP-RM) and the High Level Expert Group on Key Enabling Technologies. All of these joint undertakings provide insights about the needs and thinking of other stakeholders, which are sometimes part of the same value chain or which have similar challenges on different technologies. The stakeholders consultations are a key element of the European Union way of defining actions and priorities, thus it is almost a duty for companies active in this market to contribute to the best of their knowledge.

6   Financing the Innovation Efforts

Private companies active in the medium-to-high-tech technology industry invest typically between about 3–8 % of their annual turnover in R&D&I activities. Benchmarking these activities in between companies of different sectors, or even within one company with a broad portfolio of activities, is facilitated by the use of a common definition of the scope of R&D&I activities. A helpful guideline for this can be found in the so-called Frascati manual of the OECD. The percentage of the annual turnover invested in

R&D&I activities is also a good key performance indicator for input into the innovation process. Typically medium- to large-size companies pay for their R&D&I efforts through their cash flows. Sometimes, however, for large-sized projects, special bank loans can be used in addition, such as the ones granted by the European Investment Bank (EIB). It is expected that this offering could be enlarged in the framework of the European Fund for Strategic Investments (EFSI) initiative of the EIB. For smaller-sized companies the venture capital market offers interesting opportunities.

Companies can also count on support of public funding sources. Typically, for a company with a solid record of accomplishment of innovations leading to job creation and a professional way of dealing with the funding projects, an order of magnitude of about 10 % of the R&D&I budget can be funded through public sources. Usually, various funding instruments, such as regional level ones and EU Horizon 2020 ones, can be combined in the R&D&I portfolio, each for different purposes and for different projects, of course. The use of various funding channels is justified by the different purpose of each one. Regional funding instruments can typically have specific expectations about the creation of jobs locally through the valorization of the innovation results. They can also attach for medium- to large-sized companies a requirement on the growing of the local innovation ecosystem along with the funded innovation project. Other funding agencies define their evaluation of the return of a funded innovation project more on a monetary basis. This includes then, for example, licenses that are sold for granted patents resulting from the funded innovation project. Some funding agencies have a long-term strategic objective and wish to contribute to ensuring that a specific technology competency is grown in the geographic area. High-level funding instruments such as the EU Horizon 2020 target the promotion of EU-wide collaborations in between companies, universities, and RTOs from different EU countries. Also strategic considerations are increasingly implemented, for example, by "earmarking" projects that apply for funding when they address a common strategic objective such as ensuring the supply of critical raw materials to the European technology industry.

Next to the project-based funding approach, and also longer term program-based funding initiatives exist. One example described above is the multiyear funding by the European Institute of Innovation and

Technology on the basis of the business plan of a KIC. Other examples are the funding through the European Space Agency (ESA).

Finally, some countries apply direct cost-reduction measures for R&D&I activities by the elimination of some of the indirect cost elements associated with employment.

The R&D&I investments to be done are decided and reviewed typically during the annual budgeting process. The construction of the budget proposal usually starts as a bottom-up initiative, structured to a substantial degree on the work programs and work packages needed to move technologies up the TRL scale. This has in several companies elements of a "zero-budget-basis" approach, in which it is assumed at the beginning of a business cycle that there is no budget need if there are no work packages defined. Added to that are budget wishes related to longer term and more generic competency needs, including the filling up of the HR pipeline for technical skilled coworkers. The latter budget part has a higher intrinsic degree of continuity over a time horizon of about 5 years, thus it doesn't start from a "zero budget basis," and it constitutes typically around 20 % of the total R&D&I budget. Experience suggests that the sum of these bottom-up wishes needs to be balanced against the expected business situation for the next business year. That is the more "top-down" part of the budgeting process. For this balancing effort it is generally helpful to have defined a kind of "top ten" ranking of the most important technology development programs. Such a ranking typically spans several business years for materials technology activities. Priority can then be given to ensure the budget needs of these top ten strategic programs. For the remaining part of the budget proposals usually a scaling down of the desired efforts is needed. This scaling down can be achieved in several ways. One approach is to look for a lower intensity of the proposed work packages. This usually leads to a delay of the milestone resulting from that work package. Another approach is to look out for a different way to do the experiments—such as using a smaller scale of equipment—or even to replace some of them with computer simulations. Alternatively, one can look out for a more cost-effective—external—supplier that takes care of doing the work defined in the work package. However, it is unusual to make compromises that risk the reduction of the fidelity of experimental results, for example, by reducing the number of experimental data points proposed.

In recent years it has become common practice to treat one part of the R&D&I efforts as expenses that are fully paid within one business year, and another part as investments that are written off over a longer period.

Managers of industrial R&D&I activities know that their role in the budgeting process is to clearly communicate about the "devil's triangle." Budget processes are ultimately about which position a company wishes to occupy within the triangle between cost—quality—speed for its technology work packages, and programs. An objective of high quality and high speed comes almost automatically with a high cost, and vice versa.

7 Applying Best Practices from an Industrial Perspective

Industrial activities are deployed in a truly globalized world. More than any public agency in the world, a private company needs to find ways to continuously adapt to global competition, which means among others to fast changing boundary conditions. This has led to the ability to quickly adopt best practices from the global industrial experience pool. A few examples will be explained below. They have been chosen because of the positive experiences made with them, and because of the fact that they are to our knowledge less commonly applied in public science and technology undertakings in the field of materials technology.

A first example worthwhile to document is the drive of the industry to systematically apply quality assurance methods in their R&D&I undertakings. The methodology of quality assurance measures was developed in the mid-twentieth century, and gained widespread popularity in the worldwide automotive industry, both with the original equipment manufacturers (OEM) as with their Tier 1 and 2 suppliers, in the second half of that century. Nowadays, it is not only common practice but even a basic requirement for operation in this sector—and others—to have a high-level, certified quality assurance system in place. At first glance, when preparing to introduce such a methodology, one is tempted to see only the additional efforts required and the costs associated with them without an immediate return. For example, a quality assurance system requires quite some level of documentation of the activities: the experimental procedures have been explicitly described, the maintenance and repairs to experimental equipment need to be recorded, and the decision processes elaborated, and so on. Industry experience shows that this process is healthy as it quickly helps to remove ambiguity and to trace back origins of unexpected results. Also a very common experience is that the fidelity of the experimental results is increased by the rigid requirements of regular calibration of the measurement tools, and by the thorough upfront analysis of the reliability of the measurement tool and of the measurement procedure for the parameters sought to be evaluated (Measurement System Analysis, MSA). Then the "good old habit" of repeating experiments to enable statistical evaluations of the experimental results is promoted again. Equally, the laborious effort to make a measurement error analysis enjoys renewed popularity. All of this is highly valuable especially for the work at the low TRL level. While this work has characteristics of discovery and inventions, it is the basis for substantial subsequent investments, thus the experimental foundation must be rock solid. At the higher TRL levels the value lies in performing extensive failure mode and effects analysis (FMEA). In a nutshell this method calls for a systematic desktop analysis of what can go wrong during the manufacturing but also utilization of a materials technology. For each of the theoretically identified failure modes an assessment of how frequently this could happen and what the effects are on the product quality when it happens must be done. The product of potential frequency and possible effect yields the criterion for defining preventive actions and potential remediations. The value of these exercises is that it forces the development actors to really think thoroughly about their product and its performance in a system. The results support a stable operation of the production and a constant quality of the product.

Discussing this with nonindustrial stakeholders in the field of materials technology, especially the ones that contribute to the invention/ discovery phase (TRL1), usually yields the comment that rigid quality assurance procedures kill creativity. University stakeholders refer to the peer review process of publications as the preferred way to guarantee quality. Both are not correct in our experience, and therefore we plea for defining constructive approaches to increase the adaptation of these best practices throughout all the actors in the innovation ecosystem.

The second example we want to highlight has to do with people's characters and with cultural habits. In a global competition environment such as in today's industrial undertakings, one develops both the openness to deal with being challenged regularly as well as the willingness to implement corrective measures resulting from these challenges. Failure to do so usually results in organizational changes at the personal level and economic stress at a company/ sector level. Many examples are available in the public domain to document this. These challenges can be structured as internal audits in which company colleagues critically review what topics are worked at in which way. Internal benchmark experiences can then generate proposals for improvement of the operations. Other internal ways to achieve this goal are to implement key performance indicators (KPI) also for the innovation work. Value was found in defining a portfolio of indicators, with some relative to the input parameters (e.g., R&D&I budget as percentage of turnover), some to the process of the innovation work (e.g., percentage of milestones reached on time) and some about the output (e.g., percentage of sales resulting from new products). A systematic follow-up of these indicators and a thorough analysis of reasons for change and for non-attainment of the targets give insight into areas for improvement. Finally, of course external consultants can be engaged as well to generate a critical review and to offer external benchmarks.

A third example deals with the flexibility to transgress company/ sector boundaries and to engage in collaborations. Some examples of collaboration initiatives have been described above; they are relevant typically for the innovation work on a low TRL level. For the high-TRL-level work, when finishing the definition of a new product, for example, value is found in engaging in selected collaborations along the value chain in both directions, upstream and downstream. An upstream value chain collaboration is, for example, with a raw material supplier. Here the intensive interaction can yield cost reductions by the joint definition of the product specification, so that only the relevant parameters are recorded. Also the cost of the quality checks can be reduced along the chain if they are only done once, for example, only at the supplier side. Moreover, if the raw material supplier has an insight in the next processing steps done with the downstream partner, he can come up with innovative product characteristics that facilitate these subsequent steps. A downstream value chain collaboration is established with the customer that integrates the materials technology in a system that performs a function. For example, an automotive emission control catalyst is supplied through the intermediate of a canning company to a car maker (OEM). The car maker integrates this materials technology into the powertrain of the vehicle. For reasons of optimal performance and durability, this integration requires quite some programming of the engine management system (EMS). A deep understanding of this interplay between materials science aspects of the automotive catalyst on one hand, and the performance characteristics as part of an integrated system on the other hand, is important to the optimization of the cost of the whole system.

To conclude it should be mentioned that industry has developed the insight that there is a lot of value in the regular exchange of best practices about innovation and about other elements of business undertakings. For the aspect of innovation, this exchange, fully within the boundaries of the competition laws, is facilitated very well by the dedicated industry association called the European Industrial Research Managers Association (EIRMA). Particular value is generated by the possibility to share lessons learned and best practices developed about innovation processes across the industry sector boundaries. Some large RTOs are also members, and a structured interchange with the European University Association (EUA) as well as with the European Association of Research and Technology Organizations (EARTO) takes place. These exchanges between crucial stakeholders of parts of the innovation value chain will add to the needed resilience capacity of innovation in the European Union.

8 Take Away

There is a continuous need for innovation to secure the technology basis of the enterprises in the European Union for their business success in a globalized word. Both public and private actors play their crucial individual roles in the innovation process. Alignment and orchestration of their contributions is increasingly needed to deliver top-quality-level successes on time in a fast changing environment. This coordination process should be guided more by flexibility, dynamism, ability to learn across borders, and the willingness to accept best practices from a global pool, rather than primarily by rule setting. Enterprises have developed these basic skills of resilience to be able to exist and blossom in an environment of global competition. The innovation processes in the European Union will benefit from even more by valuing this way of doing things.

Acknowledgments The author thanks colleagues at Umicore, many friends in industry and in industry associations, and a few close family members for their critical and constructive review and the format of the messages.

9   Appendix

CEA	Commissariat à l'énergie atomique et aux énergies alternatives (French Alternative Energies and Atomic Energy Commission) www.cea.fr
EARTO	European Association of Research and Technology Organizations www.earto.eu
EIB	European Investment Bank www.eib.eu
EIP-RM	European Innovation Partnership on Raw Materials
EIRMA	European Industrial Research Management Association www.eirma.org
EIT	European Institute of Innovation and Technology www.eit.europa.eu
EFSI	European Fund for Strategic Investments, an investment initiative of the EIB
EMIRI	Energy Materials Industrial research Initiative www.emiri.eu
EMS	Engine Management System, the computer that controls and steers the operation of the engine
ESA	European Space Agency
EU	European Union
EUA	European University Association, www.eua.be
EU Horizon 2020	The funding program of the EU launched in 2014
FLAMAC	Flanders Materials Center www.flamac.be
FMEA	Failure Mode and Effect Analysis
Fraunhofer	A leading organization for technology development in Germany (www.fraunhofer.de)

(continued)

(continued)

IMEC	A world-leading research institute in the field of nanoelectronics, located in Belgium www.imec.be
Innotek	A business incubation center located in Belgium www.innotek.be
KIC	Knowledge and Innovation Community
KPI	Key Performance Indicator
MOOCS	Massive Open Online Courses
MSA	Measurement System Analysis
OECD	Organisation for Economic Cooperation and Development, www.oecd.org
OEM	Original Equipment Manufacturer, a designation for car companies
R&D&I	Research & Development & Innovation
RTO	Research and Technology Organization
SBO	Strategic basic research (Strategisch Basis Onderzoek), a governmental funding program type in Flanders
SET	Strategic Energy Technology, an initiative of the EU
Umicore	www.umicore.com
vito	a leading European independent research and technology organization headquartered in Belgium www.vito.be

14

Recommendations and Their Effects: Tiptoeing in Unchartered Territory

Klaus Gretschmann and Stefan Schepers

In our two reports of 2013 and 2014, we have suggested and reflected upon a whole series of recommendations to policy makers. The recommendations are meant for all those who bear responsibility for setting the parameters/ framework of growth, prosperity, and innovation right: heads of states and governments, ministers of the economy, competitiveness, industry, and research as well as the European Commission and the European Parliament. Some ideas and recommendations are specifically targeted at institutions or member states' governments. Moreover, many ideas and recommendations are addressed to stakeholders such as business, academia, and civil society organizations taking account of their role and importance in interactive and collaborative innovation ecosystems.

K. Gretschmann (✉)
President, Competence and Advisory Team Europe (CATE), Germany
e-mail: klaus.gretschmann@kgr-consilium.eu

S. Schepers
Director, European Public Policy Advisors (EPPA), Brussels
Henley Business School, UK
e-mail: stefan.schepers@eppa.com

© The Editor(s) (if applicable) and The Author(s) 2016
K. Gretschmann, S. Schepers (eds.), *Revolutionising EU Innovation Policy*,
DOI 10.1057/978-1-137-55554-0_14

Some ideas are far-reaching and may primarily serve to stimulate further discussion in the marketplace of ideas about the future of Europe.

The set of recommendations was also meant to contribute to the setting of corporate strategic priorities: It brings forward important proposals regarding (1) the interaction between the private and the public sectors, as well as with academia and the research world; (2) recommendations aim at fully unfolding the potential of Public–Private–People Partnerships (PPPPs); (3) the significance of innovation-carrying public procurement is pinpointed; (4) a widening of the debate about intellectual property; and (5) suggestions on how to activate and make use of new financing strategies are meant to help business and firms frame their innovation policies in a more strategic and all-encompassing way.

They involve the regular use of European Council meetings for a comprehensive discussion of a citizen-centered theme; measures to reduce the innovation divide in the single market and assistance in building national innovation ecosystems; measures to radically improve policy coherence and impact assessments, through the design and implementation of new models for impact assessments; the option to create a EU Commission vice president without a portfolio, responsible for strategic collaboration, mentoring, and coherence in innovation policy management; the regular discussion of innovation ecosystems' development in joint and inclusive Council meetings; a review of the "comitology" procedures and a rapid and significant reduction of regulatory rigidities and costs. In what follows, the reader will find the original recommendations as well as some comments about their rationale and their effects and follow-ups.

Even though the authors and contributors to this book have a deep sympathy for Europe and are aware of the benefits of European integration, they are equally convinced that Europe is in urgent need of a fresh conception and possibly even a new paradigm necessary for regaining its attractiveness. However, in order to sharpen their arguments and contribute to a high-quality public discourse, the authors feel it useful to be outspoken and to think "outside the box." Therefore, we may not always appear kind in dissecting the dysfunction of the present EU "regime"[1]or

---

[1] In political science, a *regime* is the form of government and the set of rules and norms, etc., that regulate the operation of a government, intergovernmental institutions, and interactions with societies.

the repeated failures to develop meaningful policies, notably for promoting innovation and economic and social well-being, in a coherent way.

Yet, there are already a number of elements in place that may lend themselves to become part of an innovation ecosystem approach. And the Commission seems intent on taking further steps forward, treading pragmatically, carefully, cautiously, and even hesitantly. This is reflected in President Juncker's quote[2] from many years ago: "We take a decision and wait to see what happens; if nothing, we move forward to the point of no return."

Obviously, the Commission, like all proud and self-confident administrations, believes it may be best to invent all good ideas itself. So the 2014 EU Commission started with good sense when dividing portfolios and tasks to nominate vice presidents with a policy-steering and coordinating role; any resemblance with our recommendations (see below) to ensure more coherence in EU policymaking may be purely coincidental. The establishment of the "European Policy Strategy Center" as the EU president's inside think tank is another interesting incremental innovation. However, in order to merit the term *radical innovation*, the EPSC, like the Joint Research Center (JRC) should not be part of the administrative hierarchy, but fully autonomous. The reorganization of impact assessment promises some improvement, but also falls short of the need for full independence, which the High Level Group advocated (see below).

For the first time, the 2014 Commission introduced a first vice president with the politically important responsibility of better regulation; a first step toward regulatory innovation. His first piece of work, the Communication on Better Regulation, though, falls short of real regulatory innovation, but is nonetheless a remarkable improvement compared to previous thinking about better regulation or regulatory simplification, that is, concerning consultation processes and impact assessment in all co-decision-making institutions. But more than mere hope it doesn't yet offer, while the internal opposition of powerful bureaucrats and external ones as in the traditionalist European Parliament give us reason for wariness.

Digitalization and social inclusion have moved up in political importance. The new commissioner for research is investigating innovative funding possibilities—a good start—but what about coordination with

---

[2] J. C. Juncker (1999), Interview in *Der Spiegel* 52/1999, p. 136.

national and private funding and strategic alignment? Even more applause will come if he takes on those who impose the most outlandish bureaucratic procedures (up to 70 pages for a single project), excessive fragmentation of sectors, and planning as if research is not a journey into the unknown. Attempts for a digital union or an energy union merit intensified pursuance, because both, and the cross-fertilization between them, are essential for the postindustrial economy, but the keys to research and innovation need to be turned simultaneously to have competitive effects. The Commission must have the courage to design all its research funding together with industrial and research hubs in order to seek maximum economic and social benefits and minimum costs. And the Parliament should control the Commission, but not muddle in its work.

The Commission package on a circular, resource-efficient economy can be the starting point of a new, more resilience and innovation and less regulation-bent approach to sustainability, and eventually it should become an overarching political objective. This is a key challenge for the two new senior advisors for innovation and sustainability respectively and the vice presidents looking after policy coherence. Moreover, the elaboration will require taking into account the different implementation challenges that will emerge both in the business-to-business sector and in the business-to-consumer sector.

In the setting of objectives and the organization of the key directorate-general for growth the right choices are being made: completion of the single market, supporting a high-performing industrial base, and better regulation. It recognizes that the main drivers in the economy today are digitalization, resource scarcity, and industry services links, and their impact on business models, financing, and regulation. It seeks more cross-fertilization and synergies between industry and services in the single market, and facilitates more policy coherence, as advocated in our recommendations.

While there may be more reforms on the drawing board, one cannot help but notice that overcoming silo thinking and turf defense will require a strong steering role by the vice presidents and the president himself, supported firmly by the European Council. It concerns after all the better realization of our Common Good, and the very credibility of the EU itself.

There is even a nucleus of regulatory innovation and of new consultations with stakeholders, but both still fail the radical innovation test, not least because conservative veto players, some industries, some nongovernmental organizations and, alas, the European Parliament still hold their ground.

1 Appendix I: Recommendations by the Independent High Level Group on Innovation Policy Management (2013)

Recommendations for unleashing effective innovation.
Effective innovation requires a set of seven key activities:

* Optimize the embryonic European innovation ecosystem
* Improve policy coherence
* Reduce regulatory complexity and rigidity
* Eliminate obstacles and provide new funding to innovation
* Facilitate industrial cooperation and re-interpretation of competition law
* Take an encompassing and inclusive view of intellectual property
* Increase the innovation potential through user and consumer drive

This section examines each recommendation in detail.

1. Optimize the embryonic European innovation ecosystem

Our core recommendation is to optimize the embryonic European innovation ecosystem. Instrumental recommendations relating to policy and management below are derived from this core recommendation.

Europe still urgently needs refreshed efforts to change minds and practices about what stimulates or inhibits innovation, even though a lot has been done in recent years. Efforts need to move away from linear thinking toward dealing with the interactions of the various factors and actors. The world's most competitive economies show that it can be done.

However, it requires the broadening of traditional R&D and the funding approach. Both need to involve products, processes, and intangible innovations (such as design), and to cover industry and services, business models, management, and public governance. Optimum governance and management of the innovation ecosystem is needed to ensure all available resources are used.

A temporary, independent tripartite advisory group, composed of experts from governments, business, universities, or national innovation bodies, is an indispensable tool. The advisory group will complete the innovation ecosystem by developing strong and unconditional relationships with the key stakeholders, and by encouraging action. It should provide advice to the responsible European and national authorities on:

* managing the complexities of innovation and the multiple interfaces;
* converting perspectives in a globalized economy;
* guarding strategic agility and a market oriented, bottom-up approach;
* redesigning governance tools;
* university-business, stakeholder cooperation, and peer review mechanisms;
* impact assessment for competitiveness;
* transmission between multiple levels of governance and between economic sectors;
* stimulating entrepreneurship; and
* facilitating social acceptance of innovation.

The EU must adapt its emergent innovation policy to both generic and specific characteristics of each sector and avoid applying a uniform approach to heterogeneous markets. It must also focus more on cross-sector innovation opportunities, and on digitalisation in all economic sectors (including government). Business strategies and public policy objectives need to be mutually supportive and aligned, and particular attention needs to be paid to the innovation, competitiveness, and employment resulting from these relationships. Critical factors that could undermine business success have to be eliminated quickly.

Independent peer review of regulatory simplification is necessary to reduce wasteful regulations, and to review excessively rigid application of these regulations. Peer reviews will also help to simplify structures and institutional bodies of every kind, particularly those of little current value.

A determined effort for cultural change will result from the executive development of those involved, and from transparency and communication within relevant institutions. Revising human resource policies in institutions could also ensure more diverse recruitment, and a result-based promotion system may also help to encourage cultural change.

To achieve change, we need to focus on a few key policies, rather than focusing lightly on many. We need to ensure coherent policy making through efficient coordination (from the top); to review the sometimes anti-innovative and/or politicized use of the precautionary principle; and to enable independent testing and assessment of the competitiveness of all proposals.

The EU needs to rethink how societies can better recoup some of the multiple benefits from innovation, such as publicly funded innovation that has commercial use. Broadcasting the benefits of innovation, together with evidence-based policymaking and transparency, could encourage public acceptance of innovations (even those misunderstood or contested). The role of the chief scientific advisor should be strengthened in alliance with national science advisory bodies to ensure more scientific input in policymaking and policy support.

Finally, we need to ascertain the public acceptance of innovations to avoid premature "death" of novel ideas and potentially useful developments. Social acceptance is determined by partnering, and by democratic, consensus-building mechanisms. Therefore, the public needs objective information about contested innovative ideas. This information needs to include in-depth, peer reviewed scientific analyses, detail about benefits and risks, and about risk management

2. Improve policy coherence

In the view of all the HLG members, this is the most urgent requirement.

We need mechanisms to overcome fragmentation in innovation policy inside EU institutions. These mechanisms also need to address fragmentation among member states and between them and EU authorities; between business and public authorities; and between administration and citizens. Therefore, there needs to be one overarching authority with full responsibility for innovation and competitiveness within the EU institutions and in each member state. This single authority will guarantee overall coherence between countries, sectors, clusters, departments, and their rules and actions. The authority will address the ecosystem in its entirety to ensure that the innovation-policy mix is coherent.

To encourage cooperation between relevant stakeholders and actors, criteria need to be set for giving guidance for public governance; for exchange of good practice; for independent peer review; and for adapting governance methods to new technologies. Governance capabilities need to be continually refined to meet present-day needs and to adapt to new technologies (e.g., e-governance). Better framework conditions and alignment between European and national policies aimed at stimulating innovation requires observing key (global and trans-national) competitive elements by sectors, setting agreed benchmarks, and ensuring horizontal, vertical, temporal, and systemic coherence.

We need an integrated approach, similar to the one that existed during the development phase of the Single Market: an explicit agreement, a kind of covenant, between all the relevant actors, public and private. This agreement will make fostering innovation, and its effects on competitiveness and employment, the overarching and imperative goal of EU policies. Achieving this goal requires a different mind-set and policy toolbox from what we see in today's regulation and policy design, and a fundamental overhaul of the government-business relations and consultation processes. Policy makers need to approach innovation competitively. To set the framework conditions right, the approach needs a sector and cross-sector perspective to determine where the key competitive advantages of Europe may lay dormant. The approach then needs to focus on these advantages.

3. Reduce regulatory complexity and rigidity

At the interface between the European and national levels, and in the various preparatory and decision-making bodies, all officials need to

* have a realistic understanding of how "naked" research results are transposed into markets;
* work on the basis of the evidence produced by internationally recognized and peer reviewed science;

* have a comprehensive view of what innovation and competitiveness require; and
* know which rules and regulations need urgent streamlining, a reinterpretation of their application, or even elimination.

While respecting the prerogatives of the institutions, it is imperative to set up an interinstitutional, independent EU Impact Assessment mechanism (ex ante and ex post). This mechanism will cooperate with national centers to assess the economic and social impact of proposals and amendments on innovation and competitiveness. In this context, benchmarking and comparing strengths and weaknesses with Europe's main global competitors should be standard practice for new regulations, and for revising or interpreting existing regulations. Growth and employment are too important to be blocked in the icy sea of the status quo.

We need an end to the distortion of the Single Market through the additive regulation by regional governments. And we need an end to the anticompetitive side effects of advisory agencies or committees due to selective (if not populist) interpretations of science or of the impact of new technologies.

Regulatory simplification must be accomplished bottom-up, and concrete proposals from stakeholders should be mandatory to be considered by the EU Commission within a short timeline. Interpretations of regulations should take into account new research and technologies for innovative risk management and competitiveness, as well as speedy market access.

4. Eliminate obstacles and provide new funding to innovation

Many obstacles in member states and in the EU itself still prevent or restrain innovation efforts and opportunities. These obstacles include

* limited market access;
* lack of efficient intellectual property systems;
* prohibitive regulations;
* fiscal disincentives;

* lack of skilled labor force;
* lack of motivated and top-qualified researchers;
* lack of entrepreneurial spirit; and
* discontinuity and absence of perseverance in R&D and innovation policymaking.

The EU and national governments need to eliminate these obstacles. They can do this within their own areas of competence, but in close cooperation, and against the backdrop of an innovative ecosystem.

Therefore, improved cooperation is needed between the public and private sectors. The EU and member states may be asked to encourage universities to spend a significant part of public research funding on public–private partnerships, or on business–university partnerships. The renewal of management education may also be necessary. New ways to stimulate closer cooperation are needed to align contrasting stakeholder agendas with a company's commercial objectives, and with government policy objectives. This cooperation will ensure effective knowledge transfer and rapid market use.

Best practices, as well as current and foreseeable problems in public–private partnerships (PPP), should be identified to help establish and operate national and transnational PPPs in innovation.

Cross-border cooperation between research centers should be based on intrinsic needs and desires, not artificially because of EU funding requirements.

To raise funds for innovation projects, we recommend creating a new mechanism for incubator and seed capital (rather than focus on venture capital which is less suited to the EU model of fund raising). This new mechanism requires public funding, depending on the risks involved. A fund which can spend a significant amount over a period of 5–10 years could be accumulated by bringing all EU R&D and innovation work under one authority, and will avoid fragmentation and waste. The budget for Horizon 2020 should not be fragmented over many innovation partnerships without a single overarching authority and cross-sector objectives. The Seventh and Eighth RFP, Horizon 2020, and the Structural Funds financing mechanisms should be coordinated to optimize research and innovation processes. New funding should be considered for innovative forms of business-university cooperation, such as joint strategic knowledge centers which allow for cross-sector engagement.

Moreover, the existing funding possibilities should be redesigned in order to ensure a cumulative mix of funding throughout the chain, from research to pre-market access. Special attention must be given to cross-sector projects, and to the inclusion of small and medium-sized enterprises (SMEs) for which simplicity of regulation and procedure is essential. In this context, the idea of innovation bonds should be examined again.

5. Facilitate industrial cooperation and re-interpretation of competition law

Clusters should focus on market- and society-driven needs, but should also identify age-old indigenous skills, creativity, equipment, traditions, and technologies. Innovation clusters can also rest upon these capabilities on which innovation clusters can also rest. Locally successful clusters built upon models of "flexible specialization" in traditional home industry regions could serve as excellent examples. Such clusters should be identified and supported.

To concentrate innovation policy primarily on SMEs would be insufficient. The role of corporate "locomotives" must be recognized: in particular, their leverage in the supply and distribution chains, and the symbiotic relations with SMEs, although some may follow different trajectories to growth.

Unintended side effects of other policies that can be counterproductive for innovation must be eliminated. In particular, an overly strict and sometimes misguided application of competition law (though not its principles) must be revised and overhauled to facilitate and stimulate industry cooperation in the R&D and innovation chain.

6. Take an encompassing and inclusive view of intellectual property

The EU must go beyond a focus on patents and ensure adequate protection of all forms of intellectual property: brands (including cultural and local brands), geographic indicators, trademarks, data, and copyrights. Intellectual property must be tailored to the needs and requirements of individual sectors. Particular attention must be paid to Europe's competitive position in design, creativity, history, and culture-based innovation and branding.

However, we must maintain a careful balance so as not to paradoxically hinder innovation. There needs to be a sensible balance between sharing information and building on ideas to allow innovation. Equally important, the rights of creators must be balanced against other commercial freedoms to allow for full economic potential.

The EU must eliminate the problem of counterfeiting and illegal imports at source by making it a key condition in trade agreements with third-party countries. It should enforce respect for all forms of intellectual property in the new media. This may help to protect innovations, vis-à-vis imitation by international competitors.

Patents can be legitimately used to offer protection, but it should be examined if some dormant patents could still play a useful role in creating value.

Finally, the EU should seek ways to avoid asset stripping by financial operators that may destroy our intellectual properties and manufacturing basis.

2. Increase the innovation potential through user and consumer drive

Demand-driven efforts need to complement the up until now primarily supply-driven approach to innovation. Innovation processes can either be pushed or pulled. A pushed process is based on newly invented technology that an organization has acquired, has access to, and seeks profitable applications for. A pulled process seeks areas where customers' needs are suspected but are not yet met, and then focus efforts to find solutions to those needs.

The European Innovation Partnerships (EIPs) need to be reformed to make them primarily business driven, which will ensure

* a bottom-up and market-relevant approach;
* coherence in the R&D and innovation chain;
* interaction between partnerships; and
* participation of EU and national academic experts and business.

The EIP needs to be linked to the lead market's concept and its development. This can be done before even creating an overarching authority for innovation.

A result-oriented control system needs to replace (within 1 year) the excessive bureaucratic mechanisms. All EIPs need to be brought under a single authority for innovation and competitiveness to ensure coherence and true innovation.

The number of partners in PPPs needs to be reduced to become more focused and to ensure efficiency and effectiveness, and they need to be combined with a systematic demand policy.

Scouting for new ideas, projects, and research needs to happen both locally in Europe and globally to create first mover advantages. Industries, even small and medium-sized companies, need to operate in European and global markets. This must be the focus of all innovation policy efforts.

1.1 Conclusions

A new ecosystem approach needs to start soonest, after the midterm evaluation of the 2020 Strategy, to ensure that no more time is lost on the way to strengthening the embryonic innovation ecosystem throughout the EU.

A temporary brain trust should be established to provide out-of-the-box thinking, based on the best practices in various countries worldwide, to EU and member state governments. A blueprint for a new innovation policy approach needs to be developed and implemented. The blueprint needs clearly defined objectives and a schedule, as we saw in the successful realization of the white paper on the Single Market.

A more daring approach will encourage new growth, competitiveness, and employment.

2 Appendix II: Recommendations on Inspiring and Completing European Innovation Ecosystems—A Blueprint (2014)

2.1 Innovate the Competitiveness Framework

The Single European Market itself is one outstanding driver for innovation, for corporations and start-ups alike, but it needs urgent completion and proper implementation in order to ensure an innovation-conducive playing field. There are strong public and private research capabilities in Europe, but a lot of potential value cannot be realized due to slow commercialization. There is a lot of entrepreneurial spirit out there, but it meets a lot of obstacles. Risk aversion in Europe is higher than in other parts of the world. Social innovation presents opportunities that go unused, users can play a role, but equally important is forward-looking interaction between public authorities and suppliers. There is no shortage of money, but it is not used efficiently enough due to fault lines in the EU system and between member states in spite of successful experiences. Sector policies and cross-fertilization need to be brought in line with overarching political priorities. To harvest more value out of our potential, we need to fully develop or complete both the European and the national innovation ecosystems.

Recommendation 1.1: Set Criteria for Ecosystem Development and Completion

A series of criteria need to be developed to guide priority setting in order to move toward such European innovation ecosystems that is a *shared responsibility of all the actors* in it, be they the Commission and governments, companies, or research centers. Crucial questions to ask and elements to scrutinize include the following:

* Does the innovation ecosystem create synergies with or between national innovation ecosystems, and does it facilitate and increase their efficacy?
* Does it respond to a strategic, common European challenge?
* Does it draw on the aggregate societal demand in member states and does it involve citizens in the innovation processes?
* Does it have significant effects on growth and employment, if not in the short term, at least medium to long term, and in which sectors?
* Does it have a positive effect on the Single Market for enterprises in all sectors, including in removing obstacles to market and on global competitiveness?
* Does it stimulate entrepreneurship and create space for experimentation?
* Does it contribute to the modernization of the welfare systems of the member states?

- Does it improve ecological sustainability without hindering competitiveness?
- Does it build on existing knowledge-based and industrial strongholds or develop radical new ones and stimulate cross-fertilization across sectors?
- Does it contribute to collaboration and the alignment of interests between the public sector, private sector, and knowledge institutions?

The more these questions are answered with a YES, the closer to perfection an innovation ecosystems is!

Recommendation 1.2: Strengthen Mutuality Between Key Components in Innovation Ecosystems

The advancement, fostering, and maintenance of innovation ecosystems requires achieving a *shared vision* and mutual understanding as well as *collaboration and alignment* of long-term objectives and standards in order to ensure true *commitment* to change. This must be the overarching approach to developing strategies that take account of the specificities of each sector and of their interconnections.

1.2.1   Stimulate co-creation and a learning mind-set among innovation actors

- A more open and diversity-stimulating recruitment policy in public administrations and in private enterprises will deliver positive results and stimulate innovations in the longer term. Creativity, initiative and experimentation, transparency, and stakeholder collaboration need to be rewarded through innovations in human resources management.
- In the short term, executive development efforts must be made primarily in public administrations to foster understanding of the impact of new technologies, of (incremental and radical) innovations in all sectors of the European economy involving cross-fertilization and inter-sector developments. Special capabilities are required for coaching innovation in the age of digitalization of the whole economy and society.

* Companies, the principal partner for public authorities for competitiveness and employment, should mirror the effort in the public sector to include public policy challenges in their strategy development and to investigate their public value (i.e., their contributions to the Common Good), in order to bring a more cooperative and aligned business-government interaction and culture.

1.2.2   Achieve alignment between market and policy actors

* There is often little synchrony between business strategies aimed at global markets and policy cycles aimed at national elections. While these dis-synchronies are inevitable in democratic market economies, they can constitute a systemic weakness for long-term investments in research and innovation. Some of Europe's competitors, operating with different government models and in different cycles, do not face such difficulties to the same extent. It is therefore important to explore the bottlenecks for R&D&I upfront, for each sector and inter-sector.

Recommendation 1.3: Facilitate Co-creation for Global Competitiveness

In order to be competitive in a globalized and ever more competitive environment, companies, large and small, increasingly cooperate and enter into partnerships, often also with public authorities or user groups. These partnerships allow them to reduce the uncertainty of R&D investments, minimize R&D (transaction) costs, and exploit complementary know-how. Risk can be shared, costly duplication of efforts avoided, innovative products and technologies more rapidly developed, and user reactions can be tested.

1.3.1   Align competition law application with companies' innovation objectives

* To facilitate cooperation between companies, the way in which competition law is applied in the EU should be aligned with Europe's innovation objectives. The Commission could act more in line with enabling rather than controlling business co-operation for the sake of

promoting innovation efforts, allowing experiments in company cooperation, in particular in the R&D&I phase.

1.3.2 Use competition law to stimulate innovation by eliminating rent seeking

* European competition law can play a useful role in stimulating innovation by eliminating monopolies and cartels and all forms of rent seeking, which distort the market functioning and cause inequalities in society. The Commission should put more emphasis on ex post verification in cases where competition law has been violated or market competition restricted rather than prohibiting cooperation endeavors a priori when they can have a positive effect on innovation.

1.3.2.1 Facilitate academia-company cooperation

* More than ever, the university of the future has three key tasks to fulfill: education, research, and entrepreneurship. Research cooperation with companies will benefit all three tasks. Cooperation should go beyond technical and scientific knowledge creation and extend to social sciences in order to enhance the public and social value of joint research projects.
* Networks are key components in the digital economy. They will naturally emerge bottom-up; but a top-down approach may sometimes be needed and may be complementary. The EU and/ or interested groups of member states (variable geometry should apply) or even wider groups, such as Eureka, should support emerging or potential ecosystems by incentivizing and facilitating cooperation between companies and universities and by jointly eliminating obstacles, including traditional mind-sets and mobility of human capital from abroad.
* The networks that could benefit most from steering from the top would be those aiming at developing a new "grand European project" (such as Airbus or ITER, etc.). However, it is essential that in developing such a project only qualitative criteria of a European character are applied and national criteria are sidelined and abandoned. It could be helpful to seek the advice of non-European experts and universities. In the Single Market, member states will profit from such projects, even if they are not directly involved.

* The idea of "big" projects is worth considering serving as an integrator of innovation ecosystems in the Single Market. But it is only worthwhile if from the start such projects are carried out without "national" considerations, and are focused purely on research and the global market. Therefore, strict quality criteria must be established up front, by a group of experts which include non-Europeans, too. Such projects can serve not only to keep high-added-value jobs in Europe, but also to attract top talent from outside. Project design and development should be done transparently and with stakeholder involvement. Ideas mentioned but not further developed concern health (e.g., brain), energy (e.g., CO_2 capture and use, electricity storage) and digital networks (e.g., big data analytics). Special attention should be given to the uptake of new or emerging technologies in traditional sectors including promotion and development in indigenous industries and to social innovation, which has a huge potential for cross-sector cooperation.

Recommendation 1.4: Broaden the Public Funding Approach

A principal challenge to innovation financing in Europe is a severe fragmentation of funding mechanisms, sources, and approaches alongside overly bureaucratic procedures, rather than a lack of funding as such. The EU and member states must improve the way funding is channeled into innovative activities, while keeping an eye on market diffusion and business opportunities.

1.4.1   Broaden the traditional R&D funding to include products and services, processes and intangibles

* This is already laid out in Horizon 2020, but this approach should become good practice in all funding schemes and strategies by the EU and member states. What is required is a widening of R&D funding instruments and their integration with enterprise policy.
* In particular they should help to create open innovation ecosystems.

1.4.2   Provide support for funding public–private–people partnerships (PPPPs)[3] and business–university partnerships (BUPs)

* Deepening and widening current initiatives of the Commission, the EU and member states in particular need to incentivize universities to spend a meaningful part of public research funding in PPPPs and BUPs and to jointly seek rapid elimination of impediments.
* Such funding can help to align contrasting stakeholder agendas with a company's commercial objectives and with government policy objectives. In innovation ecosystems, collaboration between science and industry is a key aspect of gaining a competitive edge. Cross-border cooperation between research centers should be based on intrinsic needs which are not created artificially to fulfill EU funding requirements.

1.4.3   Create new mechanisms for incubator and seed capital

* New mechanisms for incubator and seed capital should be designed to attract more capital in the real economy. Depending on the risks involved, this requires public co-funding.
* The creation of independent seed capital fund(s) with public money should be considered. It should be managed by private experts to ensure financial expertise, a strong science base and market orientation. Such a fund should provide up to 80 % in seed capital, in the form of a loan repayable at an attractive interest rate, if the product or service enters the market. If a newly created company—thus financed— were later sold to a non-European company, there should be a high enough compensation and return to the seed capital fund.
* A fund specifically to support private investors in high-risk innovation projects and that operates with various forms of capital provisions could be very useful.

---

[3] Based on the principle of public-private partnerships (PPP), public-private-people partnerships (PPPP, or P4) directly include and engage people as major stakeholder in both designing and implementing PPP schemes. PPPPs thereby apply a bottom-up and participative strategy, making people and civil society more visible in collaborative undertakings.

1.4.4   Offer innovation bonds by expert bodies and innovation financing agencies

* "Innovation bonds" could prove useful during the present "credit crunch" and could be offered by expert bodies and innovation financing agencies created by member states for the careful vetting of innovation projects and their feasibility. Those projects deemed solid and attractive would receive the right to issue long-term "innovation bonds" at a fixed interest rate which, although low, would provide a positive real rate of return.

1.4.4.1 Increase European research funds through institutional austerity measures

Available European funds can be significantly increased through budgetary re-allocation in those EU institutions and projects that have exceeded their validity date and whose contributions and benefits have turned negligible or negative. The funds can also be increased by reducing the many satellite institutions and centers once created for political reasons where an independent audit shows a lack of economically useful output. Both efforts should be undertaken within a short time frame.

* European publicly funded bodies, regardless of their nature, should only be set up with precise targets, independent, transparent annual evaluation, and in some cases even limited time frames (sunset clause), in order to ensure that they remain strategically agile and vigilant to deliver added value to the economy and society. Renewal of their mandate and funding must depend on meeting well-defined targets.
* Research funds could also be strengthened by channeling penalties from competition violations to novel and innovative enterprises.
* In light of public budget shortages, special attention should be paid to the important role of defense R&D, since defense spending has many civil and innovation spin-offs and offers competitive advantage for quite some companies. But the EU must secure better conversion of military R&D spending to civil use since it could increase the competitiveness and efficiency of all R&D funding.

1.4.5   Develop a portfolio approach for European research funds

* More of the available funds might be spent through a portfolio approach. The energy and digital sectors, but also the space or health sectors offer some scope for it. Europe may be behind some of its competitors in ICT, but it can still "leap frog," given a concentration of its capabilities. This may be a way to help co-shape innovation eco-systems, stimulate forward-looking policy planning, and facilitate buy-in of stakeholders.
* In any case, the present dispersive spending methods which aim to ensure that everyone gets something (*juste retour* in terms of the EU budget), abets a waste of public resources. Procedures must be established to eliminate this outdated approach.

1.4.6   Adjust taxation strategies to ensure sufficient capital allocation for productive investments

The tax systems of member states can be a powerful policy instrument for supporting innovation and can be used to reduce its investment costs. Macroeconomic policy, taxation, and monetary policies together should ensure that there is sufficient capital allocation for productive investments. Escape routes and tax loopholes should be closed, yet an incentive-compatible return on investment should be ascertained. Tax policies should help favor long-term investments in innovation over short-term and speculative ones.

* Efforts should be made to provide well-focused tax benefits related to the costs of promoting innovation (expenses toward experimental development, basic and applied research, and related supporting activities, etc.).
* Innovation will also benefit from accelerated depreciation schemes for innovation-related capital and reduced labor taxes on scientists and researchers. Zero-rate and reduced-rate VAT and lower corporate tax rates for innovation-related profits may lend themselves as instruments for promoting innovations. In particular very young enterprises would see their potential enhanced.

* The taxation on IPR has become a global tax competition issue. It would be in the collective interest of member states to ensure a level European playing field and seek ways to avoid leakage of IPR out of Europe for tax reasons.

Recommendation 1.5: Take an Inclusive View on Intellectual Property

Strong and effective IPR is crucial in an innovation ecosystem. The EU's current system of IPR protection needs considerable improvement: it is complex, fragmented, and expensive. It fails to provide legal certainty, it allows data leakage in certain procedures, and it is not up-to-date to deal with new technologies and their rapid evolution and penetration.

With regard to patents, major problems for the uptake of innovation arise with regard to high costs and complex procedures for companies to patent innovation, legal uncertainty due to different legal frameworks in the member states and EU, and the European Patent Office's increasing incapacity to handle its rapidly growing workload. Consequently, it reduces the opportunities for developers and users of technology to launch creations on markets, in particular in a cross-border context.

1.5.1   Implement a truly European patent system

* The EU must implement and enforce without any further delay the European patent system including a truly European patent to establish greater harmonization, legal certainty, and reduce administrative hurdles and costs.
* In order to facilitate co-creation, an open approach must be envisaged. It will help and support the opportunities for developers and users of technology to launch creations on European markets first.

1.5.2   Regulate the ownership of data

* The ownership of data must be regulated: it cannot be considered automatic and users/ consumers must be given clear and easy choices to opt in or out of potential uses of their personal data.

* IPR on life and nature itself should be forbidden because they must be considered common goods. Only when there is a proven and significant scientific intervention can the latter be protected. But in that case there should be clear rules for sharing the benefits with local communities. The EU should elaborate a policy that can serve as a global standard.

1.5.3 Exploit other forms of IP protection and strike a balance between protecting knowledge and disseminating it

* The EU must broaden its focus and look beyond patents to ensure adequate protection of all forms of intellectual property: brands (including cultural and local brands), geographical indications (except their potential use as a protectionist tool), trademarks, data, and copyrights. Intellectual property must be tailored to the needs and requirements of individual sectors. Particular attention must be paid to Europe's competitive position in design, creativity, history and culture-based innovation and branding.
* Furthermore, the EU must strike the right balance between protecting knowledge and disseminating it. Intangible knowledge and skills must be solidly protected from unauthorized exploitation in order to reward innovative ideas and discoveries, maintain and increase business' competitiveness, and provide incentives for investment in innovative R&D.
* Along with the classic four freedoms of the Internal Market, the free movement of knowledge must be further enabled and access to it facilitated in order to process and implement this knowledge for the creation of new knowledge and innovation in the most efficient way.

1.5.4 Vigorously address the issue of counterfeiting with conditions in trade agreements

* The EU must resolutely address the problem of counterfeiting and illegal imports at the source by making it a key condition in trade agreements with third countries. It should enforce respect for all forms of intellectual property in the new media and elsewhere. This may help to protect innovations from imitation by international competitors.
* The EU and member states should ensure that the IPR of all money spent, including scholarships abroad, remain or return here and that commercialization takes place in Europe.

* Given the value loss caused by counterfeiting for European companies and employment, R&D investment in new technologies to avoid it should be considered.

Recommendation 1.6: Expand the Use of Public Procurement to Promote Innovation

This is undoubtedly a key support mechanism for innovation ecosystems. Given the importance of the public sector in Europe, public procurement can provide a major stimulus for bringing cooperative suppliers and pro-active users together, for ensuring consumer-added value, for bringing innovation rapidly to market and for knowledge transfer and for keeping high value-added jobs in Europe. This should be stimulated using existing EU methods and funding and new ones (collaborative governance) across the Single Market and at all levels of public administration and in all sectors.

The recent EU public procurement reforms need rapid and full implementation and strong political support. So does the Platform on PP, which should network actively with major innovation ecosystems and their key actors.

There is vast scope for innovation and public budget savings too by breaking down artificial barriers between (parts of) defense and civil procurement.

1.6.1   Develop an innovative cost-benefit approach in public procurement

* Any surplus price in a given innovative public procurement project is often a very useful investment if one looks at the whole life cycle, the improvement of public services and transversal benefits in other economic sectors. Innovative ways can be found with corporations to ensure that successful launches also provide a return for cooperative public authorities. This similarly supports cost reduction and standardization of welfare provisions, which not only helps competitiveness but also public budget saving.

* By bringing stakeholders together, public authorities from various member states can develop joint public procurement and have a significant impact on innovation and even be market makers. This is an important element in the Single Market. Moreover, faster commercialization is much needed for Europe's competitiveness and employment creation and in this way they can help companies and operate a virtuous circle.

1.6.2 Use public procurement to create demand for innovative goods and stimulate research and knowledge transfer

* Smart customers are just as important as smart suppliers in terms of ensuring innovative outcomes of public procurement processes. The Public Procurement Platform could help to design qualitative criteria for how to increase technical know-how and its availability, how to ensure that potential customers are aware of new solutions and services and how to e-manage the processes.
* Public procurement can also help to develop open innovation ecosystems through cooperation across borders between regional and local authorities to help create and rapidly enlarge the markets for innovation, to enable user engagement and co-creation in the spirit of the quadruple helix innovation (Dublin Declaration on Innovation).
* Criteria and targets should be better used by public authorities to ensure that a certain part of public procurement budgets is targeted directly at innovative solutions together with measurement indicators. Having more challenging desired outcomes and upfront transparency will help to avoid risk aversion. It would also support innovative solution finding since it allows suppliers to be more creative. A clear identification of these public procurement offers within public budgets as "innovative public procurement" can raise awareness of their relevance among stakeholders.

1.6.3 Use public procurement to support an SME sector engaged in research and innovation and provide early markets for lead users

* Only a very small part of Europe's large SME sector is engaged in research and innovation. A more significant part plays a role in inno-

vation as suppliers to large corporations or in niche markets and in traditional sectors. Innovative SMEs and start-ups need to be nurtured by ensuring that they can take part in public procurement early on and that standard setting, regulations and procedures do not hinder risk taking and growth. The requirement that companies should have a number of years of existence makes little sense in fast-developing sectors, and other criteria about company solidity must be established.

* Innovative activities are also promoted by allowing different SMEs to work on finding a solution for a project, even though only one solution is chosen in the end. The de-selected innovative solutions might still represent the desired option in other contexts.
* A special effort needs to be made to facilitate lead markets for innovative goods and services and for the growth of start-up companies in innovative sectors through light touch regulation or restricted application during a well determined phase of their development.

2.2   Innovate for Social Acceptance, Connectivity and Inclusiveness

I do not understand why people would be scared of new ideas. I am scared of the old ones.

—John Cage, American composer.

Every technological advance, every innovation, carries societal effects and radically new technologies and processes—such as ICT—have radical effects on society. They create disruptions which unsettle many people while benefitting others. Not knowing beforehand who will win and who will lose, citizens are afraid and shy away from risks and hazards coming along with innovation, particularly when benefits are not immediately clear to them. Notably, they are afraid of unanticipated effects and potential dangers to their own working and living conditions.

Therefore, both governments and corporations should share a common concern for compensating for and outbalancing the negative social effects of any innovation within reasonable limits: first, by focusing as much on delivering public value as on short-term profitability; and second, by providing novel frameworks for societies to adapt and for economies to function in the general interest. If this cannot be achieved, reticence and resistance to innovation and challenging fault lines will arise, such as tensions between the smart and knowledgeable users of the internet and those lacking the skill sets to do so and between those benefiting from innovations and those who may lose in terms of jobs and security. Social protection and helping people to cope with the unintended side effects of change processes is primarily a responsibility of nation-states.

But collaborative governance methods among EU member states and between them and the EU can be a great help to move more efficiently and rapidly toward the unavoidable adaptation measures. Though the above problem was not strictly part of the requests made to the HLG, it was deemed so important that a number of recommendations on social adaptation, inclusiveness and connectivity have been included in this blueprint. After all, citizens and users are fundamental driving forces behind innovative activities. They must therefore become an integral part of the innovation process by being involved in co-shaping and determining what value an innovation should deliver to the intended user.

Recommendation 2.1: Give the Problem of Skepticism, Fears, and Worries on the Part of the Citizens vis-à-vis Innovation a Prominent Place in Innovation Ecosystems

Whereas invention is only a scientific act that in itself does not provide the ability to transform lifestyles, innovation is the implementation of a discovery that comes with a lot of intended and unintended effects. It is therefore a social process that permeates society, politics, and institutions.

In the Schumpeterian theory, innovations cause "disruptions" (creative destruction) which become the main cause of both the growth of new industries and companies and the demise of old ones. For some, direct and indirect consequences will be desirable while others will suffer. Notably, citizens are afraid of unanticipated effects, "surprises," and potential dangers to their own working and living conditions. *Any innovation policy and business strategy needs to take account of such "problems of acceptance" and "redistribution of opportunities and risks" by adapting and providing new fitting structures and measures for social bolstering, inclusiveness and connectivity.*

Recommendation 2.2: Include and Enlarge "Social Innovation" in Innovation Policy Management Schemes

Social innovations encompass novel strategies, concepts, ideas, and institutional arrangements that help boost the social well-being of citizens and social groups. In generic terms, social innovation is about how we can improve societies' capacities to solve present and future social problems. It is about new methods to mobilize the ubiquitous intelligence that exists within any society. Examples abound: social entrepreneurship, social media, new ways of self-organized social protection, nonprofit enterprises, the share economy, empowering of social groups, and new human networks, etc.

Features of modern society—for example, high levels of education or new information and communication technologies, especially social networking and new media—are making social innovation a widespread and powerful force in shaping societies. Still, until 2011 there was no ecosystem to support social innovation and little support for the innovators themselves. Today, however, we find the flagship program "Innovation Union Europe 2020" in which the EU Initiative "Social Innovation Europe" plays a prominent role. For this we recommend enlargement!

Recommendation 2.3: Develop an Inclusive Approach to Innovation to Address Social Inequality and Poverty

According to the World Bank, inclusive innovation not only increases productivity and competitiveness but also plays a crucial role in addressing problems of inequality, poverty, and uneven initial endowment.[4] Governments have a key responsibility in this regard, as they must create an enabling environment that facilitates, finances, incentivizes, and commercializes innovative products and solutions, not least through cooperation and collaboration. At the end of the day, government's central objective must be to utilize innovation to share its benefits equally with all groups of society and help serve people's needs at the base of the social pyramid.

---

[4] World Bank, 2012.

In order to realize this recommendation, the HLG recommends to

2.3.1 Create an interinstitutional agreement to safeguard, enhance, and innovate national welfare societies and share experiences

* Governance arrangements appropriate for a digital economic context should be made to ensure that the objective to safeguard, enhance, and innovate national welfare societies is made an equal priority and that it is taken fully into account in all policy areas. Respecting Treaty provisions, collaborative governance methods need to be developed to share experiences and peer review reforms. However, a balance needs to be found between fixing detailed European rules and the great diversity in the Union because it can stifle social and economic innovation.

2.3.2 Improve and innovate welfare systems through careful impact assessment of proposed policies and regulation

* While respecting the competences of the EU and member states, the new format of the Impact Assessment as proposed should also include a full assessment of whether and how proposed policies and regulations impact national welfare state systems.
* Early estimation of collateral impacts key social protection provisions by member states will allow designing more comprehensive European policies, reducing potential antagonism, boosting creativity and transversal, and vertical collaborations throughout the EU system.
* In addition, it can lead more rapidly to innovation in those systems through stimulation of research and the use of public procurement in order to achieve multiple related objectives in innovation ecosystems.

2.3.3 Improve welfare systems through the use of digitalization and innovation to reduce running costs

* Innovation and especially digitalization, can strongly contribute to reducing the running costs of welfare systems, thus mitigating budget pressures and enhancing competitiveness in delivering high-quality services to citizens at low costs.
* In line with the ambitious objectives of Horizon 2020, the European Commission and the member states should collaborate to bring the

advantages of public cost reduction and improved products and service delivery to citizens as soon as possible. The improvement of larger data sets ("big data") could bring considerable advantages in terms of cost-effectiveness and operational efficiency in a broad variety of sectors, health care being just one of them. The achievement of this goal would allow the EU to take a global lead in this domain, attracting the rest of the world to align to EU standards.

* European welfare states and their public finances are currently under pressure from budget constraints and a lack of innovation capacity. Innovation can be encouraged and activated through novel forms of cooperation between companies and public authorities in innovation partnerships to deliver new welfare services. Such arrangements could involve experimental initiatives enabling companies, in close cooperation with the public sector and users, to search for innovative solutions to societal challenges. The development of a more holistic and value-based procurement model, rather than price-driven ones, could make it easier to integrate consumer experience in areas such as health care, social care, elderly care or education.

Recommendation 2.4: Innovate Education at All Levels

Europe's significant strength is its cultural diversity and its intellectual force, which are pivotal to enabling creativity and innovation at the micro level. Likewise, the general attitude in Europe toward technology is positive and quality oriented. Europe's education systems should allow it to provide high-skill labor and attract the most creative researchers worldwide. An open attitude and attractive conditions are therefore essential.

To realize this recommendation, the HLG recommends to

2.4.1   Conciliate traditional curricula with innovative, "skills"-oriented ones based on continuous learning and life-long education

* The European education paradigms need to be reviewed with the aim of reconciling traditional curricula with a system more attentive to scientific, technological, and entrepreneurial education as well as to continuous, lifelong education and learning. This will result in the

creation of an approach which is fit for a rapidly changing economic context and the digital economy.

* It requires fostering more positive attitudes toward entrepreneurship and risk taking, encouraging creativity instead of conformity. Education policies need to better introduce creative practices and methods in teaching. Focus must be given to training teachers to increasingly use thinking tools which trigger creativity and at the same time improve their general technological and IT knowledge. To this end, business actors should not act as mere passive "financiers" but engage actively as partners with education institutes in order to give students and researchers a comprehensive view of the innovation value chain and entrepreneurship. Involvement from businesses is fundamental in providing guidance on entrepreneurial aspects such as how to develop and manage start-ups.

* Alongside the promoting of digital skill at all education levels, is the need to overcome the skills gap in advanced manufacturing and engineering. Innovation and the industry transition toward advanced and high-quality manufacturing ("factory 4.0") require capabilities and knowledge of manufacturing management principles and technological components, preferably from an intersectional perspective. Learning of these dimensions would help develop skills in problem solving and solution finding, both essential in enabling the innovation required to meet the present and future needs of businesses and public sectors.

2.4.2   Stimulate systems of apprenticeships based on existing best practices and reevaluate polytechnic education

* In order to contribute to solving unemployment among the young, cooperation and collaboration should be launched between the Commission and the member states as well as between the member states themselves to develop an EU-wide system of apprenticeships based on already existing best-practice experience.

* Polytechnic schools can provide useful education leading to much needed job opportunities, but they sometimes have an image and funding problem. Efforts should be made to reevaluate them and prepare them to deliver for the needs of the digital economy. Incentives

could also be put forward to better encourage students to engage with industry research which often is lagging behind.

2.4.3 Promote digital education and Massive Open Online Courses (MOOC)

* Digital education will make the classic education system increasingly obsolete. Drawing on evolving technological progress and its influence on citizen's behavior and needs, Europe should assign greater priority to ICT and promote Massive Open Online Courses (MOOC), an online university tool and engagement platform aimed at participation and open access via the web. Besides offering traditional course materials such as videos and problem sets, MOOCs provide forums that stimulate interactive participation among students, professors, and teachers. If well combined with some of the traditional educational tools, MOOC could promote the skill sets demanded, but also more specific skills relating to entrepreneurship, digital know-how and technological and innovative advancements.

2.4.4 Develop teleworking

* Instead of moving workers, the digital economy makes it possible to move the work. Teleworking has the potential to create employment and enhance the connectivity of workers as well as increase global scouting through expanding recruitment processes to the global level where a broader pool of knowledgeable workers is available. However, there are multiple obstacles to be removed before this potential to create employment can be fully used and certain sectors, such as those linked to ICT and education, might be more suited for teleworking.

Recommendation 2.5: Stimulate Research and Incentivize Researchers at All Levels

2.5.1 Provide incentives for researchers to focus on emerging sectors

* Encourage researchers to engage in "creative system disruption" (report from Key Technologies Expert Group, DG Research 2005), where

researchers focus on emerging sectors where research is lacking and where Europe can potentially take a leading role through research and innovative activities.

2.5.2   Facilitate cross-border research

* One of the most crucial components of the success of the European Research Area (ERA) is an adequate flow of competent researchers with high levels of mobility between institutions, sectors and countries. Programs such as the *Marie Curie Actions* or *Erasmus* are an important first step in the right direction but still do not provide comprehensive solutions for problems such as complex provisions regarding the cross-border taxation, health insurance, and social security of mobile researchers or inconsistency in the area of family benefits and pension rights that arise from regulatory fragmentation in the member states.

2.5.3   Provide greater assistance for mobility of researchers

* Intercontinental mobility and cooperation of researchers is crucial in facilitating networking, spillover, and the transfer of scientific knowledge between researchers from different regions and continents. Europe must widen up the ERA to the world, with special emphasis on highly innovative countries and must actively scout for excellent researchers and offer attractive conditions to work within the Union.
* In parallel, the EU must actively encourage stronger participation of private companies within the ERA, in particular emerging new innovators and SMEs, in the form of public–private partnerships and cooperation between research centers and enterprises. It is also important to enhance intersectional innovation capacity by better linking together researchers from different sectors, since many innovative breakthroughs take place at the intersection of sectors, fields, and cultures.
* The European IPR system must ease the sharing of knowledge for participants in the ERA. It would be useful to build a support infrastructure to share information across the EU to facilitate the way data is stored, shared, used, and reused as well as networking and interaction. More focus must also be given to support interuniversity cooperation and networking which facilitates knowledge transfer of key aspects on

innovation management and industrial research between universities of excellence and those universities lagging behind.

* Incentives should be developed for scientists to also be more entrepreneurial and to move into business or governance and back. This would help to bridge the gaps that sometimes exist between science and markets and societal improvements resulting from their work.

2.5.4   Create an open portal providing peer reviewed and evidence-based information

* To restore trust in science and encourage more evidence-based policymaking, an online portal should be created to provide peer reviewed and evidence-based information to citizens, policymakers, and media alike. Together with a reformed Impact Assessment, this will also contribute to increasing innovation acceptance and will help to avoid that constructed risk dominates public debates.

2.5.5   Launch an initiative to form a group of top-level research institutes to support competitive networking and cross-fertilization

A major strength of competitive innovation ecosystems relies upon their capacity to achieve high-level cross-fertilization and networking, in particular since top research and higher education institutions act as a kind of innovation hub or flagship. Though on average such a capacity inside the European Union is not dramatically low, it nevertheless needs to be improved quite massively. Its academic fabric could and should contribute faster, better and at a lower cost—including in terms of public funding—in combining research and education and cross-fertilizing the innovation ecosystem of the future.

More specifically, an initiative should be launched as soon as possible to support the emergence of a critical mass of top-level research universities and technology institutes evidencing the potential to play a focal role in the European and national innovation ecosystems. They would be selected whatever their institutional status and the country where they are located. They would be chosen according to five main requirements:

* their current academic production in research and education already satisfies international top-level quality criteria in a sustainable way;
* they evidence the skills and ability to bridge with enterprises and other stakeholders of the innovation ecosystem (policymakers, socioeconomic actors, other universities);
* they are active in fields that are key for the coming years;
* they successfully operate with interdisciplinary frameworks;
* the propose research agendas sensitive to innovation requirements and achievements.

This program would give support and allocate relevant means—with a midterm perspective—as any successful ecosystem-building policy requires. It should be supervised by a specific agency. Its members would basically be independent top-level academics and successful science managers from the business world. They would not act as representatives of member states or of the EU Commission. Its officers would work full time and be appointed for a time period of around 6 years. The agency would have full responsibility for handling and allocating its budget based on contributions from EU institutions, member states, and the private sector.

2.3   Innovate Governance Tools and Mechanisms: Toward an Innovative Governance System for Tomorrow's Challenges

Ever tried, ever failed. No matter. Try again, fail again. Fail better.
—Samuel Beckett, Nobel Prize Winner in Literature.

Stimulating growth and employment through the promotion of innovation carries inevitable institutional consequences. The groundwork and principles of EU policymaking were established in the 1950s in a community of six and later nine member states with the aim of integrating national goods markets. In contrast, the EU of today which has acquired and been assigned competences in many more policy areas (from service markets, labour markets, financial markets to research, enterprise, trade, competition, health, social, and environment policies), appears in urgent need of a profound and all-encompassing governance overhaul. Between the traditional Community Method and the Open Method of Coordination, it requires new instruments for Collaborative Governance.[5] In present circumstances, this should be done and can be done without Treaty changes, though in the long term a review of the division of competences between EU institutions and member states as well as between private and public actors in line with economic and societal requirements will be unavoidable.

At the moment, EU governance is excessively focused on regulation and not enough on mentoring, collaboration, stewardship, and peer review. The latter are essential to complete and manage the complexities of innovation for sustainability and competitiveness and to move toward a European innovation ecosystem as an overarching entity bringing together the different national innovation ecosystems effective in the EU.

Therefore, it is necessary to complement the European governance system based on the so-called Community Method, with methods of open, collaborative governance that are less hierarchical and legalistic and more suited to manage innovation complexity. Stewardship of innovation policy may stay with the Commission, but if it does not wish to use its right of initiative, any member government, business, or academic stakeholder could initiate and coach such collaboration. Variable geometry should be used more often, given the diversity in the EU-28, provided it remains open and transparent in its goals and working methods.

In addition to removing all obstacles to innovation and modernizing methods and tools for innovation policy, completion of the European

---

[5] Over the past few decades, a new form of governance has emerged to replace hierarchical, adversarial, and managerial modes of policymaking and implementation. Collaborative governance, as it has come to be known, brings public and private stakeholders together in a collective forum with public agencies to engage in consensus-oriented decision making. This definition involves six criteria: (1) the forum is initiated by public agencies or institutions, (2) participants in the forum include non-state actors, (3) participants engage directly in decision making and are not merely "consulted" by public institutions, (4) the forum is formally organized and meets collectively, (5) the forum aims to take decisions by consensus (even if consensus is not achieved in practice), and (6) the focus of collaboration is on public policy or public management. Cf.: Chris Ansell, Alison Gash (2008). "Collaborative Governance in Theory and Practice," in *Journal of Public Administration Research and Theory, Vol. 18, pp. 543–571*

innovation ecosystems is imperative for reaping the benefits of innovation and to marshal public acceptance and support.

Recommendation 3.1: Establish an Overarching Focus on Citizen-Centered Themes

For a variety of reasons, the EU has become widely unpopular with its member states, companies, and citizens. This is not merely due to the fallout from the financial and Euro crises, but rather the Union suffers from self-inflicted damage resulting from its contested goals and top-down, centralized, and legalistic actions. Contrary to its lip service, the EU—it seems—no longer has a shared mission that is supported by the majority of its citizens, while companies find it a less attractive place to invest and to do business. The best young entrepreneurs often leave. It increasingly deviates from the aggregate priority concerns of citizens, which are prosperity, growth, employment, and safety and security, as well as democratic self-determination in a rapidly globalizing world and from the essential needs of companies for competitiveness in a global economy.

EU policymaking must again become people centered as it once was designed as a grand project to make wars obsolete and preserve peace among the people of Europe. This is the overarching challenge for the coming decade: to rebuild confidence by being people centered and ready to innovate and reform its structures and processes according to peoples' preferences and concerns.

Against this background the HLG recommends to

3.1.1   Regularly use a European Council meeting for a comprehensive discussion of a citizen-centered theme

* With a multidisciplinary and multi-perspective preparation and taking inspiration from the best thinkers worldwide, EU Heads of States and Governments may wish to devote analysis and discussion to individual themes and problems close to the hearts of the people of Europe during selected summits. This will help to increase the EU's attractiveness and credibility and instill novel and innovative ideas into the EU policymaking process at the highest level.

3.1.2   Reduce the innovation divide and assist in building national innovation ecosystems

* The Commission Innovation Scoreboard and the more comprehensive Global Innovation Index show great disparities between member states (including regions and cities), affecting the Single Market and the joint position in the global economy. A special effort needs to be made urgently to ensure that all member states catch up with developing innovation ecosystems, as part of a European ecosystem and that they create the conditions for knowledge-based growth and for continuous improvements in innovation governance.

* To achieve this will require decisions about how best to combine for research excellence and wider stimulation of research potential (promising in development) and the functioning of the innovation value chain (from research to market). The EU may need to recognize also those who will be excellent tomorrow. Plans for a "*stairway* to excellence" in EU policies primarily target newer member states and it is unclear where this leaves southern Europe often suffering from cutbacks in research budgets. A tripartite group involving multidisciplinary academic experts, business representatives, and senior civil servants may assist those governments and administrations below the innovation average with what to do and how to catch up.

Recommendation 3.2: Radically Improve Policy Coherence

There is an urgent need for mechanisms to overcome systemic fragmentation, duplication, and even contradiction, in the design and implementation of innovation policy inside EU institutions, between member states and EU institutions, but also between companies and public authorities and between administrations and civic societies.

In particular, Europe needs an inclusive approach to promote innovation in the member states and the EU and between them, together with a new all-encompassing toolkit to ensure coherence between all the policies and actions in an innovation ecosystem.

The key challenges of the future, for example, resource efficiency, modernization of education and social protection provisions, new materials development, energy savings (in particular electricity storage and CO_2 storage and use), new communication and networking infrastructures, and the development of closed industrial systems or research of the brain all require transversal policymaking and collaboration between the Commission, governments, and stakeholders and in particular industry and research centers.

Governance capabilities need to be continually refined to meet present-day needs and adapt to new technologies, in particular e-governance. Better framework conditions and alignment between European and national policies aimed at stimulating innovation require horizontal, vertical, temporal, and systemic coherence.

In order to fulfill this need, the HLG recommends considering the following:

3.2.1 Create Commission vice presidents without portfolio, responsible for strategic collaboration, mentoring, and coherence

* In the Commission, the overarching priority of innovation and competitiveness should be entrusted to a vice president, whose core team should comprise other commissioners with responsibilities directly relevant for innovation policy. This vice president should not have a specific portfolio but should be in charge of ensuring strategic collaboration, mentoring, and coherence.
* Similarly, other vice presidents without portfolio can be charged to ensure strategic collaboration, mentoring, and coherence over other areas (such as sustainability, inclusiveness).
* Finally, given that research networks are global, a commissioner could be given a geographic responsibility, in cooperation with the EEAS, for permanently scouting for research and innovation developments in the world and for developing strategic cooperation with other regions on specific grand R&D&I challenges (e.g., with Africa on water) which can boost research and innovation and economic and trade relationships.

3.2.2   Develop regular peer review mechanisms among member states

* Peer reviews of governance quality have proven useful in other parts of the world; they can be in Europe, too. In order to stimulate the further development and completion of innovation ecosystems in all member states, to learn from best practice, to ensure maximum use of capacities available in individual countries, business sectors and research centers and to bring maximum cross-fertilization, for the benefit of all in the Single Market, a coherent peer review mechanism should be elaborated. However, without a strong political commitment for change the effects of peer review and similar mechanisms will be negligible.

3.2.3   Strengthen the role of independent advice as a meaningful input for policy improvement

* Functioning innovation ecosystems require regular, open dialogue and alignment processes between the interests of various stakeholders. This would entail a new governance culture and methods. Constructive criticism should serve as a contribution to more effective problem solving. Therefore, experts with different multidisciplinary and multi-experience backgrounds must be involved regularly to provide the inputs necessary for taking decisions of high quality and social acceptance.
* The former decision of the outgoing commission president to appoint a chief scientific adviser (CSA) should be maintained. But the role should be strengthened and enlarged to oversee the elaboration and application of new methods of impact assessment of EU legislation as a key input for improving policy and regulatory quality. The CSA's task should also involve the tracking and tracing of forefront scientific development, surveying and overviewing science and innovation communication, and delivering foresight studies. Since science is by definition science, all works and recommendations of the CSA must be public, including any dissenting opinions.
* The Science and Technology Advisory Council (STAC) should enlarge its perspective from new technologies and new scientific developments to the entire innovation value chain. It should also include experts on strategic governance, management, and social sciences in order to stimulate multidisciplinary thinking and advice.

3.2.4 Reorganize and strengthen existing innovation steering structures and mechanisms for the development of innovation ecosystems

* The EU and its member states need mechanisms to stimulate alignment, create or complete the innovation ecosystems, and overcome multiple fragmentations. To achieve this objective, there should be a clearly defined mechanism with overarching responsibility for innovation and competitiveness within the EU institutions and each member state.
* This collaborative steering mechanism responsible for innovation ecosystem emergence and completion should, in particular

    * focus on the "innovation quadruple helix"[6] (where government, academia, industry, and citizens collaborate to drive structural changes far beyond the scope any one organization could achieve on its own) which is the basis for open innovation;
    * set up a network of formal and informal, public and private sector actors whose activities and interactions initiate, import, modify, and diffuse new technologies;
    * support individual actors whose incentive structures and competencies determine the rate and direction of technological learning;
    * oversee the elimination of all barriers to innovation with a strict time frame;
    * allow the emergence of kernels for change and islands of experimentation and ensure their influence on other sectors if proven beneficial;
    * create and facilitate experimentation and prototyping in real world settings, including in policymaking;
    * challenge the independent advisory groups for novel ideas and methods, bold association thinking and foresight; and
    * coordinate their efforts with the needs of preservation and modernization of welfare societies.

---

[6] The innovation quadruple helix refers to an innovation concept where government, academia, industry, and the citizens collaborate together to drive structural changes beyond the scope of what an organisation could achieve by its own. See the Dublin Declaration on Open Innovation 2.0 for additional information at http://www.slideshare.net/DCSF/martin-curley-closing-final.

* These mechanisms must guarantee overall coherence between countries, sectors, networks, clusters, departments, and their rules and actions. They must address the innovation ecosystem in its entirety to ensure that the innovation-policy mix is coherent. They will also have a major role to play in the alignment of perceptions, preferences and objectives regarding innovations, technologies, and institutions and in ensuring institutional adaptability to change and the resilience required.
* Given the overall high professional quality of the Commission administration, advisory groups are only useful if they bring truly independent, creative, "outside the box," multidisciplinary, transversal thinking to those operating the system. They should not necessarily be permanent or allowed to prolong their operation beyond their original mandate.[7]
* A temporary, interdisciplinary brain trust is set up to advise on an overarching approach to innovation and consisting of individuals drawn from (innovative) business sectors and academia (such as experts in innovation economy, management and stewardship, education, strategy, and collaborative governance methods, etc.), but also from civil society organizations, all operating independently and in their own name, chosen (also from non-EU countries) on the sole basis of competence and experience. This "brain trust" should provide advice on managing the complexities of innovation and the multiple interfaces, converting various perspectives into a coherent approach, facilitating social acceptance, guarding strategic agility and a bottom-up approach, redesigning collaborative governance tools and peer review mechanisms; scanning and converting innovation perspectives; redesigning stakeholder involvement; review of impact assessments; innovation in welfare societies.

3.2.5   Regularly discuss innovation ecosystems development in joint and inclusive Council meetings

* At EU level, a mechanism should be modeled on the Ecofin Council, though with adaptations, perhaps through a regular merger of the research and industry parts of the Competitiveness Council (InnoComp), which would exercise overarching responsibility for innovation ecosystems in the EU and its member states and for their effective interactions.

---

[7] Therefore, the members of the HLG decided to set an example and not accept a presidency suggestion for another mandate.

- It should make a six-monthly review of progress, among other things using reporting from the peer review mechanism and the innovation ecosystems steering and coordination mechanism (see above 1.2.2) and an annual science progress report from the CSA.
- Given the macroeconomic importance of innovation, there should be an effective cooperation between these two councils (EcoFin and InnoComp). The key role is transversal coordination and alignment of various ideas and measures.

Recommendation 3.3: Foster the Dedication, Involvement, and Commitment of all Stakeholders in Innovation Policy

Helping to address innovation as an interactive system for value creation requires the redesign of policies and strategies relevant for innovation in the EU, in the member states, and in their interface. This requires firm guidance from the top but also strongly decentralized interaction and collaboration among all stakeholders. Innovative methods are needed to build consensus on strategic issues and pathways.

The enhancement and advancement, the fostering and maintenance of innovation ecosystems requires guidance, leadership, and stakeholder engagement that go beyond traditional hierarchical procedures and established practices. In the same vein, the tools need to reach beyond the technocratic and mechanistic stakeholder consultations that are routine in EU procedures and involve the representative stakeholders that can truly contribute to problem solving.

It is necessary to develop a learning mind-set both for individual actors and institutions and for stakeholders. Cross-disciplinary research and multi-experience inputs, as well as open-mindedness and incentives and finally tolerant handling of failures, will be necessary elements in the process of unfolding strategic innovation capacity. Reducing conflicts in priorities is a key ingredient for creating positive cumulative effects in any innovation ecosystem.

In order to achieve significant improvements, the HLG recommends

3.3.1   Go beyond outdated bureaucratic procedures and develop new forms of collaborative governance, in line with the requirements of open innovation

* In addition to the so-called Community Method, which serves specific purposes, collaborative governance methods can better serve other objectives, in particular the stimulation and completion and coaching of innovation ecosystems. It demands a different mind-set from those involved, be they Commission or governments, business, academia, or civic society organizations, a focus on outcomes and not on procedures and legalistic frameworks, on trust and not on hierarchy, on aligning perspectives and interests among stakeholders, on sensitivity to interrelated factor, on transparency and priority for evidence-based analysis.

* Collaborative governance arrangements go beyond the traditional interactions between EU, stakeholder groups, and other actors of the innovation ecosystem, in that rules are produced jointly, in an open and institutionalized, collective, decision-making process that is deliberative and that builds on consensus. In these kinds of governance settings, stakeholders are encouraged to take responsibility and ownership of the rules agreed upon, which again helps to increase transparency, democratic legitimacy, and accountability of the decisions made and incentivizes the owners of the decisions to ensure proper implementation.

* Collaborative governance refers to a series of methods to achieve public objectives through (transparent and open) alignment and cooperation between stakeholders which seeks to combine the nonhierarchical characteristics, collaboration and peer review, of the Open Method of Cooperation with the stewardship inherent in the Community Method, though without its regulatory outcomes. It well suits the variable geometry among governments provided for in the Treaties and today's challenge of managing complex system dynamics, but in most cases also requires the involvement of the two key actors for innovation, namely business and research centers. It does not aim at regulation, though this may be part of it, but at a collective outcome achieved through the (inter)actions of the individual actors in the process.

* Instead of merely consulting stakeholders, the EU should give them the opportunity to actively engage in co-shaping legislation. Collaborative governance implies that private actors, including citizens, engage with public ones in a direct and formal fashion and not merely on an advisory or consultative basis. This requires quality of

dialogue between decision makers and enterprises, logical alignment, including openness to consider a different approach and the quality of engagement of internal and external stakeholders.

* However, no method will produce a constructive process and outcomes if there is no trust between the key actors themselves or among them and those affected by it. Trust must be nourished, but the process can be helped by the reality check which a good IA provides and by objective agenda setting and procedures which avoid manipulation.

3.3.2 Develop a merit-based and result-oriented Human Resources Policy

* Revise human resource policies in EU institutions and member states with more diverse recruitment, in order to bring a variety of disciplines and professional experiences together. Movement between public administrations (EU and national ones), academia, and business should be facilitated and encouraged by change of rules.
* In addition, a result-based promotion system should bring cultural change in public administrations, in order to adapt mental maps to the requirements of new leadership and management of collaboration with stakeholders in the digital age, when linear thinking has to make place for complexity management, transparency and communication.

3.3.3 Review "comitology" procedures

* While respecting the necessary checks and balances, the system must be made transparent and accountable. The members of each committee, advisory group, or task force should be made public, together with regular updates on procedures and calendar for decisions. This information should be made public in a user-friendly database/portal accessible to all EU citizens.
* At the start and before final decisions are made, a method of consultation (e.g., hearing) with the addressees of the new regulation needs to be developed. Concrete operational proposals made by stakeholders need to be considered and in case of nonacceptance, justification must be provided.

3.3.4   Give priority to informed choice and own responsibility at the expense of hierarchical and authoritative approaches

* To a large extent public credibility of European policymaking and its social acceptance depends on alignment processes between stakeholders and on giving priority to informed choice and own responsibility. Lobbies for single issues are not necessarily representative of the views and expectations of the majority of citizens. This requires a change of paradigm in certain policy areas which tend to favor a hierarchical and authoritative approach while intruding on personal lifestyle and consumer choice. It would reduce antagonism toward the EU if it focused on grand, common interests and left many other issues to member states better placed to deal with social and cultural diversity and collateral attitudes.

Recommendation 3.4: Reduce Regulatory Rigidities and Costs to Stimulate Innovation

Well-crafted regulations can help to create markets and new business opportunities and provide incentives for innovative undertakings. However, regulatory rigidity and the associated burdens and costs for businesses, which weigh even more on SMEs and innovative start-ups, result from the specific procedures of policy and rulemaking in the EU, from the lack of comprehensive and independent Regulatory Impact Assessments, from fault lines within the EU institutions as well as between them and national governments (and in some cases regional governments), from ineffective alignment of discordant positions and sometimes from unconstructive lobbying by civic society organizations and business alike.

In order to reduce regulatory rigidity and costs to stimulate innovation, the HLG recommends to

3.4.1   Strengthen current regulatory simplification efforts with a sector approach and add clear timelines

* Decisive efforts have already been made to improve regulatory simplification at the EU and member state level, for example, in the work of

the High Level Group of Independent Stakeholders on Administrative Burdens (2011) or the European Commission's Regulatory Fitness and Performance Programme (REFIT), initiated in December 2012, which are an important first but belated step in the right direction. Regulatory fragmentation and inconsistency remains a major problem in the EU and the perceived administrative burdens for companies, most notably those in their start-up phase and early years, are still extremely high. Likewise and as the European Commission itself states, the process needs "constant reinvigoration to keep up the momentum."[8] However, the process also needs cooperation from and with national, and in some countries regional, authorities which also bear responsibility for the heavy regulatory burdens and costs on industry and services in Europe.

3.4.2   Update regulation and implementing guidelines more rapidly on the basis of scientific developments

* Maintaining existing regulations for too long or pursuing the same regulatory trajectory can create obstacles for new market entrants and hinder innovation in the Single Market. This creates a competitive disadvantage in the medium and long term. Methods must be developed that allow a more rapid adaptation and possibly change or even elimination of regulation in accordance with the most up-to-date scientific and technological developments.
* Simplify, merge or abolish the vast number of advisory groups of all kind to strengthen coherence. Reorganize their remit and composition and give them a sunset clause as a rule.
* However, set up temporary new task forces for each economic sector to advise the European Commission and Council with the specific task of simplifying and streamlining rules and regulations, bottom-up, to reinterpret their application in accordance with economic realities and eliminate them if necessary. Such task forces should comprise experts from large corporations and SMEs in the specific sector concerned, as well as independent experts in management and digitalization.

---

[8] COM(2013) 685 final: http://ec.europa.eu/smart-regulation/docs/20131002-refit_en.pdf.

* Strongly consider concrete operational proposals from the addressees of the regulation concerned and if they are not taken up, justification must be provided to the Competitiveness Council. Priority should be given to the digitalization of procedures to simplify them, speed them up, and increase user-friendliness. A strict timetable needs to be established and outcomes need to be made an integral part of the annual evaluation of EU officials and of career prospects.
* Allow and encourage policy and regulatory experimentation and prototyping to foster innovation. One cannot be efficient in the digital global economy with the methods inherited from the past.

3.4.3   Adapt regulatory requirements to facilitate growth of innovative SMEs

* A small part of SMEs, only around 1 %, deliver innovative activities in a market context. This group of SMEs not only needs extra targeted funding, but also space for experimentation and an adjusted regulatory framework to support its development throughout Europe. In order to protect innovative SMEs from regulatory obstacles, especially in their early phase, and eliminate artificial barriers for their development into mature companies, the EU should examine a new approach for applying the precautionary principle in the experimental phase.

Recommendation 3.5: Implement a New Model for Impact Assessments

Policies and regulations must be based on evidence to be effective and receive adherence. Great improvements have been made in the way the Impact Assessment was introduced in EU policymaking, despite severe structural deficiencies in its conception, development and consistency throughout the decision-making process requires a new conception of how and by whom the Impact Assessment should be carried out.

A significant effort should be made for independent continuous impact assessments, reviewing whether regulatory trajectories decided on long ago have delivered the desired outcomes or are in need of change, taking into account feedback from industry and society, new scientific and technological developments, and effects on competitiveness.

A two-step (national and European), bottom-up approach needs to be designed to facilitate upfront dialogue that is necessary to build trust, credibility, and acceptance through informed choice and alignment of various perspectives and interests. Key to this is acceptance that there are multiple impacts with different feedback within interacting economic and ecological systems and that these can differ within member states, in Europe as a whole, in markets and societies and individuals, the so-called quadruple helix.

This will contribute to Europe's competitive advantage by improving the coherence and inclusiveness of policies and regulations and putting the focus on outcome instead of procedure.

3.5.1   Establishment of an independent European Impact Assessment Center, based on a network of top research centers

* While respecting the prerogatives of the institutions, it is essential that impact assessments are carried out independently, continuously at every stage of the co-decision process, by a network of research centers selected only on the basis of excellence and not necessarily based in the EU. Therefore an independent European Impact Assessment institution or mechanism should be set up to ensure more effective and transparent policymaking and disclosing complex, interrelated effects from legislation on the economy and society. Impact assessments are very important to avoid that measures in one sector, or a lack of them, create a domino effect in others.

* The procedure to select the research institutions which will cooperate with the new IA institution should be conducted by the chief scientific adviser (CSA), focusing only on globally recognized academic quality criteria. Also, a restructured Joint Research Center could be a useful partner for the CSA.

* Research institutions carrying out national IA of EU proposals need to operate transparently according to the same criteria as applied at EU level, with stewardship being provided by the CSA. Their sources of funding should be disclosed when selected to be part of this network

and as a rule research institutions from another member state(s) should also be involved in such work.

* A positive list of research centers for European IA work should be easily accessible to the public and updated by the CSA on a very regular basis.
* In order to ensure real independence, the European IA institution or mechanism should be self-funded through an endowment grant provided jointly by governments and companies.

3.5.2   Include new criteria in Impact Assessments

* Clear priorities for impact assessment need to be established, such as policy and sector interfaces, checking the impact on monetary and macroeconomic policy, on innovation and creation of global competitive advantage, on employment, on EU and national research funding, potential outcomes and market access, on the welfare state (social protection) mechanisms and their funding, on regulatory stability and impact on long-term investments in many industry sectors. It should also evaluate the effects of rules and their application (or lack of it) in other major economies because this often creates competitive disadvantage. Once the evidence has been produced, all those affected by its possible implementation should be actively involved, allowing them to comment and advise and offer proposals.
* Extensive and solid competitiveness proofing, often neglected in practice, should be made a priority by the commission president and secretary-general and ensured in all impact assessments. The competitiveness proofing should check whether proposed or already existing regulation negatively impacts competitiveness, and if so, measures must be taken immediately to revise or eliminate such regulation.
* R&D&I policies should focus on creation and on exploitation; an overemphasis on inputs will not necessarily lead to innovation in markets. Therefore, impact assessments of programs need to show if and how they will stimulate innovation in reality. They equally need to address properly potential issues of innovation acceptance which would stimulate interdisciplinary research (between social and natural sciences).

* Equally important are experimentation and prototyping which are key components of a forward-looking IA process. Ideally, IA must become an iterative process.

3.5.3   Conduct Impact Assessments at all stages of the legislative process and in all regulatory and policy decisions

* On request, systemic impact assessment should be triggered using a formula that ensures rapid policymaking involving the institutions, member states and external stakeholders throughout the decision-making process.
* Regulatory Committees ("comitology") also need to take account of the impact assessment made at the start of the regulatory process and of any intermediate IAs. They must also take ex ante relevant, independent scientific advice throughout their deliberations, via the CSA of the Commission, in particular when new technologies, their likely evolution and their impact are concerned. Implementation guidelines in comitology should also be screened by Impact Assessments to check whether they are compatible with desired outcomes.

3.5.4   Apply risk-benefit analysis and reality checks in addition to theoretical models

* The benefits of a given product or policy need to be researched in equal measure as its potential risks, including the risks of nonaction. Therefore, Impact Assessments need to include a risk-reward ratio (RRR) which is applied rationally in business economics and, instinctively, by citizens in daily life.
* This approach demands the involvement of research and business up front in order to define a possible risk in real operating contexts and to develop appropriate risk management methods, as well the rewards of different forms of intervention in the quadruple helix.
* This analysis must be made in the context of their real operations and usage and not (only) in theoretic modeling. It must be complemented by social science research in order to increase public knowledge.

Recommendation 3.6: Innovate by Means of Resilience Policy and Ensure Better Science Communication

The EU should maintain its global leadership in ecological sustainability, both from the public and private angles. However, sustainability is not single, but plural, as there are several additional dimensions to sustainability: economic sustainability, such as the creation of comparative advantages and social and cultural sustainability, an integral component of welfare societies and of national identities.

Therefore, the present, mainly regulatory approach of the EU to ecological sustainability needs to be enriched and enlarged with new models, based on the latest scientific insights. Resilience theory is a way to describe and understand the complex dynamics which are triggered when we change one parameter politically without taking account of the whole ecosystem. We'll need to consider restoration, stressor reaction, self-adaptation, or self-restoration, even evolution. Resilience thinking seeks to understand the life cycles and complexity of ecosystems (including the innovation ecosystems!) in order to better manage them, placing specific issues within a comprehensive context.

This opens a vast new space for scientific research and innovation in both the public and private sectors which may lead to new insights in systemic risk and how to deal with it. However, not only academic research needs to be involved, also "experts in the field," those operating in these ecosystems that have acquired a practical understanding which complements academic research.

A new approach is important for two reasons: to achieve sustainability and greening of the economy more efficiently and to avoid competitive disadvantages. Over half of industrial production costs in Europe are related to its legalistic sustainability policies, while some key competitors have few or no concerns about it, leading to price competition and negative effects on employment.

3.6.1 Apply new findings and methodologies to the precautionary principle

* The precautionary principle is a cornerstone of policies aiming at sustainability in all areas, but its effectiveness and acceptability depends, first of all, on correctly defining the issue.

* Given the complexity of all systems, single-issue approaches must be replaced by multidimensional ones. These should be included in the IA together with practical solution finding: resilience science focuses on steering the dynamics in complex systems to preserve or restore their ecological sustainability, instead of dealing with issues in isolation from each other. Europe's "ban it" regulatory approach must be replaced by an "innovate and manage it" collaborative governance approach.
* This requires new collaborative mechanisms between stakeholders (research, business, and responsible citizen organizations), with a focus on how research and technological innovation can solve specific issues or manage related inevitably to all economic and human activity and which can create new competitive advantages simultaneously. This requires change in existing regulations to create more space for issue management, or at least a more open minded, reality-based interpretation of its application.

3.6.2   Develop a portal to provide peer reviewed and evidence-based information

* To restore trust in science, a portal should be created to provide peer reviewed and evidence-based information to citizens and media alike. This will help to bring more innovation acceptance too and avoid constructed risks dominating the debates.

3.6.3   Establishment of an independent body or network to ensure proper scientific information and communication in the media

* Given the rapid development of scientific discoveries and widespread difficulties of understanding for nonscientists, there should be an independent body, or network of such bodies already operating in some member states, in order to ensure proper scientific information and communication in the media.

3.6.4   Engage business scientists and other societal players alongside academic scientists in agency studies

* The various agencies that have been set up by the EU in order to pro- vide independent scientific advice for regulatory implementation

operate in a theoretical vacuum if they do not have access to real world developments. This leads to insufficiently multidimensional advice, ignoring the realities and missing opportunities for innovation through the combination of various perspectives.

* Therefore, procedures must be adapted to engage mixed academic-business research teams, open to other relevant societal players linked to the issue at stake, during the first phase of work, followed by independent peer review. On this basis, the actors can then prepare a final, comprehensive, theory and reality-based input for the regulators.

By Way of Conclusion

In what follows, the editors summarize the thrust of the present volume. Based upon 14 contributions from several authors, this book combines viewpoints, aspects, and perspectives to accentuate and substantiate the need for reforms that venture deep into the EU and its innovation policy. In order to redefine new interfaces and new ways of cooperation between business, politics, and the civil society, a new narrative of Europe's future may be required.

Indeed, after years of sclerosis in the 1970s and early 1980s, followed by several decades of smooth and incremental EU policymaking routine, today the EU seems to be faced with deep crises jeopardizing its very existence. In order to regain stability and attractiveness the EU and her policies are in urgent need of major overhaul, new ideas, new goals, new institutional design, and new policies.

The editors and the authors of this volume suggest focusing on innovation as an overarching and permeating objective of a renewed Union, as well as innovation in the business world, academia, government, and the European societies as a whole. Such a new goal must lend itself to improving people's lives and well-being. The common weal of the peoples of Europe necessitates a renewed innovation approach.

© The Editor(s) (if applicable) and The Author(s) 2016
K. Gretschmann, S. Schepers (eds.), *Revolutionising EU Innovation Policy*,
DOI 10.1057/978-1-137-55554-0

As a matter of fact, in order to make the EU into a "Union of Innovation," a new approach regarding innovation policy, R&D, industrial and environmental policies, etc., is needed. We have suggested in this volume to **"revolutionize" EU innovation policy** by means of opening up and revealing the possibilities of a wide-reaching innovation ecosystem supposed to replace former piecemeal approaches.

In the preceding chapters, the basic preconditions and the basic features of such an ecosystem have been rolled out; its benefits as well as the difficulties which might arise have been analyzed, and political recommendations have been developed. Each contribution is a single piece of an entire mosaic whose full picture will become clear when the reader considers the different chapters as a whole.

In Chap. 1 we describe and analyze the functioning and the basic construct of an innovation ecosystem as well as its prerequisites, its advantages over narrower approaches, and its potential political merits.

In Chap. 2 the author uses ample empirical material for analyzing in detail the benefits of strong innovation policies notably for economic development and international competition.

The focus of Chap. 3 is the analysis of the difficulties of comprehensive innovation policy systems. The author identifies obstacles and opposition and argues in favor of new sobriety in innovation policy beyond rebuff and hype.

Chapter 4 underlines the significance of clusters for a stimulating innovation ecosystem. It focuses on three factors that make clusters particularly well suited to develop effective and successful open innovation strategies: access to finance, cross-specialization, and local trust.

Chapter 5 deals with the complexities and intricacies of innovation policy inside administrations, where short-term and long-term decisions need to be reconciled, different actors and their interest are to be aligned, and interministerial policy coordination need to be ascertained.

In Chap. 6 the authors delve into a particularly important element of innovation, viz. funding and financing, suggesting that fresh thinking is somewhat imperative in order to overcome financial barriers and frictions and provide the funds needed to kick-start innovations.

Chapter 7 concentrates on the role of collaborative governance and argues that promoting innovation in the EU requires a fundamental change in the EU's governance approach. Proponents of economic paradigms calling for innovation will have to recognize that without equally significant governance innovation, their case is a lost cause. Both forms of innovation facilitate each other and are indispensable for any innovation ecosystem to work.

The significance of collaborative governance is deepened in Chap. 8, arguing that new forms of all-encompassing governance, that is, interactive and value generating, are to be designed and implemented. The crucial role of institutional arrangements as well as of governance in aligning all the driving forces and actors in favor of radical change is emphasized as a prerequisite.

Chapter 9 questions the ability of the EU system of governance to help business and research to unfold their innovative potential: The European Union is a complex system constituted by a myriad of different actors with often discordant political agendas and interests and a dominant, rigid, and regulatory approach. The author argues that notably the EU regulatory system is no longer able to successfully manage complex policies as in the case of R&D or innovation and is in strong need of overhaul.

Chapter 10 turns to one of the central cornerstones of the innovation system: a stimulating higher education and research environment. Academic institutions are key contributors and stakeholders to fuel economic and societal dynamics. Building a stronger academic capacity inside the EU is an ambition and must overcome the difference between the three basic models of higher education and research: the Anglo-Saxon, the German Humboldtian, and the French Napoleonic models.

Chapter 11 widens the perspective by enlarging the picture beyond education and by dealing with the broader issue of culture and the implications of cultural diversity for any innovation ecosystem. European "cultural industries" require cross-sectoral innovation and collaboration based on diversity, and provides an important economic and cultural asset. Politics, so the author argues, need to foster both innovation of culture and a culture of innovation!

In Chap. 12 our perspective is broadened again: The author explores the role of foresight studies and summarizes principal challenges resulting from scientific, ethical, economic, ecological and geopolitical developments for the innovation ecosystem. Foresight strengthens the urgency of cutting-edge innovation ecosystems and is a useful tool to explore the interactions in complex systems.

Chapter 13 emphasizes and explains the crucial role of enterprises and the functioning of a particularly innovation-led firm. From this micro-level analysis comes a macroeconomic dimension of an intensive, innovation-driven economy.

Finally, we end this volume by resubmitting a series of political recommendations from 2013 and 2014 and with subsequent evaluations thereof. Chapter 14 enumerates and explains the sets of recommendations made by the authors and editors working together in a HLG on IPM. In this chapter we elucidate and exemplify some of the attention and disregard that our recommendations have so far been received.

Let's summarize: Overarching innovation policy is the key tool in the postindustrial, digitalized, and global economy to stimulate economic growth and strengthen competitiveness and employment opportunities for Europe's millions of unemployed. By reordering, upgrading and enriching decisive elements of the presently rudimentary, rather than comprehensive, approach of EU innovation policy, an innovation-conducive environment can be provided.

Whereas the traditional linear model of innovation prioritizes scientific research as the basis of innovation and suggests that change happens in a successive fashion from research via invention to innovation to diffusion and marketing, the model put forward in this book provides a much richer picture of the way innovation works and how it can be stimulated and fostered.

The authors deploy the idea of innovation ecosystems, that is, a set of ideas, attitudes, institutions, instruments, policies, regulations, and factors that determine the level, direction, outcome, productivity, and degree of competitiveness from innovations, not just in the European economy, but in national societies, in regions and cities. A realm characterized by clear, simple, efficient, smart, low-complex, competition-based and socially accepted features will be best suited and conducive to prompt promotion of innovation. Such a novel approach is best suited to the complex interrelations of technology, economy, finance, and governance in today's globalized world. Factors, such as legal provisions, administrative support, entrepreneurial skills, risk propensity, and public opinion, etc., define an environment more or less conducive to innovation. The removal of bottlenecks and obstacles to innovation are the tall order of the day, within all layers of the EU system.

Innovation environments should be tailored and matched to the needs, requirements, properties, etc., of the targeted firms, businesses, organizations, and institutions. As the Single Market or the Common Currency once were, a **European Decade of Innovation** should be the new overarching vision for the EU, a benchmark for its actions. This European Decade of Innovation is meant to serve the **European Common Good**: the best living and working conditions for the peoples of Europe, the modernization and maintenance of its unique societal model—based on civil rights, humanistic values, and cultural diversity. It requires overcoming the system failures in a supranational governance model, such as the EU, once designed for other purposes in the less complex economic and political world and for culturally different societies of more than half a century ago.

Unfortunately, one rediscovers today the same pattern in operation for the last 50 years: the required reforms are evident for everyone; a lot of lip service is paid to them, but the supranational system is unable to produce them timely and consistently. Had the Lisbon Treaty not introduced the European Council of Heads of State and Government, which at least is able to deal with crises, the edifice could have crumbled already.

However, in the multilayered EU system, one cannot just blame the Commission for this; it has shown on occasion the right vision, only to be watered down by Member governments and a navel-gazing European Parliament. With every lower election turnout, the Parliament has become more interested in its own power extension than in defining the European Common Good and steering the EU toward it—some exceptions, such as defense of Europeans' civil rights, notwithstanding. The key economic actors, corporations large and small, have lost the supportive attitude that they once had, and in the void sometimes unaccountable nongovernmental organizations have captured a role disproportionate to their capabilities. The once high credibility of the EU has sunk ever lower as a result, and this when the EU, though a radically reformed one, is more needed than ever.

In a multilayered governance system, comprehensive innovation also requires the closing of the innovation gap between member states, for which there is neither even a policy nor funds, let alone the political consciousness in a considerable number of them. Although this book deals primarily with the EU system, not with national innovation or governance, we cannot avoid noting that only a small group of member states take economic and social innovation seriously enough and attempt to make reforms, and within this group there is an even smaller group of countries that succeed to make it to the top in global rankings. There are new fault lines in the Single Market and the Eurozone as a result, and one day, these will lead to political, economic, and monetary instability, jeopardizing the whole Union. An innovation deficit may not offer as much drama as a budgetary deficit, but it will surely have equally serious consequences.

When one considers what would be needed ideally, and the quite realistic recommendations for short- to mid-term reforms by the independent tripartite High Level Group on Innovation Policy Management, as did other expert groups before them,[1] and what is actually being done in the EU institutions, then the conclusion can only be that we are still far away from revolutionizing innovation policy. It is high time to get it going. Yet, we do hope that this volume can contribute to take the bull, on which Europe is currently sitting uneasily, by the horns and take on the challenge!

---

[1] See Esko Aho Report—*Creating an Innovative Europe* (European Commission 2006).

Index

Printed in the United States
By Bookmasters